The International Handbook of Competition

D1434871

Edited by

Manfred Neumann

Professor Emeritus of Economics,
University Erlangen-Nürnberg, Germany

Jürgen Weigand

Professor of Economics, WHU Otto Beisheim Graduate
School of Management, Vallendar, Germany

Edward Elgar

Cheltenham, UK • Northampton, MA, USA

Published by
Edward Elgar Publishing Limited
Glensanda House
Montpellier Parade
Cheltenham
Glos GL50 1UA
UK

Edward Elgar Publishing, Inc.
136 West Street
Suite 202
Northampton
Massachusetts 01060
USA

A catalogue record for this book
is available from the British Library

ISBN   1 84376 054 1 (cased)

Printed and bound in Great Britain by MPG Books Ltd, Bodmin, Cornwall

Contents

Contributors

David B. Audretsch, Indiana University, Bloomington, USA and Director, Max-Planck Institute for Research into Economic Systems, Jena, Germany

Jürgen Basedow, Max-Planck-Institute for Foreign and International Civil Law, Hamburg, Germany

Eric Bond, Vanderbilt University, Nashville, USA

Arnoud Boot, University of Amsterdam, The Netherlands

Marcel Canoy, CPB Netherlands Bureau for Economic Policy Analysis, The Netherlands

Paul Geroski, London Business School and Chairman, Competition Commission London, UK

Rachel Griffith, London Business School, London, UK

Christian Kirchner, Humboldt University, Berlin, Germany

Stephen Martin, Krannert Business School, Purdue University, West Lafayette, USA

Dennis C. Mueller, University of Vienna, Austria

Manfred Neumann, University of Erlangen-Nürnberg, Germany

Anne Rathbone, The Locke Institute, Fairfax, Virginia, USA

Patrick Rey, IDEI, Université Toulouse I, France

Charles Rowley, George Mason University and The Locke Institute, Fairfax, Virginia, USA

Eric van Damme, University of Tilburg, The Netherlands

Jürgen Weigand, WHU Otto Beisheim Graduate School of Management, Vallendar, Germany

Introduction

Manfred Neumann and Jürgen Weigand

Competition is a constitutive property of a market economy following immediately from the right of each individual to pursue his or her own interest. Therefore competition policy is a cornerstone of economic policy in a market economy. In fact, following the lead of US antitrust, most industrialized countries now have introduced some kind of competition policy. In particular, in the European Union competition policy has been accorded a constitutional status. As stated in Article 4 of the EC Treaty, the economic policy of the member states and the Community shall be conducted in 'accordance with the principle of an open market economy and free competition' and Article 3, lit g, says that competition must not be distorted, either by private restraints or by government interference.

In the history of ideas, competition as a salient feature of a free society can be traced back at least to John Locke (1690) who propounded that everybody has the unalienable right to pursue his or her own happiness. This idea gathered momentum from its propagation in the Bill of Rights of Virginia and the ensuing constitution of the United States of America. Given limited resources, the endeavor of countless individuals to improve their well-being by acquiring command over goods is necessarily conducive to competition. This idea found its way into legislation of the USA by the Sherman Act of 1890 which prohibits restraint of competition in most general terms.

This legislation originally found hardly any support among economists. It was only with the 1930s that economic theory began to furnish theoretical support for competition policy. Since then quite a lot has been accomplished in this direction. Today, in the USA antitrust has come to rely to a substantial degree on economic theory, and in the EC competition policy a 'more economic approach' has increasingly won ground. Hence modern competition policy rests on two pillars: on economic theory, in particular industrial economics, and legal reasoning.

This *Handbook* is intended to provide a scholarly review of the state of the art regarding principles of economic theory, empirical evidence and standards of legal evaluation in a way accessible to a wide audience. Therefore the following chapters focus on basic issues rather than on particular points which are of interest mainly for specialists in theory and legal practice.

This introduction should serve as a road map for understanding the role of competition in a market economy and clarifying the interrelation between the various chapters of the book. Readers interested in more theoretical details and a more comprehensive treatment of competition policy are referred to Martin (2001) and Neumann (2001), respectively.

Why competition and competition policy?

Unfettered competition of countless individuals is likely to give rise to warfare, as suggested by Hobbes (1588–1679) in his *Leviathan*, a struggle of everybody against everybody (*homo lupus hominem est*). This idea was echoed by Eddy (1912) who bluntly stated that 'competition is war, and war is hell'. He thus gave lively expression to the widespread belief that a market economy is characterized by chaos, unless peace is enforced by the government.

In fact, the notion of markets as being necessarily chaotic has been successfully refuted both by theory and by experience. Admittedly under somewhat restrictive and even unrealistic assumptions, for a market economy populated by individuals maximizing their utility, an equilibrium has been proved (by Debreu, 1959, and others) to exist where nobody can be made better off without somebody else being made worse off. Even though this proof had been accomplished under somewhat restrictive and unrealistic assumptions, experience suggests that a market economy, driven by individual interests, is far from being a Panglossian Utopia; rather it is a powerful machinery to create wealth for the great majority of people and potentially for everybody. The pursuit of individual interest encompasses the never-ending search for improving efficiency and probing new ideas and goods. In fact, competition is the most effective method of discovery (Hayek, 1968), by which in a market economy dispersed knowledge and expertise is brought to fruition. No central planning body would be able to be equally successful. This has most effectively been demonstrated by the breakdown of the central planning regimes favored by socialist countries.

The question then arises which kind of government intervention is required to avoid a Hobbesian chaotic struggle. Although the competitive process is likely to yield increasing wealth for the entire economy it also implies what Schumpeter (1942) called 'creative destruction'. Competitors of pioneering enterprises will be driven from the market because innovations make incumbent products and processes obsolete. Individual competitors are thus not immune from being adversely affected by creative destruction. This kind of adverse effect must be admitted in order to keep the competitive process going. Overall, however, it can be expected to work for the benefit of most people, as emphasized by Adam Smith ([1776] 1950, vol. I, p. 90).

It is in the progressive state while the society is advancing to further acquisition rather than when it has acquired its full complement of riches, that the condition of the great body of the people seems to be happiest and the most comfortable.

On the other hand, from the viewpoint of ethics, limits on the pursuit of one's own happiness are required insofar as it must not deprive others of their freedom or impede their efforts to obtain it (J.S. Mill, 1861, p. 22). According to this principle the competitive process should be governed by fairness so that malicious intent to destroy competitors should be prohibited. The ethical principle enunciated by John Stuart Mill implies that competition policy should disallow restraints of competition rather than attempt to create competition which is deemed to enhance economic welfare as seen by the authorities. Hence the upshot of granting maximum freedom entails everything being allowed unless specifically forbidden, rather than prohibiting everything unless specifically allowed.

Pervasiveness of restraints of competition
Even though competition is the most effective way to improve the well-being of people in the long run, for an individual the absence of competition may, in the short run, be preferable. The most compelling reason for this preference is certainly that collusion among competing firms is conducive to profits exceeding those compatible with competition. However, given monopoly power, excessive profits are subject to being dissipated by rent seeking, so that profits no longer are the immediate incentive to create or maintain a monopoly. In a more extended perspective the most highly valued advantage of a monopoly seems to be a quiet life. This perspective has, on one hand, been given vivid expression by John Stuart Mill (1871, p. 748) who confessed that he

> was not charmed with the ideal of life held out by those who think that the normal state of human beings is that of struggling to get on; that the trampling, crushing, elbowing, and treading on each other's heels ... are the most desirable lot of human kind.

The alluring prospect of a quiet life has given rise to widespread attempts to restrain competition. As observed by Adam Smith (1950, vol. I, p. 144), 'People of the same trade seldom meet together, even for merriment and diversion, but the conversation ends in a conspiracy against the public, or some contrivance to raise prices.'

This observation for the time of Adam Smith has been amply corroborated by Ashton (1964) in his treatise on the history of the Industrial Revolution in England. The same story is told by the history of cartels in the USA before the advent of antitrust legislation towards the end of the 19th century, in

Germany prior to World War II (Neumann, 2001) and in England before
the legislation prohibiting cartels in 1956 (Symeonidis, 2002). Even the
prohibition of cartels in the USA and Europe has not been a panacea
against the emergence of cartels in violation of the law, as recent spectacular
cases like the international vitamin cartel and the cement cartel reveal.

Welfare loss attributable to monopoly
Evaluating the welfare loss caused by monopolistic market power has been
a contentious issue. The welfare loss attributable to monopoly has usually
been measured by the loss of consumer surplus which arises insofar as the
price exceeds marginal costs (see Charles Rowley and Anne Rathbone, this
volume). In the case of oligopoly the welfare loss can be approximated by
one-half of profits of a representative firm of the industry (Cowling and
Mueller, 1978). This static measure does not, however, tell the full story.
If monopoly power results from a merger, a trade-off between monopoly
power and efficiency may arise. Increasing size may help exploit economies
of large scale so that marginal costs of the monopolistic firm may fall
short of marginal costs of the previously existing firms absorbed by the
merger. The price-raising effect of monopoly power which gives rise to a
loss in consumer welfare, may be offset by the efficiency-enhancing scale
effect which implies a gain in consumer surplus due to lower post-merger
marginal costs. (Williamson, 1968; Rowley and Rathbone, this volume). On
the other hand it must be taken into account that monopoly power may
engender rent-seeking behavior which causes costs to increase. Monopoly
power may, and most likely does, diminish incentives for innovation and
thus inhibits economic growth. In the long run these adverse effects may
dwarf any welfare gains entailed in static economies of large scale.

   A first attempt undertaken by Harberger (1954) to quantify the static
welfare loss of monopoly came up with disappointing results for those
who assumed monopoly to be a social evil of substantial weight. Harberger
suggested that the loss in consumer surplus attributable to a misallocation of
resources due to monopoly power in US manufacturing from 1924 to 1928
was unlikely to exceed one-tenth of one per cent of value added. This result
of course casts doubts on whether antitrust policy is worthwhile. However,
on closer examination it became clear that the evaluation proposed by
Harberger is flawed for at least two reasons. First, the underlying assumption
that monopoly power does not affect costs of production is questionable
even in a static environment. Second, it has to be taken into account
that a monopoly is less likely than a competitive industry to enhance
technical progress.

   Regarding costs of production the crucial argument has already been
advanced by Adam Smith ([1776] 1950), vol. II, p. 278) who observed,

By a perpetual monopoly, all the other subjects of the state are taxed very absurdly in two different ways, first, by the high price of goods, which, in the case of free trade, they could buy much cheaper, and secondly, by their total exclusion from a branch of business, which it might be both convenient and profitable for many of them to carry on. It is for the most worthless of all purposes too that they are taxed in this manner. It is merely to enable the company to support negligence, profusion, and malversation of their own servants, whose disorderly conduct seldom allows the dividend of the company to exceed the ordinary rate of profit in trades which are altogether free, and very frequently makes it fall even a good deal short of that rate.

This argument has been amply elaborated by invoking the notions of X-inefficiency (Leibenstein, 1966) and rent-seeking (Tullock, 1967; Posner, 1975; Cowling and Mueller, 1978) which implies excessive costs. Assuming costs to be the same under competition and monopoly will thus cause a substantial understatement of the static welfare loss of monopoly.

With regard to dynamics, Arrow (1962) suggested that incentives for innovation are stronger under competition than in the case of monopoly. In particular, newcomers to an industry need not care about losses incurred by incumbents following technological obsolescence. This may explain why drastic innovations like the replacement of the mail-coach by railways or the mechanical calculator by the PC have been introduced, not by incumbents, but by new firms, which started small and rapidly grew large. It can likewise be shown even for non-drastic innovations that in an oligopoly the incentives to innovate increase with a rising number of competing firms (Neumann, 2001, p. 53). A further argument why innovations are impeded by monopoly power is contained in the statement of Adam Smith quoted above. He identifies the power of a monopoly with the power of the state to levy taxes which are subsequently wasted. There is ample evidence for taxation of this kind to inhibit economic growth (Neumann, 2001, p. 94). Hence monopoly power can be expected to exert an adverse effect on economic growth which dwarfs the static welfare loss. This provides strong support for the necessity of competition policy.

Limits of competition
The emergence of giant firms during the later decades of the 19th century gave rise to gloomy predictions regarding the viability of a competitive economy. Even though the predictions of Karl Marx and his followers of an ever-increasing concentration and the eventual demise of capitalism has not come true, horizontal concentration has undoubtedly increased and, following a succession of merger waves, the size of firms has increased. As has been pointed out by Sutton (1991), particular industries, iron and steel for example, in various countries display a similar degree of horizontal

concentration. This suggests that concentration, to a large extent, is caused by technological factors and thus appears inevitable. On the other hand it must not be overlooked that in quite a few cases technological developments overturned tendencies which favored large size. Examples are the substitution of electrically powered machinery for engines powered by steam or the triumph of the PC over giant computers.

This mixed picture gives rise to the question to what extent economies of large scale do determine the size of firms and to what extent horizontal concentration must be attributed to this cause. Stephen Martin (in this volume) gives a comprehensive account of available empirical evidence and comes to the conclusion that economies of large scale are usually exhausted at quite a limited size, in most cases far below the actual size of big firms in the respective industry. In view of the evidence he argues that the greatest limitations to competition in global markets may lie in a political unwillingness to accept the resource allocations that are part and parcel of the benefits following from globalization.

In fact, globalization contributes to the viability of a competitive economy by mitigating the concentration effect of scale economies. A larger market can accommodate a larger number of firms which, given free entry into the industry, are at least able to just cover average costs where, in the example of a firm producing a single good the average cost curve is tangential to the declining individual demand curve. An increase in the size of the market may be conducive to an increase in the size of individual firms either by internal growth or by merger. Still, horizontal concentration need not increase; on the contrary, it is more likely to decrease. This applies even if a larger firm may employ a superior technique characterized by higher fixed costs and lower marginal costs (Neumann *et al.*, 2001).

Regardless of whether fixed costs do exist or not, free entry implies that, even though in the short run excess profits may arise, in the long run excess profits can be expected to be eroded.

Empirical studies in the tradition of the structure–conduct–performance paradigm have, despite some methodological problems, overwhelmingly documented that, first, price-cost margins (that is, price minus marginal costs over price) are positively associated with horizontal concentration of supply and, second, that the same applies to excess profits. These cross-section studies, regardless of whether they pertained to industries, lines of business or firms, left unanswered the question to what extent profits are persistent or subject to erosion by competition. In a series of studies, covering various countries, it has been shown that substantial erosion does in fact occur. However, it takes place only sluggishly. The competitive process thus works only imperfectly (Mueller, 1990).

Mergers and acquisitions

Mergers and acquisitions may be undertaken to reorganize industry structure in response to a changing environment and to utilize technological opportunities. From the viewpoint of an individual firm, acquiring another firm is just an investment undertaken to improve profitability. Higher profitability may be expected from raising efficiency in production by utilizing economies of scale or from product or process innovations. In the past mergers have occurred in waves corresponding closely to business cycles. So, at first sight, the interpretation of mergers and acquisitions as ordinary investment activity driven by the desire to enhance efficiency appears to have some merit. However, mergers and acquisitions may also, or alternatively, be undertaken to create or increase monopolistic market power. Both kinds of expectations may be mistaken and a merger may thus turn out as a failure.

In fact, using a novel methodology, Dennis Mueller (in this volume) demonstrates for a large international sample of merger cases that quite a few mergers actually improve efficiency. Nevertheless, a substantial share of mergers and acquisitions give rise to increased monopoly power. Finally, some mergers are simply failures from the viewpoint both of the firms involved and of the economy at large. In quantitative terms the results suggest that for every merger that yields an unambiguous increase in social welfare there are two that unambiguously reduce social welfare, divided roughly equally between mergers that lower efficiency and mergers that increase market power. Mueller suggests that these results imply that competition policy toward mergers should rest on a strong presumption *against* mergers to take place rather than a presumption in their favor.

Innovations

A closely connected aspect is whether innovations are more likely to be undertaken by small firms or by big ones. Regarding this question Schumpeter, in his *Theory of Economic Development* (1912) suggested that it is the newcomer, the pioneering entrepreneur, who is most likely to promote technical change. However, 30 years later, Schumpeter (1942) came to the conclusion that in modern times innovations are mostly coming from the laboratories of big firms. These hypotheses have given rise to a voluminous literature with respect to both theory and empirics. In particular the latter are comprehensively reviewed by David Audretsch (in this volume). The upshot is that both claims have some merit and that in particular small and medium-sized firms are responsible for a substantial share of innovative activity. Whilst until quite recently it was fashionable to agree with Chandler (1990) who concluded that 'to compete globally you have to be big', in view of overwhelming evidence to the contrary, scholarship has changed in its assessment of the role of small firms in the process of innovation and technological change, from being mostly unimportant to playing a central role.

International trade

The size of the market is larger and competition ordinarily more vigorous the more an economy is open to international trade. International trade is thus conducive to counteracting restraints of competition caused by a high concentration of supply in national industries or collusive practices. A review of the relevant literature is given by Eric Bond (in this volume).

In particular, tendencies for collusion are undermined by international trade. For collusion to be stable requires mutual trust. This condition is most likely to be satisfied in a closed society where 'people of the same trade meet for merriment and diversion', as put by Adam Smith and definitely less likely in an economy open to international trade. This general observation does not exclude the possibility of international cartels emerging and being maintained for an extended period of time. In fact, for West Germany it has been shown that imports exert an adverse effect on price-cost margins of firms in recessions but not in business cycle upswings (Neumann *et al.*, 1983; 1985). So international trade is not a panacea for overcoming any restraints of competition originating in the domestic economy. This is particularly true since foreign trade policy in quite a few cases is used as a device to 'further national interest to the detriment of trading partners' by strategic trade policy (Brander and Spencer, 1985) or by permitting export cartels. In addition, domestic industries have frequently tried to ward off import competition by raising complaints about dumping and requesting the government to levy anti-dumping duties (Messerlin and Reed, 1995). Nieberling (1999) found for various US industries that adoption of anti-dumping measures led to an increase in monopolistic market power, as revealed by price-cost margins.

The failure of international trade to undermine domestic restraints of competition completely and to offset their results cannot exclusively be attributed to inadequate economic policy. One should remember that even Adam Smith, who otherwise ardently propagated free trade, gave clear priority to defense over opulence. In fact some restraints of international trade may be justified for reasons of national security. Therefore the burden of competition policy falls mainly on domestic policy.

Financial institutions

Competition is a fundamental economic mechanism to achieve efficiency and enhance consumer welfare. In the financial sector, however, competition may lead to inefficient and unwanted market outcomes, such as credit crunches or bank runs, because there is a tendency for market failures to arise from indivisibilities, externalities and informational problems.

The financial sector in both Europe and the USA has undergone a deep transformation process over the past decade. Deregulation and globalization have intensified competitive pressures on the incumbent players. New market players, such as insurance companies, credit card providers and non-financial companies, have been entering market segments which used to be banks' territories.

Increased competition may induce financial institutions to engage in riskier activities to make up for squeezed profits. Higher overall risk and lower profitability may then raise the probability and frequency of bank failures and thus trigger banking crises. Competition can thus be a threat to the stability of the financial system. Therefore the financial sector has traditionally been subject to regulation and supervision rather than to market forces and the watchful eye of competition authorities alone.

It has frequently been argued that firm size and the scope of activities matter in banking, that in particular a banking system with large and diversified banks may be better protected from instability. Therefore a lot of research has been devoted to examining the importance of scale and scope economies in banking. Arnoud Boot (in this volume) reviews the existing evidence. Boot judges the evidence to be 'sobering' and not really helpful in explaining the current wave of restructuring and consolidation in the financial sector. Rather he argues that strategic positioning resulting from first-mover advantages, learning and market power explain much better the patterns to be observed recently.

Principles of competition policy

Competition policy aims at establishing and maintaining a competitive order by seeking to support competitive structures in industry and to entice or even enforce competitive behavior. Given these aims, competition policy may be governed by two opposing views which may be termed constructivism and the evolutionary approach, respectively. Constructivism rests on the presumption that an optimal structure of industry can be derived from economic theory and implemented by government intervention. By contrast, adherents of the evolutionary approach deny that an optimum can be conceived of a priori and insist on competition itself being a process capable of yielding an outcome which may be found optimal only ex post. This view rests on admitting that, on logical grounds, innovations cannot be foreseen, an insight most forcefully expressed by Karl Popper (1957): 'we cannot anticipate today what we shall know only tomorrow'. Still, even though the specific outcome of the competitive process is unknown, economic theory is helpful in identifying circumstances under which a maximum of economic welfare can be expected to come forth. Competition policy in the spirit of the evolutionary approach therefore primarily focuses on setting rules to remove restraints of competition rather than devising structures which are deemed to be optimal.

In practice competition policy, as conducted in most industrialized countries, is governed by both views. Therefore antitrust is presumably the most politicized field of law. Terms like 'monopolize', 'market dominance', 'substantial lessening of competition' and so forth are not self-evident but need interpretation. Economics may and has been used to give them meaning. But antitrust is more than just economics. Law has its own claims and its own tradition (Bork, 1965, p. 780). Since competition law is thus open to interpretation, political interests are coming in. Charles K. Rowley and Anne Rathbone (in this volume) give an account of the political economy of antitrust. They examine to what extent political interest groups have been shaping thrust and vigor of competition policy in the United States. However, in order for a stable framework to be maintained, reliable rules of law, enforced by courts of justice, clearly deserve to be preferred to the vagaries of changing political majorities to determine the stance of competition policy.

Containing restraints on competition can be achieved by structural remedies or by regulation of economic behavior. It can also be done by setting rules or by discretionary decisions. To understand where these principles apply we shall look at some examples outlined in Table 1. The outstanding example of a structural remedy by rule is the per se prohibition of so-called 'hardcore' cartels as adopted in the USA. The same applies in practice in the European Union. Price fixing and collusive market sharing have come to be presumed as predominantly harmful. Efficiency enhancement which has frequently been claimed by cartels to be achievable have come to be considered as irrelevant for hardcore cartels. As stated most succinctly by the court in the 'Trenton Potteries Case' in the USA in 1927 (Neale, 1966, p. 36):

> The power to fix prices, whether reasonably exercised or not, involves power to control the market and to fix arbitrary and unreasonable prices. The reasonable price fixed today may through economic and business changes become the unreasonable price of tomorrow. Once established, it may be maintained unchanged because of the absence of competition.

In fact, a cartel leaves the legal autonomy of its members untouched and is thus a relatively loose arrangement which aims at balancing partially conflicting interests. Innovations adopted by an individual firm have the potential to upset the apple cart. Unless an innovation can be expected to yield an overwhelmingly large advantage for the innovating firm it may be withheld by the potential innovator in order to maintain the monopolistic advantage of the cartel. Therefore, in the case of hardcore cartels, the rejection of an efficiency defense appears to be well taken.

Table 1   Rules or discretion

	Rules	Discretion
Structural remedies	Per se prohibition of cartels	Substantial lessening of competition for mergers
Regulation	Predation	Natural monopolies

However, restraints of competition may be only ancillary to the main purpose of a horizontal or vertical cooperation among firms which aims at enhancing efficiency by joint R&D or exploiting synergies in production or distribution. Generally, albeit with some reservation, horizontal cooperation of this kind has come to be evaluated by applying a 'rule of reason' both in the USA and in the European Union. Cooperative agreements tend to be considered innocuous if the welfare-enhancing elements outweigh the restraints of competition.

The 'rule of reason' has in particular come to be applicable in the case of mergers. Most of them are presumably undertaken to improve efficiency, whilst restraints of competition are incidental and of minor weight. Whether this is true or whether restraints of competition are dominant must be examined case by case. Hence, as a structural remedy by discretion, a merger may be disallowed. In the USA, according to the Clayton Act, this applies if the effect of the merger 'may be to substantially lessen competition or to create a monopoly' and in the EC if a merger is conducive to creating or strengthening market dominance, meaning that the emerging firm is immune from substantial competition. These criteria, 'substantial lessening competition' and 'acquiring market dominance' are in practice almost equivalent.

Even so, both are subject to interpretation. Antitrust authorities and courts of justice so far have been inclined to find them satisfied if the merged entity is essentially immune from competition and the industry may be able to raise prices above marginal costs without being thwarted by competition. Obviously, a presumption of this kind to be justified is extremely hard to prove. Actually, the Court of First Instance in the EC recently turned down decisions of the EC Commission regarding mergers because of insufficient proof of market dominance under the above meaning. In fact, however, a 'substantial lessening of competition' (SLC) need not be identified with the likelihood of collusion regarding prices and market shares to arise. As argued by Marcel Canoy, Patrick Rey and Eric van Damme (in this volume), whether SLC applies should be interpreted in the light of the theory of oligopoly which implies that an increase in horizontal concentration yields the excess of the price over marginal costs to rise and thus to engender a monopoly welfare loss regardless of whether this tendency is reinforced by collusion. This applies both to markets for homogeneous goods and in the case of product differentiation. This hypothesis has found ample support by empirical studies in the USA as well as in Europe (Neumann, 2001, p. 78) Still, according to theory, the positive association between horizontal concentration of the industry and the ensuing welfare loss is largely continuous. Therefore some threshold of concentration must be fixed where competition is deemed to be lessened to such an extent as to justify disallowing a merger. Moreover, since market dominance following from high concentration of supply may be threatened by entry of new competitors, the degree of horizontal concentration alone is not sufficient to decide whether competition is likely to be sufficiently lessened.

Thus both criteria require an arbitrary decision as to when a merger is likely to lessen competition substantially. Merger guidelines in the USA and the Regulation regarding mergers in the EC which enumerate conditions with respect to market shares, concentration measures and an evaluation of the likelihood of competitive entry are rules at face value. They nevertheless bear some element of discretion and seem to be an outgrowth of a deliberate intervention in the market. Naturally, political value judgments are coming into play for designing merger policy.

The chapter by Canoy, Rey and van Damme also provides an extensive discussion from both an economic and a legal perspective regarding the prerequisites for and the consequences of abusing market power, such as predatory conduct and monopolistic exploitation.

A first and crucial step in determining the existence of market dominance is defining and delineating the relevant market. In principle, the relevant market comprises all those goods considered to be sufficiently close substitutes. Usually antitrust authorities have been inclined to use a narrow definition of the relevant market whilst industry interests would rather favor a broad definition. Paul Geroski and Rachel Griffith (in this volume) review the present state of the art and suggest invoking both demand and supply substitution simultaneously to delineate the relevant market. In particular, they reflect on the well-known SSNIP (Small but Significant Non-transitory Increase in Price) test used by US antitrust authorities to determine the boundary of the relevant market. Geroski and Griffith show that this test – although theoretically appealing – faces complications arising for intermediate markets, multi-market effects or endogenous technology changes, among others.

Since decisions regarding the admissibility of a merger are subject to a 'rule of reason' the merging firms may raise an efficiency defense to justify the merger. This amounts to investigating whether the consumer welfare loss following an increase in monopolistic market power can be expected to be offset by efficiency gains caused by the merger.

An example of regulation by rules is the handling of predatory conduct by requiring strict preconditions for predation to be recognized. For illegal predation to be assumed requires a twofold condition. First, the price must not cover costs and, second, initial losses must be likely to be subsequently compensated by higher prices (Cabral and Riordan, 1997).

Regulation by discretion applies to natural monopolies. A precondition for a natural monopoly to be identified is economies of large scale or, more generally, so-called 'subadditivity' of the cost function (Baumol *et al.*, 1982) for joint production, meaning that at any level of output costs are lower than costs which would arise if production were to be carried out separately. If, in addition, costs are sunk, government regulation of the natural monopoly is deemed to be called for either by ex ante regulation exercised by a regulatory authority or by ex post abuse control practiced by competition authorities. Christian Kirchner (in this volume) discusses the relationship between competition policy and government regulation. In the traditional view competition policy and regulation are non-competing instruments of government intervention. However, in certain situations, such as privatization of former state monopolies and deregulation of markets, competition policy and regulation can be competing in the sense that the goals to be achieved by the instruments are conflicting. Kirchner suggests a framework for identifying and resolving areas of conflict.

Extraterritorial effects and harmonization of competition policy
In an open economy restraints of competition exert effects across national borders. Cartels may comprise firms from different countries and mergers in one country may affect output and prices in other countries as well because the merging firms are exporting or even maintain affiliates abroad. Legal remedies and political problems arising in applying competition law across national borders is discussed by Jürgen Basedow (in the present volume). It is by now well established that restraints of competition arising in a foreign country insofar as they take effect in the domestic country can in general be prosecuted by domestic authorities ('effects doctrine'). Given the present globalization of economic activities it would of course be preferable if restraints of competition were treated all over the world following identical rules. Despite some steps taken in this direction under the auspices of the World Trade Organization (WTO) there is a long way to go to achieve this most desirable end. At the present time only US antitrust law and

competition law of the EU have come closer so that some cooperation is feasible.

Social framework of competition policy

In concluding, a brief look at the social framework for competition seems to be in order. As competition policy is a constitutive part of economic and social policy it is subject to the impact of conflicting tendencies and interests. From the point of view of economics, the enhancement of efficiency appears to be the guiding principle. From a broader perspective, other objectives such as distributional justice and the maintenance of a decentralized economy as a safeguard of democracy or international rivalry, with the aim of occupying a leading position may come into play and influence the stance of the competition policy adopted. Still, for a free society, the overriding objective should be safeguarding economic freedom with limits as expounded by John Stuart Mill in his *Utilitarianism* (1861, p. 22). Following this principle industrial policy and in particular competition policy should guarantee a level playing field with equal chances for small and big firms alike. This implies in particular that distributional issues, such as supporting economic activities of particular groups of society to compensate for losses entailed by competitive pressures, should not be pursued by restraining competition but rather by helping them to compete effectively. Following this principle industries may, under certain conditions, be supported by subsidies from the government in order to stand up against foreign competition. Even though it is true that international trade flows are governed by comparative advantage, it has to be recognized that comparative advantage does not fall from heaven. To a substantial degree comparative advantages have been created by investing in private and public (both non-human and human) capital. Government subsidies to create and improve comparative advantages are thus legitimate unless they distort competition by favoring particular firms. Therefore, within the European Union, government aid is put under the surveillance of the Commission to maintain a level playing field. Beyond that the WTO should be called upon.

References

Arrow, K.J. (1962): 'Economic welfare and the allocation of resources for invention', in National Bureau of Economic Research (ed.), *The Rate and Direction of Inventive Activity: Economic and Social Factors*, Princeton: Princeton University Press.

Ashton, T.S. (1964): *The Industrial Revolution 1760–1830*, New York: Oxford University Press.

Baumol, W.J., J.C. Panzar and R.D. Willig (1982): *Contestable Markets and The Theory of Industry Structure*, New York: Harcourt Brace Jovanovich.

Bork, R.H. (1965): 'The rule of reason and the per se concept: price fixing and market division', *The Yale Law Review* 74, 775–847.

Brander, J. and B. Spencer (1985): 'Export subsidies and international market share rivalry', *Journal of International Economics* 18, 83–100.

Cabral, L.M.B. and M.H. Riordan (1997): 'The learning curve, predation, antitrust and welfare', *Journal of Industrial Economics* 45, 155–69.

Chandler, A. (1990): *Scale and Scope: The Dynamics of Industrial Capitalism*, Cambridge, MA: MIT Press.

Cowling, K. and D.C. Mueller (1978): 'The social costs of monopoly power', *Economic Journal* 88, 727–48.

Debreu, G. (1959): *Theory of Value. An Axiomatic Analysis of Economic Equilibrium*, New Haven and London: Yale University Press.

Eddy, A.J. (1912): *The New Competition. An Examination of the Conditions Underlying the Radical Change that is Taking Place in the Commercial and Industrial World – the Change from a Competitive to a Cooperative Basis*, Chicago, IL: McClury.

Harberger, A. (1954): 'Monopoly and resource allocation', *American Economic Review* 44, 77–92.

Hayek, F.A. (1968): *Wettbewerb als Entdeckungsverfahren*, Kiel: Institut für Weltwirtschaft.

Leibenstein, H. (1966): 'Allocative efficiency and X-efficiency', *American Economic Review* 56, 392–415.

Martin, S. (2001): *Industrial Organization: A European Perspective,* Oxford: Oxford University Press.

Messerlin, P.A. and G. Reed (1995): 'Antidumping policies in the United States and the European Community', *Economic Journal* 105, 1565–75.

Mill, J.S., ([1861] 1957): *Utilitarianism*, Indianapolis and New York: The Library of Liberal Arts.

Mill, J.S., ([1871] 1965): *Principles of Political Economy*, 7th edn, New York: Augustus M. Kelley.

Mueller, D.C. (ed.) (1990): *The Dynamics of Company Profits: An International Comparison*, Cambridge, UK: Cambridge University Press.

Neale, A.D. (1966): *The Antitrust Laws of the United States of America*, Cambridge, UK: Cambridge University Press.

Neumann, M. (2001): *Competition Policy. History, Theory and Practice*, Cheltenham, UK and Northampton, MA, USA: Edward Elgar.

Neumann, M., I. Böbel and A. Haid (1983): 'Business cycles and industrial market power: an empirical investigation for West German industries', *Journal of Industrial Economics* 32, 187–96.

Neumann, M., I. Böbel and A. Haid (1985): 'Domestic concentration, foreign trade and economic performance', *International Journal of Industrial Organization* 3, 1–19

Neumann, M., J. Weigand, A. Gross and M. Münter (2001): 'Market size, fixed costs and horizontal concentration', *International Journal of Industrial Organization* 19, 823–40.

Nieberling, J.F. (1999): 'The effect of U.S. antidumping law on firms' market power: an empirical test', *Review of Industrial Organization* 14, 65–84.

Popper, K.R. (1957): *The Poverty of Historicism*, London: Routledge & Kegan Paul.

Posner, R.A. (1975): 'The social costs of monopoly and regulation', *Journal of Political Economy* 83, 807–27.

Schumpeter, J.A. (1912) *Theorie der wirtschaftlichen Entwicklung* (5th edn 1952), Berlin: Duncker & Humblot.

Schumpeter, J.A. (1942): *Capitalism, Socialism and Democracy*, New York: Harper.

Smith, A. ([1776] 1950): *An Inquiry into the Nature and Causes of the Wealth of Nations*, Cannan edn, London: Methuen.

Sutton, J. (1991): *Sunk Costs and Market Structure*, Cambridge, MA: MIT Press.

Symeonidis, G. (2002): *The Effects of Competition. Cartel Policy and the Evolution of Strategy and Structure in British Industry*, Cambridge, MA: MIT Press.

Tullock, G. (1967): 'The welfare costs of tariffs, monopolies and theft', *Western Economic Journal* 5, 224–32.

Williamson, O. (1968): Economies as an antitrust defense: the welfare trade-offs', *American Economic Review*, 58, 18–36.

1 Globalization and the natural limits of competition

*Stephen Martin**

1 Introduction

The debate on competition and its limits, which has its roots at the very foundation of economics as a discipline, has a phoenix-like quality. It periodically flares up, burns itself out and rises again, but largely without memory, unconscious of its previous incarnations. Certain themes appear and reappear: competition in the sense of structure, or of conduct, or of performance; potential distinguished from actual competition; advertising as a source of information or a means of persuasion; antitrust or competition policy seen as the heavy hand of government regulation or as the last best alternative to the heavy hand of government regulation, but each iteration seems to begin more or less anew, with different parties staking out positions that to them seem new but in fact are new only to them.

The issues raised by globalization at the dawn of the 21st century were also raised, on a smaller but still ample stage, by the forging of a continent-wide economy in the United States in the generation after the US Civil War. Contrasting positions on those issues were laid out in a debate on competition and its limits that preceded passage of the Sherman Act of 1890. Those positions appeared again in policy debates in the run-up to the 1914 passage of the Clayton Act and the Federal Trade Commission Act. They appeared yet again in US debates about the depression-era National Industrial Recovery Act of 1933, in the early 1950s,[1] and again in the 1970s.[2]

I will argue in this chapter that, while globalization – 'a catch-all to describe the phenomenon of an increasingly integrated and interdependent world economy, one that exhibits supposedly free flows of goods, services, and capital, albeit not of labor' (Obstfeld and Taylor, 2002, p. 6) – may have triggered yet another cycle in the debate on competition and its limits, the terms of that debate are not new, and that it is useful to draw lessons from earlier considerations of these same issues.

In Section 2 I review the various meanings that have been given to the word 'competition'. Section 3 takes up the question of limits to actual rivalry, in particular the nature of returns to scale. Section 4 deals with limits to potential rivalry.[3] Section 5 considers the relationship between competition policy, governments' commitment to the market mechanism as a resource allocation mechanism and competition. Section 6 draws conclusions.

2   The natures of competition

Competition is a word that is given many and different meanings. The result is persistent miscommunication. Sometimes such miscommunication is understandable, as when an economist gives the term 'competition' a technical meaning in a context that is clear to other economists but open to misinterpretation by noninitiates. But economists themselves often apply the term 'competition' to different phenomena, without sufficiently laying out what is intended. In the words of Fetter (1941, p. 398):

> Every economic discussion is beset with misunderstandings by reason of the shifting senses in which words are used by speakers or are understood by hearers. Words are often used with conscious sophistry to mislead; more often speakers and hearers alike are innocently misled by the same confusion of words; again, their minds fail to meet because they are talking about very different things under the same name.

Stigler ([1957] 1965, p. 237) discerns five preconditions for competition in Adam Smith's *The Wealth of Nations*:[4,5]

1. The rivals must act independently, not collusively.
2. The number of rivals, potential as well as present, must be sufficient to eliminate extraordinary gains.
3. The economic units must possess tolerable knowledge of the market opportunities.
4. There must be freedom (from social restraints) to act on this knowledge.
5. Sufficient time must elapse for resources to flow in the directions and quantities desired by their owners.

Condition 1, which refers to competition in the sense of conduct, says that the effectiveness of the invisible hand as a resource allocation mechanism is limited if suppliers do not behave in a rivalous way. Condition 4 refers to constraints on the range of permissible conduct: the effectiveness of the invisible hand is reduced if firms are restricted by society from behaving in a rivalous way.

Condition 2 refers to competition in the sense of elements of market structure, the number and size distribution of actual firms and costs facing firms that contemplate entry: the effectiveness of the invisible hand is limited if the number of actual and potential rivals is insufficient. The effectiveness of the invisible hand is limited if suppliers are unaware of profit opportunities or if consumers are unaware of alternative sources of supply and the terms they offer (3). The invisible hand is of limited effectiveness in time periods so short that rivalry cannot make itself felt (5).

Globalization might be thought to make it more likely that the second condition is met, by increasing the number of actual and potential rivals. With globalization comes a greater knowledge, on the part of firms at least, of opportunities in once-distinct geographic markets. Globalization thus makes it more likely that the third condition is met. To the extent that firms are less likely to be able to collude or tacitly collude, the greater the number of actual rivals, globalization makes it more likely that the first condition is met as well.

The impact of globalization on the fourth precondition for competition is two-sided. Throughout the globalization process, governments have negotiated safeguards to ensure the reciprocal open access that will allow their home firms access to other geographic markets. At the same time, governments have negotiated escape hatches that allow them to impede access of foreign firms to their home geographic markets. Sequential negotiations see some such escape hatches close, while others seem inevitably to open. The protectionist instincts of governments around the world are deeply rooted.[6]

Table 1.1   Competition as rivalry

Ely (1901, p. 58)	Competition, in a large sense, means a struggle of conflicting interest.
Eddy (1913, p. 21)	… competition is on a level and practically synonymous with terms such as 'struggle,' 'contest,' 'rivalry'.
Lilienthal (1952, p. 54)	To most of us laymen, competition means struggle, contest, rivalry, matching of wits or strength. … To the non-economist, competition *in business* is but one manifestation of this spirit of conflict and rivalry of ideas.
Stigler (1957; 1965, p. 235)	'Competition' entered economics from common discourse, and for long it connoted only the independent rivalry of two or more persons.

The term 'competition' is perhaps most often used in the lay sense of rivalry among actual competitors (Table 1.1).[7,8] In a broader sense, competition in the sense of rivalry may be thought to include rivalry between actual and potential sellers and rivalry for a prize, as in an innovation race or a contest for promotion (Lazear, 1995).

Rivalry between actual and potential rivals is often made the linchpin of yet another definition of competition, competition in the sense of the absence of barriers to entry (Table 1.2).[9] This view of competition is a precursor of the theory of contestable markets (Baumol *et al.*, 1982), and might also be thought of as a device to shoehorn general equilibrium relationships into a partial equilibrium framework.[10]

Table 1.2   Competition as the absence of barriers to entry and exit

Liefmann (1915, p. 316)	Competition … is then not merely the presence of several sellers in the market. One might define it as the possibility of the free movement of labor and capital. Competition, latent at least, is present as long as the appearance of a new seller in a branch of industry is not precluded.
Machlup (1942, p. 2)	In the succeeding discussion … the expression perfect competition … will exclusively denote free and easy entry into the industry.
Stigler ([1957] 1965, pp. 264–5)	It seems preferable, therefore, to adapt the concept of competition to changing conditions by another method: to insist only upon the absence of barriers to entry and exit from an industry in the long-run normal period; that is, in the period long enough to allow substantial changes in the quantities of even the most durable and specialized resources.
Andrews (1964)	The essential characteristic of an industry which is in open competition … is nothing more than that such an industry is formally open to the entry of new competition. … it will follow from my later argument that an industry with only one firm in it might well have to be analysed as though it were competitive.

Competition in the sense of rivalry also includes the view of competition as an evolutionary triage mechanism, selecting in the fit and selecting out the unfit (Table 1.3).[11] Marshall expressed a certain caution on this point. He wrote ([1892] 1909, p. 140) of 'the law that the struggle for existence causes those organisms to multiply which are best fitted to derive benefit from their environment' and commented that 'This law is often misunderstood; and taken to mean that those organisms tend to survive which are best fitted to benefit the environment. But this is not its meaning. It states that those organisms tend to survive which are best fitted to utilize the environment for their own purposes.'

Table 1.3   Competition as a selection mechanism

Ely (1901, p. 64)	Competition is the chief selective process in modern economic society, and through it we have the survival of the fit.
Encyclopaedia Britannica (quoted in Eddy, 1913, p. 19)	Competition, in the sense in which the word is still used in many economic works, is merely a special case of the struggle for survival. … Competition, in the Darwinian sense, is characteristic, not only of modern industrial states, but of all living organisms.

Competition has also been defined by negation, as the absence of monopoly (Table 1.4).[12] Like the definition of competition in the sense of rivalry, competition in the sense of the absence of monopoly is conceived of as a particular type of conduct, but a type of conduct that is very different from the lay conception of rivalry: price-taking firms in no sense engage *price-setting?* in strategic or rivalrous behavior.

Competition, it would appear, is a many-splendored thing. But the feasibility of competition in the various senses reviewed above depends largely on a common set of underlying factors. The equilibrium number of actual competitors and the impact of potential competition on the conduct of actual competitors depend both on the underlying technology. Particularly important characteristics of the technology are the nature of returns to scale and scope, the presence or absence of network economies and the extent to which investments required to operate in the industry are sunk. It is to a consideration of such technology-based factors that we now turn.

Table 1.4   Competition as price-taking behavior

Chamberlin (1933, p. 7)	Monopoly ordinarily means control over the supply, and therefore over the price. A sole prerequisite to pure competition is indicated – that no one have any degree of such control.
Lerner (1934, p. 157)	… the monopolist is confronted with a falling demand curve for his product … while the seller in a purely competitive market has a horizontal demand curve …
Stigler ([1957] 1965, p. 262)	If we were free to redefine competition at this late date, a persuasive case could be made that it should be restricted to meaning the absence of monopoly power in a market.

3   Actual rivalry and its limits

3.1   Equilibrium market structure

It is to Henry Adams and his analysis of late 19th-century American industry that we owe the distinction between technologies characterized by decreasing, constant and increasing returns to scale. Adams saw the nature of returns to scale as determining whether or not competition among incumbents would be an effective resource allocation mechanism (1887, p. 519):

> all industries … fall into three classes, according to the relation that exists between the increment of product which results from a given increment of capital or labor. These may be termed industries of constant returns, industries of diminishing returns, and industries of increasing returns. The first two classes of industries are adequately controlled by competitive action; the third class, on the other hand, requires the superior control of state power.

For Adams, competition failed as an organizing framework of increasing returns to scale industries because the equilibrium number of suppliers in such industries was one (ibid., p. 528): 'There are many other lines of business which conform to the principle of increasing returns, and for that reason come under the rule of centralized control. Such businesses are by nature monopolies.' The railroad industry was the quintessential example of a sector that came to be supplied by firms that were large in relation to the size of the market because the technology exhibited increasing returns to scale (Hadley, 1886, p. 41): 'in those lines of industry which involve large capital, under concentrated management, the old theory of free competition is as untenable as it was in the case of railroads.'

Furthermore, it was thought that the rise of railroads and complementary technologies was the prerequisite for the rise of large firms in other sectors (van Hise, 1912, p. 7):

> The development of transportation and communication furnished the fundamental basis for concentration of industry, because through them it became possible at a moderate cost to transport goods long distances in a short time and easy to communicate with the customer who desired goods.

It is now understood, as it was by Adams and some of his contemporaries, that, where large-scale enterprise arose endogenously,[13] it carried with it efficiency advantages (Clark, 1887, p. 46):[14]

> In manufacturing industries the balance of power had been disturbed by steam, and the little shops of former times were disappearing. The science adapted to such conditions was an economic Darwinism. ... Though the process was savage, the outlook which it afforded was not wholly evil. The survival of crude strength was, in the long run, desirable. Machines and factories meant, to every social class, cheapened goods and more comfortable living.

This late 19th-century literature made a distinction between competitive and monopolistic market structures: between a large equilibrium number of suppliers and a single equilibrium supplier. We would now distinguish between monopoly, small-numbers oligopoly, large-numbers oligopoly, and competitive equilibrium market structures. What is critical for the limits of competition in this structural sense – the equilibrium number of suppliers – is not absolute firm size, but firm size relative to market size (Stigler, 1955, p. 181):

> We all recognize that in a properly defined industry, if the largest firm has less than ten per cent of the output, competition will be effective – in the absence of collusion which itself generally will be less probable and effective when concentration is low. And when one firm has forty or fifty per cent or more, or two to five firms have seventy-five per cent or more of the industry's output, competition will seldom plague the industry.

The equilibrium number of firms in an industry should not, in the long run and in the absence of government intervention, be more than that implied by the expectation that firms will operate at efficient scale. What evidence is there, it seems reasonable to ask, about the nature of efficient operation in different industries?

Scale economies The conventional measure of returns to scale in neoclassical economic theory is the function coefficient, the elasticity of output with respect to a proportional change in the use of all inputs.[15] The function coefficient is, under the usual assumptions, the ratio of average cost to marginal cost (Ferguson, 1969, p. 160; Baumol *et al.*, 1982, p. 21). It is also the inverse of the elasticity of cost with respect to output (Ferguson, 1969, pp. 158–60). The function coefficient can be generalized in a natural way to a multiproduct technology (Panzar and Willig, 1977).

Patinkin (1947; see also Dewey, 1969, ch. 3) notes that a multiplant firm, operating in a region of rising average cost in any one plant, can slide down those average cost curves by incurring the fixed cost associated with opening a new plant. The result is a scallop-shaped average cost curve that is, after an initial region of declining average cost as output rises from a low level in a single plant, approximately horizontal. This theoretical result takes on a certain interest in light of the results of the empirical studies surveyed below.

Managerial loss of control in large firms is the most commonly cited source of diseconomies of large-scale operation.[16] The multidivisional firm may be thought of as an organizational device to mitigate such diseconomies (Chandler, 1962).

Economies of scale may be inherent in physical relationships (in the nature of the technology). A common example is a change in the radius of a pipeline by a factor λ, which means an increase in the volume of the pipeline by a factor λ^2. The point of Adam Smith's famous pin factory example is that increasing scale, supported by appropriate reorganization of production relationships, permits division of labor and can vastly increase output per worker. The division of labor and of physical capital are among several factors leading to increasing returns to scale that are noted by Scherer *et al.* (1975, pp. 19–20):

> The unit cost reductions associated with increasing plant size can have numerous causes: increased specialization of machinery and labor; indivisibilities making it worthwhile to spread the cost of lumpy equipment and special skills over a large output; technological relationships permitting equipment to be scaled up at less than a proportional increase in investment outlays; economies gained in high-volume purchasing and shipping; and 'massed reserves' advantages permitting a large plant to retain proportionately fewer repair men and backup machines to hedge against randomly occurring breakdowns.

Increased labor productivity with a greater division of labor is akin to, but distinct from, the learning curve phenomenon of lower unit cost with greater cumulative output.[17]

Economies of scale are in turn distinct from economies of scope (Bailey and Friedlaender, 1982, p. 1026): 'There are said to be positive economies of scope when a single firm can produce a given level of output of each product line more cheaply than a combination of separate firms, each producing a single product at the given output level.' Economies of scope may arise as overhead costs are spread over production of multiple product lines (Clark, 1973) or may be inherent in the technology (Baumol *et al.*, 1982, pp. 71–2).

There may also be economies of multiplant operation (Scherer *et al.*, 1975); at the plant level, some of these would appear as economies of scale; at the firm level, as economies of scope. In the diagnosis of natural monopoly, the neoclassical concept of economies of scale and the more recent concept of economies of scope are subsumed at a theoretical level in the subadditivity or lack of it of the cost function, due to Faulhaber (1975), (Bailey and Friedlaender, 1982, p. 1037): 'subadditivity is said to exist if the costs of joint production are less than the costs of separate production for any scale of output or combination of outputs'.

The early empirical literature was, and much of the recent literature remains, organized in terms of estimating some version of the function coefficient or of minimum efficient scale. Subadditivity, involving as it does global properties of a relevant multiproduct cost function, is difficult to test in a definitive way. Results of some approximate and local tests of subadditivity are cited below.

When the world, or at least the field of industrial organization, was young, neither microeconomic theory nor econometric techniques were sufficiently developed to estimate measures of returns to scale like the function coefficient. Industrial economists therefore developed techniques that permitted them to assemble some evidence on the determinants of market structure. One such class of evidence was based on analyses of the size distribution of plants or firms in an industry.

Bain (1956, ch. 3) reported engineering estimates of minimum optimal plant (p. 72) and firm (p. 86) scale, 'the smallest scale at which a plant or firm may achieve the lowest attainable unit cost' (p. 53), as a fraction of industry output. Compilation of engineering estimates involves unavoidable subjective judgments. It is also highly labor-intensive, limiting its use to samples of a small number of industries.

Efforts to get at the same concept, later more often referred to as 'minimum efficient scale', for large cross-sections of industries most often relied on one of two variables that could be mechanically computed from (often, government census) data on the size distribution of firms in an industry. One of these variables was the average size of the largest plants accounting for at least 50 per cent of industry shipments, as a percentage of industry shipments. The second was average shipments of plants in the mid-point size category, as a percentage of industry shipments.[18,19]

Stigler put forward the survivor technique for estimating minimum efficient scale (1958; 1968, p. 73).[20]

Classify the firms in an industry by size, and calculate the share of industry output coming from each class over time. If the share of a given class falls, it is relatively inefficient, and in general is more inefficient the more rapidly the share falls.

Saving (1961) applied the survivor methodology to data on 200 US 4-digit S.I.C. manufacturing industries. He was obliged to discard results for 43 industries that showed two or more distinct size classes with increasing market shares. For remaining industries he finds (p. 580) that 'in most cases, the magnitudes of ... optimum sizes are quite small relative to the size of the industries. In fact, 71.9 per cent of the industries for which we have estimates of optimum plant size have minimum optimum sizes of less than 1 per cent of their respective industry's total value added' and that there is often a large range of efficient scales of operation (p. 582) 'over 65 per cent of the industries in the sample have maximum optimum sizes which are greater than five times their respective minimum optimum sizes'.

Early econometric evidence on the nature of returns to scale came from statistical analyses of the relation between output and some more or less appropriately adjusted measure of accounting cost.[21] Often a main purpose of these studies was to marshal evidence on the extent to which average and marginal cost curves for real-world plants and firms resembled the familiar U-shaped curves beloved of intermediate microeconomics courses. Short descriptions of the results of typical studies are given in Table 1.5. The findings typically imply that, after falling over an initial range of low output, the average cost curve is relatively flat (Johnston, 1960, p. 168):[22]

Two major impressions ... stand out clearly. The first is that the various short-run studies more often than not indicate constant marginal cost and declining average cost as the pattern that best seems to describe the data that have been analyzed. The second is the preponderance of the L-shaped pattern of long-run average cost that emerges so frequently.

Early production function studies' estimates of Cobb–Douglas and CES (constant elasticity of substitution) production functions, often with what now appear to be overly aggregated data, form a bridge between the types of studies discussed in Section 3 and later, more micro-based, estimates of cost and production functions. Ferguson (1967), who estimates Cobb–Douglas production functions for 2-digit U.S. Census of Manufactures industries

Table 1.5   Result of typical early cost function studies

Johnston (1960)	
Electric power (UK, 1946–7)	'The minima of successive AVC lie on a practically horizontal straight line … the envelope to these curves is only the first component of long-run average cost, but if Fig. 4–10 is a reliable indication of the second (capital cost) component, then long-run average cost is approximately constant over long ranges of output … the economies of scale in electricity generation can be fully exploited by firms of medium size'
Passenger road transport (1 large UK firm, late 1940s–early 1950s)	Declining short-run average cost throughout observed output range
Passenger road transport (24 UK firms, 1951)	Unable to reject hypothesis of constant long-run average costs
Multiproduct food processing firm (UK, 9/1950–6/1951)	Constant marginal cost for each of 14 products.

Dean (1976)	
Furniture factory (single plant, 1932–4)	Constant marginal cost, declining average cost over observed output range.
Leather transmission belt shop (1935–8)	Constant marginal cost, declining average cost over observed output range.
Hosiery mill (1935–9)	Constant marginal cost, declining average cost over observed output range.
Department store (1931–5)	Hosiery department, shoe department: constant marginal cost, declining average cost; coat department: declining marginal cost.

using state-by-state data, is typical of this literature.[23] He interprets his findings as showing that (p. 215):

> there is not sufficient evidence to reject the broad hypothesis of constant returns to scale in the American manufacturing sector. Using aggregate results alone, three industries showed increasing returns to scale (Food and Kindred Products, Primary Metals and Electrical Machinery) and three showed decreasing returns to scale (Textiles, Apparel and Related Products and Chemicals and Allied Products). Such inter-industry differences are to be expected; but taking all results into consideration, one must conclude on balance that the hypothesis of constant returns to scale cannot be rejected.

Cost and production relationships in a few industries have been the subject of repeated study, in part because of data availability, in part because of their inherent policy interest (the former, of course, may be influenced by the latter). Studies of such industries are reviewed here.[24]

White (1971) estimates minimum efficient automobile production scale at about 400 000 vehicles per year. Taking into account the risk implied by long design lead times and the difficulty in predicting public tastes far in advance, he concludes that for long-term viability, an automobile manufacturer should produce two makes of automobile and distribute them through separate dealer networks. Relating market concentration to this estimate of minimum efficient firm scale, he writes (p. 268):

> a minimum-size efficient firm would require a volume of 800,000 units annually through two makes. Thus an 8-million-unit car market could theoretically support ten efficient firms. In fact, there are only four, with one, American Motors, currently in the 250,000-unit category.

Cost–output relationships in the automobile industry have been a frequent subject of econometric analysis. Table 1.6 lists some exemplary studies. Among these studies, Friedlaender *et al.* (1983) estimate a linear hedonic cost function from time-series cross-section data for the Big Three US automobile manufacturers (GM, Ford, Chrysler) for the years 1955–79. They classify outputs into three categories, compact and subcompact cars, full-size and luxury cars, and trucks, and find evidence of varying returns to scale (1983, p. 18): 'the global cost surface is decidedly not convex, but exhibits variable regions of increasing and decreasing returns to scale and increasing and decreasing returns to multiple production'. At the sample mean, Chrysler and General Motors appeared to operate where there were increasing returns to scale (generalized function coefficients 1.16 and 1.23, respectively), Ford where there were decreasing returns to scale (generalized function coefficient 0.88).[25] The implied industry average function coefficient, 1.05, was not distinguishable from constant returns to scale.

Table 1.6   Returns to scale in automobile production

Friedlaender *et al.* (1983)	Firm-level annual data, US Big 3, 1955–79: at sample mean, GM and Chrysler IRS, Ford DRS, 'typical firm' CRS.
Fuss and Waverman (1992, p. 122)	Annual industry data: increasing returns to scale at the sample mean (scale elasticities Canada 1.17, Japan 1.07, Germany 1.1, USA 1.09).
Truett and Truett (2001, p. 1508)	Spanish industry data, 1967–92; increasing returns to scale at the sample mean, marginally significant decreasing returns to scale at maximum output in the sample.

Fuss and Waverman (1992) estimate a translog cost function from annual data for Canada, Germany, Japan and the United States, with observations for each country covering slightly varying intervals of the 1960s to the early 1980s. They report estimated function coefficients at the sample mean of 1.17 (Canada), 1.07 (Japan), 1.10 (Germany) and 1.09 (United States).

Truett and Truett (2001) estimate a translog industry cost function for the Spanish automobile sector using annual data for the period 1967–92. They find a cost elasticity that is less than one at the 5 per cent level at the sample mean, greater than one at the 10 per cent level at the maximum output in the sample. (The corresponding function coefficients are 1.319 at the sample mean, 0.773 at the maximum sample output.) They conclude that adaptation to the Single European Market will allow Spanish automobile firms to realize some economies of scale.

Berger *et al.* (1987) give references to econometric studies of economies of scale and scope in banking[26] in the 1980s. Their own results, for US banks and for 1983, suggest that there are modest economies of firm scale for banks with deposits up to $25 million, with essentially constant or modest diseconomies of scale up to deposits of $1 trillion, in states that allow branch banking.[27] Results for states that do not allow branch banking suggest statistically significant diseconomies of scale for banks with deposits of or greater than $200 million.

The results of several more recent studies of cost–scale relationships in the banking sector are summarized in Table 1.7. The bulk of this literature has been concerned with US banking, and for such studies see Cavallo and Rossi (2001, p. 516):

The main conclusions of the empirical literature concerned with the US experience ... are that overall the average cost curve is relatively flat, with some evidence of scale efficiency gains for small banks. ... constant or slight diseconomies of scale prevail in the case of large banks.

Such results for the USA seem sensitive to the treatment of risk and diversification, although studies that take risk and diversification explicitly into account do not yield a consensus. Hughes *et al.* (2001) use a specification that allows for utility maximization by managers in a risky environment, and find evidence of increasing returns to scale throughout their sample. Dealing with the presence of risk in another sample – Japanese commercial

Table 1.7   Returns to scale in banking

Altunbas *et al.* (2000) (Japanese commercial banks, 1993–6)	Scale economies for banks of asset size up to Yen 2 trillion, diseconomies of scale for larger banks (mean sample asset size about Yen 5 trillion, maximum sample asset size about Yen 75 trillion).
Hughes *et al.* (2001) (U.S. bank holding companies, 1994)	Estimates that allow for utility maximization by managers show increasing returns to scale throughout the sample range.
Wheelock and Wilson (2001) (US commercial banks, 1985, 1989, 1994)	'banks could achieve potential economies by expanding the size of their output and adjusting their output mix toward those banks with at least $300–$500 million of assets. Although we find some evidence of scale economies for banks as large as $1 billion, our point estimates are not estimated precisely across all methodologies and, hence, we do not draw firm conclusions ... The wide range over which we cannot reject constant returns to scale suggests ... that banks of many sizes could be competitively viable, though firm conclusions are difficult to draw because the density of banks exceeding $1 billion of assets is low'.
Cavallo and Rossi (2001) (Banks in 6 EU member states, 1992–7)	Increasing returns to scale for small and medium-size banks, constant returns to scale for large banks.
Carbo *et al.* (2002) (EU savings banks, 1989–96)	Constant returns to scale at smallest asset size classes; increasing returns to scale that rise with size class thereafter.

banks – and in another way, by including risk proxies directly in estimating equations, Altunbas *et al.* (2000) find the economies of scale are exhausted, and diseconomies of scale set in, at relatively low asset sizes. Studies of EU banking show the presence of economies of scale over some size ranges, without consensus on where (if at all, in sample ranges) economies of scale are exhausted.

Weiss (1971, pp. 89–90) writes:[28]

> Electric power involves three major processes: (1) production ...; transmission ...; and distribution and sales. The economies of scale in distribution seem obvious. ... The presence of two or more sets of poles, wires, transformers, and meter readers would almost always imply so much unnecessary capacity that almost all observers accept the need for monopoly in the 'retailing' of electricity. ... Transmission from the power plant to the consuming centers also involves very large economies of scale. When transmission capacity over a given distance is doubled, investment in transmission lines increases by only about 2/3. ... There are also economies of large scale in generation, but they do reach a limit.

More recent studies (Table 1.8) reach a similar conclusion: there are increasing returns to scale in the electric power industry, but they seem to be exhausted at levels that permit effective competition (Christensen and Greene, 1976, p. 656):[29]

> We conclude that a small number of extremely large firms are not required for efficient production and that policies to promote competition in electric power generation cannot be faulted in terms of sacrificing economies of scale.

The six studies noted in Table 1.9 examine four different healthcare-related markets. Cowing and Holtmann (1983) find increasing returns to scale in hospitals at their sample mean, and also that returns to scale decline as hospital size increases. Roughly half the hospitals in the Eakin and Knieser sample produce under conditions of increasing returns to scale, half under conditions of decreasing returns to scale, with the sample mean implying decreasing returns to scale.

Given (1996) and Town (2001) employ different techniques but both find constant returns to scale in health maintenance organizations, beyond low enrollment levels. Okunade (2001) gets similar results for hospital pharmacies.

Cockburn and Henderson (2001) find evidence of economies of scope in the probability that a drug development project will lead to permission to market a drug, but no evidence of economies of scale.

As noted above (Section 3.1), it was with the railroad sector that economists' and policymakers' concern with the nature of returns to scale began. Many

Table 1.8 Returns to scale in electric power

Christensen and Greene (1976, p. 656)	'Our primary finding . . . is that the U.S. electric power industry can be characterized by substantial scale economies at low levels of output. But the implied decreases in average cost diminish in importance for larger firms, resulting in an average cost curve which is very flat for a broad range of output'.
Berndt (1991, p. 83)	'. . . the econometric literature on estimated returns to scale in the electric utility industry in the United States appears to suggest that substantial economies of scale have been available, that such scale economies may have been largely exploited by the early 1970s, and that [in 1991] the bulk of electricity generation comes from firms generating electricity at the bottom of their average cost curves.
Lee (1995) (70 investor-owned US electric utilities)	Price-cost margins between monopoly and perfect competition; constant returns to scale at the sample mean.
Thompson (1997) (major US investor-owned electric utilities, 1977, 1982, 1987, 1992; p. 294)	'average-sized firms expanding output to a fixed number of customers in a given area will experience decreasing average costs for sales volumes well beyond sample mean levels. . . . firms that expand output, numbers of customers, and service territory proportionately will not experience decreasing average cost if the firm's values are at or above the sample mean'.
Filippini (1998) (39 Swiss electricity utilities, 1988–91)	Economies of output density and customer density; economies of scale for all except the largest utilities.
Atkinson *et al.* (2003)	Modestly increasing returns to scale in steam electric power generation.

studies have estimated short-run cost–output relationships, treating network size as given. Most such studies (see Table 1.10) find evidence that there are economies of density;[30] that is, that the marginal cost of increasing traffic on a network of fixed size is less than the average cost.

Table 1.9   Returns to scale in health care-related sectors

Cowing and Holtmann (1983) (340 New York State hospitals, 1975)	Increasing returns to scale at the sample mean, decreasing as scale increases.
Eakin and Kniesner (1988) (331 US hospitals, 1975–6)	165 hospitals operate with decreasing returns to scale, 166 with increasing returns to scale; decreasing returns to scale at the sample mean.
Given (1996) (California HMOs, 1986–92)	Statistically constant returns to scale at sample mean output mix from about 115 000 enrollees to sample maximum of 850 000 enrollees.
Town (2001, p. 984) (products offered by California HMOs, 1993–7)	'econometric evidence indicates that economies of scale are not present'.
Okunade (2001, p. 182) (US hospital pharmacies, 1981–90)	'Our results indicate an L-shape relationship of average cost of hospital pharmacy operations to bed size. There is no large cost differential effect of bed sizes between the largest hospital pharmacies (> 500 beds, the base) and those with 400–499 and 200–299 beds. Positive and significant cost differences of 12.12%, 5.16%, 3.5% and 2.21% exist, however, for smaller and mid-sized hospitals with 0–49, 50–99, 100–199 and 300–399 bed capacities'.
Cockburn and Henderson (2001, p. 1052) (drug development projects at 10 US pharmaceutical firms, between 1960 and 1990)	'drug development projects are more likely to result in [permission to market a drug] in firms which have significantly more diverse development efforts, rather than in those firms that simply spent more on development in total. Scale effects ... have a weak positive association with a project's success when entered alone, but this effect disappears when we control for scope.'

Griliches (1972) and Keeler (1974) find constant returns to scale if the length of track size is adjusted optimally. Atkinson *et al.* (2003) estimate an input shadow distance system for four inputs (freight ton miles, passenger miles, average passenger trip length in miles, average freight haul in miles) and find some evidence of increasing returns to scale.

Bitzan (2000) tests the subadditivity of an estimated multiproduct cost function for US railroads by comparing estimated cost functions for one and two firms. He finds that a single railroad network is a natural monopoly, while combined operation of end-to-end networks is not a natural monopoly.

Table 1.10   Returns to scale, US railroads

Griliches (1972) (97 US railroads, 52 of which with more than 500 miles of track, 1957–61)	Constant returns to scale for railroads with more than 500 miles of track.
Keeler (1974) (51 US railroads, freight, 1968–70)	Long-run constant returns to scale (gross ton-miles), increasing returns to traffic density
Harris (1977) (55 US essentially freight railroads, 1973–4)	Increasing returns to density.
Caves *et al.* (1981) (US Class I railroads, freight and passenger traffic 1955, 1963, 1974)	'… fairly strong, statistically significant, scale economies if output increases come in the form of increased haul and trip lengths. … only slight, statistically insignificant scale economies if output is increased with length of haul and trip held fixed'.
Caves *et al.* (1985, p. 99) (US Class I railroads, 1951–75)	'… increasing returns to scale for small carriers, but for medium to large railroads returns to scale are nearly constant. … substantial increasing returns to density that persist over a larger range of output than has been found in any prior study'.
Braeutigam *et al.* (1982, 1984) (firm-level data, one small US railroad, one large US railroad, quality of service taken into account)	Important economies of density, both railroads.
Vellturo *et al.* (1992) (Class I US railroads, 1974–86)	Substantial returns to scale, short run and with way and structures and route miles variable.
Bitzan (2000) (US Class I railroads, 1983–97)	Natural monopoly on a network of a given size, not on end-to-end networks.
Atkinson *et al.* (2003) (US Class I railroads, 1951–75; four inputs, four outputs)	'average returns to scale [generalized function coefficient] 1.17 … assuming [allocative efficiency]' (p. 606); 'For all firms, the average cost savings resulting from [technical efficiency], from [allocative efficiency], and from both … are approximately 63%, 12%, and 75%, respectively' (p. 609).

The study of the nature of economies of scale and/or scope in telecommunications has been contentious (see, for example, Charnes *et al.*, 1988; Evans and Heckman, 1988).[31] Waverman (1989, pp. 83–90) summarizes 20 such studies (of AT&T and Bell Canada) that were published between 1977 and 1986, covering intervals ranging from 1947 to 1978. Of the results of these studies, he writes (p. 87):

> The evidence on overall economies of scale ... would appear to favor the presence of such economies. In only two cases does the lower-bound estimate of overall economies of scale (95 per cent confidence region below the mean estimates) fall below unity.

Waverman outlines methodological shortcomings of the literature. He sees some of those same difficulties in his own results, and in conclusion writes (1989, p. 94), 'My view is that neither scale nor scope was significant in the 1947–77 period at the level of a firm such as AT&T before divestiture' and 'It is unlikely that significant economies of scale existed in interchange service between 1950 and 1980.'

Röller (1990a) addresses some of Waverman's points, and finds evidence of economies of scale in US telecommunications before 1979. Shin and Ying (1992) estimate that there are modest economies of scale in local exchange carriers, but reject subadditivity of the multiproduct cost function. Local exchange carriers, by these estimates, are not natural monopolies. Sung (2002) finds statistically constant returns to scale, on average, for US local telephone exchanges. Bloch *et al.* (2001) find no evidence of economies of scale for Australian telecommunications.

Despite the intuitively appealing and long-held notion that the telecommunications sector should be thought of as a natural monopoly, there is evidence both for and against that proposition, and the verdict at this writing must be 'not proven'.[32] Table 1.11 summarizes the surveyed studies.

Tables 1.12 and 1.13 give capsule indications of the results of studies of the nature of returns to scale (and occasionally, scope) in 12 different sectors. There is some evidence of some increasing returns to scale in some of these studies: Geehan (1977) for Canadian insurance, Betancourt and Malanoski (1999) for supermarket distribution, and the four studies of food-processing industries. Other studies suggest that such increasing returns to scale as are present decline with firm size, or over time. None of these studies finds returns to scale that are so persistent as to suggest that the sector studied might be thought of as a natural monopoly.

Much of the extensive literature on the nature and determinants of trends in total factor productivity carries out empirical work at an extreme level

Table 1.11   Returns to scale in telecommunications

Röller (1990a) (Bell System, annual data, 1947–79; estimated quadratic cost function constrained to display theoretically expected properties)	'strong overall economies of scale … at all output levels observed between 1947 and 1979,' economies of scope; subadditivity not rejected; 'the data are consistent with the natural monopoly hypothesis'.
Bloch *et al.* (2001) (Australia, annual data, 1926–91)	Economies of scope, no economies of scale along the three rays examined.
Guldmann (1991) (44 LECs, New York, 1980)	With territory size fixed, minimum average cost at 51 053 telephone lines (sample range 874 to 552 868, median 7000, mean 27 957).
Shin and Ying (1992), Ying and Shin (1993) (58 LECs, 1976–83, 1976–87)	Modest economies of scale at the sample mean; cost function not globally subadditive.
Sung (2002) (8 LECs, annual data, 1950s-1991)	'the bulk of [local exchange carriers] are operating in the essentially flat area of the average cost curve'; 'small and medium firms have slightly increasing returns to scale while large firms suffer from slightly decreasing returns to scale'.

of aggregation, such as the US manufacturing sector. Studies with less aggregated data, like those of Baily *et al.* (1992), Burnside *et al.* (1995) and Klette (1999), report as a joint product with their productivity estimates findings of constant returns to scale. Studies with two-digit industries, which are much less aggregated than the whole manufacturing sector but far too aggregated to constitute meaningful industries in an economic sense, report finding increasing returns to scale (Morrison, 1990), and are inconsistent with the bulk of the micro-level evidence.[33]

A possible reconciliation of these differing results lies in an appeal to increasing returns to factors of production external to firms or industries, such as human capital and the state of knowledge. The results of Morrison and Siegel (1997) are at least suggestive of this explanation.[34]

It may be the case that studies with aggregate data indicate increasing returns to scale because they are picking up external economies based upon the public good aspects of knowledge, while studies with industry, firm and plant data find constant returns to scale to factors of production that are internal to the firm. Such a conclusion suggests that there should be public support for public and private investment in knowledge. This support might

Table 1.12   Returns to scale, various sectors

Baumol and Braunstein (1977) (56 academic journals, several publishers, 1969, 1971, 1973)	Evidence of economies of scope: 'costs increased more slowly with increases in circulation than with increases in pages, and in both cases costs per journal declined as the number of journals per publisher increased.' Firms in the sample appear to be operating at efficient size.
Geehan (1977) (43 Canadian life insurance companies, 1970)	Some evidence of statistically significant increasing returns to scale, not of economically significant returns to scale.
Wang Chiang and Friedlaender (1985) (105 US trucking firms, 1976)	'At the grand sample mean, the [generalized function coefficient was] 0.998, while at the sample mean of the "large" carriers, [it was] 0.929. Thus the "typical" firm operating at the sample [mean] appears to be operating under constant returns to scale, while the representative "large" firm is subject to moderate diminishing returns.' Economies of scope at the sample mean, not for the representative 'large' firm.
Kumbhakar (1993) (Utah dairy farms)	'In general, the small farms, as a group, are found to be less efficient relative to the class of medium and large farms. ... We find that the returns to scale of the small farms are much higher when compared to the medium and large firms'.
Kerkvliet *et al.* (1998) (US beer brewing; annual industry data, 1952–92)	Estimated efficient firm scale rose from at most 608 000 barrels of beer per year in 1960 to at most 1.3 million barrels of beer per year in 1970; from at least 2.653 million barrels of beer per year in 1975 to at least 5.008 million barrels of beer per year in 1990; by late 1980s, national producers larger than necessary to exploit economies of scale.
Betancourt and Malanoski (1999) (US supermarkets, 1982)	Estimated constant returns to scale with respect to output, increasing returns to scale with respect to distribution services.

Table 1.12 continued

MacDonald and Ollinger (2000) (hog slaughter; establishment data, Census years, 1963–92)	Modestly increasing returns to scale at the sample mean; returns to scale rising over time; largest plants operate near constant returns to scale.
Buccola *et al.* (2000) (US food-processing industries; 4-digit SIC data, 1958–94)	Largest economies of scale in bakery products, smaller in flour milling, near-constant in rice milling and feed milling.
Callan and Thomas (2001) (municipal solid waste disposal and recycling, Massachusetts, 1997)	At the sample mean, estimated constant returns to scale in waste disposal, economies of scale in recycling and economies of scope between disposal and recycling.
Morrison Paul (2001) (US meat packing, SIC 2011, 1958–91)	Substantial economies of scale early in the sample period, near constant returns to scale by the end of the sample period.
Hollas *et al.* (2002) (33 US natural gas utilities, 1975–94)	'The pattern of changes suggests promotion of competition has generally moved gas distributors "to the left" on their long-run average cost curves. After restructuring, 37 per cent of gas distributors are in either the increasing or constant scale categories compared to 24.2 per cent and 23.0 per cent [before 1978] and [between 1978 and 1992] periods, respectively.'
Drake and Simper (2002) (police forces, England and Wales, 1992/93–1996/97)	Economies of scale, less than 3000 staff members; constant returns to scale, 3001 to 4500 staff members; diseconomies of scale, more than 4500 staff members.
Xia and Buccola (2002) (4 4-digit SIC meat-processing industries, 1973–94)	With productivity growth, average cost curves become lower, flatter over time; economies of scale at the sample mean.

take the form of the promotion of international technology alliances, as well as more traditional national policies.[35] Such a result would not overturn the conclusion suggested by studies based on less aggregate data that economies of scale within firms and plants are typically exhausted at outlet levels far below those of global markets.

Table 1.13   Evidence on returns to scale from productivity studies

Morrison (1990, p. 28) (17 2-digit US manufacturing industries, 1952–86)	'short and long-run scale economies exist and are quite substantial in a number of industries. Scale economies also appear to be increasing, especially in industries which tend to be more capital-intensive and have experienced productivity growth stagnation' (p. 29). 'The procyclicality of the [elasticity of cost with respect to output] is evident … declines are evident for most industries in the downturns of 1969–70, 1974–5 and 1982–3. To a large extent cyclical movements in [the elasticity of cost with respect to output] are driven by utilization fluctuations, since potential scale economies appear to be increasing over time rather smoothly'.
Baily *et al.* (1992) (Longitudinal Research Database; plant-level data; 23 4-digit SIC industries, 4 Census years)	'The general word among researchers at the Center for Economic Studies at the Census Bureau has been that there are constant returns to scale in the LRD panel. Our results are unlikely to change that conclusion. If anything, there is some sign of decreasing returns'.
Burnside *et al.* (1995) (26 3-digit SIC industries, 1977–92)	'… inference about returns to scale is quite robust across the three specifications of technology that we considered. There just is not much evidence in our data sets against the hypothesis of constant returns to scale.'
Klette (1999) (14 2/3 digit ISIC Norwegian manufacturing industries, 1980–90)	'… the average firm in most industries seems to face constant or moderately decreasing returns to scale'.

Network externalities   There are network externalities if the utility enjoyed by any one consumer of a good is greater, the greater the total consumption of the good.[36] Telephone service is a classic example of a direct network externality: the more consumers there are joined to the network, the more phone calls any one consumer can choose to make. Indirect network externalities arise from the interaction of quantity consumed (installed customer base) and the provision of complementary goods. That Windows operating systems have an effective monopoly for personal computers encourages software developers to write packages that are compatible with Windows. This makes personal computer users better off, as they have a wider range of available applications.

Intuition honed on markets without network externalities can go astray in their presence. Economides and Flyer (1997) show that equilibrium market structure in the presence of strong network economies is typically asymmetric, with entrants attaining at most a fringe position and having little impact on the price set by the leading firm.[37] Further, consumer welfare and net social welfare are typically greater when one firm has an asymmetrically larger market share, as this maximizes the network externalities enjoyed by consumers. Where network externalities are strong, the link between competition (in most of senses noted in Section 2) and good market performance is broken.

An implication is that globalization in network industries may lead to increased overall welfare and improved performance in the global market, but not to market structures that are competitive in the sense of having a large number of actual rivals of broadly similar sizes or in which the threat of potential competition would temper the conduct of incumbents. It can be presumed that regional political leaders in such a global market will not be indifferent to income transfers from their region to a network leader based in some other region. Possible consequences include the policies (less optimistically) to erect barriers to globalization and (more optimistically) to support local suppliers of products complementary to those of the network leader.

Endogenous sunk costs   Sutton (1991, 1998) analyzes the relationship between endogenous sunk costs – spending on advertising and on research and development – and equilibrium market structure.[38] Where the sunk costs that must be covered by a firm supplying a market are given by the technology, his models show, market concentration goes to zero as market size becomes large. Where the costs that are sunk are the cost of choice variables of the firm, variables that increase consumers' willingness to pay for a product, equilibrium seller concentration is bounded away from zero.[39] Evidence from the food sector (1991) supports the predicted impact of advertising on seller concentration (1991). Evidence from a cross-section of high R&D intensity industries supports the predicted impact of R&D spending on market concentration (1998).[40]

Globalization implies the reduction of costs incurred by suppliers located in one regional submarket that supply (either directly or by direct foreign investment) other regional markets. Globalization implies the reduction of costs incurred by consumers located in one regional submarket who wish to obtain a product variety offered by a supplier based in some other regional market.[41] Sutton's work suggests that, to the extent that globalization leads to a reduction in exogenous sunk entry costs, globalization should lead to lower levels of concentration in larger, more nearly global, markets. Where the sunk costs of operating in global markets are endogenous, however, reductions in the equilibrium level of market concentration need not materialize.

Globalization should not be expected to lead to an increase in competition in the sense of the equilibrium number of rivals in markets where endogenous sunk costs are a significant factor.

3.2   Competition, efficiency and market structure

Efficient operation   The notion that rivalry promotes efficient operation long antedates Leibenstein and the analysis of X-efficiency.[42] For example, Chadwick (1859, p. 409) writes:[43]

> I recognise as a fact of common experience, that where a single tradesman is permitted to have the entire and unconditional possession of a field of service, as in remote rural districts, he generally becomes indolent, slow, unaccommodating, and too often insolent, reckless of public inconvenience, and unprogressive. To check these evils, competition of a second is no doubt requisite.

A modern rationale for the existence of technical inefficiency, and the possibility that the degree of inefficiency is itself the product of economic forces, is given by Caves and Barton (1990, pp. 4–5):[44]

> If costs are elevated X per cent above the minimum attainable, we must suppose that it pays somebody to reduce them. A satisfactory theoretical story must explain why that opportunity is not seized. The main part of the answer lies in second-best bargains struck between principals and agents – whether the owners of equity shares in firms and their hired managers or managers at any level within the enterprise and the persons whom they hire and supervise. The potential for second-best outcomes of such bargains and the implied strong possibility that the degree of nonoptimality will vary from case to case supply one basis for explaining technical efficiency.

A body of empirical research suggests that rivalry promotes technical efficiency. Primeaux (1977) studies the average costs of monopoly and duopoly US electric public utilities and finds (p. 107) that 'average cost is reduced, at the mean, by 10.75 per cent because of competition'.[45]

In their analysis of the efficiency of U.S. manufacturing industries, Caves and Barton (1990) find that a greater share of imported supplies promotes efficiency in domestic establishments, which seems to be greatest in industries where the four-firm seller concentration ratio is around 40 per cent.[46] A successor study of efficiency in six industrialized countries finds (Caves, 1992, p. 12) that: 'In every country high concentration is found hostile to technical efficiency. In four of them a quadratic relationship indicates that maximum efficiency comes at an intermediate level of concentration. ... In the other two a linear negative effect dominates.'

Hay and Liu (1997) study the efficiency of 181 leading firms in 21 3- or 4-digit UK manufacturing industries for the period 1970–89. They find that firm efficiency increases with greater efficiency of firms in the same industry and as own market share falls.[47] Both results are consistent with the view that rivalry promotes efficiency.

Specific instances of deregulation allow case studies of natural (or, some might say, unnatural) experiments in the impact of increased rivalry on market performance. Graham *et al.* (1983) is an early study, followed by many more, suggesting that deregulation of US airlines increased operating efficiency. That deregulation would decrease flight frequency and increase load factors had been anticipated by advocates of deregulation. Emergence of the hub-and-spoke system had not been anticipated. Eckel *et al.* (1997) report evidence (lower fares as well as stock market effects) suggesting that the privatization of British Airways similarly improved market performance.

Ng and Seabright (2001) estimate a frontier production function for 12 EU and 7 US major airlines for the period 1982–95, and report, among other results, (p. 610):[48]

> An increase of one percentage point in the proportion of a carrier's international routes on which it faced competition from a third airline (holding its market share constant) would lower rents to employees by 3 per cent and costs to the airline by about 2 per cent.

> ... a reduction of ten percentage points in the share of public ownership would be associated (other things equal) with a 10 per cent reduction in rents and therefore about an 6.5 per cent reduction in costs.

Lien and Peng (2001) compute an efficiency measure for a sample of 25 OECD telecommunications operators over the period 1980–95. Efficiency is estimated to be lower for markets and years where there are at most one or two operators. Similar comparisons with company-level data seem to confirm the country-level results.

Efficient market structure   There is evidence that rivalry promotes the development of a cost-minimizing market structure. One class of such evidence is that on the development of the hub-and-spoke system in the US post-deregulation passenger airline industry, noted above.

Elliott and Gribbin (1977), Broadberry and Crafts (1992) and Symeonidis (1998, 2002) analyze a quantum ratcheting-up of the toughness of UK competition policy toward collusion in the mid-1950s. The result seems to have been a quantum reduction in the ability of trade associations to deliver 'the quiet life' to members, a shake-out of high-cost firms, and an increase in the market shares of low-cost firms.

Hay and Liu (1997) examine UK manufacturing and estimate that the market shares of less efficient firms erode over time. But they find no simple pattern of types of product or market structure to explain the speed of such erosion, and caution (pp. 610–11): 'The results are a warning against attempts to categorise the state of competition in a market a priori, on the basis of market structure and degree of product differentiation.'

On balance, empirical evidence supports the view of rivalry as a selection mechanism.

3.3   Competition and the exercise of monopoly power[49]

It is a robust result of static models of imperfectly competitive markets that the noncooperative equilibrium level of market power falls as the number of firms rises. In repeated-game models, noncooperative collusion is generally less likely to be an equilibrium, the greater the number of firms. Much economic theory also leads one to suspect that actual collusion, as well as its tacit counterpart, is less likely to be stable, the greater the number of firms.[50]

Turning to empirical evidence, although cross-section studies of market performance are out of style, it should be noted that a multitude of such studies suggest that competition from foreign suppliers tempers the ability of domestic suppliers to hold price above marginal cost.[51]

Market integration in the European Union generates continuing data about the impact of increased competition on market performance. Allen *et al.* (1998) examine the impact of the EU's Single Market Programme on 15 3-digit NACE[52] industries for the period 1976–94. Their results suggest (p. 452): 'On average, after allowing for other influences on pricing, price-cost margins have fallen by 3.9 per cent since 1991 across the fifteen sectors studied.' Working with a sample of 745 Italian firms, Bottasso and Sembenelli (2001) find that for firms in tradable goods sectors that estimated price-cost margins between 15.8 per cent and 19 per cent for 1982–7 and between 6.6 per cent to 10.7 per cent for 1988–93. Siotis (2003) finds a reduction in price-cost margins for Spanish manufacturing with integration into the EU.

Of course, not all increased competition comes from lowering the barriers that separate suppliers located in different geographic markets. The US Congressional Budget Office (1998) estimated that measures to permit increased competition between generic and brand-name pharmaceuticals from the 1980s onward (p. ix) 'have lowered average returns from marketing a new drug by roughly 12 per cent'.[53]

Lowering barriers to trade brings increased competition (actual and potential rivalry) and improves market performance. It is equally to be expected that vigorous domestic competition will hone efficiency (promote competitiveness) and promote success on international markets. Sakakibara and Porter (2001) present empirical evidence that the vigor of competition in Japanese domestic markets has contributed to Japan's strong exporting track record.

3.4 Rivalry and dynamic market performance

It was Emerson's phrase that 'A foolish consistency is the hobgoblin of little minds', and 'little minds' is a category into which Schumpeter certainly did not fall. The terms of the debate between the Joseph Schumpeter (Schumpeter Mark I) of *The Theory of Economic Development* (1934), who argued that it would most often be new firms that drive innovation, and the Joseph Schumpeter of *Capitalism, Socialism and Democracy* (1943) (Schumpeter Mark II), who argued that large firms with static market power would be responsible for most innovation, is too well known to require detailed review.[54]

There is evidence that competition, in various senses, promotes productivity growth.[55] Baldwin (1993, ch. 9), examining data on a sample of Canadian manufacturing plants, finds (p. 235) that 'some 40 to 50 per cent of productivity growth is due to plant turnover' which he takes as evidence that 'a Darwinian replacement process is at work. Progress is made as the successful displace the unsuccessful'.

Olley and Pakes (1996), who limit their attention to a single industry (telecommunications equipment) also find evidence that productivity growth is driven by a plant-level selection effect (1996, p. 1292):

the changes in the telecommunications industry improved performance by inducing a reallocation of capital to more productive plants. This reallocation process seems to be facilitated by entry and exit. ... it is the reallocation of capital, rather than an increase in the efficiency of the allocation of variable inputs or in average productivity, that seems to underlie the increase in productivity that followed the deregulation of the telecommunications industry.

Baily and Gersbach (1995) examine nine industries in Germany, Japan and the United States. They classify each industry for each country as locally, regionally or globally competitive and find a broadly positive relationship between labor productivity and the breadth of competition. They also construct a globalization index based on exposure of lower-productivity industries to the rivalry of the high productivity industry via either imports or direct foreign investment, and find that greater globalization in this sense is associated with greater relative productivity. Börsch-Supan (1998) similarly finds a pattern of relative capital productivity across the three countries consistent with the hypothesis that globalization promotes efficient use of capital.

Nickell *et al.* examine U.K. firm-level panel data and 'see in the data ... a time series association between increases in market share and falls in the level of productivity combined with a cross-section association between higher market share and higher rates of productivity growth.' (1992, p. 1072). Nickell (1996) finds that firm-level productivity growth is higher, the lower the level of economic rents, the greater the number of competitors, and the lower is market share. Nickell *et al.* (1997) find that firm-level productivity growth is lower, the higher the level of economic rents.[56]

Carlin *et al.* analyze UK establishment data for 1980–92 and report (2001, p. 76):

> Only about one-half of productivity growth takes place within surviving establishments, with net entry accounting for about another 30 per cent. ... the survival and growth of some entrants and the cumulative impact of exit have a significant effect on productivity growth over a decade or more. An even more important contribution comes from the net effect of the opening and closure of plants by multi-product firms.

They also find that product-market competition raises the level and growth of productivity.[57]

Tybout and Westbrook (1995) examine the impact of late-1980s Mexican trade liberalization on Mexican manufacturing. They find evidence of productivity increases, in part due to cost reductions, in part due to market share increases of more efficient plants. They do not find evidence of gains due to the realization of scale economies.[58]

Hay looks at the consequences of Brazil's 1990 opening up to trade and finds (2001, p. 620) 'the main effects of trade liberalisation as a reduction of market shares in the domestic market, a sharp fall in profits, and a marked increase in the efficiency of large Brazilian manufacturing firms'.

Pavcnik (2002) finds that Chilean trade liberalization induced higher productivity in continued plants and exit of less productive plants. In a remark that anticipates the discussion in Section 5, she writes (2002, p. 271): 'the barriers to plant turnover are important determinants of the success of trade liberalization'.

Amato and Amato (2001) look at productivity growth in a sample of 274 US 4-digit SIC industries for the years 1977, 1982, 1986 and 1992, and find that productivity growth is greater, all else equal, the greater the growth rates of either import or export sales.

4   Potential rivalry and its limits

The idea that one can rely on potential rivalry alone to support good market performance is one of the periodically recurring themes in industrial economics.[59] Gunton (1888, p. 403) writes of trusts:

> they have therefore a direct interest in keeping prices at least sufficiently low not to invite the organization of counter enterprises which may destroy their existing profits. If the gates for the admission of new competitive capital are always open, the economic effect is substantially the same as if the new competitor were already there; the fact that he may come any day has essentially the same effect as if he had come, because to keep him out requires the same kind of influence that would be necessary to drive him out.[60]

Along the same lines, Van Hise writes (1912, p. 84):

> In making the statement that prices of many articles, from the great natural monopolies to matches, are controlled by some form of combination or agreement, it is not meant to imply that any price can be charged for an article. There is a limit beyond which, if the price be raised, competitors will enter a business. This so-called potential competition makes the combinations careful not to place the prices at so high a level as to lead to additional competition.[61]

Machlup (1942) again emphasized the impact of potential competition on market performance. The importance of potential competition was a central element of the structure–conduct–performance framework, which emphasized the importance of barriers to entry precisely because the height of such barriers was thought to determine the extent to which potential competition could work its effect. Baumol *et al.* (1982) renovated the doctrine of potential competition, rebaptized it as the theory of contestable markets, and put forward the airline industry, with its 'capital on wings' as a likely prototype of a real-world analogue of a contestable market.

The finding of Eads *et al.* (1969) that pilots and co-pilots could be treated as a fixed resource in the short run might be thought to raise the possibility of a range of increasing returns to scale on the supply side of the passenger airline market. Caves *et al*. (1984) find that what is at work is economies of density rather than economies of scale in the strict sense.[62] Later work confirms that the passenger airline industry cannot be said to be contestable.

The results of some such studies are indicated in Table 1.14. From the point of view of obtaining good market performance, potential rivalry may be good; actual rivalry is better.[63]

Table 1.14   Returns to scale in and contestability of the airline industry

Eads *et al*. (1969) (12 local carriers, quarterly data, 1Q 1958–4Q 1966)	Input of pilots and co-pilots treated as a fixed factor in the short run. No evidence of substantial increasing returns to scale.
Graham *et al*. (1983) (194 local US airline markets, 4Q 1980, 1Q 1981)	'… fares seem to be positively related to concentration, thereby indicating that potential competition is not strong enough at present to eliminate all attempts to raise price in concentrated markets'.
Caves *et al*. (1984) (annual observations, trunk and local airlines, 1970–81)	Constant returns to scale (proportional increases in network size and output), economies of density (increases in output, network size constant).
Borenstein (1989) (1508 city-pair routes serviced by at least 2 of the 9 largest US airlines, 3Q 1987)	'… dominance of major airports by one or two carriers, in many cases the result of hub formation, appears to result in higher fares for consumers who want to fly to or from these airports' (p. 362).
Berry (1992) (1219 US city-pair markets, 1980)	'… profits decline fairly rapidly in the number of entering firms. … efforts to decrease city pair concentration by increasing airport access will be to some degree offset by competition within city pairs: even as the number of potentially profitable firms increases, within-market competition will limit the number of entering firms' (p. 914).
Brueckner *et al*. (1992) (US round trips with change at hub, 4Q 1985)	'… addition of the first competitor to a monopoly market lowers fares by 7.7%. Addition of a second or third competitor reduces fares by a further 3.4% … addition of an extra competitor beyond three lowers fares by a further 0.6%. … addition of a potential competitor to the market … lowers fares by 1.6%' (pp. 325–6).

This empirical literature suggests that it is not useful to analyze the passenger airline industry as if it were contestable. The broader implication for the impact of globalization on market performance is that, in a wide range of industries, apparently minor market characteristics will often offer incumbents the opportunity to engage in strategic behavior that raises the cost of entry, blunting the force of potential competition. The extent to which incumbents are able to effect such strategic behavior depends on the commitment of public authorities to market competition as a resource allocation mechanism.

5   Globalization and the limits of competition as a policy

When I write of 'competition as a policy', I have in mind not merely what is called in the EU 'competition policy' and in the USA 'antitrust policy', but rather a public commitment to the market mechanism as a resource allocation mechanism. Certainly such a commitment includes application of competition policy: in the words of Stigler (1955, p. 177), 'An antitrust policy is employed by a society which wishes to use the competitive market, rather than powerful private or public bodies, to regulate most economic activity.' Global trade evoked a World Trade Organization, and it seems likely that global markets will in due course evoke a Global Competition Organization (Scherer, 1994). That global markets bring with them business behavior that is typically condemned in national markets seems beyond dispute (Connor, 2001).

But public commitment to the market mechanism is more than having an antitrust policy. Competition or antitrust policy is but one in a menu of public policies that impact the functioning of the market mechanism. These include, among others, the boundary between the public and the private sector and the differences in the nature of the economic environment on either side of that boundary,[64] the nature of local programs to promote economic development, rules governing trade flows, labor market and workplace safety legislation, consumer protection legislation, property development (zoning) rules and environmental protection legislation. A commitment to markets as a resource allocation mechanism includes not only using antitrust policy to promote effective market performance but also ensuring that these other elements of public policy are not applied in such a way as to short-circuit the functioning of markets. Full realization of the benefits of globalization requires that governments let the market mechanism work.

Examples of public policies that sidestep the market mechanism are all too easy to find. Countries that maintain a vigorous competition policy for their own domestic market typically permit their suppliers to collude for sale on export markets. This is difficult to justify in its own right, and ignores the fact that explicit collusion with respect to foreign markets facilitates tacit collusion with respect to the domestic market.

The historical record of trade distortion via voluntary export restraints is well known. So is the indefensible application of WTO anti-dumping provisions, the rule of which seems to be, as in *Romeo and Juliet*, 'all are punish'd'.[65] US safeguard tariffs on steel (March 2002) represent a practical departure from reliance on competitive international markets. So do US farm policies and the EU's Common Agricultural Policy.

Subsidies to firms by EU member states have a track record of keeping inefficient firms alive, blocking one of the avenues for gains from EU market integration (Martin, 2001, ch. 10). Similar prisoners' dilemma races to promote local economic development occur in the USA. The EU has a better policy track record than the USA in this area, in principle at least, in that the distortionary nature of state aid is recognized and control of state aid is an element of EU competition policy.[66]

Beyond policy measures that explicitly distort markets to accomplish a goal that is not otherwise reachable, or not otherwise reachable at acceptable political cost, national packages of product and labor market regulations may have the practical effect of shielding domestic firms from the buffeting winds of competition. Nicoletti *et al.* (2000) report the results of an OECD evaluation of national product and labor market policies in terms of their impact on product market competition. The study evaluates regulations, administrative procedures, barriers to entrepreneurship, barriers to trade and other economic policies conditioning the ability of rivals to compete.

The results of these evaluations are combined, using factor analysis, to construct an index of product market regulation, with lower values representing less restrictive regulation. A similar index is constructed for employment protection regulation.[67] These rankings are depicted in Figure 1.1, along with a simple regression line fitted to the observations.[68] It is evident that there is a tendency for countries where product market regulation is less cordial towards competition also to have intensive labor market regulations.

Scarpetta *et al.* (2002) report evidence that restrictive product and labor market regulations of the kind described in Figure 1.1 have a negative impact on multifactor productivity and limit the market access of small and medium-sized firms. Djankov *et al.* (2002) carry out a cross-section analysis of entry regulations for 85 countries and find (p. 35) 'that heavier regulation of entry is generally associated with greater corruption and a larger unofficial economy'. They do not directly analyze the relation between the nature of entry regulation and productivity growth, but do report the heavier regulation of entry is not associated 'with better quality of private or public goods'. (ibid.).

Employment
protection
legislation

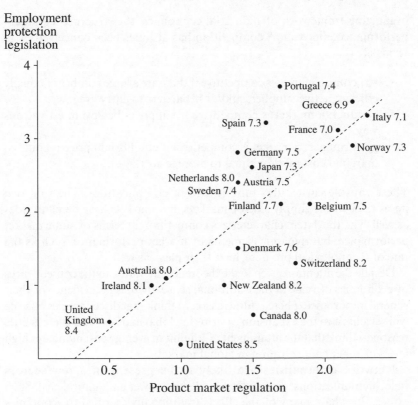

Sources: Nicoletti *et al.* (2000), Gwartney and Lawson (2002).

Figure 1.1 Product market regulation and employment protection regulation

Figure 1.1 also shows, for each country, its 'Economic Freedom' ranking (Gwartney and Lawson, 2002), on a scale of 0 (low economic freedom) to 4 (high economic freedom). The subjective nature of this ranking means that it may be questioned by reasonable parties.[69] It nonetheless seems worthwhile to note that countries found by the OECD to have competition-friendly product and labor market regulations tend to rank high on the subjective economic freedom scale.

6 Conclusion
The large literature on competition is made obscure by the fact that some of its components deal with competition in one sense, some in another, with various, to use the phrase of Vickers (1995), concepts of competition, concepts not always clearly distinguished. Harking back to the classic

organizing framework of industrial economics, the structure–conduct–performance approach,[70] competition has at times been conceived of in terms of

- structure: a market is competitive if there are a large number of equally efficient active suppliers and/or if barriers to entry are low;
- conduct: a market is competitive if suppliers behave in a rivalrous way;
- performance: a market is competitive if equilibrium price is equal to marginal cost (and/or equal to average cost).

These capsule caricatures hint at further complications. The first two items refer to the supply side of markets, but markets have demand sides as well. The third item characterizes competition in terms of static market performance, but dynamic elements of market performance, such as the rate of technological progress, have their place as well.

Despite the attention given in the theoretical literature to the consequences of economies of scale in the traditional sense, there is no evidence of their general importance. There is little reason to think that diseconomies of scale will set a limit to the expansion of firms in global markets, and there is little reason to think that the attainment of minimum average cost mandates high levels of seller concentration in global markets.

Network externalities are likely to be present in a few sectors (telecommunications; distribution of electric power and natural gas). Such externalities have many of the effects traditionally ascribed to economies of scale in production.

Outside of such sectors, there is no compelling evidence for the presence of natural monopoly. The initial reaction to any claim of natural monopoly should be scepticism. Where network economies are present, they imply that the best equilibrium market performance will be characterized by substantial rent transfers to a single leading supplier. In global markets, such an outcome may well be politically unacceptable.

Competition in the sense of rivalry seems clearly to promote efficient operation and productivity growth. Full realization of these and other benefits of globalization requires governments to accept the resource reallocations that more competitive, more rivalrous, markets bring. An unwillingness to do this may well prove to be the most serious limitation to competition in global markets.

Notes
*   I am grateful to the editors for offering me the opportunity to prepare this chapter, and to Dennis Mueller, Manfred Neumann and Lars-Hendrick Röller for comments. Responsibility for errors is my own.

1. See among others Lilienthal (1952), Dirlam and Kahn (1954).
2. See among others Demsetz (1974), Bork (1978).
3. I do not discuss limits to competition stemming from possible market failures, including the failure of competitive equilibrium to exist (Telser, 1988), tragedies of the commons (Gould; 1972; Clark, 1973; Smith, 1975) and demand-side behavior (Scitovsky, 1950; Diamond, 1971; Waterson, 2003).
4. McNulty (1967) reviews the pre-Smith literature on competition and writes (1967, p. 396) 'by the time the Wealth of Nations appeared, competition was a familiar concept in economic writing and . . . its analytical function was its recognized tendency to bring market price to a level which would eliminate both excessive profits and unsatisfied demand, that is, to the lowest level sustainable over the long run.' See also McNulty (1968).
5. Stigler himself (1942, pp. 2–3) put forward a definition of workable competition that included specifications about the number of actual competitors, the conduct of actual competitors, and the nature of entry conditions: 'An industry is workably competitive when (1) there are a considerable number of firms selling closely related products in each important market area, (2) these firms are not in collusion, and (3) the long-run average cost curve for a new firm is not materially higher than for an established firm.'
6. The connection between protectionist tariffs and domestic market performance was made by some during US Senate debates on the Sherman Act (remarks of Senator Vest, 21 Cong. Rec. 2466, 21 March 1890). Others denied any such connection. Simons (1936, p. 72) called for 'Gradual but complete abolition of the gigantic federal subsidies implicit in [the U.S.] tariff structure and rapid termination of subsidies and production control for agriculture' and clearly saw a link between tariff policy and domestic market performance: 'The open season on consumers must be abolished; for, if the direction of tariff changes is not reversed, we cannot hope to prevent wholesale extension of tariff politics into interference with internal trade.'
7. Van Hise (1912, pp. 72–5) writes of competition in quality, competition in price and competition in service, but in all three dimensions it is competition in the sense of rivalry that is meant. Adelman (1948, p. 1303) writes that 'Competition requires rivalry in buying and selling among business firms which are not in collusion. But rivalry alone is not competition' and cites an instance in which rivalry in advertising was thought to be an instrument of exclusion.
8. As noted by Vickers (1995, footnote 6), Bork has objected to the characterization of competition, for (US) antitrust purposes, in terms of rivalry on the ground that (1978, p. 58) 'It is a loose usage and invites the further, wholly erroneous conclusion that the elimination of rivalry must always be illegal' and 'It makes rivalry an end in and of itself, no matter how many or how large the benefits flowing from the elimination of rivalry.' Vickers addresses this comment by observing that his own discussion goes beyond the framework of US antitrust policy. For my part, I point out that a well-known exchange between Senator Kenna and Senator Edmunds during debate on the Sherman Act (21 Cong. Rec. 3151–2), to which Bork himself refers (1978, p. 68, footnote) makes clear that the elimination of less efficient rivals by more efficient rivals was not intended to violate the Sherman Act. To write that the identification of competition with rivalry invites the conclusion that any and all elimination of rivalry is illegal is argument, not analysis.
9. Andrews (1951, p. 142) reads Marshall as using the term competition in the sense of freedom of entry. The characterization of market competition as the absence of barriers to entry to the market is paralleled by Becker's (1958, p. 106) characterization of free political competition as the absence of barriers into the political arena. It draws on themes central to the too-maligned structure–conduct–performance paradigm and, by its reference to specialized resources, anticipates the emphasis given to sunk investments by the theory of contestable markets.
10. For descriptions of competition in a general equilibrium sense, see Holmes (1910, p. 412), Triffin (1940, p. 88), and Stigler ([1957] 1965, p. 263). Most industrial economists have resisted the temptation to go up what Mason (1959, p. 5) called 'the garden path' of general equilibrium, and so will I. See, however, Lankford and Stewart (1980) and Suzumura

(1995, ch. 2), and for an effort by general equilibrium theorists, Dierker and Grodal (1998). Stigler (1949) offers a withering view of general equilibrium approaches.

11. See also Clark (1887, p. 46, cited below), and the discussion of the survivor technique in Section 3.

12. See also Triffin (1940, p. 5 and the references in footnote 4) and Lerner (1944, pp. 73–4). Mason's ([1937] 1949, p. 28]) statement is more nuanced:

> The antithesis of the legal conception of monopoly is free competition, understood to be a situation in which the freedom of any individual or firm to engage in legitimate economic activity is not restrained by the state, by agreements between competitors or by the predatory practices of a rival. But free competition thus understood is quite compatible with the presence of monopoly elements in the *economic* sense of the word monopoly. For the antithesis of the economic conception of monopoly is not free but pure competition, understood to be a situation in which no seller or buyer has any control over the price of his product. Restriction of competition is the legal content of monopoly; control of the market is its economic substance.

13. And, we would now add, in the absence of strategic entry-deterring behavior.

14. Non-efficiency political and social goals have of course been put forward in debates about public policy toward business behavior. Judge Hand accurately states one of the original goals of US antitrust policy *(U.S.* v. *Aluminum Company of America* 148 F. 2nd 416 at 429 (1945)): 'Throughout the history of [US antitrust and related] statutes it has been constantly assumed that one of their purposes was to perpetuate and preserve, for its own sake and in spite of possible cost, an organization of industry in small units which can effectively compete with each other.' Such views may be thought to relate to the fourth precondition for competition found by Stigler in *The Wealth of Nations*, freedom from social restraints to act on the knowledge of market opportunities. It is probably accurate to say that the development of US antitrust law has ostensibly read such goals out of US competition policy. See, however, Section 5.

15. Ferguson (1967, footnote 1) attributes the term 'function coefficient' to Carlson (1939). See also Ferguson (1969, pp. 79–80).

16. See, for example, Robinson (1958, pp. 39–49).

17. See Fudenberg and Tirole (1980), Ghemawat (1985) and, for an application, Gruber (1994).

18. For discussions, see Scherer (1974) and Weiss (1974, pp. 224–5), Davies (1980) and Gupta (1981). Strickland and Weiss (1976, p. 1112) prefer the mid-point size–class-based MES measure on the ground that it is more correlated with engineering-based measures than the top 50 per cent based measure. Saving (1963) draws conclusions about the shape of average cost function using an approach that generalizes Gibrat's Law. De Brabander and Vanlommel (1978) and Fuss and Gupta (1981) use estimated cost functions to infer the minimum efficient scale output level.

19. Another variable used by Bain was absolute capital requirements, the investment needed to set up a plant of minimum efficient size. Caves *et al.* (1975) introduced the cost disadvantage ratio, value-added per worker in plants in the upper half of the industry plant-size distribution divided by value-added per worker in plants in the lower half of the industry plant-size distribution.

20. For an earlier statement, see Stigler (1950; 1968, pp. 98–9). For critical views, see Weiss (1964), Shepherd (1967) and Bain (1969). For a comparison of survivor, engineering and Census of Manufactures-based estimates, see MacPhee and Peterson (1990).

21. Friedman's (1955) remarks on the futility of analyzing accounting cost data should be noted. Read narrowly, these remarks may be seen as an argument that accounting measures of the value of a firm's capital stock are poor indicators of the corresponding economic value. This argument has been taken up by others (Fisher and McGowan, 1983; Fisher, 1987). It is probably a fair reading of the literature to say that this argument is accepted as correct in principle, although (by revealed preference) not in practice fatal to the use of appropriately adjusted accounting data in empirical research by industrial and

other economists. Read broadly (Friedman, 1955, pp. 235–6), Friedman's remarks may be seen as the precursor of the panglossian view that there is no such thing as economic profit, only efficiency rents (see Dick and Lott, 1990, and the references therein).

22. Heflebower (1955, p. 370) reaches a similar conclusion.
23. For other such studies, see Besen (1967) and Moroney (1967). Griliches and Ringstad (1971) find evidence of economies of scale, declining with firm size, using Norwegian data. Atack (1985, p. 178) obtains results broadly constant with the presence of constant returns to scale in nineteenth-century U.S. manufacturing.
24. Studies of the airline industry are taken up in Section 4.
25. Friedlaender *et al.* also present evidence on returns to scope (1983, pp. 16–7): 'The results indicate that for all of the firms there appear to be marked economies of joint production from combining the production of large cars with small cars and trucks, varying diseconomies from combining the production of trucks with the production of small and large cars, and varying economies and diseconomies from combining the production of small cars with the production of large cars and trucks.'
26. Arnoud Boot, in this volume, discusses in more detail the role of scale and scope for the banking industry and competition therein.
27. See their Table 1, firm results using the production approach, p. 512.
28. An entry for the electric power industry appears in Table 1.5. See Walters (1963, Table VIII) for references to other early studies of electricity cost functions; also see Nelson and Wohar (1983).
29. For another survey of this literature, see Cowing and Smith (1978).
30. Caves *et al.* (1985, p. 97): returns to density reflect the relationship between inputs and outputs with the rail network held fixed. Returns to scale reflect the relationship between inputs and the overall scale of operations, including both outputs and network size.
31. See Röller (1990b) for a particularly useful discussion of Evans and Heckman (1983) and Charnes *et al.* (1988). See also Diewert and Wales (1991) for a discussion of the Evans and Heckman results.
32. Schankerman and Nadiri (1986) analyze annual data for the Bell System for 1947–76 and find a long-run elasticity of cost with respect to output 0.57, implying substantial economies of scale. Their functional form implies the presence of some economies of scale; they treat R&D as an input.
33. Caves and Barton (1990, p. 23) similarly note 'Broadly based estimates of Cobb–Douglas and CES production functions in manufacturing ... typically find statistically significant economies of scale. However, a considerable weight of evidence from the field of industrial organization suggests that plant cost curves in narrowly defined manufacturing industries typically take the shape of a letter J lying on its side, indicating scale economies (which may or may not be substantial) at small scales of operation that diminish and give way to constant returns over an extensive range of large scales.'
34. Henderson (1999) finds decreasing returns to labor, capital and materials with plant-level data, but evidence of external economies from agglomeration of own-industry plants in the same region.
35. For discussion of which, see Martin and Scott (2000).
36. See the Spring 1994 issue of the *Journal of Economic Perspectives* for a symposium on network externalities, the October 1996 issue of the *International Journal of Industrial Organization* for a special issue on the topic, and Shy (2001). For references to the broader topic of path dependence, see Liebowitz and Margolis (1990, 1999) and David (1985, 2001).
37. Of course, that the equilibrium which emerges in the absence of strategic behavior and has a market structure that involves a dominant firm is not the same thing as an observed market structure with a dominant firm having emerged with strategic behavior by that dominant firm. See Borenstein (1989) for passenger airlines, Weiman and Levin (1994), Gabel (1994) for the US telephone industry.
38. For reviews, see Bresnahan (1992) and Scherer (2000). See also Sutton (2000).

39. The lower bound for seller concentration implied by high levels of R&D spending depends on the extent to which firms supplying a market employ similar technology trajectories; see Sutton (1998, Section 3.6).
40. See Robinson and Chiang (1996) for other supporting evidence.
41. For consumer goods, the reduction in purchasing transaction cost of an individual consumer will be via the intermediary of a reduction in costs to a wholesale or retail distributor of supplies from a foreign firm. In such cases, at least, the supply-side and demand-side impacts of globalization are, to borrow a metaphor, the two blades of a pair of scissors.
42. On which, see Perlman (1990) and the references therein.
43. Chadwick is in turn anticipated by Adam Smith, who notes that one consequence of the opening up of roads is to bring competition to previously isolated regions, and writes that one of the advantages of such competition is that (Smith, [1776] 1937, p. 147) 'Monopoly, besides, is a great enemy to good management, which can never be universally established but in consequence of that free and universal competition which forces everybody to have recourse to it for the sake of self-defence.' Not long after Chadwick, Adams (1887, p. 501) wrote that 'Again, wherever the conditions for competitive action are maintained, society has a guarantee that goods will be produced at the lowest possible cost; for the hope of personal gain leads to the best disposal of labor, to invention, and to the adoption of the best machinery.' Judge Hand's often-quoted observation (148 F. 2d 416 at 427) that 'immunity from competition is a narcotic' is well known.
44. For theoretical contributions, see Horn *et al.* (1995), Bertoletti and Poletti (1996, 1997), Schmidt (1997), Barros and Macho-Stadler (1998), and Wright (2003), among others.
45. Hausman and Neufeld (1991) compare the efficiency of publicly-owned and privately-owned US electric utilities in 1897–8 and find publicly-owned utilities to be more efficient. As they note (p. 420), ownership and competition effects are distinct influences on efficiency.
46. They also note that efficiency appears to fall with enterprise diversification and (1990, p. 63) that: 'A major puzzle ... is a highly significant negative correlation between estimated efficiency and the number of plant observations used to estimate the production function.'
47. I am indebted to Dennis Mueller for the observation that a finding that the efficiency falls as market share rises is inconsistent with the efficiency argument of Demsetz (1974), and suggests that the positive coefficient of market share commonly found in studies of line-of-business profitability (Martin, 1983; Ravenscraft, 1983; others) is evidence of the exercise of market power.
48. They also find increasing returns to both scale and density. See Table 1.14 for results of other studies touching on these points.
49. I defer discussion of the impact of potential rivalry on the exercise of market power to Section 4.
50. See, generally, Scherer (1970, ch. 6).
51. See Esposito and Esposito (1971), Caves (1980), Neumann *et al.* (1985), and Katics and Petersen (1994), among others.
52. Nomenclature générale des activités économiques dans les Communautés Européennes. See EC Commission (1996).
53. Allen *et al.* (1998, p. 451) report improved market performance in EU pharmaceuticals under the Single Market Programme.
54. See, generally, Winter (1984). The evolution in Schumpeter's views is noted by Samuelson (2003, p. 90).
55. Satisfactory treatment of the large empirical literature relating alternative measures of innovation input or innovation output to market and firm characteristics would require a separate chapter. The results of empirical studies of factors explaining differences in productivity growth rates may in any case be more easily related to the matter of the impact of globalization on dynamic market performance.

56. High debt levels or the presence of a dominant shareholder substitute for low economic rent in promoting productivity growth. See also Kovenock and Phillips (1997), who find evidence of strategic influences on plant closing decisions in oligopoly.
57. Carlin *et al.* (2001) also analyze a sample for Eastern European transition economies. They find evidence of restructuring, without much indication of concomitant productivity growth.
58. This result is plausible, given the findings of the literature reviewed in Section 3.1, that in most industries available economies of scale can be realized at relatively low output levels.
59. Demsetz (1968, p. 57, footnote 7) cites Chadwick (1859) in connection with Demsetz' monopoly franchise argument questioning the theoretical rationale for regulation of natural monopoly. The citation of Chadwick in this context is not without peculiar aspect, as Chadwick himself (1859, p. 408) presupposed ongoing administrative supervision of the conduct of a successful 'bidder for the field'. From the point of view of the modern theory of regulation, it would be thought doubtful that the informational requirements Chadwick mentions for such supervision could be met. Nor did Chadwick limit the scope of his proposal to natural monopoly (Dnes, 1994). What Chadwick put forward was an argument for a form of regulation, not an argument that regulation was unnecessary.
60. Giddings (1887, p. 76) makes much the same argument.
61. See also Liefmann (1915), Marshall (1923, p. 524).
62. The nature of these results is similar to those reported by Caves and various sets of co-authors for railroads; see Table 1.10.
63. The results of Bresnahan and Reiss (1987, 1991) on the impact of entry in local markets are consistent with this view.
64. That there is a public sector is not, in and of itself, inconsistent with reliance on the market mechanism. It becomes so if public firms are given immunity from the rules that apply to private firms.
65. For a more complete discussion of trade-distorting policy measures, see Martin (2001, ch. 9).
66. Incorporation of control of state aid into US antitrust policy would need to navigate treacherous shoals of the US federal system of government.
67. With regard to which, the industrial economics adage that barriers to exit are barriers to entry comes to mind. Where it is difficult for firms to discharge employees, firms are reluctant to hire employees. Employee protection legislation very often appears to be legislation that protects workers with jobs at the expense of would-be workers who do not have jobs.
68. Austria, Sweden and The Netherlands have identical values of both indexes.
69. The treatment of intellectual property rights in making the economic freedom ranking seems positively wrongheaded. Excessive intellectual property rights are not conducive to economic freedom, as is recognized by Milton Friedman in his preface to Gwartney and Lawson (2002).
70. The structure–conduct–performance framework is largely superseded in academic research by a game-theoretic approach that grafts industrial economics onto the neoclassical microeconomic theory of the firm (and, it can be argued, reproduces many of the results obtained using the S–C–P approach).

Bibliography

Adams, H.C. (1887): 'Relation of the state to industrial action', *Publications of the American Economic Association* 1, January, 471–549.

Adelman, M.A. (1948): 'Effective competition and the antitrust laws', *Harvard Law Review* 61, 1289–1350.

Allen, C., M. Gasiorek and A. Smith (1998): 'The competition effects of the single market in Europe', *Economic Policy* 27, 439–69.

Altunbas, Y., M.-H. Liu, P. Molyneux and R. Seth (2000): 'Efficiency and risk in Japanese banking', *Journal of Banking & Finance* 24, 1605–28.

Amato, L.H. and C.H. Amato (2001): 'The effects of global competition on total factor productivity in U.S. manufacturing', *Review of Industrial Organization* 19, 407–23.

Andrews, P.W.S. (1951): 'Industrial analysis in economics', in T. Wilson and P.W.S. Andrews (eds), *Oxford Studies in the Price Mechanism*, Oxford: Clarendon Press, pp. 139–72.

Andrews, P.S.W. (1964): *On Competition in Economic Theory*, London: Macmillan.

Atack, J. (1985): *Estimation of Economies of Scale in Nineteenth Century United States Manufacturing*, New York and London: Garland Publishing.

Atkinson, S.E., R. Färe and D. Primont (2003): 'Stochastic estimation of firm inefficiency using distance functions', *Southern Economic Journal* 69, 596–611.

Bailey, E.E. and A.F. Friedlander (1982): 'Market structure and multiproduct industries', *Journal of Economic Literature* 20, 1024–48.

Baily, M.N. and H. Gersbach (1995): 'Efficiency in manufacturing and the need for global competition', *Brookings Papers on Economic Activity Microeconomics*, 307–47.

Baily, M.N., C. Hulten and D. Campbell (1992): 'Productivity dynamics in manufacturing plants', *Brookings Papers on Economic Activity Microeconomics*, 187–267.

Bain, J.S. (1956): *Barriers to New Competition*, Cambridge, MA: Harvard University Press.

Bain, J.S. (1969): 'Survival ability as a test of efficiency', *American Economic Review* 59, Papers and Proceedings, 99–108.

Baldwin, J.R. (1993): *The Dynamics of Industrial Competition*, Cambridge, UK: Cambridge University Press.

Barros, F. and I. Macho-Stadler (1998): 'Competition for managers and product market efficiency', *Journal of Economics & Management Strategy* 7, 89–103.

Baumol, W.J. and Y.M. Braunstein (1977): 'Empirical study of scale economies and production complementarity: the case of journal production', *Journal of Political Economy* 85, 1037–48.

Baumol, W.J., J.C. Panzar and R.D. Willig (1982): *Contestable Markets and the Theory of Industry Structure*, New York: Harcourt Brace Jovanovich.

Becker, G.S. (1958): 'Competition and democracy', *Journal of Law and Economics* I, 105–9.

Berger, A.N., G.A. Hanweck and D.N. Humphrey (1987): 'Competitive viability in banking: scale, cope, and product mix economies', *Journal of Monetary Economics* 20, 501–20.

Berndt, E.R. (1991): *The Practice of Econometrics*, Reading, MA: Addison-Wesley Publishing Company.

Berry, S.T. (1992): 'Estimation of a model of entry in the airline industry', *Econometrica* 60, 889–917.

Bertoletti, P. and C. Poletti (1996): 'A note on endogenous efficiency in Cournot models of incomplete information', *Journal of Economic Theory* 71, 303–10.

Bertoletti, P. and C. Poletti (1997): 'X-inefficiency, competition and market information', *Journal of Industrial Economics* 45, 359–75.

Besen, S.M. (1967): 'Elasticities of substitution and returns to scale in United States manufacturing: some additional evidence', *Southern Economic Journal* 34, 280–82.

Betancourt, R.R. and M. Malanoski (1999): 'An estimable model of supermarket behavior: prices, distribution services and some effects of competition', *Empirica* 26, 55–73.

Bitzan, J. (2000): 'Railroad cost conditions – implications for policy', Manuscript.

Bloch, H., G. Madden and S.J. Savage (2001): 'Economies of scale and scope in Australian telecommunications', *Review of Industrial Organization* 18, 219–27.

Borenstein, S. (1989): 'Hubs and high fares: dominance and market power in the U.S. airline industry', *Rand Journal of Economics* 20, 344–65.

Bork, R.H. (1978): *The Antitrust Paradox: A Policy at War with Itself*, New York: Basic Books.

Börsch-Supan, A. (1998): 'Capital's contribution to productivity and the nature of competition', *Brookings Papers on Economic Activity Microeconomics*, 205–44.

Bottasso, A. and A. Sembenelli (2001): 'Market power, productivity and the EU Single Market program: evidence from a panel of Italian firms', *European Economic Review* 45, 167–86.

de Brabander, B. and E. Vanlommel (1978): 'Economies of scale, minimum optimal plant size and effectiveness of market structure in Belgian industry anno 1970', *European Economic Review* 11, 363–77.

Braeutigam, R.R., A.F. Daughety and M.A. Turnquist (1982): 'The estimation of a hybrid cost function for a railroad firm', *Review of Economics and Statistics* 64, 394–404.

Braeutigam, R.R., A.F. Daughety and M.A. Turnquist (1984): 'A firm-specific analysis of economies of density in the railroad industry', *Journal of Industrial Economics* 33, 3–20.

Bresnahan, T.F. (1992): 'Sutton's sunk costs and market structure: price competition, advertising, and the evolution of concentration, *Rand Journal of Economics* 23, 137–52.

Bresnahan, T.F. and P.C. Reiss (1987): 'Do entry conditions vary across markets?', *Brookings Papers on Economic Activity Microeconomics*, 833–81.

Bresnahan, T.F. and P.C. Reiss (1991): 'Entry and competition in concentrated markets', *Journal of Political Economy* 99, 977–1009.

Broadberry, S.N. and N.F.R. Crafts (1992): 'Britain's productivity gap in the 1930s: some neglected factors', *Journal of Economic History* 52, 531–58.

Brueckner, J.K., N.J. Dyer and P.T. Spiller (1992): 'Fare determination in airline hub-and-spoke networks', *Rand Journal of Economics* 23, 309–33.

Buccola, S., Y. Fujii and Y. Xia (2000): 'Size and productivity in the U.S. milling and baking industries', *American Journal of Agricultural Economics* 82, 865–80.

Burnside, C., M. Eichenbaum and S. Rebelo (1995): 'Capital utilization and returns to scale', *NBER Macroeconomics Annual*, 67–110.

Callan, S.J. and J.M. Thomas (2001): 'Economies of scale and scope: a cost analysis of municipal solid waste services', *Land Economics* 77, 48–60.

Carbo, S., E.P.M. Gardener and J. Williams (2002): 'Efficiency in banking: empirical evidence from the savings bank sector', *The Manchester School* 70, 204–28.

Carlin, W., J. Haskel, and P. Seabright (2001): 'Understanding "the essential fact about capitalism": markets, competition and creative destruction', *National Institute Economic Review* 175, January, 67–84.

Carlson, S. (1939): *A Study on the Pure Theory of Production*, Stockholm Economic Studies no. 9, London: P.S. King & Sons.

Cavallo, L. and S.P.S. Rossi (2001): 'Scale and scope economies in the European banking systems', *Journal of Multinational Financial Management* 11, 515–31.

Caves, D.W., L.R. Christensen and J.A. Swanson (1981): 'Productivity growth, scale economies, and capacity utilization in US railroads, 1955–74', *American Economic Review* 71, 994–1002.

Caves, D.W., L.R. Christensen and M.W. Tretheway (1984): 'Economies of density versus economies of scale: why trunk and local service airline costs differ', *Rand Journal of Economics* 15, 471–89.

Caves, D.W., L.R. Christensen, M.W. Tretheway and R.J. Windle (1985): 'Network effects and the measurement of returns to scale and density', in A.F. Daughety (ed.), *Analytical Studies in Transport Economics*, Cambridge, UK: Cambridge University Press.

Caves, R. and D. Barton (1990): *Efficiency in US Manufacturing Industries*, Cambridge, UK: Cambridge University Press.

Caves, R.E. (ed.) (1980): 'Symposium on international trade and industrial organization', *Journal of Industrial Economics* 29.

Caves, R.E., J. Khalilzadeh-Shirazi and M.E. Porter (1975): 'Scale economies in statistical analyses of market power', *Review of Economics and Statistics* 57, 133–40.

Caves, R.E. (ed). (1992): *Industrial Efficiency in Six Nations*, Cambridge, MA: MIT Press.

Chadwick, E. (1859): 'Results of different principles of legislation and administration in Europe of competition for the field, as compared with competition within the field, of service', *Journal of the Royal Statistical Society* 22, 381–420.

Chamberlin, E.H. (1933): *The Theory of Monopolistic Competition*, Cambridge, MA: Harvard University Press.

Chandler, A.D. Jr. (1959): 'The beginnings of "Big Business" in American industry', *Business History Review* 33, 1–31, reprinted in T.K. McCraw (ed.), *The Essential Alfred Chandler*, Boston, MA: Harvard Business School Press, 1988.

Chandler, A.D. Jr (1962): *Strategy and structure: chapters in the history of industrial enterprise*, Cambridge, MA: MIT Press.

Charnes, A., W.W. Cooper and T. Sueyoshi (1988): 'A goal programming/constrained regression review of the Bell System breakup', *Management Science* 34, 1–26.

Christensen, L.R. and W.H. Greene (1976): 'Economies of scale in U.S. electric power generation', *Journal of Political Economy* 84, Part 1, 655–76.

Clark, C.W. (1973): 'Profit maximization and the extinction of animal species', *Journal of Political Economy* 81, 950–61.

Clark, J.B. (1887): 'The limits of competition', *Political Science Quarterly* 2, 45–61.

Cockburn, I.M. and R.M. Henderson (2001): 'Scale and scope in drug development', *Journal of Health Economics* 20, 1033–57.

Congressional Budget Office (1998): 'Congress of the United States. How increased competition from generic drugs has affected prices and returns in the pharmaceutical industry', Washington, DC.

Connor, J. (2001): *Global Price Fixing*, Dordrecht: Kluwer Academic Publishers.

Cowing T. and A. Holtmann (1983): 'Multiproduct short-run hospital cost functions: empirical evidence and policy implications from cross-section data', *Southern Economic Journal* 49, 637–53.

Cowing, T.G. and V.K. Smith (1978): 'The estimation of a production technology: a survey of econometric analyses of steam-electric generation', *Land Economics* 54, 157–70.

David, P.A. (1985): 'Clio and the economics of QWERTY', *American Economic Review* 75, 332–7.

David, P.A. (2001): 'Path dependence, its critics, and the quest for "Historical Economics"', in P. Garrouste and S. Ioannides (eds), *Evolution and Path Dependence in Economic Ideas: Past and Present*, Cheltenham, UK and Northampton, MA, USA: Edward Elgar.

Davies, S. (1980): 'Minimum efficient size and seller concentration: an empirical problem', *Journal of Industrial Economics* 28, 287–301.

Dean, J. (1976): *Statistical Cost Estimation*, Bloomington, IN: Indiana University Press.

Demsetz, H. (1968): 'Why regulate utilities?', *Journal of Law and Economics* 11, 55–65.

Demsetz, H. (1974): 'Two systems of belief about monopoly', in H.J. Goldschmid, H.M. Mann and J.F. Weston (eds), *Industrial Concentration: the New Learning*, Boston: Little, Brown & Company.

Dewey, D. (1969): *The Theory of Imperfect Competition*, New York: Columbia University Press.

Diamond, P. (1971): 'A model of price adjustment', *Journal of Economic Theory* 3, 156–68.

Dick, A.R. and J.R. Lott, Jr (1990): 'Comment on "The role of potential competition in industrial organization"', *Journal of Economic Perspectives* 4, 213–15.

Dierker, E. and B. Grodal (1998): 'The price normalization problem in imperfect competition and the objective of the firm', Center for Industrial Economics working paper 98–08.

Diewert, W.E. and T.J. Wales (1991): 'Multiproduct cost functions and subadditivity tests: a critique of the Evans and Heckman research on the U.S. Bell System', discussion paper 91–21, Department of Economics, University of British Columbia.

Dirlam, J.B. and A.E. Kahn (1954): *Fair Competition*, Ithaca, NY: Cornell University Press.

Djankov, S., R. La Porta, F. Lopez-de-Silanes and A. Shleifer (2002): 'The regulation of entry', *Quarterly Journal of Economics* 117, 1–37.

Dnes, A.W. (1994): 'The scope of Chadwick's bidding scheme', *Journal of Institutional and Theoretical Economics* 150, 524–36.

Drake, L. and R. Simper (2002): 'X-efficiency and scale economies in policing: a comparative study using the distribution free approach and DEA', *Applied Economics* 34, 1859–70.

Eads, G., M. Nerlove, and W. Raduchel (1969): 'A long-run cost function for the local service airline industry: an experiment on nonlinear estimation', *Review of Economics and Statistics* 51, 258–70.

Eakin, B.K. and T.J. Kniesner (1988): 'Estimating a non-minimum cost function for hospitals', *Southern Economic Journal* 54, 583–97.

EC Commission (1996): *NACE Rev.* 1, Luxembourg: Office for Official Publications of the European Communities.

Eckel, C., D. Eckel and V. Singal (1997): 'Privatization and efficiency: industry effects of the sale of British Airways', *Journal of Financial Economics* 43, 275–98.

Economides, N. and F. Flyer (1997): 'Compatibility and market structure for network goods', manuscript, Stern School of Business, New York University, November.

Eddy, A.J. (1913): *The New Competition*, Chicago: A.C. McClurg & Co.

Elliott, D.C. and J.D. Gribbin (1977): 'The abolition of cartels and structural change in the United Kingdom', in A.P. Jacquemin and H.W. de Jong (eds), *Welfare Aspects of Industrial Markets*, Leiden: Martinus Nijhoff, pp. 345–65.

Ely, R.T. (1901): 'Competition: its nature, its permanency, and its beneficence', *Publications of the American Economic Association*, 3rd Series, 2, February, 55–70.

Esposito, L. and F.F. Esposito (1971): 'Foreign competition and domestic industry profitability', *Review of Economics and Statistics* 53, 343–53.

Evans, D.S. and J.J. Heckman (1983): 'Multiproduct cost function estimates and natural monopoly tests for the Bell System', in D.S. Evans (ed.), *Breaking Up Bell*, Amsterdam: North-Holland, pp. 253–82.

Evans, D.S. and J.J. Heckman (1988): 'Rejoinder: natural monopoly and the Bell System: response to Charnes, Cooper and Sueyoshi', *Management Science* 34, 27–38.

Faulhaber, G.R. (1975): 'Cross-subsidization: pricing in public enterprise', *American Economic Review* 65, 966–77.

Ferguson, C.E. (1967): 'Substitution, relative shares, and returns to scale: some statistical regularities and curiosa', *Southern Economic Journal* 34, 209–22.

Ferguson, C.E. (1969): *The Neoclassical Theory of Production and Distribution*, Cambridge, UK: Cambridge University Press.

Fetter, F. (1941): 'The fundamental principle of efficiency in mass production', Appendix D, TNEC Monograph No. 13, *Relative Efficiency of Large, Medium-Sized, and Small Business*, Senate Committee Print, 76th Congress, 3d Session, Washington, DC: U.S. Government Printing Office.

Filippini, M. (1998): 'Are municipal electricity distribution utilities natural monopolies?', *Annals of Public and Cooperative Economics* 69, 157–74.

Fisher, F.M. (1987): 'On the misuse of the profit–sales ratio to infer monopoly power', *Rand Journal of Economics* 18, 384–96.

Fisher, F.M. and J.J. McGowan (1983): 'On the misuse of accounting rates of return to infer monopoly profits', *American Economic Review* 73, 82–97.

Friedlaender, A.F., C. Winston and K. Wang (1983): 'Costs, technology, and productivity in the U.S. automobile industry', *Bell Journal of Economics* 14, 1–20.

Friedman, M. (1955): 'Comment', in National Bureau of Economic Research conference report, *Business Concentration and Price Policy*, Princeton: Princeton University Press, pp. 230–38.

Fudenberg, Drew and Jean Tirole (1980): 'Learning-by-doing and market performance', *Bell Journal of Economics* 14, 522–30.

Fuss, M.A. and V.K. Gupta (1981): 'A cost function approach to the estimation of minimum efficient scale, returns to scale, and suboptimal capacity', *European Economic Review* 15, 123–35.

Fuss, M.A. and L. Waverman (1992): *Costs and Productivity in Automobile Production*, Cambridge, UK: Cambridge University Press.

Gabel, D. (1994): 'Competition in a network industry: the telephone industry, 1894–1910', *Journal of Economic History* 54, 543–72.

Geehan, R. (1977): 'Returns to scale in the life insurance industry', *Bell Journal of Economics* 8, 497–514.

Ghemawat, P. (1985): 'Building strategy on the experience curve', *Harvard Business Review* 63, 143–9.

Giddings, F.H. (1887): 'The persistence of competition', *Political Science Quarterly* 2, 62–78.

Given, R.S. (1996): 'Economies of scale and scope as an explanation of merger and output diversification activities in the health maintenance organization industry', *Journal of Health Economics* 15, 685–713.

Gould, J.R. (1972): 'Extinction of a fishery by commercial exploitation: a note', *Journal of Political Economy* 80, 1031–8.

Graham, D.R., D.P. Kaplan and D.S. Sibley (1983): 'Efficiency and competition in the airline industry', *Bell Journal of Economics* 14, 118–38.

Griliches, Z. (1972): 'Cost allocation in railroad regulation', *Bell Journal of Economics* 3, 26–41.

Griliches, Z. and V. Ringstad (1971): *Economies of Scale and the Form of the Production Function*, Amsterdam: North-Holland.

Gruber, H. (1994): *Learning and Strategic Product Innovation*, Amsterdam: North-Holland.

Guldmann, J.M. (1991): 'Economies of scale and density in local telephone networks', *Regional Science and Urban Economics* 20, 521–35.

Gunton, G. (1888): 'The economic and social aspect of trusts', *Political Science Quarterly* 3, 385–408.

Gupta, V.K. (1981): 'Minimum efficient scale as a determinant of concentration: a reappraisal', *The Manchester School of Economic and Social Studies*, 153–164.

Gwartney, J. and R. Lawson (2002): *Economic Freedom of the World 2002 Annual Report*, Vancouver: Fraser Institute.

Hadley, A.T. (1886): 'Private monopolies and public rights', *Quarterly Journal of Economics* 1, 28–44.

Hand, Learned (1945): *U.S.* v. *Aluminum Company of America*, 148 F. 2d 416 (C.C.A. 2d, 1945).

Harris, R.G. (1977): 'Economies of traffic density in the rail freight industry', *Bell Journal of Economics* 8, 556–64.

Hausman, W.J. and J.L. Neufeld (1991): 'Property rights versus public spirit: ownership and efficiency of U.S. electric utilities prior to rate-of-return regulation', *Review of Economics and Statistics* 73, 414–23.

Hay, D.A. (2001): 'The post-1990 Brazilian trade liberalisation and the performance of large manufacturing firms: productivity, market share, and profits', *Economic Journal* 111, 620–41.

Hay, D.A. and G.S. Liu (1997): 'The efficiency of firms: what difference does competition make?', *Economic Journal* 107, 597–617.

Heflebower, R.B. (1955): 'Full costs, cost changes, and prices, in National Bureau of Economic Research' (ed.), *Conference report. Business Concentration and Price Policy*, Princeton: Princeton University Press, pp. 361–92.

Henderson, V. (1999): 'Marshall's scale economies', NBER working paper 7358, September.

Hollas, D.R., K.R. Macleod and S.R. Stansell (2002): 'A data envelopment analysis of gas utilities' efficiency', *Journal of Economics and Finance* 26, 123–37.

Holmes, J. (1910): Dissenting opinion, *Dr. Miles Medical Co.* v. *Park & Sons Co.*, 220 U.S. 373.

Horn, H., H. Land and S. Lundgren (1995): 'Managerial effort incentives, X-inefficiency and international trade', *European Economic Review* 39, 117–38.

Hughes, J.P., L.J. Mester and C. Moon (2001): 'Are scale economies in banking elusive or illusive? Evidence obtained by incorporating risk-taking into models of bank production', *Journal of Banking & Finance* 25, 2169–2208.

Johnston, J. (1960): *Statistical Cost Analysis*, New York: McGraw-Hill.

Katics, M.M. and B.C. Petersen (1994): 'The effect of rising import competition on market power: a panel data study of US manufacturing', *Journal of Industrial Economics* 42, 277–98.

Keeler, T.E. (1974): 'Railroad costs, returns to scale and excess capacity', *Review of Economics and Statistics* 56, 201–8.

Kerkvliet, J.R., W. Nebesky, C. Horton Tremblay and V.J. Tremblay (1998): 'Efficiency and technological change in the U.S. brewing industry', *Journal of Productivity Analysis* 10, 271–88.

Klette, T.J. (1999): 'Market power, scale economies and productivity: estimates from a panel of establishment data', *Journal of Industrial Economics* 48, 451–76.

Kovenock, D. and G.M. Phillips (1997): 'Capital structure and product market behavior: an examination of plant exit and investment decisions', *Review of Financial Studies* 10, 767–803.

Kumbhakar, S.C. (1993): 'Short-run returns to scale, farm-size, and economic efficiency', *Review of Economics and Statistics* 75, 336–41.
Lankford, R. and J.F. Stewart (1980): 'A general equilibrium analysis of monopoly power and the distribution of income', in J.J. Siegfried (ed.), *The Economics of Firm Size, Market Structure and Social Performance*, Washington, DC: Bureau of Economics, Federal Trade Commission.
Lazear, E.P. (1995): *Personnel Economics*, Cambridge, MA: MIT Press.
Lee, B.J. (1995): 'Separability test for the electricity supply industry', *Journal of Applied Econometrics* 10, 49–60.
Lerner, A.P. (1934): 'The concept of monopoly and the measurement of monopoly power', *Review of Economic Studies* 1, 157–75.
Lerner, A.P. (1944): *Economics of Control*, New York: Macmillan; reprinted New York: Augustus M. Kelley Publishers, 1970.
Liebowitz, S.J. and S.E. Margolis (1990): 'The fable of the keys', *Journal of Law and Economics* 33, 1–26.
Liebowitz, S.J. and S.E. Margolis (1999): *Winners, Losers, & Microsoft: Competition and Antitrust in High Technology*, Oakland, CA: The Independent Institute.
Liefmann, R.L. (1915): 'Monopoly or competition as the basis of a government trust policy', *Quarterly Journal of Economics* 29, 308–25.
Lien, D. and Y. Peng (2001): 'Competition and production efficiency: telecommunications in OECD countries', *Information Economics and Policy* 13, 51–76.
Lilienthal, D.E. (1952): *Big Business: A New Era*, New York: Harper & Brothers Publishers.
MacDonald, J.M. and M.E. Ollinger (2000): 'Scale economies and consolidation in hog slaughter', *American Journal of Agricultural Economics* 82, 334–46.
Machlup, F. (1942): 'Competition, pliopoly, and profits', *Economica* 9, 1–23, 153–73.
MacPhee, C.R. and R.D. Peterson (1990): 'The economies of scale revisited: comparing Census costs, engineering estimates, and the survivor technique', *Quarterly Journal of Business and Economics* 29, 43–67.
Marshall, A. ([1892] 1909): *Economics of Industry*, 4th edn, 1909, London: Macmillan.
Marshall, A. (1923): *Industry & Trade*, 4th edn, London: Macmillan.
Martin, S. (1983): 'Market, firm, and economic performance', Salomon Brothers Center for the Study of Financial Institutions Monograph Series, 1983–1.
Martin, S. (2001): *Industrial Organization: A European Perspective*, Oxford: Oxford University Press.
Martin, S. and J.T. Scott (2000): 'The nature of innovation market failure and the design of public support for private innovation', *Research Policy* 19, 437–47.
Mason, E.S. ([1937] 1949): 'Monopoly in law and economics', *Yale Law Journal* 47, 34–49; reprinted in American Economic Association, *Readings in the Social Control of Industry*, Philadelphia and Toronto: The Blakiston Company, 1949, pp. 25–47. (Page references are to the reprinted version.)
Mason, E.S. (1959): *Economic Concentration and the Monopoly Problem*, Cambridge, MA: Harvard University Press.
McNulty, P.J. (1967): 'A note on the history of perfect competition', *Journal of Political Economy* 75, 395–9.
McNulty, P.J. (1968): 'Economic theory and the meaning of competition', *Quarterly Journal of Economics* 82, 639–56.
Moroney, J.R. (1967): 'Cobb–Douglas production functions and returns to scale in U.S. manufacturing', *Western Economic Journal* 6, 39–51.
Morrison, C.J. (1990): 'Market power, economic profitability and productivity growth measurement: an integrated structural approach', NBER working paper 3355, May.
Morrison, C.J. and D. Siegel (1997): 'External capital factors and increasing returns in U.S. manufacturing', *Review of Economics and Statistics* 79, 647–54.
Morrison Paul, C.J. (2001): 'Cost economies and market power: the case of the U.S. meat packing industry', *Review of Economics and Statistics* 83, 531–40.
Nelson, R.A. and M.E. Wohar (1983): 'Regulation, scale economies, and productivity in steam-electric generation', *International Economic Review* 24, 57–79.

Neumann, M., I. Böbel and A. Haid (1985): 'Domestic concentration, foreign trade and economic performance', *International Journal of Industrial Organization* 3, 1–19.

Ng., C.K. and P. Seabright (2001): 'Competition, privatisation and productive efficiency: evidence from the airline industry', *Economic Journal* 111, 591–619.

Nickell, S., S. Wadhwani and M. Wall (1992): 'Productivity growth in U.K. companies, 1975–86', *European Economic Review* 36, 1055–91.

Nickell, S., D. Nicolitsas and N. Dryden (1997): 'What makes firms perform well?', *European Economic Review* 41, 783–96.

Nickell, S.J. (1996): 'Competition and corporate performance', *Journal of Political Economy* 104, 724–45.

Nicoletti, G., S. Scarpetta and O. Boylaud (2000): 'Summary indicators of product market regulation with an extension to employment protection legislation', OECD Economics Department working papers no. 226.

Obstfeld, M. and A.M. Taylor (2002): 'Globalization and capital markets', NBER working paper 8846.

Okunade, A.A. (2001): 'Cost–output relation, technological progress, and clinical activity mix of US hospital pharmacies', *Journal of Productivity Analysis* 16, 167–93.

Olley, G.S. and A. Pakes (1996): 'The dynamics of productivity in the telecommunications equipment industry', *Econometrica* 64, 1263–97.

Panzar, J.C. and R.D. Willig (1977): 'Economies of scale in multi-output production', *Quarterly Journal of Economics* 91, 481–94.

Patinkin, D. (1947): 'Multi-plant firms, cartels, and imperfect competition', *Quarterly Journal of Economics*, 173–205.

Pavcnik, N. (2002): 'Trade liberalization, exit, and productivity improvements: evidence from Chilean plants', *Review of Economic Studies* 69, 245–76.

Perlman, M. (1990): 'The evolution of Leibenstein's X-efficiency theory', in K. Weiermair and M. Perlman (eds), *Studies in Economic Rationality*, Ann Arbor: University of Michigan Press, pp. 7–25.

Primeaux, W.J. (1977): 'An assessment of X-efficiency gained through competition', *Review of Economics and Statistics* 59, 105–8.

Ravenscraft, D.J. (1983): 'Structure–profit relationships at the line of business and industry level', *Review of Economics and Statistics* 65, 22–31.

Robinson, E.A.G. (1958): *The Structure of Competitive Industry*, Cambridge, UK: Cambridge University Press.

Robinson, W.T. and J. Chiang (1996): 'Are Sutton's predictions robust? Empirical insights into advertising, R&D, and concentration', *Journal of Industrial Economics* 44, 398–408.

Röller, L.-H. (1990a): 'Proper quadratic cost functions with an application to the Bell System', *Review of Economics and Statistics* 72, 202–10.

Röller, L.-H. (1990b): 'Modelling cost structure: the Bell System revisited', *Applied Economics* 22, 1661–74.

Sakakibara, M. and M.E. Porter (2001): 'Competing at home to win abroad: evidence from Japanese industry', *Review of Economics and Statistics* 83, 310–22.

Samuelson, P.A. (2003): 'Pure theory aspects of industrial organization and globalization', *Japan and the World Economy* 15, 89–90.

Saving, T.R. (1961): 'Estimation of optimum sized plant by the survivor technique', *Quarterly Journal of Economics* 75, 569–607.

Saving, T.R. (1963): 'The four parameter lognormal, diseconomies of scale and the size distribution of manufacturing establishments', *International Economic Review*, 105–13.

Scarpetta, S., P. Hemmings, T. Tressel and J. Woo (2002): 'The role of policy and institutions for productivity and firm dynamics: evidence from micro and industry data', OECD Economics Department working papers no. 329.

Schankerman, M. and M.I. Nadiri (1986): 'A test of static equilibrium models and rates of return to quasi-fixed factors, with an application to the Bell System', *Journal of Econometrics* 33, 97–118.

Scherer, F.M. (1970): *Industrial Market Structure and Economic Performance*, Chicago: Rand McNally & Company.

Scherer, F.M. (1974): 'The determinants of multi-plant operation in six nations and twelve industries', *Kyklos*, 124–39.

Scherer, F.M. (1994): *Competition Policies for an Integrated World Economy*, Washington, DC: The Brookings Institution.

Scherer, F.M. (2000): 'Professor Sutton's "Technology and Market Structure"', *Journal of Industrial Economics* 48, 215–23.

Scherer, F.M., A. Beckenstein, E. Kaufer and R.D. Murphy (1975): *The Economics of Multi-Plant Operation: An International Comparisons Study*, Cambridge, MA: Harvard University Press.

Schmidt, K.M. (1997): 'Managerial incentives and product market competition', *Review of Economic Studies* 64, 191–213.

Schumpeter, J.A. (1934): *The Theory of Economic Development*, Cambridge, MA: Harvard University Press.

Schumpeter, J.A. (1943): *Capitalism, Socialism and Democracy*, New York: Harper & Row.

Scitovsky, Tibor (1950): 'Ignorance as a source of oligopoly power', *American Economic Review* 40, Papers and Proceedings, 48–53.

Shapiro, C. and H.R. Varian (1999): *Information Rules*, Boston, MA: Harvard University Business School Press.

Shepherd, W.G. (1967): 'What does the survivor technique show about economies of scale', *Southern Economic Journal* 34, 113–22.

Shin, R.T. and J.S. Ying (1992): 'Unnatural monopolies in local telephone', *Rand Journal of Economics* 23, 171–83.

Shy, O. (2001): *The Economics of Network Industries*, Cambridge, UK: Cambridge University Press.

Simons, H.C. (1936): 'The requisites of free competition', *American Economic Review* 26, 68–76.

Siotis, G. (2003): 'Competitive pressure and economic integration: an illustration for Spain, 1983–1996', *International Journal of Industrial Organization*, 21, 1435–60.

Smith, A. ([1776] 1937): *An Inquiry Into the Nature and Causes of the Wealth of Nations*, Cannan edn, 1937, New York: The Modern Library.

Smith, V.L. (1975): 'The primitive hunter culture, Pleistocene extinction, and the rise of agriculture', *Journal of Political Economy* 83, 727–56.

Stigler, G.J. (1942): 'The extent and bases of monopoly', *American Economic Review* 32, 1–22.

Stigler, G.J. (1949): 'Monopolistic competition in retrospect', *Five Lectures on Economic Problems*, London: Longmans, Green and Co.

Stigler, G.J. (1950): 'Monopoly and oligopoly by merger', *American Economic Review* 40, 23–34; reprinted in G.J. Stigler (1968): *The Organization of Industry*, Homewood, IL: Richard D. Irwin. (Page references are to the reprinted version.)

Stigler, G.J. (1955): 'Mergers and preventive antitrust policy', *University of Pennsylvania Law Review* 104, 176–84.

Stigler, G.J. (1957): 'Perfect competition, historically contemplated', *Journal of Political Economy* 65, reprinted in G.J. Stigler (1965): *Essays in the History of Economics*, Chicago and London: The University of Chicago Press, 234–67. (Page references are to the reprinted version).

Stigler, G.J. (1958): 'Economies of scale', *Journal of Law and Economics* 1, 54–71; reprinted with an addendum in G.J. Stigler (1968): *The Organization of Industry*, Homewood, IL: Richard D. Irwin. (Page references are to the reprinted version.)

Strickland, A.D. and L.W. Weiss (1976): 'Advertising, concentration, and price-cost margins', *Journal of Political Economy* 84, 1109–21.

Sung, N. (2002): 'Measuring embodied technical change in the US local telephone industry', *Applied Economics* 34, 77–83.

Sutton, J. (1991): *Sunk Costs and Market Structure*, Cambridge, MA: MIT Press.

Sutton, J. (1998): *Technology and Market Structure*, Cambridge, MA: MIT Press.

Sutton, J. (2000): *Marshall's Tendencies: What Can Economists Know?*, Cambridge, MA: MIT Press.

Suzumura, K. (1995): *Competition, Commitment, and Welfare*, Oxford: Oxford University Press.

Symeonidis, G. (1998): 'The evolution of UK cartel policy and its impact on conduct and structure', in S. Martin (ed.), *Competition Policies in Europe*, Amsterdam: North-Holland.

Symeonidis, G. (2002): *The Effects of Competition: Cartel Policy and the Evolution of Strategy and Market Structure in British Industry*, Cambridge, MA: MIT Press.

Telser, L.G. (1988): *Theories of Competition*, Amsterdam: North-Holland.

Thompson, H.G. (1997): 'Cost efficiency in power procurement and delivery service in the electric utility industry', *Land Economics* 73, 287–96.

Town, R. (2001): 'The welfare impact of HMO mergers', *Journal of Health Economics* 20, 967–90.

Triffin, R. (1940): *Monopolistic Competition and General Equilibrium Theory*, Cambridge, MA: Harvard University Press.

Truett, L.J. and D.B. Truett (2001): 'The Spanish automotive industry: scale economies and input relationships', *Applied Economics* 33, 1503–13.

Tybout, J.R. and M.D. Westbrook (1995): 'Trade liberalization and the dimensions of efficiency change in Mexican manufacturing industries', *Journal of International Economics* 39, 53–78.

Van Hise, C.R. (1912): *Concentration and Control*, New York: Macmillan.

Vellturo, C.A., E.R. Berndt, A.F. Friedlaender, J.S. Wang Chiang and M.H. Showalter (1992): 'Deregulation, mergers, and cost savings in Class I U.S. railroads, 1974–1986', *Journal of Economics & Management Strategy* 1, 339–69.

Vickers, J.S. (1995): 'Concepts of competition', *Oxford Economic Papers* 47, 1–23.

Walters, A.A. (1963): 'Production and cost functions: an econometric survey', *Econometrica* 31, 1–66.

Wang Chiang, J.S. and A.F. Friedlaender (1985): 'Truck technology and efficient market structure', *Review of Economics and Statistics* 67, 250–58.

Waterson, M. (2003): 'The role of consumers in competition and competition policy', *International Journal of Industrial Organization* 21, 129–50.

Waverman, L. (1989): 'U.S. interchange competition', in R.W. Crandall and K. Flamm (eds), *Changing the Rules*, Washington, DC: The Brookings Institution.

Weiman, D. and R. Levin (1994): 'Preying for monopoly? The case of Southern Bell Telephone Company, 1894–1912', *Journal of Political Economy* 102, 103–26.

Weiss, L.W. (1964): 'The survival technique and the extent of suboptimal capacity', *Journal of Political Economy* 72, 246–61.

Weiss, L.W. (1965): 'The survival technique and the extent of suboptimal capacity: a correction', *Journal of Political Economy* 73, 300–301.

Weiss, L.W. (1971): *Case Studies in American Industry*, 2nd edn, New York: John Wiley.

Weiss, L.W. (1974): 'The concentration-profits relationship and antitrust', in H.J. Goldschmid, H.M. Mann, and J.F. Weston (eds), *Industrial Concentration: the New Learning* Boston: Little, Brown & Company.

Wheelock, D.C. and P.W. Wilson (2001): 'New evidence on returns to scale and product mix among U.S. commercial banks', *Journal of Monetary Economics* 47, 653–74.

White, L. (1971): *The Automobile Industry Since 1945*, Cambridge, MA: Harvard University Press.

Winter, S.G. (1984): 'Schumperian competition in alternative technological regimes', *Journal of Economic Behavior and Organization* 5, 287–320.

Wright, D.J. (2003): 'Managerial incentives and firm efficiency in the presence of competition for managers', *International Journal of Industrial Organization* 21, 419–37.

Xia, Y. and S. Buccola (2002): 'Size, cost, and productivity in the meat processing industries', *Agribusiness* 18, 283–99.

Ying, J.S. and R.T. Shin (1993): 'Costly gains to breaking up: LECs and the Baby Bells', *Review of Economics and Statistics* 75, 357–61.

2   Efficiency versus market power through mergers

Dennis C. Mueller

1   Introduction

The 20th century began with the first great merger wave in the United States and the United Kingdom. It ended with another great wave that engulfed virtually every developed country in the world. As befits a global economy, many of the mergers taking place at the end of the century were cross-border deals. In between these two great waves there were three additional waves in the United States at the end of the 1920s, 1960s and 1980s. These mergers have obviously transformed the companies involved in them. In 1950, Philip Morris was a relatively non-leading, specialized company in the tobacco industry. Later it became the largest cigarette producer in the world, thanks to its introduction of the Marlboro brand in the mid-1950s, and the world's leading retail food manufacturer, thanks to its many acquisitions over the years, including in particular its acquisitions of food company giants Kraft Foods and General Foods. Other than changing the shapes and sizes of the merging companies, what have been the effects of the many thousands of mergers that have occurred in the United States and increasingly in all corners of the globe and, in particular, what have been their effects on efficiency and market power?

This would seem to be the most obvious and important question to ask about mergers both with respect to our understanding of the merger process and for the design of merger policy. Unfortunately, after more than a century and a vast number of theoretical and empirical studies of mergers, studies by economists and students of business do not agree on what the answer to this question is. There are a number of reasons for this disagreement, some having to do with the *types* of methodologies that have been employed, some having to do with *how* they have been employed. My goal in this chapter is not to give a detailed account of the many studies that have been undertaken and to try and explain why they have reached different conclusions, but rather to look at the results themselves and try to come up with an answer to the questions posed above, namely to what extent have mergers led to increases in economic efficiency, and to what extent have they led to increases in market power? As we shall see, there is a third question that is also relevant: to what extent have mergers resulted in *decreases* in economic efficiency?

We proceed as follows. In the following section the leading hypotheses as to why mergers occur are reviewed. Section 3 examines by far the largest branch of the literature: studies in business finance. We then turn in Sections 4 and 5 to evidence of the effects of mergers on profitability and market shares or sales growth. In Section 6 the results of the two preceding sections are relied upon to give answers to the questions just posed. Some additional relevant evidence is examined in Section 7, with conclusions and policy implications drawn in Section 8.

2   Hypotheses about why mergers occur

If the market values of two merging firms correctly reflect the present discounted values of their profit streams, and the managers of the acquiring (surviving) firm maximize profits, a merger occurs only if it is expected to lead either to an increase in price for one or more of the firm's products, or a reduction in costs. Numerous hypotheses have been put forward as to why each might occur.

2.1   Mergers that increase market power

Horizontal mergers   The first great merger wave at the end of the 19th century witnessed the creation through merger of such near-monopolies as American Tobacco, Standard Oil of New Jersey and American Sugar. The increases in market power that these mergers generated were sufficiently transparent to result in their subsequent undoing through the enforcement of the newly passed Sherman Antitrust Act. That some mergers have occurred for the purpose of raising price is unquestionable.

Horizontal mergers can also increase market power and product price, when they fall short of creating a monopoly. If we assume that each firm i maximizes the following objective function,

$$O_i = \pi_i + \theta \sum_{j \neq i}^{n} \pi_j, \tag{2.1}$$

where π_i is firm i's profit and θ is the *degree of cooperation*, then it will choose price and output to satisfy the following first-order condition:

$$\frac{\pi_i}{S_i} = \frac{1}{\eta} \left(\frac{m_i}{\sigma} - \theta m_i + \theta \right), \tag{2.2}$$

where S_i is firm i's sales, m_i is its market share, η is the industry elasticity of demand, and σ is the degree of product differentiation ($0 \leq \sigma \leq 1$) (Mueller, 1986, pp. 54–6). A degree of cooperation, θ, equal to 1 leads to the perfect collusion outcome, $\theta = 0$ is the Cournot outcome and a negative θ such that the term in parentheses in (2.2) is zero produces the Bertrand equilibrium, price equal to marginal costs (assumed here to equal average costs). If we assume that two merging firms could always choose the same price and quantity combinations after a merger as before, a horizontal merger between firms i and j leads to the following objective function for the post-merger company i (ibid., p. 189)

$$O_i = \pi_i + \pi_j + \theta \sum_{k \neq i,j}^{n} \pi_k.$$

(2.3)

The horizontal merger effectively leads to perfect collusion between the two merging firms. As long as there was not perfect collusion among all firms in the industry before the merger, or Bertrand competition afterwards, the merger must lead to a higher price and reduced output after the merger. Thus, all horizontal mergers should be accompanied by some manifestations of a market power increase.[1]

Horizontal mergers can also lead to an effective increase in market power and higher prices if the reduction of the number of sellers increases the degree of cooperation, θ, for at least some firms in the industry.

Vertical mergers   The only anti-competitive effects of vertical mergers that have not by now been totally discredited are that they can raise entry barriers by requiring that an entrant at one stage in the production chain enter at all others, or that they can facilitate predatory actions (Comanor, 1967).

Conglomerate mergers   Conglomerate mergers might seem the least likely to produce market power increases, but they can when they lead to *multimarket contact*. Scott (1989) presents a case study of one merger that was clearly intended to increase multimarket contact, and both Scott, (1993) and Evans and Kessides (1993) present evidence of higher profits and prices in markets where substantial multimarket contact is present among the sellers. Other hypotheses concerning the anticompetitive effects of mergers are more speculative, although examples of anticompetitive behaviour through reciprocal price relationships, or from the elimination of a potential entrant do exist.[2]

2.2   Mergers that increase efficiency

Horizontal mergers   The easiest efficiency gain to envisage is between two firms in an industry with significant scale economies, where at least one of the merging firms is of less than minimum efficient size. Technological changes that greatly expand the minimum efficient size of a firm have led to merger waves within industries. The gains from a horizontal merger in the presence of scale economies are greatest for the smallest companies. This explanation of mergers leads one to expect the smaller firms in an industry to be most active in combining. But merging firms tend to be, if anything, bigger than the average company, and this fact casts a shadow over the general nature of scale economies as an explanation for horizontal mergers (Mueller, 1980a, 1980b; Hughes, 1989).

Merger waves can also occur in declining industries to rationalize production by ensuring that the least efficient production capacity is retired first (Dutz, 1989).

Vertical mergers   Vertical integration through merger can increase efficiency by (1) eliminating price distortions in factor inputs, when upstream producers have market power, (2) reducing the transactions costs of contracting between vertically linked firms, when asset specificity is present, and (3) reducing bargaining costs between vertically linked firms in the presence of asymmetric information (Williamson, 1989; Perry, 1989).

Conglomerate mergers   A variety of hypotheses concerning efficiency gains from diversification mergers were advanced at the time of the first conglomerate merger wave, although not all of these necessarily require that the merger be conglomerate. Most of these have been discredited either theoretically or empirically.[3]

By far the most widely held view regarding the efficiency gains from mergers and takeovers is the hypothesis that they are motivated to replace managements that fail to maximize shareholder wealth with those who will. As first put forward by Robin Marris (1964) it was intended to explain hostile takeovers, not mergers in general, but most observers holding this hypothesis apply it to evidence on both mergers and takeovers (Jensen and Ruback, 1983). Following Henry Manne's (1965) appellation, it has come to be called the 'market for corporate control' hypothesis. Those who espouse this hypothesis presume this market to be efficient, and thus the premia paid reflect the expected gains from replacing the acquired firm's management with that of the buyer. Although it is the most popular and viable of the efficiency-related hypotheses as to why conglomerate mergers occur, obviously it need not be restricted to mergers of this form.

2.3 Merger hypotheses that do not presume profit increases

The managerial discretion hypothesis Both the pecuniary and non-pecuniary rewards of managers are often linked to the growth in size of their firm (Marris, 1964, ch. 2). Mergers to increase a company's size or to avoid an eventual decline in size are most likely to be undertaken by mature firms and those in slow-growing or declining industries with sufficient cash to finance this type of expansion (Mueller, 1969, 1972; Jensen, 1986).

The hubris hypothesis As we shall see in the following section, acquiring firm shareholders are generally not better off at the time a merger is announced, and become worse off with the passage of time. The premia paid to acquire other companies totally exhaust any gains the mergers might generate. Richard Roll (1986) has hypothesized that the market for corporate control is characterized by the 'winner's curse'. The company whose management has the highest expectations of the profit potential of the target wins the bidding, but pays on average more than the true profit potential of the company justifies. Although the winner's curse explains why acquiring firm shareholders lose from mergers, it does not explain why managers, who seek to maximize their shareholders' wealth, participate in a bidding game when the 'winner' always loses. This is where hubris enters. Acquiring firm managers believe that the odds do not apply to them – they can beat the curse.

An advantage of the two hypotheses that assume that mergers do not create wealth is that they are broadly consistent with the positive correlation between stock price movements and merger activity. The constraint on managerial pursuit of unprofitable growth is the possibility that their firm will be taken over and they will be replaced. As we shall see, acquiring firms tend to outperform the market by a substantial amount over a sustained period *prior* to undertaking an acquisition. What better time could there be to announce an acquisition that will lower your shareholders' wealth than when the market is doing well, and your firm has been outperforming the market? Moreover, at such times internal cash flows are likely to be high, and the cost of raising external capital will appear low.

In a bull market all players may suffer from hubris. Recent price increases confirm the wisdom of one's past investment decisions and lead to overconfidence and overoptimism, that is to say, to hubris.[4]

3 The effects of mergers on share prices

3.1 Do mergers increase shareholder wealth?
A large literature has tried to answer this question by examining changes in stock prices occurring before, at and after merger announcements.

Although the interpretations that the authors place on these findings vary considerably, the actual patterns observed in the data are remarkably similar. The easiest results to summarize and interpret are those for the acquired firms. In almost every merger the buyer offers a premium for the acquired company's shares to induce its owners to sell. The acquired firm's share price rises to reflect this premium. This rise often begins a month or two before the public announcement of the merger, suggesting insider knowledge and trading. On average mergers are consummated six months after they are announced. Thus, in a matter of a few months, shareholders of acquired firms earn returns substantially *above* what would otherwise be expected. These have tended to fall in a range between 15 and 30 per cent of the acquirer's market value, with a median gain of around 20 per cent.[5]

The pattern for the acquiring companies is illustrated in Figure 2.1, which has been constructed from data reported by Asquith (1983) but is typical of results obtained in other studies. The figure plots the cumulative residuals estimated using the capital asset pricing model, and thus the null hypothesis is that the acquiring companies' shares would have performed as the market portfolio did for firms with comparable betas. Acquiring firms begin to earn positive abnormal returns roughly two years prior to the merger announcements. These cumulate to 14.3 per cent of the acquirers' market values by the day before the merger announcement. On that day, day 0, the bidders earn an average return of 0.2 per cent. Points to the right of day 0 represent observations following the consummation of the mergers. Starting at the time that the mergers are completed, the acquirers' abnormal returns become negative and fall a cumulative 7.0 per cent.

Virtually every study that has estimated abnormal returns from before merger announcements has found that acquirers begin earning positive abnormal returns long before the announcements (sometimes as much as five years before) and that these cumulate to substantial amounts: on average roughly 15 per cent of the acquirers' market values (see references in note 5).

The finding of an economically and statistically insignificant abnormal return to acquirers is also typical of other studies. Median values for large numbers of studies invariably are within one percentage point of a zero abnormal return.

In stark contrast to the pre-merger period, acquiring firms are generally found to earn returns substantially below the market portfolio, or other control groups over the post-merger period. In a survey of 23 studies, I found 17 with significant negative abnormal returns for long post-merger periods. The median post-merger abnormal return was –6.8 per cent (Mueller, 1995).

Thus the typical pattern of share returns for acquiring companies is as follows. Starting anywhere from two to five years prior to undertaking a

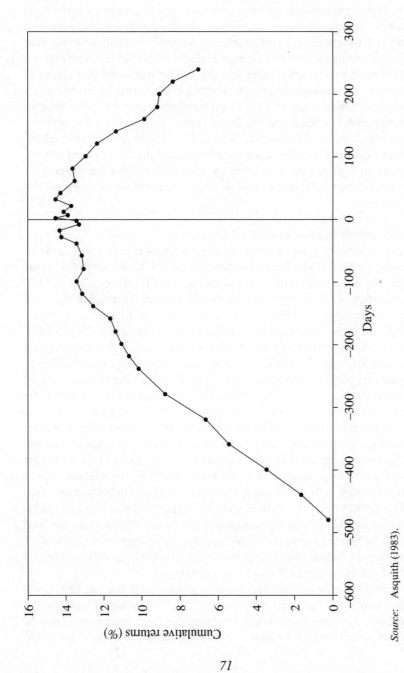

Source: Asquith (1983).

Figure 2.1 Cumulative residuals for successful bidding firms

merger, an acquirer begins to outperform the market. Since it is inconceivable that the market is reacting to a merger several years down the road, one must assume that any causal linkage between these events runs from outperforming the market to undertaking an acquisition. As noted above, growth-oriented managers are more likely to undertake unprofitable acquisitions when their company's profits are abnormally high and their shareholders have enjoyed substantial above-market returns. Managerial hubris is also more likely at these times. The announcements of mergers, on the other hand, result in a mixed pattern of returns, with the safest conclusion perhaps being 'that for the stockholders of the acquiring firms, "news" of an acquisition may not be worthwhile news' (Mandelker, 1974, p. 321). In the months that follow, the shareholders of acquiring firms suffer relative declines in their wealth, declines that continue in some cases for several years after the merger.

How can these results be interpreted? There are essentially three alternative interpretations.

3.2   Mergers have generated net wealth gains

Several observers have interpreted the findings regarding returns to acquiring and acquired firm shareholders as (1) 'consistent with value maximizing behaviour on the part of bidding firms' (Halpern, 1983, p. 314), (2) 'consistent with the operation of an efficient capital market' (Council of Economic Advisors, 1985, pp. 197–8) and (3) providing strong evidence 'that takeovers generate aggregate net benefits to the economy' (Council of Economic Advisors, 1985, pp. 197–8). These conclusions reflect the following chain of reasoning. The negligible gains to acquiring firm shareholders at the time mergers are announced are a result of bidding between actual and potential acquirers in an efficient market that results in all of the gains from a change in control being bid away. Since the capital market is efficient, the declines in returns to acquiring company shareholders over an extended period following merger announcements can be ignored. Indeed, a majority of event studies has not even bothered to estimate or report post-merger returns, since their existence is denied by the efficient capital market assumption. If post-merger declines were related to the mergers, they would have occurred immediately upon the mergers' announcements under the capital market efficiency assumption. Since the acquirers do not lose when the mergers are announced, and acquired companies' shareholders are unquestionably better off, their gains represent a net increase in corporate wealth. Society is better off by this magnitude.

Although many event studies have simply ignored the negative post-merger returns or dismissed them as 'puzzling', some recent studies have argued that they should be ignored because there are several econometric problems, which make it difficult to obtain accurate estimates of abnormal returns over long time periods (Fama, 1998; Andrade *et al.*, 2001). There are at least two reasons for rejecting this justification for ignoring the negative post-merger returns to acquirers when judging the effects of mergers.

First, the econometric problems should sometimes produce estimates of returns that are large and positive, sometimes large and negative. This has definitely not been the case, however. Estimates of post-merger returns are far more often negative and significant than positive and significant. Such systematic patterns need explaining.

Second, the negative post-merger returns do not disappear once the econometric problems are addressed.[6] Furthermore, the patterns of post-merger returns are related in a plausible way to both the types of mergers taking place and their timing. Mergers taking place during stock market booms are far more likely to be followed by significant losses than those taking place when the stock market is depressed.[7] This pattern is consistent with the hypotheses that the shares of acquirers are overvalued at the time they undertake acquisitions. Consistent with this interpretation is the finding that the returns to acquirers which finance their acquisitions entirely through exchanges in shares are significantly lower than when cash is used.[8] Finally, one must note that 'friendly' mergers are much more likely to be followed by significant losses to acquiring firms' shareholders than hostile takeovers or tender offers. It is not obvious why the econometric problems raised to explain away large negative post-merger returns to acquirers should vary so systematically with the type of merger, its timing and its means of finance.

3.3 Mergers have generated net wealth losses

The most straightforward way to interpret the pattern of returns depicted in Figure 2.1, that is consistent with the logic underlying the event study approach, is that new information about the mergers reached the market over a sustained period following their completion, and that this information was systematically *negative*. Since acquiring companies tend to be six to ten times larger than their targets, depending on the sample of mergers, a 7 per cent loss to acquirers would offset gains to targets over a range from 42 to 70 per cent. Since few studies report gains to targets of this magnitude, the mergers would have to be judged on average to be wealth destroying, once the post-merger losses to acquirers are considered.

3.4 The event study methodology is incapable of measuring whether mergers increase or reduce shareholder wealth

The third possible interpretation of the pre- and post-announcement returns of acquirers allows the market's evaluation of shares to be subject to fads and overoptimism. The market begins mistakenly to bid up the share prices of some group of firms. These firms undertake mergers while their shares are overpriced. The post-merger declines in returns to acquirers are not *caused* by the mergers, but merely reflect the market's return to a more objective evaluation of these companies' prospects.

There is much in the evidence to support this latter interpretation. Rau and Vermaelen (1998) find, for example, that the acquisitions of low book-to-market 'glamour' firms had significantly lower post-merger returns than did high book-to-market firms. They also report that glamour acquirers more frequently issued stock to finance their mergers, suggesting perhaps that the managers thought that their stock was 'overvalued'. In further support of this interpretation are the findings of several studies that post-merger cumulative returns are much lower for mergers financed through exchanges of shares, discussed above.

This interpretation is further buttressed by analyses of the market's evaluation of diversification and conglomerate mergers during the 1960s. Servaes (1996) found that the market values of diversified companies were already significantly discounted in the late 1960s and early 1970s. Matsusaka (1993) reports, however, that announcements of conglomerate acquisitions at that time were coupled with *positive* and significant abnormal returns. Why would the market bid down the shares of companies which had already diversified and simultaneously bid up the shares of companies announcing moves in that direction? An obvious answer is that conglomerate mergers were in vogue at the time. The conglomerates' managers were thought to be capable of adding value to any company they acquired. The price–earnings ratios of the conglomerates were bid up accordingly and each newly announced acquisition was greeted with still more enthusiasm.

The possibility that the pre-announcement positive abnormal returns reflect overoptimism and an overvaluation of acquirers' shares calls into question the common practice in event studies of measuring the effects of mergers using short windows. If the market can overvalue a group of companies' shares for a period of three to four years, it is possible that it will continue to overvalue them for a few days or even a month or two around the announcements of acquisitions. Indeed, if the reason for the overvaluation of acquirers prior to the announcements is a mistaken acceptance of a 'theory' about the synergistic effects of mergers – as seems to have been true of the conglomerates – the market's reaction to merger announcements is certain to have an upward bias. Thus explaining post-merger declines in acquirers' share prices by assuming their overvaluation prior to the announcements casts a shadow of doubt over both the efficient capital market hypothesis and the event study literature that rests upon it.

4 The effects of mergers on profitability

The difficulty in interpreting the results from event studies discussed at the end of the previous section implies that we must examine the effects of mergers on traditional measures of performance such as profits and sales to infer whether they increase efficiency or market power.

If managers maximize profits, they should expect the profits of their company to rise following a merger. Although all expectations will not be fulfilled, if managers have *rational expectations*, the average merger should generate positive profits. Perhaps the most surprising finding of the merger literature is that this prediction has not been generally confirmed. This surprising finding holds even for the first two great merger waves in the United States in which the mergers were largely horizontal and resulted in many cases in substantial increases in firm size and market shares (Hogarty, 1970).

One of the most comprehensive studies of the effects of mergers on profitability is an analysis of nearly 6000 lines of business between 1950 and 1977 by Ravenscraft and Scherer (1987) (hereafter R&S).[9] They regressed the profits of individual lines of business in the years 1975, 1976 and 1977 on industry dummies and a variable that measured the fraction of the line of business that had been acquired since 1950. In this way they compared the profit rate of an acquired line of business in, say, the soft drink industry with the average profit rate in soft drinks of all soft drinks producers. In addition to measuring the fraction of the line of business that was acquired, R&S attempted to control for other aspects of the merger, such as whether it was a hostile takeover or not. They also distinguished between mergers on the basis of the accounting convention employed by the acquiring firm to evaluate the acquired firm's assets.

Under the *pooling* convention the assets of the newly created company are determined by simply adding the book values of the assets of the two merging firms. Under the purchase accounting convention, the acquired unit's assets are evaluated at the price paid for them. Thus, if market values of acquired companies roughly equal the book values of their assets, a more favourable impression of the post-merger profits of acquired units will be obtained if the pooling accounting convention is employed.[10] A typical regression result follows (R&S, p. 101):

$$\pi = [257 \text{ industry dummies}] + 0.68 \ (0.60) \ POOL - 2.82 \ (2.24) \ PURCH \\ + 0.84 \ (0.83) \ NEW + 1.46 \ (1.51) \ EQUALS + 30.15 \ (5.67) \ SHR - 3.65 \\ (1.65) \ HOSTILE - 3.77 \ (1.69) \ WHITE - 2.23 \ (1.18) \ OTHER \qquad (2.4)$$
$$R^2 = 0.182 \qquad\qquad n = 2{,}732$$

The dependent variable is the profit to asset ratio of a line of business in one of the years, 1975, 1976 or 1977. The variables POOL and PURCH measure the fraction of a line of business that was acquired and whether the assets of the acquired unit were measured as their book value prior to the merger, as under the pooling convention, or their purchase price. The coefficient on POOL is insignificant, implying that the profit rate of an acquired line of business was not significantly different from that of non-acquired lines of business, when the acquired unit's assets were measured at their pre-merger book values. When the profit rates of the acquired lines of business were measured relative to the values paid for these assets, however, they were 2.82 percentage points below those of non-acquired units. The mean profit rate of manufacturing firms over the 1975–7 period was roughly 9.9 per cent, so that the lower return earned by acquired units was both economically and statistically significant (*t*-statistics in parentheses).

There is weak evidence that mergers between similar sized firms are more profitable (coefficient on EQUALS), and that units involved in hostile mergers are less profitable (HOSTILE and WHITE). The latter finding may stem from poorer than average pre-merger performance of hostile targets. The most significant variable in the equation is the firm's market share (SHR). R&S include this variable to control for the fact that acquired units tend to be smaller and have smaller market shares on average. Unfortunately, to the extent that mergers reduce the efficiency of the acquired units, as implied by the coefficient on PURCH, they also reduce the acquired units' market shares (see discussion in the following section). Thus the inclusion of market share in the regression actually controls for some of the adverse effects of the mergers, thereby biasing the coefficients on POOL and PURCH upwards.

Similarly, negative findings were obtained by Meeks (1977) in a study of over 1000 mergers since World War II in the United Kingdom. The post-merger profitability of the merging firms was significantly lower on average than their pre-merger profitability.

An examination of 19 additional studies for different countries and time periods reveals, like R&S and Meeks, some which find declines in profits following mergers, some finding increases and still others observing no significant change at all. If one weighs the evidence presented in each study by the number of observations in it, one must conclude that mergers have *at best* left profitability unchanged, and more likely have actually reduced the profits of the merging firms (Mueller, 2003a, ch. 9).

5   Effects of mergers on market share and growth

To increase profits, a merger must either shift the demand schedules of the merging firms or lower their costs. Demand schedule shifts might come about either because of changes in the market power of the merging firms or because of a change in the quality characteristics perceived by buyers due perhaps to more advertising or R&D having taken place. Each of these effects can in turn affect the market share(s) of the merging firms. An alternative way to measure the effects of mergers is to examine the changes in market shares that accompany them. Since accounting definitions of sales do not differ as greatly across companies and countries as definitions of profits and assets, this measure is perhaps to be preferred.

Under the assumption that firms face linear demand schedules and have constant average costs, and that they maximize an objective function as given in eq. (2.1), it can be shown that a merger which either increases the quality or reduces the costs of one of the merging firms must increase its market share. A merger which increases market power, on the other hand, can lead to a reduction in market share as the merging firms cut output to raise price (Mueller, 1986, pp. 184–91). To test for the effects of mergers on market shares I used a sample of 209 acquired firms from the 1000 largest US companies of 1950, and compared the market shares of firms acquired between 1950 and 1972 with those of non-acquired firms of similar size in the same industries (Mueller, 1985, 1986, ch.9). A typical regression result looked as follows:

$$MS_{72} = 0.011 \ (2.61) + 0.885 \ (45.02) \ MS_{50} - 0.705 \ (20.02) \ D \ MS_{50} \quad (2.5)$$
$$R^2 = 0.94 \qquad\qquad n = 313$$

where MS_i is a firm's market share in year i, and D represents a dummy variable that takes on a value of 1 if the firm was acquired, 0 if it was not. The equation shows that the average non-acquired firm retained 88.5 per cent of its 1950 market share in 1972. Firms among the 1000 largest of 1950 lost market share on average to smaller firms and new entrants over the 1950s and 1960s. An acquired company lost significantly more market share, however. On average it retained only 18 per cent of its 1950 market share $(0.885 - 0.705)$. Additional tests showed that the loss of market share tended to occur after the mergers took place. The earlier a firm was acquired, the greater its loss of market share.

These results were for conglomerate and vertical mergers. Companies involved in horizontal mergers also exhibited market share losses relative to non-merging companies. The losses were smaller for bigger companies, suggesting that the horizontal mergers may also have led to increases in the degree of cooperation, but the overwhelming effect of the acquisitions on companies in the largest 1000 of 1950 was to reduce their market shares, and thus it would seem to have reduced either the quality of their products or the efficiency of their operations.[11]

Baldwin and Gorecki (1990, pp. 53–73) or Baldwin (1995, pp. 242–6) also found significant declines in market shares for Canadian plants acquired in horizontal mergers, but observed no significant changes in market shares for other acquired plants. Goldberg (1973) found no significant changes in market shares in three and half years following their acquisition for a sample of 44 advertising intensive companies, as did Rhoades (1986) for 413 acquired banks for a period of up to six years following their acquisition.

A similar approach to comparing market shares is to examine merging firms' growth rates following mergers relative to matched samples or industry means. Six studies of this type, for Australia, Belgium, France, Germany, Sweden and the UK, found no significant changes in growth rates following mergers.[12] Significant *declines* in growth rates were observed in Holland and the USA (Peer, 1980; Mueller, 1980c).

Thus we reach a conclusion from studies of the effects of mergers on market shares and relative growth rates similar to that from the profitability studies. There is no evidence that mergers increase market shares and growth as we would expect if they increased product quality or efficiency. There is some evidence that mergers have a significantly negative effect on market shares, and thus on quality or efficiency.

6   Effects of mergers on profits and sales

The results regarding the profitability of mergers, although mixed, are clearly more positive than those regarding their impacts on market shares and growth. Although no studies come up with significant positive effects of mergers on market shares or growth, quite a few find that they increase profitability. Whether these increases in profitability should be interpreted as social welfare increases or not depends, of course, on whether they are the result of increases in market power or increases in efficiency. In a recent study of mergers occurring in virtually every country of the world, Gugler et al. (2003) have attempted to distinguish between mergers that increase market power and those that increase efficiency by examining their effects upon both profitability and sales.

As the discussion in the previous section indicated, a merger that improves efficiency, broadly defined to include both cost reductions and product improvements, results in an unambiguous increase in the merged firms' market share(s) and profits. If we assume that two merging firms could select the same price and output combinations after a merger as before, then a merger that increases market power – that is to say their ability to raise price – should, if they choose to exercise this market power, lead to higher prices and a reduction of sales.[13] This reasoning led Gugler et al. to make the predictions given in the second column of Table 2.1.

Table 2.1   Possible consequences of mergers

	Δ Π > 0	Δ Π < 0
Δ S > 0	1 Efficiency increase	3 Market power reduction (?)
Δ S < 0	2 Market power increase	4 Efficiency decline

Source: Gugler *et al*. (2003), Table 1.

As noted in Section 2, some mergers may take place because managers are *not* maximizing profits. Although these mergers could result in no changes in profits or sales, it is reasonable to assume that some inefficiencies accompany joining different organizational structures and 'corporate cultures' and thus that costs rise and profits and sales fall for these mergers – the prediction in the lower right-hand corner of Table 2.1. The remaining entry in the table has been called 'market power-reducing mergers' by analogy with entry 2. No managers are likely to undertake a merger with the purpose of reducing market power and so this combination of effects is a bit of a puzzle, hence the question mark in 3.

Gugler *et al*. use the changes in sales and profits of the median-sized firms in the acquiring and acquired firms' industries to project what the sales and profits of the merging firms would have been had they not mergered. One interesting finding of the study is that the effects of mergers on profits and sales are very similar across all countries and across the different types of mergers. In particular, cross-border mergers are neither more nor less successful than domestic mergers.

Table 2.2 summarizes some of the main findings of Gugler *et al*. Looking first at the effects of mergers on profits, we see that 56.7 per cent of the mergers resulted in higher profits for the merging firms five years after the mergers than were predicted on the basis of the changes in profits of the median firms in their industries. Across the full sample of 1250 mergers, the profits of the merging companies five years after the mergers averaged $17.8 million more than predicted, based on the profits of the median firms in their industry. This difference was statistically significant, but small in comparison to the mean sales of the two merging firms at the time of the merger: $2553.3 million (Gugler *et al*., 2003, Tables 2 and 4).

The bottom row of Table 2.2 indicates that a majority of mergers (55.8 per cent) resulted in lower than predicted sales for the merging companies five years after the mergers. Thus the findings of Gugler *et al*. with respect to mergers' effects on profits and sales are consistent with those of other studies, in that they find mergers to be somewhat more successful in terms of their effects on profits than in terms of their effects on sales.

Table 2.2   Classification of mergers by firm size in year t+5 (per cent of mergers)

		Δ Π > 0	Δ Π < 0
		1	3
	Small	34.7	17.5
Δ S > 0	Large	23.4*	12.7*
	All	29.1	15.1
		2	4
	Small	20.4	27.4
Δ S < 0	Large	34.8*	29.1
	All	27.6	28.2

Notes: ΔΠ>0 (ΔΠ < 0) denotes that the mergers resulted in a profit increase (decrease) relative to year t and relative to industry and country peers. ΔS>0 (ΔS<0) denotes that the mergers resulted in a sales increase (decrease) relative to year t and relative to industry and country peers. The first number in each cell is for small firms (total sales less than the median in year t–1), the second number in each cell is for large firms (total sales more than the median in year t–1), and the third number in each cell is the overall proportion. A* means that the proportion of small firms is significantly different from the proportion of large firms at the 1 per cent level, two-sided test.

Source: Gugler *et al.* (2003), Table 10.

The fraction of all mergers that leads to increases in efficiency (ΔΠ>0 and ΔS>0) is roughly the same as the fraction producing an increase in market power (ΔΠ>0 and ΔS<0), which in turn is nearly equal to the fraction resulting in a decrease in efficiency (ΔΠ<0 and ΔS<0). The somewhat puzzling category, (ΔΠ<0 and ΔS>0), accounts for the smallest fraction of mergers.

It would seem more likely that mergers between large companies would increase market power, and that mergers between small ones would yield scale economies and other efficiency gains. This conjecture is confirmed in the Gugler *et al.* results. A significantly larger fraction of mergers between small firms (34.7 per cent) resulted in efficiency increases than for large firms (23.4 per cent). The reverse was true for mergers increasing market power. On the other hand, there was no systematic relationship between the size of the merging firms and the likelihood that they would result in a decrease in efficiency. If we assume that increases in market power reduce social welfare, and that decreases in efficiency reduce social welfare, then a majority of the mergers in the Gugler *et al.* study reduced social welfare.

7 Additional evidence regarding the effects of mergers on market share and growth

The strongest evidence that mergers increase efficiency is contained in studies of changes in plant ownership. Lichtenberg and Siegel (1987), for example, found that between 1972 and 1981 productivity fell in US plants before an ownership change and rose afterward. Since many of these ownership changes would have been spin-offs of plants obtained in previous mergers, Lichtenberg and Siegel's findings in part corroborate other work suggesting that mergers in the 1960s lowered company profits and efficiency. Baldwin (1991, 1995, pp. 246–53) also found significant increases in productivity for Canadian plants acquired through spin-offs, and through horizontal mergers. McGuckin and Nguyen (1995) also observed plant productivity increases following mergers in the United States. Thus it would appear that some immediate gains in efficiency at the plant level may result from mergers.

However, these results for *changes* in plant ownership and productivity are at odds with estimates of *levels* of plant productivity for diversified firms. Both Caves and Barton (1990) and Lichtenberg (1992) found that plants held by diversified firms had lower productivity levels than plants held by undiversified firms. Since mergers are the most popular way to diversify, we are left with the puzzle of how mergers can increase productivity at the time that they occur, and yet lead to lower productivity in the long run.

The studies examining mergers' effects on productivity seem to contradict those examining their effects on profitability and sales. One explanation for this inconsistency may be that the studies of productivity effects have used samples of mergers concentrated in the 1970s and early 1980s. As we have seen in the discussion of mergers' effects on share prices, their effects can differ substantially depending upon whereabouts in the business/stock market cycle they occur.

8 Policy implications

The standard approach to measuring the effects of mergers on social welfare is to assume that managers maximize profits, and thus that mergers must increase either market power or economic efficiency, or both. If the former they are bad, and the extent of the welfare loss is measured by the lost consumers' surplus (Harberger's triangle) that follows the exercise of the increase in market power. If only efficiency increases they are good, and the welfare gain is the increased consumers' and producers' surpluses that ensue. If both effects are present, the net welfare change must be calculated. In a classic paper, Williamson (1968) demonstrated that the gains in surpluses will generally exceed the losses.[14] Unless mergers only increase market power, the bias is in favour of mergers. This bias has governed US merger policy for the past two decades, and merger policy in most other countries at all times.

There are at least two reasons to question this presumption in favour of mergers. First, there is a strong asymmetry in the intertemporal effects of mergers on market power and efficiency. In a growing economy a company eventually achieves the necessary size for economic efficiency through internal growth. With a 3 per cent growth rate, only five years are needed to achieve a 16 per cent size increase. Only in declining industries can time not achieve the same efficiency gains as mergers.[15] On the other hand, a market power increase, as measured by the change in market share, is not eliminated with time. The mergers that created the United States Steel company produced a firm that was arguably *less* efficient than its rivals, as indicated by its continual decline in market share since its creation. Yet after a century of decline, it continues to lead the remnants of the US steel industry.

A second reason to question a presumption in favour of allowing mergers to take place is that they may generate neither efficiency gains nor market power increases. Their only effects may be to increase company size and to reduce economic efficiency. A reduction in efficiency can be expected to take the form of higher costs and that will lead to higher prices. Thus, when mergers reduce efficiency, society loses *both* a welfare triangle and a welfare rectangle.

The results summarized in Table 2.2 suggest that for every merger that results in an unambiguous increase in social welfare – efficiency increases and profits and sales both rise – there are two that unambiguously reduce social welfare, divided roughly equally between mergers that lower efficiency and mergers that increase market power. These results imply in turn that competition policy towards mergers should rest on a strong presumption *against* allowing mergers to take place, rather than what has been the case until now, a presumption in their favour.

US merger policy today allows a merger to take place even when it is expected to result in an increase in market power, if the merging firms can demonstrate that accompanying efficiency gains will result in a net increase in social welfare. Similar efficiency defences are being discussed currently in the European Union. No efficiency defense is needed, however, when a merger is not expected to increase market power. Given the large fraction of mergers that have reduced the efficiency of the merging companies, this policy amounts to a strong bias towards allowing mergers that reduce social welfare. A neutral policy towards mergers would require that *all* mergers above a certain size threshold pass an efficiency defence before being allowed to take place.[16]

Notes

1. In an article that received considerable attention, Salant *et al.* (1983) demonstrated that horizontal mergers in a homogeneous product industry ($\sigma = 1$) characterized by Cournot equilibria ($\theta = 0$) are generally *unprofitable* for the merging firms, which caught the profession by surprise. Not surprisingly, it generated a medium-sized literature of its own. This counterintuitive result comes about because of the twin assumptions that the firms have Cournot reaction functions and the equilibrium is symmetric. If either of the two assumptions is relaxed, the possibility of horizontal mergers that profit the merging firms appears; see, for example, Deneckere and Davidson (1985) and Perry and Porter (1985).
2. See the discussion and examples in Steiner (1975, chs 9 and 10) and Scherer and Ross (1990, pp. 188–90).
3. See surveys by Steiner (1975), Mueller (1977, 2003a, ch. 8), Hughes et al. (1980), and Scherer and Ross (1990, pp. 159–67).
4. Shiller (1981, 1984, 2000). Just how optimistic the managers of acquiring firms must be is illustrated in the study by Alberts and Varaiya (1989). They show that, to justify the premia paid for companies in the 1970s and 1980s, managers of acquiring US firms would have to anticipate improving the performance of an acquired unit from that of an average firm to one in the top decile of all companies.
5. See surveys by Mueller (1977, 1995, 2003b); Jensen and Ruback (1983).
6. See Agrawal *et al.*, (1992), Rau and Vermaelen (1998) and, for a survey, Agrawal and Jaffe (2000). Mitchell and Stafford (2000) subject their data to exhaustive econometric adjustments and succeed in reducing, but not totally eliminating, some of the post-merger negative returns.
7. See Agrawal *et al.* (1992); Loderer and Martin (1992); Higson and Elliott (1998); and discussion in Mueller (2003b).
8. See Travlos (1987), Franks *et al.* (1991), Gregory (1997), Loughran and Vijh (1997), Rau and Vermaelen (1998) and Mitchell and Stafford (2000).
9. A 'line of business' comes close in most cases to an economic definition of an industry: tyres, soap, etc.
10. R&S (pp. 229–38) found that the choice of accounting convention was related to the pre-merger ratio of market to book value of assets of the acquired firm. The lower this ratio, the more likely it was that the purchase accounting convention was used. Thus managers (accountants?) tended to employ the accounting procedure that cast the most favourable light on the acquired unit's post-merger profitability, and thus on the profitability of the combined entity. Lintner (1971) once hypothesized that the enhanced potential to engage in 'creative accounting' was a motive for mergers. In a post-Enron and WorldCom world, perhaps this motive for mergers should be re-examined.
11. Anti-merger policy was very strict in the 1950s and 1960s, and thus horizontal mergers among major competitors were rare. But, under the more relaxed antimerger policy of the 1980s, more significant horizontal mergers did take place. Stewart and Kim (1993) have found that mergers during 1985–6 led to significant increases in market concentration and welfare losses.
12. McDougall and Round (1986, pp. 157–9), Kumps and Witterwulghe (1980), Jenny and Weber (1980), Cable *et al.*, (1980), Ryden and Edberg (1980); and Cosh *et al.* (1980).
13. In a Cournot oligopoly, Farrell and Shapiro (1990, pp. 112–13) have proved that a merger that generates no synergies must lead to a higher price.
14. See, however, Ross (1968) and DePrano and Nugent (1969), as well as Williamson's defence (1977).
15. We speak here of course of horizontal mergers only. But it is with these that the trade-off seems most likely to be at issue.
16. For further discussion of this proposal, see Mueller (1996, 1997).

References

Agrawal, A. and J.F. Jaffe (2000): 'The post-merger performance puzzle', in C. Cooper and A. Gregary (eds), *Advances in Mergers and Acquisitions*, vol.1, New York: Elsevier Science, pp. 7–41.

Agrawal, A., J.F. Jaffe and G.N. Mandelker (1992): 'The post-merger performance of acquiring firms: a re-examination of an anomaly', *Journal of Finance* 47, 1605–21.

Alberts, W.W. and N.P. Varaiya (1989): 'Assessing the profitability of growth by acquisition: a "premium recapture" approach', *International Journal of Industrial Organization* 7, 133–49.

Andrade, G., M. Mitchell and E. Stafford (2001): 'New evidence and perspectives on mergers', *Journal of Economic Perspectives* 15, 103–20.

Asquith, P. (1983): 'Merger bids, uncertainty and stockholder returns', *Journal of Financial Economics* 11, 51–83.

Baldwin, J.R. (1991): 'The dynamics of the competitive process', mimeo, Queen's University.

Baldwin, J.R. (1995): *The Dynamics of Industrial Competition*, Cambridge: Cambridge University Press.

Baldwin, J.R. and P. Gorecki (1990): 'Mergers placed in the context of firm turnover', in Bureau of the Census, *1990 Annual Research Conference, Proceedings*, Washington, DC: U.S. Department of Commerce, pp. 53–73.

Cable, J.R., P.R. Palfrey and J.W. Runge (1980): 'Federal Republic of Germany, 1964–1974', in D.C. Mueller (ed.), *The Determinants and Effects of Mergers: An International Comparison*, Cambridge, MA: Oelgeschlager, Gunn & Hain, pp. 99–132.

Caves, R.E. and D.R. Barton (1990): *Efficiency in U.S. Manufacturing Industries*, Cambridge, MA: MIT Press.

Comanor, W.S. (1967): 'Vertical mergers, market power, and the antitrust laws', *American Economic Review* 57, 254–65.

Cosh, A., A. Hughes and A. Singh (1980): 'The causes and effects of takeovers in the United Kingdom: an empirical investigation for the late 1960s at the microeconomic level', in D.C. Mueller (ed.), *The Determinants and Effects of Mergers: An International Comparison*, Cambridge, MA: Oelgeschlager, Gunn & Hain, pp. 227–70.

Council of Economic Advisors (1985): *Annual Report*, Washington, DC: Government Printing Office.

Deneckere, R. and C. Davidson (1985): 'Incentives to form coalitions with Bertrand competition', *Rand Journal of Economics* 16, 473–86.

DePrano, M.E. and J.B. Nugent (1969): 'Economies as an antitrust defense: Comment', *American Economic Review* 59, 947–59.

Dutz, M.A. (1989): 'Horizontal mergers in declining industries', *International Journal of Industrial Organization* 7, 11–33.

Evans, W.N. and I.N. Kessides (1993): 'Living by the "golden rule": Multimarket contact in the U.S. airline industry', *Quarterly Journal of Economics* 109, 341–66.

Fama, E.F. (1998): 'Market efficiency, long-term returns, and behavioral finance', *Journal of Financial Economics* 49, 283–306.

Farrell, J. and C. Shapiro (1990): 'Horizontal mergers: an equilibrium analysis', *American Economic Review* 80, 107–26.

Franks, J., R. Harris and S. Titman (1991): 'The postmerger share-price performance of acquiring firms', *Journal of Financial Economics* 29, 81–96.

Goldberg, L.G. (1973): 'The effect of conglomerate mergers on competition', *Journal of Law and Economics* 16, 137–58.

Gregory, A. (1997): 'An examination of the long run performance of UK acquiring firms', *Journal of Business Finance and Accounting* 25, 971–1002.

Gugler, K., D.C. Mueller, B.B Yurtoglu and Ch. Zulehner (2003): 'The effects of mergers: an international comparison', *International Journal in Industrial Economics* 21, 625–54.

Halpern, P. (1983): 'Corporate acquisitions: a theory of special cases? A review of event studies applied to acquisitions', *Journal of Finance* 38, 297–317.

Higson, C. and J. Elliott (1998): 'Post-takeover returns: the UK evidence', *Journal of Empirical Finance* 5, 27–46.

Hogarty, T.F. (1970): 'Profits from mergers: the evidence of fifty years', *St. John's Law Review* 44, special edition, 378–91.

Hughes, A. (1989): 'The impact of merger: a survey of empirical evidence for the UK', in J. Fairburn and J. Kay (eds), *Mergers and Merger Policy*, Oxford: Oxford University Press, pp. 30–98.

Hughes, A., D.C. Mueller and A. Singh (1980): 'Hypotheses about mergers', in D.C. Mueller (ed.), *The Determinants and Effects of Mergers: An International Comparison*, Cambridge, MA: Oelgeschlager, Gunn & Hain, pp. 27–66.

Jenny, F. and A.-P. Weber (1980): 'France, 1962–72', in D.C. Mueller (ed.), *The Determinants and Effects of Mergers: An International Comparison*, Cambridge, MA: Oelgeschlager, Gunn & Hain, pp. 133–62.

Jensen, M.C. (1986): 'Agency costs of free cash flow, corporate finance and takeovers', *American Economic Review* 76, 323–9.

Jensen, M.C. and R.S. Ruback (1983): 'The market for corporate control', *Journal of Financial Economics* 11, 5–50.

Kumps, A.-M. and R. Witterwulghe (1980): 'Belgium, 1962–74', in D.C. Mueller (ed.), *The Determinants and Effects of Mergers: An International Comparison*, Cambridge, MA: Oelgeschlager, Gunn & Hain, pp. 67–97.

Lichtenberg, F.R. (1992): 'Industrial de-diversification and its consequences for productivity', *Journal of Economic Behavior and Organization* 18, 427–38.

Lichtenberg, F.R. and D. Siegel (1987): 'Productivity and changes in ownership of manufacturing plants', *Brookings Papers on Economic Activity*, 643–73.

Lintner, J. (1971): 'Expectations, mergers and equilibrium in purely competitive securities markets', *American Economic Review* 61, 101–11.

Loderer, C. and K. Martin (1992): 'Postacquisition performance of acquiring firms', *Financial Management* 21, 69–91.

Loughran, T. and A.M. Vijh (1997): 'Do long-term shareholders benefit from corporate acquisitions?', *Journal of Finance* 52, 1765–90.

Mandelker, G. (1974): 'Risk and return: the case of merging firms', *Journal of Financial Economics* 1, 303–35.

Manne, H.G. (1965): 'Mergers and the market for corporate control', *Journal of Political Economy* 73, 110–20.

Marris, R. (1964): *The Economic Theory of Managerial Capitalism*, Glencoe: Free Press.

Matsusaka, J.G. (1993): 'Takeover motives during the conglomerate merger wave', *Rand Journal of Economics* 24, 357–79.

McDougall, F.M. and D.K. Round (1986): *The Determinants and Effects of Corporate Takeovers in Australia, 1970–1981*, Victoria: Australian Institute of Management.

McGuckin, R. and S.V. Nguyen (1995): 'On the productivity and plant ownership change: new evidence from the longitudinal research database', *Rand Journal of Economics* 26, 257–76.

Meeks, G. (1977): *Disappointing Marriage: A Study of the Gains from Merger*, Cambridge, UK: Cambridge University Press.

Mitchell, M.L. and E. Stafford (2000): 'Managerial decisions and long-term stock price performance', *Journal of Business* 73, 287–329.

Mueller, D.C. (1969): 'A theory of conglomerate mergers', *Quarterly Journal of Economics* 83, 643–59.

Mueller, D.C. (1972): 'A life cycle theory of the firm', *Journal of Industrial Economics* 20, 199–219.

Mueller, D.C. (1977): 'The effects of conglomerate mergers: a survey of the empirical evidence', *Journal of Banking and Finance* 1, 315–47.

Mueller, D.C. (ed.) (1980a): *The Determinants and Effects of Mergers: An International Comparison*, Cambridge, MA: Oelgeschlager, Gunn & Hain.

Mueller, D.C. (1980b): 'A cross-national comparison of the results', in D.C. Mueller (ed.) (1980a), pp. 299–314.

Mueller, D.C. (1980c): 'The United States, 1962–1972', in D.C. Mueller (ed.), (1980a) pp. 271–98.

Mueller, D.C. (1985): 'Mergers and market share', *Review of Economics and Statistics* 67, 259–67.

Mueller, D.C. (1986): *Profits in the Long Run*, Cambridge, UK: Cambridge University Press.

Mueller, D.C. (1995): 'Mergers: theory and evidence', in G. Mussati (ed.), *Mergers, Markets and Public Policy*, Dordrecht: Kluwer Academic Publishers, pp. 9–43.

Mueller, D.C. (1996): 'Antimerger policy in the United States: history and lessons', *Empirica* 23, 229–53.

Mueller, D.C. (1997): 'Merger policy in the United States: a reconsideration', *Review of Industrial Organization* 12, 655–85.

Mueller, D.C. (2003a): *The Corporation – Investment, Mergers and Growth*, London: Routledge.

Mueller, D.C. (2003b): 'The finance literature on mergers: a critical survey', in M. Waterson (ed.), *Competition, Monopoly and Corporate Governance: Essays in Honor of Keith Cowling*, Cheltenham, UK and Northampton, MA, USA: Edward Elgar, pp. 161–205.

Peer, H. (1980): 'The Netherlands, 1962–1973', in D.C. Mueller (ed.), *The Determinants and Effects of Mergers: An International Comparison*, Cambridge, MA: Oelgeschlager, Gunn & Hain, pp. 163–91.

Perry, M.K. (1989): 'Vertical integration: determinants and effects', in R. Schmalensee and R. Willig (eds), *Handbook of Industrial Organization*, vol. 1, Amsterdam: North-Holland, pp. 415–73.

Perry, M.K. and R.H. Porter (1985): 'Oligopoly and the incentive for horizontal merger', *American Economic Review* 75, 219–27.

Rau, P.R. and T. Vermaelen (1998): 'Glamour, value and the post-acquisition performance of acquiring firms', *Journal of Financial Economics* 49, 223–53.

Ravenscraft, D.J. and F.M. Scherer (1987): 'Mergers and managerial performance', in J.C. Coffee, Jr, L. Lowenstein and S. Rose-Ackerman (eds), *Takeovers and Contests for Corporate Control*, Oxford: Oxford University Press.

Rhoades, S.A (1986): 'The operating performance of acquired firms in banking before and after acquisition', *Board of Governors of the Federal Reserve System Staff Studies* 149, April.

Roll, R. (1986): 'The hubris hypothesis of corporate takeovers', *Journal of Business* 59, 197–216.

Ross, P. (1968): 'Economies as an antitrust defense: Comment', *American Economic Review* 58, 1371–6.

Ryden, B. and J.-O. Edberg (1980): 'Large mergers in Sweden, 1962–1976', in D.C. Mueller (ed.) (1980a), pp. 193–226.

Salant, S.W., S. Switzer and R.J. Reynolds (1983): 'Losses from horizontal merger: the effects of an exogenous change in industry structure on Cournot–Nash equilibrium', *Quarterly Journal of Economics* 98, 185–99.

Scherer, F.M. and D. Ross (1990): *Industrial Market Structure and Economic Performance*, 3rd edn, Boston: Houghton Mifflin.

Scott, J.T. (1989): 'Purposive diversification as a motive for merger', *International Journal of Industrial Organization* 7, 35–47.

Scott, J.T. (1993): *Purposive Diversification and Economic Performance*, Cambridge, UK: Cambridge University Press.

Servaes, H. (1996): 'The value of diversification during the conglomerate merger wave', *Journal of Finance* 51, 1201–25.

Shiller, R.J. (1981): 'Do stock prices move too much to be justified by subsequent changes in dividends?', *American Economic Review* 71, 421–36.

Shiller, R.J. (1984): 'Stock prices and social dynamics', *Brookings Papers on Economic Activity*, 457–98.

Shiller, R.J. (2000): *Irrational Exuberance*, Princeton, NJ: Princeton University Press.

Steiner, P.O. (1975): *Mergers: Motives, Effects, Policies*, Ann Arbor: University of Michigan Press.

Stewart, J.F. and S.-K. Kim (1993): 'Mergers and social welfare in U.S. manufacturing, 1985–86', *Southern Economic Journal* 59, 701–20.

Travlos, N.G. (1987): 'Corporate takeover bids, methods of payment and bidding firms' stock returns', *Journal of Finance* 42, 943–63.

Williamson, O.E. (1968): 'Economies as an anti-trust defense: the welfare trade-offs', *American Economic Review* 58, 18–36; reprinted with corrections in C.K. Rowley (ed.), *Readings in Industrial Economics*, London: Macmillan, 1972.

Williamson, O.E. (1977): 'Economies as an anti-trust defense revisited', in A.P. Jacquemin and H.W. de Jong (eds), *Welfare Aspects of Industrial Markets*, Leiden: Martinus Nijhoff.

Williamson, O.E. (1989): 'Transaction cost economics', in R. Schmalensee and R. Willig (eds), *Handbook of Industrial Organization*, vol. 1, Amsterdam: North-Holland, pp. 135–82.

3   Small firms, innovation and competition

David B. Audretsch

1 Introduction

From the perspective of the static model of industrial organization, the entry
of new firms is important because they provide an equilibrating function
in the market. In the presence of market power, the additional output
provided by the new entrants restores the levels of profits and prices to
their long-run competitive equilibrium. However, as Geroski (1995) points
out in his comprehensive survey on 'What Do We Know About Entry?' the
actual amount of output in markets contributed by new entrants is trivial.
He reports from an exhaustive empirical literature that the share of total
industry sales accounted for by new entrants typically ranges from 1.45 to
6.36 per cent. This would seemingly suggest that new entrants contribute
insufficient additional output to provide a competitive threat to incumbent
firms. The implications for competition policy under this static perspective
are that policies encouraging new-firm entry will contribute little in terms
of fostering market competition. Thus competition policies in both Europe
and the United States have traditionally focused on reducing barriers to
entry for existing incumbent enterprises rather than on reducing barriers
to the start-up of new enterprises.

However, a recent literature analyzing the dynamics of firms and industries
suggests that the contribution of new and small firms to the dynamics of
competition is significantly greater than found in a static analysis. There are
two reasons why new-firm entry generates more competition in the dynamic
than in the static context. The first is that the market shares of entrants,
while being inconsequential in the start-up and early years, often increase
to significant levels within several years subsequent to entry. For example,
Audretsch (1995) finds that, while the market penetration of new-firm start-
ups is low, in some industries the penetration ratio has risen to nearly 20
per cent within five years of entry. Analysis of longitudinal data bases
suggests that the market penetration of new firms has been understated by
only considering their competitive impact in the entry year.

The second, and presumably more important, reason why the contribution
of new and small firms is of greater significance is, as Geroski (1995)
also points out, that 'entry is often used as a vehicle for introducing new
innovations'. Ideas for new products, processes or organizations that cannot

flourish or be pursued within the context of incumbent firms are sometimes pursued by the start-up of a new firm. The start-up of a new firm can represent the attempt to commercialize an untried idea. As Jovanovic (1982) argues in his model of noisy selection, new firms do not know the viability of their enterprises but only discover this subsequent to start-up, struggling in the market and striving for performance. Start-ups, learning from market experience that their product is viable, grow and ultimately survive; those learning that their products are not viable stagnate and exit. Thus an important source of market competition in this dynamic context comes from the new products and processes being introduced in the market by new firms.

The dynamic contribution to competition emanating from new and small firms suggests that policies mitigating barriers to start-up of new firms as well as barriers to entry by incumbent firms should be an equally important component of competition policies. By encouraging the entry of new firms, policy can generate new competition in the form of a greater number of firms experimenting with a greater variety of approaches. Increased variety generates greater competition which, through a process of selection, results in many firms exiting and fewer surviving by providing the best novel approaches (Cohen and Klepper, 1992; Audretsch and Thurik, 2001).

Policymakers have recently recognized the potential contribution to dynamic competition that new firms can play. This has led to a shift in emphasis towards reducing barriers to start-up. A wide range of programs has been introduced by governments on both sides of the Atlantic to reduce such barriers. For example, the Small Business Innovation Research (SBIR) in the US program provides over $1.4 billion annually to high-technology small firms. The commitment of the European Union is exemplified by the European Council Meeting in Lisbon in 2000, where the EU announced the mandate to become 'the most entrepreneurial and dynamic knowledge-based economy in the world'.[1]

Just as the economy has been besieged by a wave of technological change that has left virtually no sector of the economy untouched, scientific understanding of the innovative process – that is, the manner by which firms innovate, and the impact such technological change has in turn on enterprises and markets – has also undergone a revolution, which, if somewhat quieter, has been no less fundamental. Well into the 1970s, a conventional wisdom about the nature of technological change generally pervaded. This conventional wisdom had been shaped largely by scholars such as Alfred Chandler (1977), Joseph Schumpeter (1942) and John Kenneth Galbraith (1956) who had convinced a generation of scholars and policymakers that innovation and technological change lie in the domain of large corporations and that small business would fade away as the victim of its own inefficiencies.

At the heart of this conventional wisdom was the belief that monolithic enterprises exploiting market power were the driving engine of innovative activity. Schumpeter had declared the debate closed, with his proclamation in 1942 (p. 106) that, 'What we have got to accept is that [the large-scale establishment] has come to be the most powerful engine of progress.' Galbraith (1956, p. 86) echoed Schumpeter's sentiment: 'There is no more pleasant fiction than that technological change is the product of the matchless ingenuity of the small man forced by competition to employ his wits to better his neighbor. Unhappily, it is a fiction.'

At the same time, the conventional wisdom about small and new firms was that they were burdened with a size inherent handicap in terms of innovative activity. Because they had a deficit of resources required to generate and commercialize ideas, this conventional wisdom viewed small enterprises as being largely outside the domain of innovative activity and technological change. Thus, even after David Birch (1981) revealed the startling findings from his study that small firms provided the engine of job creation in the USA, most scholars still assumed that, while small businesses may create the bulk of new jobs, innovation and technological change remained beyond their sphere.

While this conventional wisdom about the singular role played by large enterprises with market power prevailed during the first three decades subsequent to the end of World War II, more recently a wave of new studies has challenged this conventional wisdom. Most importantly, these studies have identified a much wider spectrum of enterprises contributing to innovative activity, and found that, in particular, small entrepreneurial firms as well as large established incumbents play an important role in the innovation and process of technological change.

Taken together, these studies comprise a new understanding about the links between entrepreneurship, firm size and innovative activity. The purpose of this chapter is to identify this new understanding about the role that entrepreneurship and small firms play with respect to technological change and innovation and to contrast it with the previous conventional wisdom. This chapter begins with the most prevalent theory about innovation and technological change: the model of the knowledge production function. Just as the conventional wisdom was shaped largely by the available empirical data and analyses, so it is with the newer view. Thus, in the following section of this chapter, issues arising when trying to measure innovative activity are discussed.

The debate and the evidence regarding the relationship between innovative activity and firm size is examined in the third section. In the fourth section, the impact that the external industry environment exerts on technological change is identified. The role that knowledge spillovers and geographic location play in innovative activity is explained in the fifth section. This leads to a reinterpretation of the knowledge production function when entrepreneurial activity is considered in the sixth section.

Finally, a summary and conclusions are provided in the last section. A key finding is that the conventional wisdom regarding the process of innovation technological change is generally inconsistent with the new understanding about the role of entrepreneurship in innovative activity. The empirical evidence strongly suggests that small entrepreneurial firms play a key role in generating innovations, at least in certain industries. While the conventional wisdom is derived from the Schumpeterian hypothesis and assumption that scale economies exist in R&D effort, for which there is considerable empirical evidence, more recent evidence suggests that scale economies bestowed through the geographic proximity facilitated by spatial clusters seems to be more important than those for large enterprises in producing innovative output.

2 The knowledge production function

The starting point for most theories of innovation is the firm (see, for example, Baldwin and Scott, 1987; Cohen and Levin, 1989; Scherer, 1984, 1991; Dosi, 1988). In such theories the firms are exogenous and their performance in generating technological change is endogenous (Scherer, 1984, 1991; Cohen and Klepper, 1991, 1992; Arrow, 1962).

For example, in the most prevalent model found in the literature of technological change, the model of the 'knowledge production function', formalized by Zvi Griliches (1979), firms exist exogenously and then engage in the pursuit of new economic knowledge as an input into the process of generating innovative activity.

The most decisive input in the knowledge production function is new economic knowledge. As Cohen and Klepper conclude, the greatest source generating new economic knowledge is generally considered to be R&D (Cohen and Klepper, 1991, 1992).

When it came to empirical estimation of the knowledge production function, it became clear that measurement issues played a major role. The state of knowledge regarding innovation and technological change has generally been shaped by the nature of the data which were available to scholars for analyses. Such data have always been incomplete and, at best, represented only a proxy measure reflecting some aspect of the process of technological change. Simon Kuznets observed in 1962 that the greatest obstacle to understanding the economic role of technological change was a clear inability of scholars to measure it. More recently, Cohen and Levin (1989) warned:

> A fundamental problem in the study of innovation and technical change in industry is the absence of satisfactory measures of new knowledge and its contribution to technological progress. There exists no measure of innovation that permits readily interpretable cross-industry comparisons.

Measures of technological change have typically involved one of the three major aspects of the innovative process: (1) a measure of the inputs into the innovative process, such as R&D expenditures, or else the share of the labor force accounted for by employees involved in R&D activities; (2) an intermediate output, such as the number of inventions which have been patented; or (3) a direct measure of innovative output.

These three levels of measuring technological change have not been developed and analyzed simultaneously, but have evolved over time, roughly in the order of their presentation. That is, the first attempts to quantify technological change at all generally involved measuring some aspects of inputs into the innovative process (Scherer, 1965a, 1965b, 1967; Grabowski, 1968; Mueller, 1967; Mansfield, 1968). Measures of R&D inputs (first in terms of employment and later in terms of expenditures) were only introduced on a meaningful basis enabling inter-industry and inter-firm comparisons in the late 1950s and early 1960s.

A clear limitation in using R&D activity as a proxy measure for technological change is that R&D reflects the resources devoted to producing innovative output, but not the amount of innovative activity actually realized. That is, R&D is an input and not an output in the innovation process. In addition, Kleinknecht (1987, 1991), Kleinknecht and Verspagen (1989) and Kleinknecht et al. (1991) have systematically shown that R&D measures incorporate only efforts made to generate innovative activity that are undertaken within formal R&D budgets and within formal R&D laboratories. They find that the extent of informal R&D is considerable, particularly in smaller enterprises.[2] And, as Mansfield (1984) points out, not all efforts within a formal R&D laboratory are directed towards generating innovative output in any case. Rather, other types of output, such as imitation and technology transfer, are also common goals in R&D laboratories.

As systematic data measuring the number of inventions patented were made publicly available in the mid-1960s, many scholars interpreted this new measure not only as being superior to R&D but also as reflecting innovative output. In fact, the use of patented inventions is not a measure of innovative output, but is rather a type of intermediate output measure.

A patent reflects new technical knowledge, but it does not indicate whether this knowledge has a positive economic value. Only those inventions which have been successfully introduced in the market can claim that they are innovations as well. While innovations and inventions are related, they are not identical. The distinction is that an innovation is 'a process that begins with an invention, proceeds with the development of the invention, and results in the introduction of a new product, process or service to the marketplace' (Edwards and Gordon, 1984, p. 1).

Besides the fact that many, if not most, patented inventions do not result in an innovation, a second important limitation of patent measures as an indicator of innovative activity is that they do not capture all of the innovations actually made. In fact, many inventions which result in innovations are not patented. The tendency of patented inventions to result in innovations and of innovations to be the result of inventions which were patented combine into what Scherer (1983a) has termed the *propensity* to patent. It is the uncertainty about the stability of the propensity to patent across enterprises and across industries that casts doubt upon the reliability of patent measures.[3] According to Scherer (1983a, pp. 107–8), 'The quantity and quality of industry patenting may depend upon chance, how readily a technology lends itself to patent protection, and business decision-makers' varying perceptions of how much advantage they will derive from patent rights. Not much of a systematic nature is known about these phenomena, which can be characterized as differences in the propensity to patent.'

Mansfield (1984, p. 462) has explained why the propensity to patent may vary so much across markets: 'The value and cost of individual patents vary enormously within and across industries ... Many inventions are not patented. And in some industries, like electronics, there is considerable speculation that the patent system is being bypassed to a greater extent than in the past. Some types of technologies are more likely to be patented than others.' The implications are that comparisons between enterprises and across industries may be misleading. According to Cohen and Levin (1989), 'There are significant problems with patent counts as a measure of innovation, some of which affect both within-industry and between-industry comparisons.'

Thus, even as new and superior sources of patent data have been introduced, such as the new measure of patented inventions from the computerization by the US Patent Office (Hall *et al.*, 1986; Jaffe, 1986; Pakes and Griliches, 1980, 1984) as well as in Europe (Schwalbach and Zimmermann, 1991; Greif, 1989; Greif and Potkowik, 1990), the reliability of these data as measures of innovative activity has been severely challenged. For example, Pakes and Griliches (1980, p. 378) warn that 'patents are a flawed measure [of innovative output]; particularly since not all new innovations are patented and since patents differ greatly in their economic impact'. And in addressing the question, 'Patents as indicators of what?', Griliches (1990, p. 1669) concludes that, 'Ideally, we might hope that patent statistics would provide a measure of the [innovative] output ... The reality, however, is very far from it. The dream of getting hold of an output indicator of inventive activity is one of the strong motivating forces for economic research in this area.'[4]

It was not before well into the 1970s that systematic attempts were made to provide a direct measure of the innovative output. Thus it should be emphasized that the conventional wisdom regarding innovation and technological change was based primarily upon the evidence derived from analyzing R&D data, which essentially measure inputs into the process of technological change and patented inventions, which are a measure of intermediate output at best.

The first serious attempt to measure innovative output directly was by the Gellman Research Associates (1976) for the National Science Foundation. Gellman identified 500 major innovations that were introduced into the market between 1953 and 1973 in the United States, the United Kingdom, Japan, West Germany, France and Canada. The data base was compiled by an international panel of experts, who identified those innovations representing the 'most significant new industrial products and processes, in terms of their technological importance and economic and social impact' (National Science Board, 1975, p. 100).

A second and comparable data base once again involved the Gellman Research Associates (1982), this time for the US Small Business Administration. In their second study, Gellman compiled a total of 635 US innovations, including 45 from the earlier study for the National Science Foundation. The additional 590 innovations were selected from fourteen industry trade journals for the period 1970–79. About 43 per cent of the sample was selected from the award winning innovations described in the *Industrial Research & Development* magazine.

The third data source that has attempted to measure innovation activity directly was compiled at the Science Policy Research Unit (SPRU) at the University of Sussex in the United Kingdom.[5] The SPRU data consist of a survey of 4378 innovations that were identified over a period of 15 years. The survey was compiled by writing to experts in each industry and requesting them to identify 'significant technical innovations that had been successfully commercialized in the United Kingdom since 1945, and to name the firm responsible' (Pavitt *et al.*, 1987, p. 299).

The most recent and most ambitious major data base providing a direct measure of innovative activity is the US Small Business Administration's Innovation Data Base (SBIDB). The data base consists of 8074 innovations commercially introduced in the USA in 1982. A private firm, The Futures Group, compiled the data and performed quality-control analyses for the US Small Business Administration by examining over one hundred technology, engineering and trade journals, spanning every industry in manufacturing. From the sections in each trade journal listing innovations and new products, a data base consisting of the innovations by four-digit standard industrial classification (SIC) industries was formed.[6] These data were implemented by Acs and Audretsch (1987, 1988, 1990) to analyze the relationships between firm size and technological change and market structure and technological change, where a direct rather than indirect measure of innovative activity is used.

In their 1990 study (ch.2), Acs and Audretsch compare these four data bases directly measuring innovative activity and find that they generally provide similar qualitative results. For example, while the Gellman data base identified small firms as contributing 2.45 times more innovations per employee than do large firms, the SBIDB finds that small firms introduce 2.38 more innovations per employee than do their larger counterparts. In general, these four data bases reveal similar patterns with respect to the distribution of innovations across manufacturing industries and between large and small enterprises. These similarities emerge, despite the obviously different methods used to compile the data, especially in terms of sampling and standard of significance.

Just as for the more traditional measures of technological change, there are also certain limitations associated with the direct measure of innovative activity. In fact, one of the main qualifications is common among all three measures: the implicit assumption of homogeneity of units. That is, just as it is implicitly assumed that each dollar of R&D makes the same contribution to technological change, and that each invention which is patented is equally valuable, the output measure implicitly assumes that innovations are of equal importance.[7] As Cohen and Levin (1989) observe, 'In most studies, process innovation is not distinguished from product innovation; basic and applied research are not distinguished from development.' Thus the increase in the firm's market value resulting from each innovation, dollar expended on R&D, and patent, is implicitly assumed to be homogeneous – an assumption which clearly violates real-world observation.

In order at least to approximate the market value associated with innovative activity, FitzRoy and Kraft (1990, 1991) follow the example of Connolly and Hirschey (1984), Pakes (1985) and Connolly *et al.* (1986). Using data for 57 West German firms in the metalworking sector, FitzRoy and Kraft (1990, 1991) measure innovation as the 'proportion of sales consisting of products introduced within the last five years'. Presumably the greater the market value of a given product innovation, the higher would be the proportion of sales accounted for by new products.

Similarly, von der Schulenburg and Wagner (1991) are able to provide one of the first applications of a direct measure of innovative activity in West Germany. Their measure is from the IFO Institute and is defined as the 'percentage of shipments of those products which were introduced recently into the market and are still in the entry phase'.[8] Like the measure of innovative activity used by FitzRoy and Kraft (1990, 1991), the von der Schulenburg and Wagner measure reflects the market value of the innovation and therefore attempts to overcome one of the major weaknesses in most of the other direct and indirect measures of innovative activity.

The knowledge production function has been found to hold most strongly at broader levels of aggregation. The most innovative countries are those with the greatest investments in R&D. Little innovative output is associated with less developed countries, which are characterized by a paucity of production of new economic knowledge. Similarly, the most innovative industries also tend to be characterized by considerable investments in R&D and new economic knowledge. Industries such as computers, pharmaceuticals and instruments are not only high in R&D inputs that generate new economic knowledge, but also in terms of innovative outputs (Audretsch, 1995). By contrast, industries with little R&D, such as wood products, textiles and paper, also tend to produce only a negligible amount of innovative output. Thus the knowledge production model linking knowledge generating inputs to outputs certainly holds at the more aggregated levels of economic activity.

Where the relationship becomes less compelling is at the disaggregated microeconomic level of the enterprise, establishment or even line of business. For example, while Acs and Audretsch (1990) found that the simple correlation between R&D inputs and innovative output was 0.84 for four-digit SIC manufacturing industries in the United States, it was only about half, 0.40, among the largest US corporations.

The model of the knowledge production function becomes even less compelling in view of the recent wave of studies revealing that small enterprises serve as the engine of innovative activity in certain industries. These results are startling because, as Scherer (1991) observes, the bulk of industrial R&D is undertaken in the largest corporations; small enterprises account only for a minor share of R&D inputs.

3   The role of firm size

At the heart of the conventional wisdom has been the belief that large enterprises able to exploit at least some market power are the engine of technological change. This view dates back at least to Schumpeter, who in *Capitalism, Socialism and Democracy* (1942, p. 101) argued, 'The monopolist firm will generate a larger supply of innovations because there are advantages which, though not strictly unattainable on the competitive level of enterprise, are as a matter of fact secured only on the monopoly level.' The Schumpeterian thesis, then, is that large enterprises are uniquely endowed to exploit innovative opportunities. That is, market dominance is a prerequisite to undertaking the risks and uncertainties associated with innovation. It is the possibility of acquiring quasi-rents that serves as the catalyst for large-firm innovation.

Five factors favoring the innovative advantage of large enterprises have been identified in the literature. First is the argument that innovative activity requires a high fixed cost. As Comanor (1967) observes, R&D typically involves a 'lumpy' process that yields scale economies. Similarly, Galbraith (1956, p. 87) argues, 'Because development is costly, it follows that it can be carried on only by a firm that has the resources which are associated with considerable size.'

Second, only firms that are large enough to attain at least temporary market power will choose innovation as a means for maximization (Kamien and Schwartz, 1975). This is because the ability of firms to appropriate the economic returns accruing from R&D and other knowledge-generating investments is directly related to the extent of that enterprise's market power (Cohen and Klepper, 1991; Levin *et al.*, 1985, 1987; Cohen *et al.*, 1987).

Third, R&D is a risky investment. Small firms engaging in R&D make themselves vulnerable by investing a large proportion of their resources in a single project. However, their larger counterparts can reduce the risk accompanying innovation through diversification into simultaneous research projects. The larger firm is also more likely to find an economic application of the uncertain outcomes resulting from innovative activity (Nelson, 1959).

Fourth, scale economies in production may also provide scope economies for R&D. Scherer (1991) notes that economies of scale in promotion and in distribution facilitate the penetration of new products, thus enabling larger firms to enjoy a greater profit potential from innovation. Finally, an innovation yielding cost reductions of a given percentage results in higher profit margins for larger firms than for smaller firms.

There is also substantial evidence that technological change – or rather, one aspect of technological change reflected by one of the three measures discussed in the previous section, R&D – is, in fact, positively related to firm size.[9] The plethora of empirical studies relating R&D to firm size is most thoroughly reviewed in Acs and Audretsch (1990, ch.3), Baldwin and Scott (1987) and Cohen and Levin (1989). The empirical evidence generally seems to confirm Scherer's (1982, pp. 234–5) conclusion that the results 'tilt on the side of supporting the Schumpeterian Hypothesis that size is conducive to vigorous conduct of R&D'.

In one of the most important studies, Scherer (1984) used the US Federal Trade Commission's Line of Business Data to estimate the elasticity of R&D spending with respect to firm sales for 196 industries. He found evidence of increasing returns to scale (an elasticity exceeding unity) for about 20 per cent of the industries, constant returns to scale for a little less than three-quarters of the industries, and diminishing returns (an elasticity less than unity) in less than 10 per cent of the industries. These results were consistent with the findings of Soete (1979) that R&D intensity increases along with firm size, at least for a sample of the largest US corporations.

While the Scherer (1984) and Soete (1979) studies were restricted to relatively large enterprises, Bound *et al.* (1984) included a much wider spectrum of firm sizes in their sample of 1492 firms from the 1976 COMPUSTAT data. They found that R&D increases more than proportionately with firm size for the smaller firms, but that a fairly linear relationship exists for larger firms. Despite the somewhat more ambiguous findings in still other studies (Comanor, 1967; Mansfield, 1981, 1983; Mansfield *et al.*, 1982), the empirical evidence seems generally to support the Schumpeterian hypothesis that research effort is positively associated with firm size.

The studies relating patents to firm size are considerably less ambiguous. Here the findings unequivocally suggest that 'the evidence leans weakly against the Schumpeterian conjecture that the largest sellers are especially fecund sources of patented inventions' (Scherer, 1982, p. 235). In one of the most important studies, Scherer (1965b) used the Fortune annual survey of the 500 largest US industrial corporations. He related the 1955 firm sales to the number of patents in 1959 for 448 firms. Scherer found that the number of patented inventions increases less than proportionately with firm size. Scherer's results were later confirmed by Bound *et al.* (1984) in the study mentioned above. Basing their study on 2852 companies and 4553 patenting entities, they determined that the small firms (with less than $10 million in sales) accounted for 4.3 per cent of the sales from the entire sample, but 5.7 per cent of the patents.

Such results are not limited to the USA. Schwalbach and Zimmermann (1991) find that the propensity to patent is less for the largest firms in West Germany than for the medium-sized enterprises included in their sample.

A number of explanations have emerged for smaller enterprises perhaps, in fact, tending to have an innovative advantage, at least in certain industries. Rothwell (1989) suggests that the factors yielding small firms with the innovative advantage generally emanate from the difference in management structures between large and small firms. For example, Scherer (1991) argues that the bureaucratic organization of large firms is not conducive to undertaking risky R&D. The decision to innovate must survive layers of bureaucratic resistance, where an inertia regarding risk results in a bias against undertaking new projects. However, in the small firm the decision to innovate is made by relatively few people.

Second, innovative activity may flourish most in environments free of bureaucratic constraints (Link and Bozeman, 1991). That is, a number of small-firm ventures have benefited from the exodus of researchers who felt thwarted by the managerial restraints in a larger firm. Finally, it has been argued that, while the larger firms reward the best researchers by promoting them out of research to management positions, the smaller firms place innovative activity at the center of their competitive strategy (Scherer, 1991).

Scherer (1988, pp. 4–5) has summarized the advantages small firms may have in innovative activity:

> Smaller enterprises make their impressive contributions to innovation because of several advantages they possess compared to large-size corporations. One important strength is that they are less bureaucratic, without layers of 'abominable no-men' who block daring ventures in a more highly structured organization. Second, and something that is often overlooked, many advances in technology accumulate upon a myriad of detailed inventions involving individual components, materials, and fabrication techniques. The sales possibilities for making such narrow, detailed advances are often too modest to interest giant corporations. An individual entrepreneur's juices will flow over a new product or process with sales prospects in the millions of dollars per year, whereas few large corporations can work up much excitement over such small fish, nor can they accommodate small ventures easily into their organizational structures. Third, it is easier to sustain a fever pitch of excitement in small organizations, where the links between challenges, staff, and potential rewards are tight. 'All-nighters' through which tough technical problems are solved expeditiously are common.

Two other ways that small enterprises can compensate for their lack of R&D is through spillovers and spin-offs. Typically an employee from an established large corporation, often a scientist or engineer working in a research laboratory, will have an idea for an invention and ultimately for an innovation. Accompanying this potential innovation is an expected net return from the new product. The inventor would expect to be compensated for his/her potential innovation accordingly. If the company has a different, presumably lower, valuation of the potential innovation, it may decide either not to pursue its development, or that it merits a lower level of compensation than that expected by the employee.

In either case, the employee will weigh the alternative of starting his/her own firm. If the gap in the expected return accruing from the potential innovation between the inventor and the corporate decision maker is sufficiently large, and if the cost of starting a new firm is sufficiently low, the employee may decide to leave the large corporation and establish a new enterprise. Since the knowledge was generated in the established corporation, the new start-up is considered to be a spin-off from the existing firm. Such start-ups typically do not have direct access to a large R&D laboratory. Rather, these small firms succeed in exploiting the knowledge and experience accrued from the R&D laboratories with their previous employers.

The research laboratories of universities provide a source of innovation-generating knowledge that is available to private enterprises for commercial exploitation. Jaffe (1989) and Acs *et al.* (1992), for example, found that the knowledge created in university laboratories 'spills over' to contribute to the generation of commercial innovations by private enterprises. Acs *et al.* (1994) found persuasive evidence that spillovers from university research contribute more to the innovative activity of small firms than to the innovative activity of large corporations. Similarly, Link and Rees (1990) surveyed 209 innovating firms to examine the relationship between firm size and university research. They found that, in fact, large firms are more active in university-based research. However, small- and medium-sized enterprises apparently are better able to exploit their university-based associations and generate innovations. Link and Rees (1990) conclude that, contrary to the conventional wisdom, diseconomies of scale in producing innovations exist in large firms. They attribute these diseconomies of scale to the 'inherent bureaucratization process which inhibits both innovative activity and the speed with which new inventions move through the corporate system towards the market' (ibid., p. 25).

Thus, just as there are persuasive theories defending the original Schumpeterian Hypothesis that large corporations are a prerequisite for technological change, there are also substantial theories predicting that small enterprises should have the innovative advantage, at least in certain industries. As described above, the empirical evidence based on the input measure of technological change, R&D, tilts decidedly in favor of the Schumpeterian Hypothesis. However, as also described above, the empirical results are somewhat more ambiguous for the measure of intermediate output: the number of patented inventions. It was not until direct measures of innovative output became available that the full picture of the process of technological change could be obtained.

Using this new measure of innovative output from the SBIDB, Acs and Audretsch (1990) show that, in fact, the most innovative US firms are large corporations. Further, the most innovative American corporations also tended to have large R&D laboratories and be R&D-intensive. At first glance, these findings based on direct measures of innovative activity seem to confirm the conventional wisdom. However, in the most innovative four-digit SIC industries, large firms, defined as enterprises with at least 500 employees, contributed more innovations in some instances, while in other industries small firms produced more innovations. For example, in computers and process control instruments small firms contributed the bulk of the innovations. By contrast, in the pharmaceutical preparation and aircraft industries the large firms were much more innovative.

Probably their best measure of innovative activity is the total innovation rate, which is defined as the total number of innovations per one thousand employees in each industry. The large-firm innovation rate is defined as the number of innovations made by firms with at least 500 employees, divided by the number of employees (thousands) in large firms. The small-firm innovation rate is analogously defined as the number of innovations contributed by firms with fewer than 500 employees, divided by the number of employees (thousands) in small firms.

The innovation rates, or the number of innovations per thousand employees, have the advantage in that they measure large- and small-firm innovative activity relative to the presence of large and small firms in any given industry. That is, in making a direct comparison between large- and small-firm innovative activity, the absolute number of innovations contributed by large firms and small enterprises is somewhat misleading, since these measures are not standardized by the relative presence of large and small firms in each industry. When a direct comparison is made between the innovative activity of large and small firms, the innovation rates are presumably a more reliable measure of innovative intensity because they are weighted by the relative presence of small and large enterprises in any given industry. Thus, while large firms in manufacturing introduced 2445 innovations in 1982, and small firms contributed slightly fewer, 1954, small-firm employment was only half as great as large-firm employment, yielding an average small-firm innovation rate in manufacturing of 0.309, compared to a large-firm innovation rate of 0.202 (Acs and Audretsch, 1988, 1990).

The most important and careful study to date documenting the role of German SMEs (enterprises with fewer than 500 employees) in innovative activity was undertaken by a team of researchers at the Zentrum für Europäische Wirtschaftsforschung (ZEW) led by Dietmar Harhoff and Georg Licht. They analyzed the findings made possible by the Mannheim Innovation Data Base. This data base measures the extent of innovative activity in German firms between 1990 and 1992. Harhoff and Licht (1996) use the data base to identify that 12 per cent of the research and development expenditures in (West) German firms comes from SMEs.

Harhoff and Licht show that the likelihood of a firm not innovating decreases with firm size. For example, 52 per cent of firms with fewer than 50 employees were not innovative. By contrast, only 15 per cent of the firms with at least 1000 employees were not innovative. More striking is that the smallest firms that do innovate have a greater propensity to be innovative without undertaking formal research and development. While only 3 per cent of the largest corporations in Germany are innovative without undertaking formal R&D, one-quarter of the innovative firms with fewer than 50 employees are innovative without formal R&D.

The study also shows that even fewer SMEs in the five new German *Länder* are innovative than is the case in West Germany. Over two-thirds of the smallest SMEs in East Germany are not innovative, and they are less than half as likely to undertake R&D as are their Western counterparts.

Systematic empirical evidence also suggests that the German *Mittelstand* is confronted by considerable barriers to innovative activity. Beise and Licht (1996) analyzed the *Mannheimer Innovationspanel* consisting of 43 300 innovating firms to identify the main barriers to innovative activity confronting German small- and medium-sized enterprises. The major barrier to innovation listed in both 1992 and 1994 was too high a gestation period required for innovative activity. In 1994, nearly 60 per cent of German SMEs reported that too long a high gestation period required to innovate was a very important barrier to innovative activity. Other major barriers to innovative activity include legal restrictions and restrictive government policies, too long required to obtain government approval for a new product, a shortage of finance capital, a lack of competent employees and too high a risk.

Thus there is considerable evidence suggesting that, in contrast to the findings for R&D inputs and patented inventions, small enterprises apparently play an important role in generating innovative activity, at least in certain industries. By relating the innovative output of each firm to its size, it is also possible to shed new light on the Schumpeterian Hypothesis. In their 1991 study, Acs and Audretsch find that there is no evidence that increasing returns to R&D expenditures exist in producing innovative output. In fact, with just a few exceptions, diminishing returns to R&D are the rule. This study made it possible to resolve the apparent paradox in the literature that R&D inputs increase at more than a proportional rate with firm size, while the generation of patented inventions does not. That is, while larger firms are observed to undertake a greater effort towards R&D, each additional dollar of R&D is found to yield less in terms of innovative output.

4 The industry context

In comparison to the number of studies investigating the relationship between firm size and technological change, those examining the relationship between innovation and the external industry structure or environment are what Baldwin and Scott (1987, p. 89) term 'miniscule' in number. In fact, the most comprehensive and insightful evidence has been made possible by utilizing the Federal Trade Commission's Line of Business Data. Using 236 manufacturing industry categories, which are defined at both the three- and four-digit SIC level, Scherer (1983a) found that 1974 company R&D expenditures divided by sales was positively related to the 1974 four-firm concentration ratio. Scherer (1983b, p. 225) concluded that, 'although one cannot be certain, it appears that the advantages a high market share confers in appropriating R&D benefits provide the most likely explanation of the observed R&D–concentrator associations'.

Scott (1984) also used the FTC Line of Business Survey Data and found the U-shaped relationship between market concentration and R&D. However, when he controlled for the fixed effects for two-digit SIC industries, no significant relationship could be found between concentration and R&D. These results are consistent with a series of studies by Levin *et al.* (1985, 1987), Levin and Reiss (1984) and Cohen *et al.* (1987). Using data from a survey of R&D executives in 130 industries, which were matched with FTC Line of Business Industry Groups, Cohen *et al.* (1987) and Levin *et al.* (1987) found little support for the contention that industrial concentration is a significant and systematic determinant of R&D effort.

While it has been hypothesized that firms in concentrated industries are better able to capture the rents accruing from an innovation, and therefore have a greater incentive to undertake innovative activity, there are other market structure variables that also influence the ease with which economic rents can be appropriated. For example, Comanor (1967) argued and found that, using a measure of minimum efficient scale, there is less R&D effort (average number of research personnel divided by total employment) in industries with very low scale economies. However, he also found that, in industries with a high minimum efficient scale, R&D effort was also relatively low. Comanor interpreted his results to suggest that, where entry barriers are relatively low, there is little incentive to innovate, since the entry subsequent to innovation would quickly erode any economic rents. At the same time, in industries with high entry barriers, the absence of potential entry may reduce the incentives to innovate.

Because many studies have generally found positive relationships between market concentration and R&D, and between the extent of barriers to entry and R&D, it would seem that the conventional wisdom built around the Schumpeterian Hypothesis has been confirmed. However, when the direct measure of innovative output is related to market concentration, Acs and Audretsch (1988, 1990) find a pointedly different relationship to emerge. In fact, there appears to be unequivocal evidence that concentration exerts a negative influence on the number of innovations being made in an industry.

Acs and Audretsch (1987, 1988, 1990) found that market structure influences not only the total amount of innovative activity, but also the relative innovative advantage between large and small enterprises. The differences between the innovation rates of large and small firms examined in the previous section can generally be explained by (1) the degree of capital intensity, (2) the extent to which an industry is concentrated, (3) the total innovative intensity, and (4) the extent to which an industry comprises small firms. In particular, the relative innovative advantage of large firms tends to be promoted in industries that are capital intensive, advertising-intensive, concentrated and highly unionized. By contrast, in industries that are highly innovative and composed predominantly of large firms, the relative innovative advantage is held by small enterprises.

5   The geographic context

The evidence revealing small enterprises to be the engine of innovative activity in certain industries, despite an obvious lack of formal R&D activities, raises the question about the source of knowledge inputs for small enterprises. The answer emerging from a series of studies (Jaffe, 1989) is from other, third-party, firms or research institutions, such as universities. Economic knowledge may spill over from the firm or research institution creating it for application by other firms.

That knowledge spills over is barely disputed. However, the geographic range of such knowledge spillovers is greatly contested. In disputing the importance of knowledge externalities in explaining the geographic concentration of economic activity, Krugman (1991) and others do not question the existence or importance of such knowledge spillovers. In fact, they argue that such knowledge externalities are so important and forceful that there is no compelling reason for a geographic boundary to limit the spatial extent of the spillover. According to this line of thinking, the concern is not that knowledge does not spill over but that it should stop spilling over just because it hits a geographic border, such as a city limit, state line or national boundary.

A recent body of empirical evidence clearly suggests that R&D and other sources of knowledge not only generate externalities, but studies by Audretsch and Feldman (1996), Jaffe (1989), Audretsch and Stephan (1996), Anselin et al. (1997, 2000), and Jaffe et al., (1993) suggest that such knowledge spillovers tend to be geographically bounded within the region where the new economic knowledge was created. That is, new economic knowledge may spill over, but the geographic extent of such knowledge spillovers is limited.

Krugman (1991, p. 53) has argued that economists should abandon any attempts at measuring knowledge spillovers because 'knowledge flows are invisible, they leave no paper trail by which they may be measured and tracked'. But as Jaffe *et al.* (1993, p. 578) point out, 'knowledge flows do sometimes leave a paper trail' – in particular in the form of patented inventions and new product introductions.

Studies identifying the extent of knowledge spillovers are based on the knowledge production function. Jaffe (1989) modified the knowledge production function approach to a model specified for spatial and product dimensions:

$$I_{si} = IRD^{\beta_1} \times UR_{si}^{\beta_2} \times (UR_{si} \times GC_{si}^{\beta_3}) \times \varepsilon_{si}, \qquad (3.1)$$

where I is innovative output, IRD is private corporate expenditures on R&D, UR is the research expenditures undertaken at universities, and GC measures the geographic coincidence of university and corporate research. The unit of observation for estimation was at the spatial level, s, a state, and industry level, i. Estimation of equation (3.1) essentially shifted the knowledge production function from the unit of observation of a firm to that of a geographic unit.

Implicitly contained within the knowledge production function model is the assumption that innovative activity should take place in those regions, s, where the direct knowledge-generating inputs are the greatest, and where knowledge spillovers are the most prevalent. Audretsch and Feldman (1996), Anselin *et al.* (1997, 2000) and Audretsch and Stephan (1996) link the propensity for innovative activity to cluster together to industry-specific characteristics, most notably the relative importance of knowledge spillovers.

6   The knowledge production function reconsidered

The model of the knowledge production function becomes even less compelling in view of the evidence documented in Section 3 showing that entrepreneurial small firms are the engine of innovative activity in some industries, which raises the question, 'Where do new and small firms get the innovation producing inputs, that is the knowledge?'

The appropriability problem, or the ability to capture the revenues accruing from investments in new knowledge, confronting the individual may converge with that confronting the firm. Economic agents can and do work for firms and, even if they do not, they can potentially be employed by an incumbent firm. In fact, in a model of perfect information with no agency costs, any positive economies of scale or scope will ensure that the appropriability problems of the firm and individual converge. If an agent has an idea for doing something different from what is currently being practiced by the incumbent enterprises – both in terms of a new product or process and in terms of organization – the idea, which can be termed an innovation, will be presented to the incumbent enterprise. Because of the assumption of perfect knowledge, the firm and the agent would agree upon the expected value of the innovation. But to the degree that any economies of scale or scope exist, the expected value of implementing the innovation within the incumbent enterprise will exceed that of taking the innovation outside the incumbent firm to start a new enterprise. Thus the incumbent firm and the inventor of the idea would be expected to reach a bargain splitting the value added to the firm contributed by the innovation. The payment to the inventor – in terms of either a higher wage or some other means of remuneration – would be bounded between the expected value of the innovation if it was implemented by the incumbent enterprise on the upper end, and by the return that the agent could expect to earn if he used it to launch a new enterprise on the lower end.

A different model refocuses the unit of observation away from firms deciding whether to increase their output from a level of zero to some positive amount in a new industry, to individual agents in possession of new knowledge that, owing to uncertainty, may or may not have some positive economic value. It is the uncertainty inherent in new economic knowledge, combined with asymmetries between the agent possessing that knowledge and the decision-making vertical hierarchy of the incumbent organization with respect to its expected value that potentially leads to a gap between the valuation of that knowledge and its economic value.

Divergences in the expected value regarding new knowledge will, under certain conditions, lead an agent to exercise what Albert O. Hirschman (1970) has termed *exit* rather than *voice*, and depart from an incumbent enterprise to launch a new firm. But who is right, the departing agents or those agents remaining in the organizational decision making hierarchy who, by assigning to the new idea a relatively low value, have effectively driven the agent with the potential innovation away? Ex post the answer may not be too difficult. But given the uncertainty inherent in new knowledge, the answer is anything but trivial a priori.

This initial condition of, not just uncertainty, but a greater degree of uncertainty vis-à-vis incumbent enterprises in the industry is captured in the theory of firm selection and industry evolution proposed by Boyan Jovanovic (1982). The theory of firm selection is particularly appealing in view of the rather startling size of most new firms. For example, the mean size of more than 11 000 new-firm start-ups in the manufacturing sector in the United States was found to be fewer than eight workers per firm. While the minimum efficient scale (MES) varies substantially across industries, and even to some degree across various product classes within any given industry, the observed size of most new firms is sufficiently small to ensure that the bulk of new firms will be operating at a suboptimal scale of output. Why would an entrepreneur start a new firm that would immediately be confronted by scale disadvantages?

An implication of the theory of firm selection is that new firms may begin at a small, even suboptimal, scale of output and then, if merited by subsequent performance, expand. Those new firms that are successful will grow, whereas those that are not successful will remain small and may ultimately be forced to leave the industry if they are operating at a suboptimal scale of output.

An important finding of Audretsch (1995), verified in a systematic and comprehensive series of studies contained in the reviews by Caves (1998), Sutton (1997) and Geroski (1995), is that, although entry may still occur in industries characterized by a high degree of scale economies, the likelihood of survival is considerably less. People will start new firms in an attempt to appropriate the expected value of their new ideas, or potential innovations, particularly under the entrepreneurial regime. As entrepreneurs gain experience in the market they learn in at least two ways. First, they discover whether they possess 'the right stuff', in terms of producing goods and offering services for which sufficient demand exists, as well as whether they can produce that good more efficiently than their rivals. Second, they learn whether they can adapt to market conditions as well as to strategies engaged in by rival firms. In terms of the first type of learning, entrepreneurs who discover that they have a viable firm will tend to expand and ultimately survive. But what about those entrepreneurs who discover that they are either not efficient or not offering a product for which there is a viable demand? The answer is, *it depends – on the extent of scale economies as well as on conditions of demand.* The consequences of not being able to grow will depend, to a large degree, on the extent of scale economies. Thus, in markets with only negligible scale economies, firms have a considerably greater likelihood of survival. However, where scale economies play an important role the consequences of not growing are substantially more severe, as evidenced by a lower likelihood of survival. As highlighted in the recent industrial organization literature, in the presence of scale advantages the likelihood of survival for new entrants very much depends on the incumbents' strategic behaviour: whether they have the incentive to deter entry or rather to accommodate it (see Tirole, 1988, ch.8).

What emerges from the new evolutionary theories and empirical evidence on the role of small firms is that markets are in motion, with a lot of new firms entering the industry and a lot of firms leaving the industry. The evolutionary view of the process of industry evolution is that new firms typically start at a very small scale of output. They are motivated by the desire to appropriate the expected value of new economic knowledge, but, depending upon the extent of scale economies in the industry, the firm may not be able to remain viable indefinitely at its start-up size. Rather, if scale economies are anything other than negligible, the new firm is likely to have to grow to survive. The temporary survival of new firms is presumably supported through the deployment of a strategy of compensating factor differentials that enables the firm to discover whether or not it has a viable product.

The empirical evidence (Caves, 1998; Sutton, 1997; Geroski, 1995) supports such an evolutionary view of the role of new firms in manufacturing, because the post-entry growth of firms that survive tends to be spurred by the extent to which there is a gap between the MES level of output and the size of the firm. However, the likelihood of any particular new firm surviving tends to decrease as this gap increases. Such new suboptimal scale firms are apparently engaged in the selection process. Only those firms offering a viable product that can be produced efficiently will grow and ultimately approach or attain the MES level of output. The remainder will stagnate and, depending on the severity of the other selection mechanism (the extent of scale economies), may ultimately be forced to leave the industry. Thus the persistence of an asymmetric firm-size distribution biased towards small-scale enterprise reflects the continuing process of the entry of new firms into industries and not necessarily the permanence of such small and suboptimal enterprises over the long run. Although the skewed size distribution of firms persists with remarkable stability over long periods of time, a constant set of small and suboptimal scale firms does not appear to be responsible for this skewed distribution. Rather, by serving as agents of change, entrepreneurial firms provide an essential source of new ideas and experimentation that otherwise would remain untapped in the economy.

7   Conclusions

Within a generation, scholarship has produced theories, evidence and new insights that have dramatically changed the prevalent view about the role of entrepreneurship in innovation and technological change. The conventional wisdom held that small firms inherently have a deficit of knowledge assets, burdening them with a clear and distinct disadvantage in generating innovative output. This view was certainly consistent with the early interpretation of the knowledge production function. As Chandler (1990) concluded, 'to compete globally you have to be big'.

More recent scholarship has produced a revised view that identifies entrepreneurial small firms as making a crucial contribution to innovative activity and technological change. There are two hypotheses for scholarship about the role of small firms having evolved so drastically within such a short period. This first is that, as explained in this chapter, the measurement of innovative output and technological change has greatly improved. As long as the main instruments to measuring innovative activity were restricted to inputs into the innovative process, such as expenditures on formal R&D, many or even most of the innovative activities by smaller enterprises simply remained hidden from the radar screen of researchers. With the development of measures focusing on measures of innovative output, the vital contribution of small firms became prominent, resulting in the emergence of, not just the recognition that small firms provide an engine of innovative activity, at least in some industry contexts, but also of new theories to explain and understand how and why small firms access knowledge and new ideas. This first hypothesis would suggest that, in fact, small firms have always made these types of innovative contributions, but they remained hidden and mostly unobserved to scholars and policymakers.

The alternative hypothesis is that, in fact, the new view towards the innovative capacity of small firms emerged, not because of measurement improvements, but because the economic and social environment actually changed in such a way as to shift the innovative advantage more towards smaller enterprises. This hypothesis would say that the conventional wisdom about the relative inability of small firms to innovate was essentially correct, at least for a historical period of time. Rather, the new view of small firms as engines of innovative activity reflect changes in technology, globalization and other factors that have fundamentally altered the importance and process of innovation and technological change. As Jovanovic (2001, pp. 54–5) concludes, 'The new economy is one in which technologies and products become obsolete at a much faster rate than a few decades ago … It is clear that we are entering the era of the young firm. The small firm will thus resume a role that, in its importance, is greater than it has been at any time in the last seventy years or so.'

Future research may sort out which of these two hypotheses carries more weight. However, one important conclusion will remain. Scholarship has clearly changed in its assessment of the role of small firms in the process of innovation and technological change, from being mostly unimportant to carrying a central role.

The emerging literature has identified that new and small firms contribute to dynamic competition in at least two ways that are not captured by static competition (Audretsch and Thurik, 2001). The first is that their relatively modest small market shares upon entry tend to increase in subsequent years. The second, and probably more important, impact is that new and small firms are a significant source of innovative activity. Policymakers have responded by introducing a broad spectrum of instruments designed to promote dynamic competition in the form of new and small firms (ibid.). While the traditional instruments of competition policy have generally focused on restricting the freedom of (large) incumbent enterprises to contract, in terms of prohibiting mergers or certain types of conduct deemed to be predatory, these new pro-competition instruments are essentially enabling in nature, in that they encourage the start-up and growth of new innovative enterprises. Just as the more traditional competition policy has focused on reducing barriers to competition, the new enabling policy is oriented towards mitigating barriers to start-up. While one restricts the conduct of dominant incumbent enterprises, the other facilitates the entry and start-up of new enterprises. These new pro-competitive enabling entrepreneurship policies are not a substitute for the more traditional policy approach, but rather represent a welcome new addition to the arsenal of policy instruments available to policymakers to promote market competition.

Notes

1. http://europa.eu.int/comm/enterprise/entrepreneurship/green_paper
2. Similar results emphasizing the importance of informal R&D have been found by Santarelli and Sterlachinni (1990).
3. For example, Shepherd (1979, p. 40) has concluded that, 'Patents are a notoriously weak measure. Most of the eighty thousand patents issued each year are worthless and are never used. Still others have negative social value. They are used as "blocking" patents to stop innovation, or they simply are developed to keep competition out.'
4. Chakrabarti and Halperin (1990) use a fairly standard source of data for US patents issued by the US Office of Patents and Trademarks, the BRS/PATSEARCH online database, to identify the number of inventions patented by over 470 enterprises between 1975 and 1986. Of particular interest is their comparison between the propensity of firms to patent and company R&D expenditures, and a measure not often found in the economics literature, the number of published papers and publications contributed by employees of each firm. Not only do they bring together data from a number of rich sources, but they compare how the relationships between the various measures of innovative activity vary across firm size.
5. The SPRU innovation data are explained in considerable detail in Pavitt *et al.* (1987) and Rothwell (1989).
6. A detailed description of the US Small Business Administration's Innovation Data Base can be found in Chapter 2 of Acs and Audretsch (1990).
7. It should be emphasized, however, that Acs and Audretsch (1990, ch.2) perform a careful analysis of the significance of the innovations based on four broad categories ranking the importance of each innovation.
8. The data base used by von der Schulenburg and Wagner (1991) is the IFO-Innovationstest and is explained in greater detail in Oppenländer (1990), and König and Zimmermann (1986).
9. Fisher and Temin (1973) demonstrated that the Schumpeterian Hypothesis could not be substantiated unless it was established that the elasticity of innovative output with respect

to firm size exceeds one. They pointed out that, if scale economies in R&D do exist, a firm's size may grow faster than its R&D activities. Kohn and Scott (1982) later showed that, if the elasticity of R&D input with respect to firm size is greater than unity, then the elasticity of R&D output with respect to firm size must also be greater than one.

References

Acs, Z.J. and D.B. Audretsch (1987): 'Innovation, market structure and firm size', *Review of Economics and Statistics* 69, 567–75.

Acs, Z.J. and D.B. Audretsch (1988): 'Innovation in large and small firms: an empirical analysis', *American Economic Review* 78, 678–90.

Acs, Z.J. and D.B. Audretsch (1990): *Innovation and small firms*, Cambridge: MIT Press.

Acs, Z.J. and D.B. Audretsch (1990): 'R&D, firm size and innovative activity', in Z.J. Acs and D.B. Audretsch (eds), *Innovation and Technological Change: An International Comparison*, Ann Arbor: University of Michigan Press, pp. 39–59.

Acs, Z.J. and D.B. Audretsch (eds) (1991): *Innovation and Technological Change: An International Comparison*, Ann Arbor: University of Michigan Press.

Acs, Z.J., D.B. Audretsch and M.P. Feldman (1992): 'Real effects of academic research', *American Economic Review* 82, 363–7.

Acs, Z.J., D.B. Audretsch and M.P. Feldman (1994): 'R&D spillovers and recipient firm size', *Review of Economics and Statistics* 100, 336–67.

Anselin, L, A. Varga and Z.J. Acs (1997): 'Local geographic spillovers between university research and high technology innovations', *Journal of Urban Economics* 42, 422–48.

Anselin,L., A. Varga and Z.J. Acs (2000): 'Geographic and sectoral characteristics of academic knowledge externalities', *Papers in Regional Science* 79, 435–43.

Arrow, K. (1962): 'Economic welfare and the allocation of resources for invention', in R.R. Nelson (ed.), *The Rate and Direction of Inventive Activity*, Princeton: Princeton University Press.

Audretsch, D.B. (1995): *Innovation and Industry Evolution*, Cambridge: MIT Press.

Audretsch, D.B. and M.P. Feldman (1996): 'R&D spillovers and the geography of innovation and production', *American Economic Review* 86, 630–40.

Audretsch, D.B. and P.E. Stephan (1996): 'Company–scientist locational links: the case of biotechnology', *American Economic Review* 86, 641–52.

Audretsch, D.B. and R. Thurik (2001): 'Capitalism and democracy in the 21st century: from the managed to the entrepreneurial economy', in D.C. Mueller and U. Cantner (eds), *Capitalism and Democracy in the 21st Century*, Heidelberg: Physica Verlag, pp. 23–40.

Baldwin, W.L. and J.T. Scott (1987): *Market Structure and Technological Change*, London and New York: Harwood Academic Publishers.

Beise, M. and G. Licht (1996): 'Innovationsverhalten der deutschen Wirtschaft', unpublished manuscript, Zentrum für Europäische Wirtschaftsforschung (ZEW), Mannheim, January.

Birch, D.L. (1981): 'Who creates jobs?', *Public Interest* 65, 3–14.

Bound, J., C. Cummins, Z. Griliches, B.H. Hall and A. Jaffe (1984): 'Who does R&D and who patents?', in Z. Griliches (ed.), *R&D, Patents and Productivity*, Chicago, IL: University of Chicago Press, pp. 21–54.

Caves, R.E. (1998): 'Industrial organization and new findings on the turnover and mobility of firms', *Journal of Economic Literature* 36,1947–82.

Chakrabarti, A.K. and M.R. Halperin (1990): 'Technical performance and firm size: analysis of patents and publications of U.S. firms', *Small Business Economics* 2, 183–90.

Chandler, A. (1977): *The Visible: The Managerial Revolution in American Business*, Cambridge, MA: Harvard University Press.

Chandler, A. (1990): *Scale and Scope: The Dynamics of Industrial Capitalism*, Cambridge, MA: Harvard/Belknap Press.

Cohen, W.M. and S. Klepper (1991): 'Firm size versus diversity in the achievement of technological advance', in Z.J. Acs and D.B. Audretsch (eds), *Innovation and Technological Change: An International Comparison*, Ann Arbor: University of Michigan Press, pp. 183–203.

Cohen, W.M. and S. Klepper (1992): 'The tradeoff between firm size and diversity in the pursuit of technological progress', *Small Business Economics* 4, 1–14.

Cohen, W.M. and R.C. Levin (1989): 'Empirical studies of innovation and market structure', in R. Schmalensee and R. Willig (eds), *Handbook of Industrial Organization*, vol. II, Amsterdam: North-Holland, pp. 1059–1107.

Cohen, W.M., R.C. Levin and D.C. Mowery (1987): 'Firm size and R&D intensity: a reexamination', *Journal of Industrial Economics* 35, 543–65.

Comanor, W.S. (1967): 'Market structure, product differentiation and industrial research', *Quarterly Journal of Economics* 81, 639–57.

Connolly, R.A. and M. Hirschey (1984): 'R&D, market strucutre and profits: a value based approach', *Review of Economics and Statistics* 66, 682–6.

Connolly, R.A., B.T. Hirsch and M. Hirschey (1986): 'Union rent seeking, intangible capital, and the market value of the firm, *Review of Economics and Statistics* 68, 567–77.

Dosi, G. (1988): 'Sources, procedures, and microeconomic effects of innovation', *Journal of Economic Literature* 26, 1120–71.

Edwards, K.L. and T.J. Gordon (1984): 'Characterization of innovations introduced on the U.S. market in 1982', The Futures Group, prepared for the U.S. Small Business Administration under Contract No. SBA-6050-OA82.

Fisher, F.M. and P. Temin (1973): 'Returns to scale in research and development: what does the Schumpeterian hypothesis imply?', *Journal of Political Economy* 81, 56–70.

FitzRoy, F.R. and K. Kraft (1990): 'Innovation, rent-sharing and the organization of labour in the Federal Republic of Germany', *Small Business Economics* 2, 95–104.

FitzRoy, F.R. and K. Kraft (1991): 'Firm size, growth and innovation: some evidence from West Germany', in Z.J. Acs and D.B. Audretsch (1991): *Innovation and Technological Change*, Ann Arbor: University of Michign Press/Harvester Wheatsheaf, 152–9.

Galbraith, J.K. (1956): *American Capitalism: The Concept of Coutervailing Power*, rev. edn, Boston, MA: Houghton Mifflin.

Gellman Research Associates (1976): 'Indicators of international trends in technological innovation', prepared for the National Science Foundation.

Gellman Research Associates (1982): 'The relationship between industrial concentration, firm size, and technological innovation', prepared for the Office of Advocacy, U.S. Small Business Administration under award no. SBA-2633-OA-79.

Geroski, P.A. (1995): 'What do we know about entry?', *International Journal of Industrial Organization* 13, 421–40

Grabowski, H.G. (1968): 'The determinants of industrial research and development: a study of the chemical, drug, and petroleum industries', *Journal of Political Economy* 76, 292–306.

Greif, S. (1989): 'Zur Erfassung von Forschungs- and Entwicklungstatigkeit durch Patente', *Naturwissenschaften* 76, 156–9.

Greif, S. and G. Potkowik (1990): *Patente and Wirtschaftszweige: Zusammenfiihrung der Internationalen Patentklassifikation and der Systematik der Wirtschaftszweige*, Cologne: Carl Heymanns Verlag.

Griliches, Z. (1979): 'Issues in assessing the contribution of R&D to productivity growth', *Bell Journal of Economics* 10, 92–116.

Griliches, Z. (1990): 'Patent statistics as economic indicators: a survey', *Journal of Economic Literature* 28, 1661–1707.

Hall, B.H., Z. Griliches and J.A. Hausman (1986): 'Patents and R&D: is there a lag?', *International Economic Review* 27, 265–302.

Harhoff, D. and G. Licht (1996): *Innovationsaktivitäten kleiner und mittlerer Unternehmen*, Baden-Baden: Nomos Verlagsgesellschaft.

Hirschman, A.O. (1970): *Exit, Voice and Loyalty*, Cambridge, MA: Harvard University Press.

Jaffe, A.B. (1986): 'Technological opportunity and spillovers of R&D: evidence from firms' patents, profits and market value', *American Economic Review* 76, 984–1001.

Jaffe, A.B. (1989): 'Real effects of academic research', *American Economic Review* 79, 957–70.

Jaffe, A.B., M. Trajtenberg and R. Henderson (1993): 'Geographic localization of knowledge spillovers as evidenced by patent citations', *Quarterly Journal of Economics* 63, 577–98.

Jovanovic, B. (1982): 'Selection and evolution of industry', *Econometrica* 50, 649–70.
Jovanovic, B. (2001): 'New technology and the small firm', *Small Business Economics* 16, 53–5.
Kamien, M.I. and N.L. Schwartz (1975): 'Market structure and innovation: a survey', *Journal of Economic Literature* 13, 1–37.
Kleinknecht, A. (1987): 'Measuring R&D in small firms: how much are we missing?', *Journal of Industrial Economics* 36, 253–6.
Kleinknecht, A. (1991): 'Firm size and innovation: reply to Scherer', *Small Business Economics* 3, 57–8.
Kleinknecht, A. and B. Verspagen (1989): 'R&D and market structure: the impact of measurement and aggregation problems', *Small Business Economics* 1, 297–302.
Kleinknecht, A., T.P. Poot and J.O.N. Reiljnen (1991): 'Technical performance and firm size: survey results from the Netherlands', in Z.J. Acs and D.B. Audretsch (1990): *Innovation and Small Firms*, Cambridge, MA: MIT Press, pp. 84–108.
Kohn, M. and J.T. Scott (1982): 'Scale economies in research and development: the Schumpeterian hypothesis', *Journal of Industrial Economics* 30, 239–49.
König, H. and K.F. Zimmermann (1986): 'Innovations, market structure and market dynamics', *Journal of Institutional and Theoretical Economics* 142, 184–99.
Krugman, P. (1991): *Geography and Trade*, Cambridge: MIT Press.
Kuznets, S. (1962): 'Inventive activity: problems of definition and measurement', in R.R. Nelson (ed.), *The Rate and Direction of Inventive Activity*, National Bureau of Economic Research Conference Report, Princeton, NJ, pp. 19–43.
Levin, R.C. and P.C. Reiss (1984): 'Tests of a Schumpeterian model of R&D and market structure', in Z. Griliches (ed.), *R&D, Patents, and Productivity*, Chicago, IL: University of Chicago, pp. 175–208.
Levin, R.C., W.M. Cohen and D.C. Mowery (1985): 'R&D appropriability opportunity and market structure: new evidence on the Schumpeterian Hypothesis', *American Economic Review* 15, 20–24.
Levin, R.C., A.K. Klevorick, R.R. Nelson and S.G. Winter (1987): 'Appropriating the returns from industrial research and development', *Brookings Papers on Economic Activity* 3, 783–820.
Link, A.N. and B. Bozeman (1991): 'Innovative behavior in small-sized firms', *Small Business Economics* 3, 179–84.
Link, A.N. and J. Rees (1990): 'Firm size, university based research, and the returns to R&D', *Small Business Economics* 2, 25–32.
Mansfield, E. (1968): *Industrial Research and Technological Change*, New York: W.W. Norton.
Mansfield, E. (1981): 'Composition of R&D expenditures: relationship to size of firm, concentration, and innovative output', *Review of Economics and Statistics* 63, 610–15.
Mansfield, E. (1983): 'Industrial organization and technological change: recent empirical findings', in J.V. Craven (ed.), *Industrial Organization, Antitrust and Public Policy*, The Hague: Kluwer-Nijhoff, pp. 129–43.
Mansfield, E. (1984): 'Comment on using linked patent and R&D data to measure interindustry technology flows', in Z. Griliches (ed.), *R&D, Patents, and Productivity*, Chicago, IL: University of Chicago Press, pp. 462–64.
Mansfield, E., A. Romeo, M. Schwartz, D. Teece, S. Wagner and P. Brach (1982): *Technology Transfer, Productivity, and Economic Policy*, New York: W.W. Norton.
Mueller, D.C. (1967): 'The firm decision process: an econometric investigation', *Journal of Political Economy* 81, 58–87.
National Science Board (1975): *Science Indicators 1974*, Washington, DC: Government Printing Office.
National Science Foundation (1986): *National Patterns of Science and Technology Resources 1986*, Washington, DC: Government Printing Office.
Nelson, R.R. (1959): 'The simple economics of basic scientific research', *Journal of Political Economy* 67, 297–306.

Oppenländer, K.-H. (1990): 'Investitionsverhalten and Marktstruktur – Empirische Ergebnisse für die Bundesrepublik Deutschland', in B. Gahlen (ed.), *Marktstruktur and gesamtwirtschaftliche Entwicklung*, Berlin: Springer Verlag, pp. 253–66.

Pakes, A. (1985): 'On patents, R&D and the stock market rate of return', *Journal of Political Economy* 93, 390–409.

Pakes, A. and Z. Griliches (1980): 'Patents and R&D at the firm level: a first report', *Economics Letters* 5, 377–81.

Pakes, A. and Z. Griliches (1984): 'Estimating distributed lags in short panels with an application to the specification of depreciation patterns and capital stock constructs', *Review of Economic Studies* 51, 243–62.

Pavitt, K., M. Robson and J. Townsend (1987): 'The size distribution of innovating firms in the U.K.: 1945–1983', *Journal of Industrial Economics* 55, 291–316.

Rothwell, R. (1989): 'Small firms, innovation and industrial change', *Small Business Economics* 1, 51–64.

Santarelli, E. and A. Sterlachinni (1990): 'Innovation, formal vs. informal R&D, and firm size: some evidence from Italian manufacturing firms', *Small Business Economics* 2, 223–8.

Scherer, F.M. (1965a): 'Firm size, market structure, opportunity and the output of patented inventions', *American Economic Review* 55, 1097–1125.

Scherer, F.M. (1965b): 'Size of firm, oligopoly and research: a comment', *Canadian Journal of Economics and Political Science* 31, 256–66.

Scherer, F.M. (1967): 'Market structure and the employment of scientists and engineers', *American Economic Review* 57, 524–30.

Scherer, F.M. (1982): 'Inter-industry technology flows in the United States', *Research Policy* 11, 227–45.

Scherer, F.M. (1983a): 'The propensity to patent', *International Journal of Industrial Organization* 1, 107–28.

Scherer, F.M. (1983b): 'Concentration, R&D and productivity change', *Southern Economic Journal* 50, 221–5.

Scherer, F.M. (1984): *Innovation and Growth: Schumpeterian Perspectives*, Cambridge, MA: MIT Press.

Scherer, F.M. (1988): 'Testimony before the Subcommittee on Monopolies and Commercial Law, Committee on the Judiciary, U.S. House of Representatives', 24 February.

Scherer, F.M. (1991): 'Changing perspectives on the firm size problem', in Z.J. Acs and D.B. Audretsch (eds), *Innovation and Technological Change: An International Comparison*, Ann Arbor: University of Michigan Press, pp. 24–38.

Von der Schulenburg, J.-M. Graf and J. Wagner (1991): 'Advertising, innovation and market structure: a comparison of the United States of America and the Federal Republic of Germany', in Z.J. Acs and D.B. Audretsch (eds), *Innovation and Technological Change*, pp. 160–82.

Schumpeter, J. (1942): *Capitalism, Socialism and Democracy*, New York: Harper and Row.

Schwalbach, J. and K.F. Zimmermann (1991): 'A Poisson model of patenting and firm structure in Germany', in Z.J. Acs and D.B. Audretsch (1990): *Innovation and Small Firms*, Cambridge, MA: MIT Press, pp. 109–20.

Scott, J.T. (1984): 'Firm versus industry variability in R&D intensity', in Z. Griliches (ed.), *R&D, Patents and Productivity*, Chicago, IL: University of Chicago Press, pp. 233–48.

Shepherd, W.G. (1979): *The Economics of Industrial Organization*, Princeton, NJ: Prentice Hall.

Soete, L.L.G. (1979): 'Firm size and inventive activity: the evidence reconsidered', *European Economic Review* 12, 319–40.

Sutton, J. (1997): 'Gibrat's legacy', *Journal of Economic Literature* 35, 40–59.

Tirole, J. (1988): *The Theory of Industrial Organization*, Cambridge, MA: MIT Press.

4 Trade policy and competition policy: conflict vs. mutual support

Eric Bond

1 Introduction

Achieving allocative efficiency is a primary goal of trade liberalization and of competition policy. Trade barriers impose costs or restrictions on actions of foreign firms that do not apply to domestic firms. When markets are perfectly competitive, the discriminatory nature of trade barriers prevents goods from being produced in the lowest cost location. Trade liberalization is a means of achieving an efficient international allocation of resources. Competition policy, on the other hand, is primarily focused on limiting actions of firms that might restrict competition in the domestic market. The 1994 OECD interim report on convergence of competition policies notes that 'There is general agreement that the basic objective of competition policy is to protect and preserve competition as the most appropriate means of ensuring the efficient allocation of resources ... in free market economies.'

There are two problems with this simple characterization, in which trade liberalization policy is aimed at achieving equal market access by all firms and competition policy is aimed at preventing anti-competitive actions within the domestic market. The first is that countries often depart from efficiency motives in setting their trade and competition policies. Large countries may benefit at the expense of other countries by imposing tariffs, since the cost of the tariff is shifted onto the foreign suppliers. In addition, special interest groups that benefit from trade barriers may successfully lobby for the imposition of tariffs or quantitative restrictions. Similar examples can be cited where concentrated industries have used their influence to weaken the impact of competition laws.

A second problem is that the jurisdictions of the policies may overlap. Although competition policy does not discriminate between domestic and foreign firms, it could have the effect of limiting market access by foreign firms. For example, the USA has long complained that lax competition policy in Japan has allowed Japanese firms to foreclose entry by US firms, despite reductions in trade barriers. Some aspects of international trade policy also conflict with competition policy by forbidding foreign firms to take actions that would be legal for domestic firms. Anti-dumping policy prevents foreign firms from setting a lower price on their exports than on their domestic sales, but there are no restrictions that prevent home firms from engaging in the equivalent pattern of price discrimination.

The purpose of this chapter is to explore the linkages between trade policy and competition policy. Section 2 develops a simple theoretical framework for identifying the effects of changes in trade and competition policy on national welfare. Section 3 uses this framework to explore linkages between trade and competition policy for a small open economy. Section 4 examines policymaking in a large country, where policies may have spillover effects on other countries. Section 5 examines the role of interest groups in explaining observed policies, and discusses how institutional design may be used to dilute the influence of special interest groups.

2   The welfare effects of trade and competition policies

In order to illustrate the interactions between trade policy and competition policy, it is useful to derive an expression for the change in welfare of an open economy as a result of parameter changes. Consider a two-good model, and assume that the preferences of consumers can be represented by a community utility function $U(D_1, D_2)$ defined over aggregate consumption of the two goods. The change in national welfare, measured in terms of good 1, will be $dy = dD_1 + pdD_2$ where p is the domestic relative price of good 2. The budget constraint for an open economy will be $D_1 + p^w D_2 = X_1 + p^w X_2$, where p^w is the world relative price of good 2 and X_i is domestic output of good i. Home prices will differ from world prices by the vector of trade taxes $t = p - p^w$, where $t_i > 0$ indicates an import tariff (export subsidy) if good i is imported (exported). Totally differentiating the budget constraint and using the definition of dy yields

$$dy = (p - p^w)dM_2 + (dX_1 + pdX_2) - M_2 dp^w, \qquad (4.1)$$

where $M_2 \equiv D_2 - X_2$ is net imports of good 2. Equation (4.1) is a general decomposition of the change in a country's welfare into the trade volume effect, the value of production effect and the terms of trade effect.[1]

The first term in (4.1) is the trade volume effect, which captures the international allocative efficiency effect associated with changes in the volume of trade. When good 2 is an imported good with a positive tariff ($p > p^w$), an increase in the volume of imports will raise domestic welfare because the value of the good in the domestic market exceeds its cost. If good 2 is an export good that is taxed ($p < p^w$), welfare will increase if there is an increase in the volume of exports (that is, $dM_2 < 0$). Thus increases in the volume of trade will increase welfare when trade is taxed.

The second term is the production efficiency effect, which indicates that home welfare will increase if a policy change increases the value of domestic output evaluated at domestic prices. In cases where the economy is producing on the production possibility frontier, policy changes that result in a movement along the production possibility frontier will satisfy $dX_1 + cdX_2 = 0$, where c can be interpreted as the marginal cost of good 2. Substituting this into (4.1) yields

$$dy = (p - p^w)dM_2 + (p - c)dX_2 - M_2 dp^w \qquad (4.2)$$

With perfect competition in both sectors, $p = c$ and the value of production effect will be zero. If sector 2 is imperfectly competitive, $p > c$ and a policy change that increases the output of good 2 will raise the value of output.

The third term in (4.1) is the terms of trade effect. An increase in the world price of good 2 will reduce (raise) the welfare of the home country if it imports (exports) good 2. The terms of trade effect differs from the previous two effects in the sense that it reflects a redistribution of world income, rather than an efficiency effect. If the home country experiences an improvement in its terms of trade as a result of a policy change, the rest of the world experiences a worsening of its terms of trade of equal magnitude. For a small country, world prices will be unaffected by price changes, so $dp^w = 0$.

The effect of policy changes on national welfare will be the sum of the impact of these changes on the volume of trade, production efficiency and the terms of trade. We begin by discussing the case of a small country, which simplifies the analysis because there is no terms of trade effect.

3 Trade and competition policy for small countries

In this case we show that, for an open economy that is too small to affect international prices, the policy mix that maximizes national welfare is free trade combined with a competition policy that achieves allocative efficiency. We then examine how trade policy affects competitiveness when competition policy does not achieve allocative efficiency.

First consider the case where domestic industries are perfectly competitive, so that the decisions of producers will maximize the value of production at domestic prices and the production effect of a tariff change in (4.1) will be 0. A tariff reduction will unambiguously raise the welfare of the country, because a reduction in the tariff reduces the domestic price of imports and increases the volume of imports. If trade is restricted by a quota, rather than a tariff, the price differential $p - p^w$ will equal the return to owners of the licenses to import under the quota. Relaxation of the quota will cause an increase in the volume of trade and raise welfare. Free trade yields the highest welfare when industries are competitive because domestic resources are allocated according to comparative advantage.

If domestic industries are imperfectly competitive, competition policy should be used to achieve the efficient allocation of domestic resources. For example, suppose that sector 2 is an oligopolistic industry with price exceeding marginal cost. It follows from equation (4.2) that welfare can be increased by a competition policy that increases the output of sector 2. Output in sector 2 can be increased by policies that make firms compete more aggressively and set prices that are closer to marginal cost. One policy that would accomplish this outcome would be to impose price ceilings that required firms to price at marginal cost. With these first best competition policies in place, firms will be producing at the efficient point on the production possibility frontier for a given domestic price, as in the case of perfect competition. The best trade policy will then be to eliminate all tariffs, as in the competitive case.

3.1   International trade and competitiveness

In practice, such intrusive competition polices as required to achieve marginal cost pricing efficiency are rarely observed in market economies.[2] The more common practice is to have competition laws restrict actions of firms that would restrict output and raise markups, such as the outlawing of price-fixing agreements among firms. In addition, competition authorities intervene in market structure by preventing mergers or breaking up monopoly firms in order to increase competition and reduce markups. When the competition policy fails to achieve the first best outcome, changes in trade policy may have a first-order effect on national income (that is, $\partial X_1/\partial t + p\partial X_2/\partial t \neq 0$). Thus the desirability of trade liberalization must also take into account its effect on output in imperfectly competitive industries. Intuitively, one would expect that trade liberalization would have a pro-competitive effect by bringing more competitors into the market and causing foreign firms to price more aggressively.

The pro-competitive effect of trade liberalization can be illustrated most simply in the case where there is a single producer in sector 2. With no international trade the domestic producer will have a monopoly in the domestic market and price will exceed marginal cost in that sector. Assuming that foreign goods are perfect substitutes for the domestic product, consumers will have an infinitely elastic supply of goods from the world market if the government chooses any non-prohibitive tariff. This eliminates the market power of the domestic seller, so that any degree of trade will be a perfect substitute for the first best competition policy when trade is restricted by a tariff. Further reductions in the tariff will have a favorable trade volume effect, so that free trade will be the optimal policy.

If protection comes in the form of a quota, rather than a tariff, the domestic seller will still have market power because the quota limits the supply of foreign goods. However, the presence of imports will make the domestic firm's demand curve more elastic than under autarky, lowering the markup. Expansion of the quota to the point where imports equal the free trade level will result in the first best welfare level for the small country. This example illustrates that, when imported goods are perfect substitutes for domestic output, the pro-competitive effect of trade is sufficiently large for the first best level of welfare to be attained. It also illustrates the point that the form of trade policy can have an important effect on the competitiveness of the domestic market when markets are imperfectly competitive.

Helpman and Krugman (1989, ch.3) show that a pro-competitive effect of trade liberalization also exists if foreign goods are imperfect substitutes for domestic goods and the domestic industry is a Cournot oligopoly. A tariff will generally increase the markups of domestic firms, and a quota will increase markups by even more. With either form of protection, trade liberalization will make the demand curve of the domestic firms more elastic, resulting in lower markups. The primary difference from the case with perfect substitutability is that free trade will not eliminate the market power of domestic firms, so that the first best welfare level cannot be attained using trade policy alone. However, trade liberalization will be a useful complement to trade policy when competition policy is unable to achieve first best outcomes.

These results suggest that the finding that trade liberalization lowers markups, and thus has a pro-competitive effect when firms behave non-cooperatively, is quite robust. Furthermore, empirical evidence from a number of countries surveyed by Tybout (2003) suggests that trade liberalization does tend to reduce markups.

3.2   Trade policy and the sustainability of collusion

Price-fixing agreements among firms in an industry exacerbate the distortion due to imperfect competition because they cause firms to compete less aggressively and reduce their outputs. This creates a welfare reducing effect in the domestic market as shown by the second term in (4.2). As a result, competition laws in most countries contain prohibitions against price fixing agreements in the domestic markets.[3] Firms continue to attempt to evade these bans through tacit agreements to fix prices, as reflected in the large number of successful prosecutions of international cartels by the US Department of Justice in the past decade.[4]

Antitrust authorities have a number of policies that can be used to deter collusion between firms. These include the expenditure of resources to investigate price fixing complaints, the imposition of large fines for firms caught fixing prices and the provision of amnesty for executives who admit to participating in collusive behavior. The question we examine in this section is whether trade liberalization can play a role in deterring collusive agreements.

Since price-fixing agreements are illegal, firms cannot write enforceable contracts to restrict outputs. They may still be able to collude by engaging in collusive agreements by utilizing self-enforcing agreements that use the threat of a price war to punish firms that deviate from the cartel. Such an agreement will be sustainable if the pay-off under the agreement to reduce output is at least as great as can be obtained by deviating from the agreement and then suffering the punishment imposed by the cartel members. Letting π^c denote cartel profits, π^D the deviation pay-offs, π^p the pay-off in the punishment phase and δ the discount factor, the condition for the agreement to be sustainable is $\pi^c \geq (1 - \delta)\pi^D + \delta\pi^p$. Since $\pi^D > \pi^c > \pi^p$, there will be a minimum discount factor $\delta^{min} \equiv (\pi^D - \pi^c)/(\pi^D - \pi^p) \in (0,1)$ such that the cartel agreement will be sustainable if $\delta \geq \delta^{min}$.

Trade policy can be said to deter collusion if it raises δ^{min}, since this makes it less likely that a given collusive agreement is sustainable. One case in which trade liberalization would seem to deter collusion is that of extremely high trade barriers that exclude foreign firms from the domestic market completely. Since collusion is typically easier to sustain when there are a smaller number of firms, trade barriers sufficiently high to exclude foreign firms would facilitate collusion by precluding foreign firms from participating in a market-sharing agreement in the domestic market. Thus trade liberalization from extremely high levels would be a pro-competitive policy. However, this result does not generalize to indicate a monotonic relationship between tariff rates and the sustainability of collusion when tariff rates are sufficiently low for both home and foreign firms to be participating in the cartel.

Davidson (1984) analyzes the case of a home firm colluding with a foreign firm under Cournot competition. He finds a non-monotonic relationship between the tariff rate and the minimum discount factor when firms are attempting to sustain the monopoly output level. Similarly, Fung (1992) examined the sustainability of collusion between a home and a foreign firm in the domestic market assuming that firms are Bertrand competitors. He found that trade liberalization makes collusion easier to sustain if the foreign firm is the low-cost producer, but could make it harder to sustain if the foreign firm is the high-cost producer. In each of these papers firms are colluding in a single market, so that the tariff has an asymmetric effect on the cartel members. This will typically cause the minimum discount factors of firms to move in opposite directions, so that the impact on the sustainability of the cartel is ambiguous.

The effect of trade barriers on collusion is different in the case where firms are colluding in multiple markets. Bond and Syropoulos (2002) consider a two-country model with symmetric Cournot oligopolists who engage in multimarket collusion that allocates cartel member market shares across all markets. Such international market sharing has been a feature of a number of recent cartel agreements prosecuted by the Department of Justice. With multimarket agreements, reciprocal trade liberalization affects collusive agreements by changing the way in which market shares are allocated across markets. When trade barriers are high, collusive agreements take the form of geographical collusion, with firms in each market staying out of the market in the other country market. When trade barriers are low, firms divide markets in each country. Bond and Syropoulos show that, when trade barriers are high, tariff reduction makes collusion more difficult to sustain because geographic collusion is harder to sustain. However, when trade barriers are low, tariff reduction will actually facilitate collusion.

A second point that has emerged in this literature is that the form of protection will affect the ability of firms to collude. With imperfect competition, quantitative restrictions will have a different impact on the behavior of firms than will tariffs. Rotemberg and Saloner (1989) show that collusion between a home and a foreign firm in the domestic market is harder to sustain with a tariff than a quota under Bertrand competition. This occurs because it is more difficult for the foreign firm to punish a deviating home firm when the foreign firm's output is restricted by a quota.

In some cases, the manner in which protection is administered may affect the ability of firms to collude. One example is the case of US anti-dumping law, which allows US firms to petition for protection against foreign firms whose export prices are below those they charge in their domestic market. Prusa (1992) points out that, under US anti-dumping law, foreign firms can avoid penalties if they reach an agreement with the US firms that would result in a withdrawal of the petition by the home firms. In the absence of an anti-dumping petition, such agreements between home and foreign firms to raise prices would be violations of US antitrust laws. However, under the Noerr–Pennington doctrine, these agreements are not subject to antitrust laws because they are the outcome of an administrative process. Thus the anti-dumping process may allow home and foreign firms to coordinate prices and market shares in a way that would otherwise be illegal. Prusa found that approximately 20 per cent of the anti-dumping cases were withdrawn prior to a finding.

These results show that there is no robust relationship between tariff rates and minimum discount factors. The impact will depend on whether firms compete in prices or quantities and whether firms collude in single or multiple markets, so it should not be assumed that a free trade policy will be sufficient to prevent collusion among domestic and foreign firms. Active pursuit of collusion among firms is called for even in the presence of liberal trade policies. Furthermore, care should be designed in the choice of trade instruments to make sure that they do not make it easier for firms to collude.

4   Tariff and competition policy for a large country

We now turn to the setting of competition and trade policy for a country that is large enough to affect world prices. In this case the welfare effect of policy changes must take into account the effect of changes in the terms of trade in equations (4.1) or (4.2). There are two main themes in this section. The first is that a country that is attempting to maximize national welfare will no longer choose trade and competition policies that are aimed at achieving allocative efficiency. The large country will be willing to accept some inefficiency in order to improve its terms of trade. The second point is that setting of trade and competition policies can create a prisoner's dilemma for large country, because a large country fails to take into account the unfavorable terms of trade effects it imposes on other countries in setting its policies. This yields an argument for multilateral coordination on trade and competition policy.

The role of terms of trade effects can be seen most simply in the case of tariff setting by a large country when domestic industries are perfectly competitive. The effect of a tariff on good 2 and national welfare is obtained from (4.1) to be

$$\frac{dy}{dt} = \left(p - p^w\right)\frac{dM_2}{dt} - M_2 \frac{dp^w}{dt}. \tag{4.3}$$

In the case where the foreign industry is perfectly competitive, a home country tariff reduces p because it reduces the demand for imported goods. It can be seen from (4.3) that an increase in the tariff must be welfare-improving at $t = 0$, since the first term will be 0 and the terms of trade effect will raise welfare. Thus the optimal tariff will be positive in the large country case. A similar argument shows that a deviation from allocative efficiency could be welfare-improving at $t = 0$ if it has the effect of improving the terms of trade. A large country will thus have the incentive to use its trade and competition policies to manipulate its terms of trade.

Since a policy that improves the terms of trade of the home country worsens the welfare of the foreign country, a policy that maximizes home welfare is likely to impose negative spillovers on other countries. Using a similar derivation to that of (4.1), the change in foreign country welfare, dy^* can be expressed as

$$dy^* = (p^* - p^w)dM_2^* + dX_1^* + p^*dX_2^* - M_2^*dp^w, \qquad (4.4)$$

where p^* is the price in the foreign country market. Foreign trade barriers are the difference between the foreign and world prices, $t^* = p^* - p^w$. Equations (4.1) and (4.4) illustrate that the effects of policy changes in one country can be transmitted to other countries through changes in trade volumes and changes in the terms of trade. Since $dM = -dM^*$, increases in trade volume will raise welfare in both countries as long as trade is not being subsidized. In contrast, terms of trade changes will move the welfare in the two countries in opposite directions.

Tariffs will be too high when firms set tariffs unilaterally, because each country disregards the negative effect of its tariff policy on the welfare of other countries. This gives rise to a need for multilateral agreements covering tariff rates. Equations (4.1) and (4.4) can be used to show that, when markets are competitive, a multilateral tariff reduction that leaves p^w unaffected will raise welfare of both countries. Free trade will be an efficient policy from a global perspective. A similar argument can be used to show that choosing competition policy in each country to achieve allocative efficiency will lead to global efficiency. We thus obtain the result that, from a global perspective, the use of trade liberalization and competition policy to achieve efficient resource allocation is a desirable goal.

We now turn to the linkages between competition policy and trade policy. We first examine the use of tariffs in the presence of imperfectly competitive firms. We then turn to the use of competition policy instruments when trade policy is constrained by WTO obligations.

4.1   Rent extraction and profit-shifting trade policies

In the small country case it was shown that trade liberalization can be a substitute for competition policy when the first best competition policy is not in place. In this section we examine the role of tariff policy in situations where the home country can affect prices of import or exported goods because foreign firms are imperfectly competitive. In this section we provide examples indicating that a much richer set of outcomes arise in the large country case. In particular, the presence of imperfectly competitive foreign firms will create an incentive for countries to use activist trade policy. Furthermore, the chosen trade policies could include export or import subsidies.

The first example we consider, which is analyzed by Brander and Spencer (1984), is the case where the home country is using trade policy to obtain imports from a price-setting foreign firm at a more advantageous price. This is often referred to as a case of rent extraction, since trade policy is being used to reduce profits of the foreign firms. Suppose that there is a single foreign producer with market power that is selling good 2 in the home country market, and that home country firms are all competitive. Using equation (4.3), it can be seen that the home country can improve its welfare by using trade policy to induce the foreign monopolist to reduce his price. The foreign monopolist will reduce price if the trade policy causes the home import demand schedule to become more elastic. If the home country import demand curve is linear, a tariff will reduce the price received by the foreign firm and improve the home terms of trade. However, if the home import demand schedule has a constant elasticity, an import subsidy will be the optimal policy. This result contrasts with the competitive case, where the optimal policy is always a tariff. The difference between the two cases arises because, with imperfect competition, trade policy is aimed at affecting both the slope and the location of the home country demand curve in order to reduce the foreign price.

A second example occurs in the case of a home country firm that is competing with a foreign firm in a third country market. Brander and Spencer (1985) show that an export subsidy to the home firm will be welfare-improving, because it increases the market share of the home firm and shifts profits from the foreign firm to the home firm. The export subsidy has the effect of worsening the terms of trade, because the price in the third country market will fall. However, since price exceeds marginal cost for the home exporter, the favorable output expansion effect in (4.2) more than offsets the unfavorable terms of trade effect.

One characteristic of the strategic trade policies considered in this section is that they create negative spillover effects on the welfare of other countries. Although the home country may benefit from these policies, they will worsen the terms of trade of the foreign country and result in a contraction of the output of imperfectly competitive foreign firms. Both of these effects will reduce foreign welfare, so the use of trade policies to capture profits from foreign firms will give rise to a prisoner's dilemma situation. Welfare of both countries could be improved by negotiations that limited the use of profit-shifting trade instruments.

4.2   Export cartels and import buying monopolies

In the remainder of this section we examine how competition policy instruments affect trade patterns and world markets. The successive rounds of trade liberalization under the World Trade Organization (WTO) have led to significant reductions in trade barriers, particularly on trade between developed countries. Since the ability of countries to use tariffs to improve the terms of trade is limited by these trade agreements, this raises the question of whether a country might use competition policy instruments to achieve improvements in its terms of trade. Competition policy could potentially be a substitute for trade policy to attain terms of trade improvements. The WTO concept of national treatment prevents member countries from using competition policies that explicitly treat foreign firms differently from national firms. However, competition policies may still have an effect that gives domestic firms an advantage relative to foreign firms or that improves the terms of trade.

In this section we focus on how competition policies may have spillover effects on other countries, and discuss some of the evidence on whether competition policies are actually being used as a substitute for trade policy instruments. With competition policy, the spillovers between countries are affected by the fact that each country is given the right to determine the rules of competition within its own market.

The treatment of cartels and price-fixing agreements can be used to illustrate this point. Cartels in the domestic market have an adverse effect on domestic welfare because they create an inefficient allocation of resources. However, if most of the cartel's sales occur in a foreign country, the favorable effect of the cartel on the country's terms of trade might more than offset its negative effect on domestic consumer welfare. As a result, an export cartel may increase a country's national welfare. The Organization of Petroleum Exporting Countries (OPEC) is a prime example of an export cartel that raises welfare of member countries, since most oil consumption occurs in non-member countries.

This would lead to the prediction that countries would be more tolerant of cartels operating in export markets than of cartels operating in the domestic market. The treatment of export cartels under US law is a prime example of the way terms of trade considerations may be reflected in competition policy. The USA has historically been one of the most aggressive countries in pursuing price-fixing agreements operating within its borders, yet is more tolerant of export marketing agreements. The Webb Pomerene Act allows US firms to form cooperative agreements for selling in export markets, as long as the agreement does not have an adverse effect on the US market. These export cartels have an effect similar to that of an optimal export tax, since they improve a country's terms of trade by reducing the supply of the export good. In this sense, export cartels may be a substitute for the use of export taxes when the use of trade instruments is constrained by international agreements. However, the ability of export cartels to raise prices can be limited to the extent that competition authorities in the importing country may prosecute the collusive activities of these cartels.

The general rule of international law is that competition authorities have the right to pursue foreign cartels as long as the cartels do not reflect an official policy of the foreign government.[5] Thus the OPEC cartel cannot be prosecuted under US antitrust laws because it is an official policy of the governments of the oil-exporting countries. However, the fact that the Webb Pomerene Act allows US firms to form exporting marketing agreements was not considered a valid defense when these firms were accused of violating antitrust laws in the European Union. The Webb Pomerene Act allows such agreements among exporters, but the EU did not interpret this approval as rising to the level of making these export agreements an element of US government policy.

Just as an export cartel can provide the terms of trade effect of an export tax, an import buying arrangement could substitute for an import tariff. A monopoly given the right to import would take into account the fact that it faces an upward-sloping supply of exports from the rest of the world, and thus purchase a smaller quantity of imports than the free trade level in order to maintain a markup between the world price and the home market price. Thus a country prevented from imposing an optimal tariff could create an import-buying monopoly to improve its terms of trade. However, the General Agreement on Tariffs and Trade (GATT) anticipated the possibility of such a policy, and includes a statement in Article 2 that countries should not introduce import buyer monopolies that have the effect of offsetting tariff reductions that have been negotiated.

More generally, competition policy changes that have the effect of offsetting the effect of tariff reductions could give rise to a complaint under Article XXIII of the GATT. This point is emphasized by Bagwell and Staiger (2002, ch.9), who argue that a separate international agreement on competition policy may be unnecessary. Article XXIII prevents countries from taking actions that nullify or impair market access concessions made in a negotiating round, even though the policies themselves are not necessarily directly covered by GATT negotiations. For example, the USA argued (albeit unsuccessfully) that the distribution system in Japan served as a trade barrier that prevented US firms from gaining access to the market for photographic developing services in Japan, and thus had the effect of nullifying tariff concessions made by Japan.

4.3   Merger policy

Similar cross-country spillovers arise when governments are deciding whether to allow mergers of firms. In a closed economy, a merger will be welfare-improving if the cost savings from the merger are sufficiently large to offset any adverse effects on markups. In an open economy, the terms of trade effects must also be taken into account as indicated by (4.1). In addition, mergers create a problem of overlapping jurisdictions for competition policy.

The incentives for countries in influencing market structure will depend on the number of firms in each country. If the home firms are an oligopoly and there are no firms in the foreign country, it may be in the interest of the home country to allow a merger among the firms in order to obtain the monopoly profits from export sales. Such a merger would be less advantageous to the home country than allowing the firms to collude in export markets, since it also increases markups on sales to home country consumers, but it could raise home country welfare. If there are an equal number of firms in each country and firms are Cournot competitors, a merger among home firms would cause them to compete less aggressively and reduce output. Foreign firms would capture a larger market share as a result of a merger of home firms. In this case the incentive for the home country is to try to encourage entry of firms in order to obtain a larger share of world profits.

The question of how the incentive to allow mergers is affected by trade liberalization has been studied by Richardson (1999) and Horn and Levinsohn (2001). Richardson analyzes the case where governments impose tariffs, and shows that a reduction in the tariff will result in a larger number of firms if the fixed costs of entry are sufficiently large. Horn and Levinsohn consider the case in which governments are using export subsidies to their firms. They show that the effect of a reduction in export subsidies on the marginal benefit of entry is ambiguous.[6] Thus there does not exist an unambiguous relationship between trade liberalization and the incentive of countries to subsidize.

Under current practice, mergers that have significant effects on international markets must be approved by competition authorities in major market areas where the firms would be selling. For example, a merger between two firms in the USA could be blocked by competition authorities in the European Union. Such a policy requires that each jurisdiction gain from the merger. A cooperative agreement between jurisdictions that allowed negotiation on competition policy issues would generate a more lax standard on mergers. If governments can negotiate compensating transfers, a merger would be approved as long as it generated a gain to all of the jurisdictions combined.

5 The political economy of competition and trade policy

The theory of the previous sections provides an analysis of the welfare effects of changes in trade and competition policy. As such, it can provide guidelines for the development of trade and competition policies for governments that are interested in choosing policies that maximize national welfare. If governments choose policies to maximize national welfare, the theory will also yield predictions about the type of trade and competition policies that would be observed in practice. However, there is substantial evidence that organized interest groups may be able to organize and lobby the government to enact policies that benefit the interest group but reduce national welfare. For example, the fact that many small countries have high tariff levels is inconsistent with governments that have national welfare maximization as an objective. In this section we consider some of the implications of special interest politics for the linkages between trade policy and competition policy.

To illustrate how special interests may influence the choice of policy, consider the case in which firms in sector 1 are perfectly competitive and sector 2 is an oligopoly consisting of identical firms. Suppose that firms in sector 2 organize to form a lobby, and that the aggregate profits of firms in the sector can be expressed as $\Pi = pX_2 - C(X_2)$, where $C(X_2)$ is the cost function for the oligopoly. The objective of the interest group is to influence policy in such a way as to maximize the profits of firms in the sector, which would occur at the monopoly output level. This would suggest that sector 2 would lobby for trade policies that raise the price of good 2, either through protection from import competition or through export subsidies. In addition, they would lobby for lax competition policies that would allow firms to achieve outputs that are closer to the monopoly output level. In the event of trade liberalization, organized sectors may shift lobbying activities to encourage a relaxation of competition policy in order to obtain protection from foreign rivals.

The influence of the sector 2 lobby on policy can be captured by assuming that the policymaker chooses policies to maximize a weighted welfare function $W = y + a\Pi$, where y is the level of national income (including oligopoly profits). With $a > 0$ this objective function puts greater weight on the welfare of the organized group than on other interest groups, so the policymaker would be willing to accept some reduction in national income in order to raise the welfare of a special interest group. The policy that maximizes the welfare of the policymaker will be a weighted average of the policy that maximizes national welfare and the policy that maximizes the profits of sector 2 firms. This can explain the choice of protectionist policies for countries that are too small to affect the terms of trade and the choice of lax competition policies that benefit powerful producer interests.[7]

If economic efficiency is the goal of trade and competition policy, an interesting question is whether institutions can be designed in such a way that the role of special interests is reduced. For example, Gilligan (1997) argues that the Reciprocal Trade Agreements Act of 1934 played a critical role in reducing protectionist pressure in the USA. Prior to this legislation, US tariffs were set by acts of Congress and protectionist pressure from import-competing sectors. Under the Reciprocal Trade Agreements Act, the power to negotiate reciprocal trade agreements with foreign governments was delegated to the President. Since such agreements would result in lower tariffs imposed by foreign countries on US exports, exporters lobbied in favor of the Act and offset the lobbying from protectionist groups.

The anti-dumping process, on the other hand, has resulted in very protectionist outcomes. Dumping occurs when a firm sets a lower price in its export market than in its home market. The WTO allows countries to impose anti-dumping duties that are equal to the amount of this price difference if imports are shown to cause injury to the domestic industry. The determination of the dumping margin and the extent of injury is based on rules determined as part of the anti-dumping legislation. The establishment of a rules-based process has the advantage of reducing the role for lobbying in determining the outcome. However, the rules for establishing dumping margins and injury have a distinctly protectionist bias. For example, in determining injury resulting from imports, the International Trade Commission is not allowed to consider the benefits arising for consumers from reduced prices. Furthermore, the legislation has been changed over time to weaken the requirement that the injury experienced by the domestic firms be strictly a result of the dumped imports and to allow petitioners to receive the duties imposed. These rules make it much easier and more attractive for US firms to obtain protection from foreign competition.

The protectionist nature of anti-dumping policy in the USA contrasts sharply with antitrust rules that address similar pricing practices within the USA. For example, one possible explanation of dumping is that it is the result of an attempt by foreign firms to drive US firms out of business and establish a monopoly in the US market. Predatory pricing of this type is an anti-competitive practice that is illegal under the Sherman Antitrust Act because it is intended to create a monopoly in the domestic market. However, the standard of proof under US antitrust policy is much stricter than in the antidumping process. In order to establish guilt, it must be shown that the predating firm is setting prices below average variable cost and that they intend to drive other firms out of the market.

A second possible explanation of dumping is that it is part of a policy of spatial price discrimination, in which firms charge different prices in geographically separate markets. The welfare effects of price discrimination are ambiguous, and price discrimination within the USA is not per se illegal under US antitrust law. The Robinson Patman Act was intended to prevent price discrimination, and was a result of political pressure from small retailers who wanted to prevent chain stores from receiving more favorable prices from manufacturers. In this sense it has a protectionist background similar to that of the anti-dumping process. However, the judicial interpretation of the act has allowed firms to use competitive pressures and efficiency as a defense against charges of price discrimination. Furthermore, the Department of Justice rarely pursues price discrimination cases.

From an efficiency perspective, there is no reason why foreign firms should be treated differently from domestic firms with regard to the use of these practices. Negotiations in which the interests of foreign suppliers are also represented would be required in order to reduce the protectionist bias of the anti-dumping process. Some regional trade agreements, such as the European Union and the Closer Economic Union between Australia and New Zealand, have moved in this direction by eliminating anti-dumping actions against member countries. There seems little prospect of such a result under the WTO, however, without agreements that would result in the coordination of competition policies.

6   Conclusions

This chapter has provided a survey of the linkages between trade policy and competition policy. It has been shown that trade liberalization is a complement to competition policy, because it increases the degree of competition in the domestic market and lowers margins when firms are behaving non-cooperatively. However, trade liberalization is less likely to be successful at preventing collusive behavior on the part of firms. The relationship between the level of trade barriers and the ease with which collusion can be sustained is non-monotonic, and depends critically on the type of trade barriers. Thus strict enforcement of laws preventing price fixing will still be required once trade barriers have been eliminated.

A second linkage that was explored between trade and competition policy concerned the use of competition policy to protect domestic firms when trade barriers have been reduced. Trade liberalization can be undermined by competition policies that allow domestic firms to use anti-competitive actions that restrict access of foreign firms to the market. Currently, the WTO tools for dealing with this problem are somewhat limited. Countries can file complaints with the Dispute Settlement body of the WTO if actions are taken which undermine market access that has been negotiated in tariff rounds. However, such cases may be difficult to prove and this path is infrequently used. This suggests that more international cooperation may be required on competition policy issues to deal with these international spillovers.

Notes

1. Welfare decompositions of this type have a long tradition in international trade theory, as can be seen for example in Jones (1969) or Dixit and Norman (1980).
2. One reason for this is that the informational requirements to calculate the firm's marginal cost are large, and the policy could lead to shortages or surpluses in the market if errors are made in estimating marginal cost. This method of reducing markups is impractical in all but the most concentrated industries.

3. The USA, which considers price-fixing agreements to be per se illegal, has taken the most aggressive stance against price fixing. Policies in Europe have historically been more lax, but have been becoming more strict over time. See Bond (2003) for a more extensive discussion.
4. The DOJ (2000, ch.4) cites successful prosecutions of a number of cartels involving both US and foreign firms, including a food and feed additive cartel (operating from 1991 to 1995), a vitamin cartel (1990–99) and a graphite electrodes cartel (1992–7). These cartels had significant impacts on prices in the US market, with the feed additive cartel having been estimated to raise the price of citric acid by 30 per cent and the price of lycine by 70 per cent.
5. In the USA, the first prosecution of this type occurred in *US* v. *American Tobacco* (1911), in which British and American firms colluded to raise prices in the US and British markets. The US Supreme Court ruled that the Department of Justice was within its authority to pursue this case.
6. Falvey and Nathananan (2001) consider the case in which trade restrictions take the form of quotas.
7. Bagwell and Staiger (2002) argue that, in a world with policymakers who use weighted social welfare functions of the type considered here, the externality from tariffs will operate through the terms of trade. This means that the primary reason for countries negotiating trade agreements is to deal with the terms of trade externality, as analyzed in the previous section.

References

Bagwell, K. and R. Staiger (2002): *The Economics of the World Trading System*, Cambridge, MA: MIT Press.

Bond, E.W. (2003): 'Antitrust policy in open economies: price fixing and international cartels', in J. Hartigan (ed.), *Handbook of International Trade and Law*, Oxford: Blackwell.

Bond, E.W. and C. Syropoulos (2002): 'Reciprocal trade liberalization and multimarket collusion', manuscript.

Brander, J. and B. Spencer (1984): 'Tariff protection and import competition', in H. Kierzkowski (ed.), *Monopolistic Competition and International Trade*, Oxford: Blackwell.

Brander, J. and B. Spencer (1985): 'Export subsidies and market share rivalry', *Journal of International Economics* 18, 83–100.

Davidson, C. (1984): 'Cartel stability and tariff policy', *Journal of International Economics* 17, 219–37.

Dixit, A. and G. Norman (1980): *Theory of International Trade*, Cambridge, UK: Cambridge University Press.

Falvey, R. and M. Nathananan (2001): 'Tariffs, quotas, and mergers', research paper 30, University of Nottingham.

Fung, K.C. (1992): 'Economic integration as competitive discipline', *International Economic Review* 33, 837–47.

Gilligan, M. (1997): *Empowering Exporters: Reciprocity, Delegation and Collective Action in American Trade Policy*, Ann Arbor: University of Michigan Press.

Helpman, E. and P. Krugman (1989): *Trade Policy and Market Structure*, Cambridge: MIT Press.

Horn, H. and J. Levinsohn (2001): 'Merger policy and trade liberalization', *Economic Journal* 111, 244–76.

Jones, R.W. (1969): 'Tariffs and trade in general equilibrium: comment', *American Economic Review* 59, 418–24.

OECD (Organization of Economic Cooperation and Development) (1994): *Areas of Convergence in Competition Policy and Law*, Paris: OECD/GD.

Prusa, T. (1992): 'Why are so many anti-dumping petitions withdrawn?', *Journal of International Economics* 25, 339–42.

Richardson, M. (1999): 'Trade and competition policy: concordia discors?', *Oxford Economic Papers* 51, 649–64.
Rotemberg, J. and G. Saloner (1989): 'Tariffs vs. quotas with implicit collusion', *Canadian Journal of Economics* 89, 237–44.
Tybout, J. (2003): 'Plant level and firm level evidence on the new trade theories', in E. Kwan Choi and J. Harrigan (eds), *Handbook of International Trade*, Oxford: Blackwell.
US Department of Justice (DOJ) (2000): 'Final report to the Attorney General and Assistant Attorney General for antitrust', Antitrust division, international competition policy Advisory committee, Washington, DC.

5   Financial services: consolidation and strategic positioning

Arnoud Boot

1   Introduction[1]

Liberalization and deregulation of financial markets have had a tremendous effect on the financial services sector worldwide. An unprecedented wave of restructuring and consolidation has swept through the United States and Europe as well as Asia. Prominently figures the breath-taking scale of consolidation in banking through mergers and acquisitions. For the USA the consolidation of money center banks (for example the Chase Manhattan and Chemical Bank merger, and the subsequent merger with J.P. Morgan), the creation of regional megabanks (for example the expansion strategies of BankOne and Nationsbank and their mergers with, respectively, First Chicago/NBD and BankAmerica) may serve as examples in kind. And this is not the end. The most recently announced mergers bring together the merged banks that now operate under the name J.P. Morgan and BankOne, and also involve a merger between BankAmerika (the entity that includes Nationsbank and FleetBoston). On a domestic scale, Europe has seen some spectacular mergers between large universal banks. Take, for example, the acquisition of Paribas by Banque National de Paris (BNP) or the marriage of the Union Bank of Switzerland and Swiss Bank Corporation. Also a few cross-border mergers, such as the acquisitions across the Dutch–Belgian border,[2] or HSBC's acquisition of Crédit Commercial de France caught public attention. Merger mania in Japan has created some of the world's largest banks as ranked by book value of assets (for example, Mizuho, created through the merger of Fuji, Dai-Ichi Kangyo Bank and Industrial Bank of Japan).

To some extent, a parallel trend manifests itself; many banks have actually broadened their scope of activities. Even banks traditionally known for their sharpened and well-focused strategies have embarked on scope expansion. Take Bankers Trust, a key player in the corporate market, which was taken over by Deutsche Bank, a scope expanding universal bank. Scope expansion has also taken hold of investment banking where key players have redefined their product portfolios to include traditional commercial banking products. Examples are the union of Salomon Brothers (investment bank) and Smith Barney (brokerage) within Travelers (now in Citicorp), Credit Suisse's acquisition of the US stockbroker DLJ, and UBS's takeover of Paine-Webber. The spectacular cross-industry merger by Citicorp and Travelers also brings the insurance activities together with bank-oriented financial services.[3]

The motivations for mergers seem obvious to many bank executives, and many consultants. The popular financial press points to the increasingly competitive environment of banking as the trigger for the observed development. With competition in commercial banking heating up, banks feel forced to quickly and significantly improve efficiency. A short-cut to achieving efficiency gains could be a cost-saving motivated merger with another bank. A horizontal merger may allow to exploit efficiencies of scale through elimination of redundant branches and back-office consolidation. Moreover, increased competitive pressure and diminishing margins in commercial banking invite banks to look outside their traditional domain. Some non-banking activities may offer higher margins so expanding becomes attractive.

However, these popular explanations are inadequate. The empirical evidence on scale and scope economies in banking is far from conclusive. It is questionable whether these economies are large enough to justify consolidation and scope expansion on the scale that we have observed (see Berger, 1997; Berger, Hunter and Timme, 1993). Moreover, ample research in corporate finance points at the existence of a 'diversification discount'. On average, diversification seems to destroy value. There is substantial evidence that improvements in operating performance and stock returns have been experienced by firms that have refocused (see John and Ofek, 1995; Comment and Jarrell, 1995). Therefore, there are three important questions: (1) Why are there so many mergers and acquisitions taking place in the industry? (2) How does this merger wave affect efficiency and competition? and (3) how should public policy react to it? These questions become even more relevant considering the media and analyst reports that increasingly challenge the broad focus that characterizes most financial institutions.[4]

This chapter aims to address these questions. I will examine the existing empirical evidence on scale and scope economies in banking. The findings of a recent survey article by Berger, Demsetz and Strahan (1999) provide only weak and very limited support for the scale and scope hypothesis. Although their review is extensive, the presented evidence is overwhelmingly for the USA and the surveyed studies are quite dated. Therefore, the value of this evidence for explaining the current consolidation wave remains unclear. I will show that the existing evidence is of some value but there are more recent findings which prove to be more valuable. However, in conclusion I argue that the evidence does not help understand current changes in banking. Therefore, I do not have a good basis for predicting the effects of these changes on competition and suggesting appropriate public policy responses.

The low explanation value of the existing evidence is not the result of econometric and sample-selection issues. Rather, I believe that the changes are relatively unrelated to true scale and scope economies. The market environment in banking is often characterized by strategic interaction among the key players in the market. These key players are usually big in terms of absolute size (assets) or market shares but not big enough to act independently from their rivals.[5] Individual decisions on investment or pricing do not only affect individual profits but also the profits of the rivals. In a setting of strategic interaction, banks face mutual interdependencies which can be exploited *strategically*. For example, strategic interdependence can give rise to aggressive price competition ('Bertrand competition'). A strategic move could be to eliminate a direct competitor by a horizontal merger and so change the nature and intensity of competition from aggressive price competition to a more moderate, softer form of competition.[6] While this is a direct and very plausible effect, the scale and scope expansion also has a strategic component which is not (directly) aimed at market dominance. The financial services sector faces considerable uncertainty about what activities and what combinations of activities will (ultimately) offer lasting competitive advantages. This uncertainty could lead to a wait-and-see strategy where individual players try to be present in many more activities than ultimately (after the dust has settled) could be optimal. Delaying choice allows for a more informed choice later. This strategy, however, is costly and asks for 'deep pockets'. Here the competitive environment comes in. The domestic consolidation has facilitated some 'breathing room' (that is reduced competition) and also directly created deeper pockets. In a sense the consolidation facilitates delaying choices, and that might be optimal (provided one can afford it) in the current uncertain environment. In other words, the current consolidation wave and the broad scope of many of the players in the industry may be the result of strategic (re-)positioning, exploiting first-mover advantages, learning economies, and strategic advantages of market power and associated 'deep pockets'.

The recent wave of restructuring and consolidation may be seen as a transitory phase in the evolution of the industry from the old equilibrium to a new one. For this phase, strategic positioning is the optimal response to the rapid and unpredictable changes. Once the mist of uncertainty has cleared, one may observe a new type of repositioning and particularly an increase in focus. The current outsourcing wave might be a first manifestation of this. Indeed, increasing competitive pressures seem at work already and may erode the deep pockets, and scope expansion may soon become too costly.

This chapter is organized as follows. In Section 2, I briefly review the economic fundamentals of financial intermediation and banking. This research, mainly theoretical in nature, sheds light on the costs and benefits of bank funding vis-à-vis direct funding in the financial market. In this context, I discuss the impact of competition on the value of relationship banking. These insights provide a foundation for understanding the role of financial institutions in the future. Section 3 discusses the extensive empirical literature on scale and scope economies in banking. Here, I focus on scale and scope considerations which may be relevant in the future. An issue in this context is that the literature needs to differentiate more between the various activities (services and products) of financial intermediaries. Scale and scope economies have been looked at too generically. Section 4 introduces strategic considerations, in particular, the importance of *strategic positioning*. In Section 5, I discuss the public policy concerns as they relate to competitiveness and stability in banking. As I will indicate, competition policy is hampered by (only partially founded) concerns about financial stability. In section 6, I offer some thoughts on the (to be expected) disaggregation of the value chain, with a more prominent role for alliances and joint ventures. In my view, these offer a first indication that competitive pressures may finally reverse the scope expanding trend in the financial services sector. Section 7 concludes.

2   Fundamentals: the economics of banking

2.1   Introduction

What does economic theory tell us about the role of financial institutions? The relevant field of financial intermediation offers some guidance in uncovering the value-added of financial institutions. The literature has primarily focused on three issues: the role of banks in funding real activities, the value of relationships in intermediated finance versus transactions in financial markets and the prospects of liquefying bank assets, for example securitization.

We will examine what economic theory has to say on each of these issues. Of particular interest also is what the impact is of the ever more competitive environment on the value of relationship banking. This will shed some light on the competitive positioning of financial institutions and their possibly changing role. While these insights will be primarily theoretical, they provide in my view a valuable foundation for understanding the current restructuring in the financial services industry.

2.2 Traditional versus modern banking

Traditional commercial banks hold non-marketable or illiquid assets that are funded largely by deposits. There is typically little uncertainty about the value of these deposits, which are often withdrawable on demand. The liquidity of bank liabilities stands in sharp contrast to that of their assets, reflecting the banks' *raison d'être*. By liquefying claims, banks facilitate the funding of projects that might otherwise be infeasible.

The banks' assets are illiquid largely because of their information sensitivity. In originating and pricing loans, banks develop proprietary information. Subsequent monitoring of borrowers yields additional private information. The proprietary information inhibits the marketability of these loans. The access to information is the key to understanding the comparative advantage of banks. In many of their activities banks exploit their informational advantages and the related network of contacts. This relationship-oriented banking is a characteristic of value-enhancing financial intermediation. The relationship and network orientation does not apply only to traditional commercial lending but also to many areas of 'modern banking'.

One might be tempted to interpret modern banking as transaction-oriented. In this way an investment bank (IB) – generally considered a prime example of modern banking – facilitates a firm's access to public capital markets. The IB's role could be interpreted as that of a broker, matching buyers and sellers for the firms' securities. In this interpretation IBs just facilitate transactions, which would confirm the transaction orientation of modern banking. The IBs' added value would then be confined to their networks: their ability to economize on search or matching costs. As a characterization of modern banking, this would describe their economic role too narrowly. IBs do more. Almost without exception, they *underwrite* those public issues, that is absorb credit and/or placement risk. This brings an IB's role much closer to that of a commercial bank engaged in lending; the processing and absorption of risk is a typical intermediation function similar to that encountered in traditional bank lending.[7]

In lending, a bank manages and absorbs risk (for example credit and liquidity risks) by issuing claims on its total assets with different characteristics from those encountered in its loan portfolio. In financial intermediation theory this is referred to as 'qualitative asset transformation' (see Greenbaum and Thakor, 1995). Underwriting of an IB can be interpreted analogically; risk is (temporarily) absorbed and is channeled through to the claim holders of the IB. The role of IBs is therefore more than purely brokerage. Underwriting requires information acquisition about the borrower, which is supported by a relationship orientation. A relationship orientation will therefore still be present in investment banking, both in the direction of investors ('placement capacity') and towards borrowing firms.

What will also be true, however, is that, in investment banking, relationships depend much less on local presence. Nevertheless, public debt issues are relatively hands-off, with few interactions between financiers and borrowers over time (Berlin and Mester, 1992, Rajan and Winton, 1995). The full menu of financing options for borrowers includes many other products with varying degrees of relationships. In the continuum between bank loans and public debt issues, we can find, for example, syndicated loans. These are offered by investment banks and commercial banks alike and typically involve several financiers per loan. Generally, only the lead banks have a relationship with the borrower, and the relationship intensity is somewhere between a bank loan and a public debt issue (see Dennis and Mullineaux, 1999).

It is important to note that the relationship aspect does not only involve funding but also includes various other financial services, for example, letters of credit, deposits, check clearing and cash management services. I will not focus on these services per se, but one should keep in mind that these services can expand the information available to the intermediary. As some have argued, the information that banks obtain by offering multiple services to the *same* customer may be of value in lending (Degryse and Van Cayseele, 2000). For example, the use of checking and deposit accounts may help the bank in assessing a firm's loan repayment capability. Thus the scope of the relationship may affect a bank's comparative advantage.

2.3 Are bank loans special?
Some see public capital market financing as a potentially superior substitute for bank lending. This, however, stated as such, is unwarranted. Bank lending has distinct comparative advantages. In particular, it may support enduring close relationships between debtor and financier that may mitigate information asymmetries. This has several components. A borrower might be prepared to reveal proprietary information to its bank, while it would never have disseminated this information to the financial markets (Bhattacharaya and Chiesa, 1995). A bank might also be more receptive to information because of its role as enduring and dominant lender. This amounts to observing that a bank might have better incentives to invest in information acquisition. While costly, the substantial stake that it has in the funding of the borrower, and its (hopefully) enduring relationship – with the possibility of information reusability over time – increase the value of information.[8]

The bank–borrower relationship is also less rigid than those normally encountered in the financial market. The general observation is that a better information flow facilitates more informative decisions. In particular, relationship finance could allow for more flexibility and possibly value-enhancing discretion. This is in line with the important current discussion in economic theory on rules versus discretion, where discretion allows for decision making based on more subtle, potentially non-contractible, information.[9] Two dimensions can be identified. One dimension is related to the nature of the bank–borrower relationship. In many ways, it is a mutual commitment based on trust and respect. This allows for *implicit* (non-enforceable) long-term contracting. An optimal information flow is crucial for sustaining these 'contracts'. Information asymmetries in the financial market and the non-contractibility of various pieces of information may rule out long-term access to alternative capital market funding sources as well as *explicit* long-term commitments by banks. Therefore, both bank and borrower may realize the added value of their relationship, and have an incentive to foster the relationship.[10]

Another feature is that relationship banking could accommodate an intertemporal smoothing of contract terms, including accepting losses for the bank in the short term that are recouped later in the relationship. Petersen and Rajan (1995) show that credit subsidies to young or *de novo* corporations may reduce the moral hazard problems and information frictions that banks face in lending to such borrowers. However, subsidies impose losses on the bank. Banks may nevertheless provide funding if they can expect to offset these losses through the long-term rents generated by these borrowers. The point is that, without access to subsidized credit early in their lives, *de novo* borrowers would pose such serious adverse selection and moral hazard problems that no bank would lend to them. Relationship lending could make such subsidies and accompanying loans feasible because the proprietary information generated during the relationship produces rents for the bank later in the relationship and permits the early losses to be offset. The importance of intertemporal transfers in loan pricing is also present in Berlin and Mester (1998). They show that rate-insensitive core deposits allow for intertemporal smoothing in lending rates. This suggests a complementarity between deposit taking and lending. Moreover, the loan commitment literature has emphasized the importance of intertemporal tax-subsidy schemes in pricing to resolve moral hazard (Boot *et al.*, 1991) and also the complementarity between deposit taking and *commitment* lending (see Kashyap *et al.*, 1999).

The other dimension is related to the structure of the explicit contracts that banks can write. Bank loans are generally easier to renegotiate than bond issues or other public capital market funding vehicles. The renegotiation allows for a qualitative use of flexibility. Sometimes this is a mixed blessing because banks may suffer from a soft-budget constraint (the borrowers may realize that they can renegotiate ex post, which could give them perverse ex ante incentives). In reality, bank loans often have priority to resolve this problem. With priority a bank may strengthen its bargaining position and thus become tougher.[11] The bank could then credibly intervene in the decision process of the borrower when it believes that its long-term interests are in danger. For example, the bank might believe that the firm's strategy is flawed, or a restructuring is long overdue. Could the bank push for the restructuring? If the bank has no priority, the borrower may choose to ignore the bank's wishes. This is because the borrower realizes that the bank cannot credibly enforce its demands. The bank could threaten to call in the loan, but the borrower, anticipating the dreadful consequences not only for himself but also for the bank, realizes that the bank would not carry out such a threat. However, when the bank has priority, the prioritized claim may insulate the bank from these dreadful consequences. It could now credibly threaten to call the loan, and enforce its wishes upon the borrower. This then identifies an important advantage of bank financing: *timely intervention.*[12]

These observations highlight the complementarity of bank lending and capital market funding. Prioritized bank debt facilitates timely intervention. This feature of bank lending is valuable to the firm's bondholders as well. They might find it optimal to grant bank debt priority over their own claims, and in doing so delegate the timely intervention activity to the bank.[13] Consequently, the borrower may reduce its total funding cost by accessing both the bank-credit market and the financial market.

Diamond (1991) and Hoshi *et al.* (1993) further develop arguments highlighting the complementarity of bank lending and capital market funding. Hoshi *et al.* (1993) show that bank lending exposes borrowers to monitoring, which may serve as a certification device that facilitates simultaneous capital market funding.[14] Diamond (1991) shows that borrowers may want to borrow first from banks in order to establish sufficient credibility before accessing the capital markets. Again banks provide certification and monitoring. Once the borrower is 'established', it switches to capital market funding. In this explanation, there is a sequential complementarity between bank and capital market funding. In related theoretical work, Chemmanur and Fulghieri (1994) show that the quality of the bank is of critical importance for its certification role. This suggests a positive correlation between the value of relationship banking and the quality of the lender. The overall conclusion is that bank lending potentially facilitates more informative decisions based on a better exchange of information.[15] While not universally valuable, this suggests a benefit of relationship-oriented banking.[16]

2.4   Securitization: a threat to bank lending?

Securitization is an example of a financial innovation (or an innovation in funding technology) that suggests a potential gain of (transaction-oriented) markets at the expense of bank lending. Is this true? Let me first evaluate the economics of securitization.[17]

Securitization is an example of unbundling of financial services. It is a process whereby assets are removed from a bank's balance sheet. More specifically, banks no longer permanently fund assets; instead the investors buying the asset-backed securities provide funding. Asset-backed securities rather than bank deposits then fund dedicated pools of bank-originated assets. As I will emphasize, securitization does not signal the demise of banks, even if it becomes an economically important innovation (and thus substantially reduces the banks' on-balance sheet assets). To see this point, one needs to analyze the traditional lending function in some detail.

The lending function can be decomposed into four more primal activities: origination, funding, servicing and risk processing. Origination subsumes screening prospective borrowers and designing and pricing financial contracts. Funding relates to the provision of financial resources. Servicing involves the collection and remission of payments as well as the monitoring of credits. Risk processing alludes to hedging, diversification and absorption of credit, interest rate, liquidity and exchange rate risk. Securitization decomposes the lending function such that banks will no longer fund the assets but continue to be involved in the primal activities.

The economics of securitization dictates that the originating bank credit enhances the issue. Credit enhancement is typically achieved through the provision of excess collateral, guarantees or with a letter of credit. Effectively this means that the originating bank continues to bear part of the consequences (losses) if the securitized assets do not perform. The credit enhancement reduces the riskiness of the asset-backed claims from the investors' perspective but, more importantly, it addresses conflicts of interest rooted in the originating bank's proprietary information. With private information in the possession of the originating bank, the market requires assurances that the bank will truthfully reveal the quality of the assets it seeks to sell. As with a warranty in product markets, credit enhancement discourages misrepresentation by requiring the originator to absorb a portion of the losses owing to default. Similarly, credit enhancement signals to the market that the originator will perform a thorough credit evaluation and an undiminished monitoring effort. Credit enhancement therefore reduces the information sensitivity of securitized claims by enhancing their marketability.[18]

What this implies is that securitization could lead to a reconfiguration of banking. Banks would continue to originate and service assets, while also processing the attendant risk in order to sustain these activities. Banks would still screen and monitor borrowers, design and price financial claims, and provide risk management services. Consequently, securitization would preserve the incremental value of banks.[19]

How important will securitization become? I can only give a very tentative answer. So far, the securitization market is still small in Europe, but growing. The USA is much more developed. For example, the total volume of mortgage-linked securitization issues in Europe amounts to just 8 per cent of that in the USA, where it stood at US$1621 billion (source: The Bond Market Association). In the USA, securitization has spread rapidly in the last two decades but mainly for car loans, mortgages and credit card receivables. The standardization and modest size of these credits allows diversification of idiosyncratic risks upon pooling. Private information distortions (as discussed above in the context of credit enhancement) are thought to be less severe for these standardized credits.

What can be said about the larger, more customized and heterogeneous commercial loans? These tend to be more information-sensitive. Their quality is therefore more dependent on the rigor of initial screening and subsequent monitoring. Hence the pooling of commercial loans does less to dissipate their information sensitivity, attenuating the benefits of securitization. These considerations, however, do not preclude the securitization of business credits. They merely elevate the cost. For example, with more information-sensitive assets, the originating bank may need to retain a larger portion of the credit risk, while credit enhancement becomes more important. If the information sensitivity is too severe, credit enhancement, short of total recourse may not overcome the private information problem. Thus the potential advantages of securitization would largely be lost, and traditional bank lending would continue to dominate. However, for an increasing array of moderately information-sensitive assets, securitization might become the preferred intermediation technology.

In fact, over the last few years several successful examples of transactions involving the securitization of business credits have emerged. Including synthetic transactions (default swaps), the European volume of CDOs (securitization of business credits) has grown from €40 billion in 1999 to €128 billion in 2001. Moreover, a new market for the securitization of working capital (via asset-backed commercial paper, ABCP conduits) is rapidly coming to maturity.[20]

As my discussion of the economics of securitization suggests, even if securitization became prevalent, banks could continue to play an important role for most of the primal activities that were previously combined in bank lending. More importantly, the comparative advantage of banks rooted in proprietary information about their clientele could be preserved. However, the message is not totally comforting for banks. In particular, the securitization of loans may greatly benefit from standardization in the origination (lending). This may weaken the bank–borrower relationship somewhat. The securitization trend does also force banks to think about their market positioning. A key question is whether securitization skills (structuring, but also placement capacity with (end) investors) need to be developed. In other words, can the commercial bank continue just to originate assets (and let others bring in the securitization skills), or do securitization skills need to be developed in-house? For most commercial banks, it will be very difficult to develop placement capacity. Also the sheer size needed would make this a difficult proposition. Some structuring skills, however, and a better feeling for the financial markets might become indispensable.

2.5 Is relationship banking at risk?

I have argued that relationships may facilitate a continuous flow of information between debtor and creditor that could guarantee uninterrupted access to funding. Some, however, believe that more competition threatens these relationships, while others have recently argued the exact opposite. The question then is: how does elevated inter-bank competition or more intense competition from the financial market affect relationship banking?[21]

Let me first consider the viewpoint that more competition means less relationship banking. The argument here is that with more competition borrowers might be tempted to switch to other banks or to the financial market. When banks anticipate a shorter expected life span of their relationships, they may respond by reducing their relationship-specific investments. More specifically, anticipated shorter relationships inhibit the reusability of information, and thus diminish the value of information (Chan *et al.*, 1986). Banks may then find it less worthwhile to acquire costly proprietary information, and relationships will suffer. Interestingly, shorter or weaker relationships may then become a self-fulfilling prophecy.

A complementary negative effect of competition on relationship banking may come from the impact that competition has on the intertemporal pricing of loans. Increased credit market competition could impose constraints on the ability of borrowers and lenders to share surpluses intertemporally. In particular, it becomes more difficult for banks to 'subsidize' borrowers in earlier periods in return for a share of the rents in the future. Thus the funding role for banks that Petersen and Rajan (1995) see in the case of young corporations (see the discussion in Section 2.3) may no longer be sustainable in the face of sufficiently high competition. This indicates that excessive inter-bank competition ex post may discourage bank lending ex ante.[22,23]

An alternative view is that competition may elevate the importance of a relationship orientation as a distinct competitive edge. It may mitigate somewhat the negative effect that pure price competition would otherwise have on bank profit margins. Boot and Thakor (2000) show that a relationship orientation can alleviate these competitive pressures because a relationship banking orientation can make a bank unique relative to competitors. A more competitive environment may then encourage banks to become more client-driven and customize services, thus focusing more, rather than less, on relationship banking.[24]

What this discussion indicates is that the impact of competition on relationship banking is complex; several effects need to be disentangled. What seems to have emerged, though, is that greater inter-bank competition may very well elevate the value of relationship banking. Pure price competition is an unattractive alternative. However, truly creating an added value in relationship banking may require skills that many banks do not (yet) have. Without those skills a retreat from relationship banking (including, for example, 'downsizing' of the branch network) might be unavoidable.

2.6   Conclusions

The overall picture emerging from the overview of economic theory is that banks play an important role in the process of financial intermediation. Banks process information which is often proprietary. I have extensively discussed the role of banks in lending, and concluded that they will continue to have a distinct role in this activity. Securitization of bank loans has some impact but will not fundamentally affect the relationship-oriented role of banks, although obtaining some debt capital market capabilities might become necessary.

While most of the arguments in this section focus on the banks' role in lending, the applicability of the analysis is broader. Banks facilitate a fine-tuning of intermediation services, and capitalize in this way on their relationships. The growing competitive pressures in the industry will more than ever force banks to search for comparative advantages. Offering tailored, relationship-oriented financial services is only possible for those institutions that can capitalize on distinct skills. The optimal scale and scope has not been addressed. This comes next.

3   Scale and scope issues in banking

3.1   Introduction

Scale and scope economies are often cited as one of the main reasons behind the current merger and acquisition wave in banking. But are scale and scope economies truly present? And could they rationalize the current restructuring in the industry? In this section we first summarize the empirical evidence on scale and scope economies. Existing empirical evidence is quite generic. One of my conclusions is that the existing studies do not really differentiate between activities which in combination could offer scope benefits, nor do they focus on activities which generate economies of scale.

After discussing the empirical evidence and the main barriers to realizing scope and scale economies (Sections 3.2 to 3.4), I seek to identify the main sources of scope and scale economies (Section 3.5). I conclude with some observations on the activities that I consider most susceptible to scale and scope economies (Section 3.6).

3.2   Early empirical evidence on scale and scope economies

Scale and scope economies in banking have been studied extensively. A survey paper by Berger *et al.* (1999) concludes that, in general, the empirical evidence cannot readily identify substantial economies of scale or scope.[25] Scale economies could not readily be found beyond a relatively small size of banks as measured by total assets (that is, beyond $100 million up to $10 billion in total assets). The story on scope economies is even more negative. Diseconomies of scope are quite prevalent. An important caveat is that this research largely involves US studies only. Contrary to banking in many other countries, US banking has historically been quite fragmented.[26] The mergers and acquisitions that were included in most studies took place in an environment where severe constraints existed on the type and geographic dispersion of activities. It is conceivable that these restrictions made it difficult to benefit from scale and scope economies (see also Calomiris and Karceski, 1998). Moreover, most studies use data from the 1970s and 1980s. Since the structure, technology and environment of banking has changed dramatically over the last decades, it is not clear whether insights from those studies readily apply today.

In any case, most empirical researchers in the area of industrial organization will acknowledge that scale and scope economies are very difficult to measure. So, at best, only very modest conclusions could ever be drawn from these empirical studies. The presence of largely inconclusive results should not then really be surprising. Moreover, inefficiencies in managing larger organizations may mitigate possible scale and scope benefits. This would be in line with the sizable literature on the 'diversification discount'. Berger (2000) offers an illustration by observing that managerial ability to control costs creates a differentiation in bank performance that may well dominate the potential scale economies. The difference between an 'average bank' and the 'best practice bank' is about 20 per cent (of the costs of the average bank), while cost scale economies in the 1980s were not more then 5 per cent but possibly are more today. Berger also argues that managerial ability may have an equally big impact on revenue efficiency.

A complication in the empirical studies is also that increasing scale and scope may facilitate market power and thus elevate profitability in the absence of scale and scope economies. This effect might be less important in inter-geographic market mergers. Moreover, alternative distribution networks (for example, direct banking) and the proliferation of financial markets may have reduced the effective market power of locally concentrated financial institutions, and elevated the contestability of markets. This points to a more general issue: the level of concentration may no longer be a good proxy for the (non-) competitiveness of a market.

Another issue is that the level of aggregation in most studies is high and may obscure benefits to scale and scope. In particular, one should look at what type of mergers and acquisitions involve scale and/or scope benefits. For example, Flannery (1999) points to recent research that suggests that mergers with both a geographic and an activity focus are most value-enhancing.[27] Similarly, in analyzing scope and scale issues, one should focus on the type of activities. What are the scale economies in each activity? And what product mix offers true scope economies?[28]

A final concern relates to the effect of mergers on the valuation of financial institutions. A popular methodology is to look at the announcement effect of a merger. A problem with this approach is that mergers may change the structure and dynamics of the industry. If this were the case, the announcement effect could reflect all kinds of other, unobserved (unobservable) effects, including changes in expectations. Some of these and other concerns are summarized in Table 5.1.

3.3   Further evidence on scale and scope economies

Let me first focus on scope economies. In 'earlier' work (up to the mid-1990s), scope economies were measured by comparing the costs of a specialized single product financial institution to those of a financial institution producing multiple financial services. A typical study along these lines is Ferrier *et al.* (1993). The authors consider possible scope benefits of five closely related bank services: demand deposits, time deposits, real estate loans, installment loans and commercial loans. In their sample, 575 banks are represented that participated in the 1984, Federal Reserve's Functional Cost Analysis (FCA) program. The authors compare the costs of the more specialized corporations to those of the more diversified corporations. They conclude that less than 3 per cent of the banks in the sample showed scope economies, while 79 per cent had scope diseconomies. Other contemporary studies come to similar conclusions (Berger *et al.*, 1987; Pulley and Humphrey, 1993). Ferrier *et al.* (1993), also showed that diseconomies of scope were most likely for the larger banks in the sample.

Table 5.1   Some problems with the existing empirical studies on scale and scope economies

Subject	Issues
Market power analysis: effect on prices and profits	Is concentration the right measure? What about contestability of markets?
Static	Combined effect of market power and efficiency changes difficult to disentangle
	Profitability ratios affected by market power
Dynamic (effect of mergers and acquisitions)	Cost ratios via costs of deposits linked to market power. Operational costs affected by relative importance of deposits versus purchased funds
	Event studies affected by 'signaling': that is, the immediate effect of a merger announcement on stock prices incorporates all types of changes in expectations
Efficiency consequences	How to measure scope economies?
Static	Lack of data points for mega-institutions
Dynamic	Little differentiation between type of mergers and/or type of activities

More recent studies have focused on different efficiency concepts, in particular profit efficiency. Again the results are inconclusive at best. In a typical study, Berger, Humphrey and Pulley (1996) focus on the joint 'consumption' benefits of deposits and loans, in a sense the benefits of one-stop banking. Theoretically, various benefits could be envisioned, such as lower transaction and search costs, and lower information costs. However, no profit efficiency enhancement could be discovered. Observe that this does not necessarily imply that scope economies do not exist. It is (theoretically) possible that competition between financial institutions prevents banks from retaining the benefits. That is, the surplus that scope expansion creates might be passed through to the consumers. But, as a general conclusion, it is fair to say that scope economies are hard to realize. Illustrative in this respect is Saunders and Schumacher (2000), who lists 27 studies, of which 13 find diseconomies of scope, six find economies of scope and eight are neutral.

However, also in these studies 'old' data dominate. Recently Long (2001) has looked at the shareholder gains (that is, the immediate announcement effects) from focused versus diversifying bank mergers in the USA between

1988 and 1995. What he found was that focused mergers, on the level of both activity and geography, had positive announcement effects. Moreover, focus in activities was shown to be more important than geographical focus, albeit that the latter was important as well.[29] Activity-diversifying mergers had no positive announcement effects. These results point at the presence of scale rather than scope economies.

While Long's (2001) study (again) focuses on relatively small US banking institutions (market cap acquirer approximately $2 billion, and target less than $100 million), recent European evidence on much larger institutions confirms the desirability of geographical focus. Beitel and Schiereck (2001), analyzing mergers between European financial institutions between 1988 and 2000, show that domestic (intra-state) mergers on average have significantly positive combined (bidder plus target) announcement effects, but more weakly so in recent years (1988–2000). They also found that diversifying domestic mergers (particularly between banks and insurers) had on average a positive value impact. In line with this evidence, the Citigroup–Travelers merger resulted in an increase in the stock prices of both merger partners (Siconolfi, 1998). The latter insight is also confirmed in other European studies on bank–insurer mergers; for example Cybo-Ottone and Murgia (2000) find a positive effect on combined value. The distribution of the value gains is often tilted against bidders, however. Especially in cross-border bank mergers, bidding banks suffer a severe value loss (and targets come out extremely well).

The importance of geographical focus may identify problems with managing (and improving) foreign acquisitions, but also highlights the market power effect. Domestic consolidation often facilitates market power, and this is present with both scale and scope expanding mergers and acquisitions.[30]

These (and related) studies focus on stock market responses to acquisition announcements. While these announcement effects reveal the market's expectation of future cash flow, we should keep in mind that actual performance may differ from market expectations. As Long (2001) puts it, 'Although the prior conditions to predict successful mergers may exist, their presence may be difficult to discern.' This is particularly true for some of the mega-mergers that are observed today. A lack of data points and potentially radical and unprecedented shifts in the structure of banking give us (and the market) little guidance in interpreting the value consequences of these mergers. As an example, the reported significant positive announcement effects associated with bank–insurance mergers may be difficult to reconcile with the current market sentiment.

An alternative approach for analyzing scale and scope economies is to focus on structural differences between financial conglomerates and specialized institutions. Several studies have looked at the relative cost and profit efficiency (for example Berger and Mester, 1997; Berger and Humphrey, 1997). Vander Vennet (2002) has looked at this in the European context. He finds somewhat higher cost and profit efficiency for conglomerates and universal banks. This may look surprising in light of earlier comments; however, these efficiency differences cannot readily be translated into scale and scope economies. The banking industry is changing rapidly and the (traditional) inefficiencies in banking are coming under attack from competitive pressure and technological advances. Differences in efficiency may just reflect differences in the state of adjustment of these institutions, translating into temporarily diverging levels of X-efficiency, rather than indicating scale or scope economies.

3.4   Problems with realizing economies of scale and scope

It is important to observe that technological and regulatory frictions affect the potential realization of scope (and scale) economies. For example, a merger between two financial institutions may not readily lead to scale and scope economies because the integration of computer systems may take time. An interesting account on this very issue is the integration of Citicorp and Travelers. A quote from the *New York Times*:

> Citibank and Travelers say their deal is mainly about finding ways to grow rather than cutting costs. But the challenge will be finding common ground between Citicorp's traditional emphasis on advanced technology and Traveler's preference for low-cost, no frills systems. (*New York Times*, 13 April 1998, Business Day section)

In the same article it is stated that Citicorp has a backlog of past integration issues before it can even think of making its systems compatible with those of Travelers. These issues point to the potential frictions that severely hamper the realization of scale and scope benefits. For example, ultimately, technological benefits might also include the cross-use of databases from the insurance and banking side. The realization of this scope benefit might have to wait until systems are finally made compatible. The bottom line is that technological frictions may severely hamper the realization of scope (and scale) benefits.

A similar argument can be made with respect to regulatory constraints. If regulations force banking and insurance activities to be operated separately, potential scope economies may suffer. This problem was most acute in the USA where, until recently, insurance and banking activities could not be combined under one corporate roof. In many other countries, regulations are (were) less stringent but could still have a major impact on the feasibility of realizing scope economies.

In the end, implementation issues are crucial as well. As the earlier reported evidence shows, there are enormous differences between the best practice and 'average practice' financial institutions. Managerial ability may play a crucial role. A final barrier may come from political considerations. Many countries seek to protect their domestic financial institutions and, if needed, help create 'national champions' to preserve domestic ownership and control.

Table 5.2 summarizes the main barriers to realizing scope and scale economies.

Table 5.2   Possible barriers to realizing scope and/or scale economies

Barrier	Examples
Technological barrier	Incompatible computer systems, conflicting distribution channels
Regulatory barrier	Explicit limitations on activities, regulation-induced Chinese walls
Managerial barrier	Lack of leadership, cultural differences
Political considerations	'National flagship' attitude

3.5   Sources of scale and scope economies

Having presented the mixed empirical evidence, I now seek to uncover the main sources of scale and scope economies. I see the following sources: (a) information technology-related economies, (b) reputation and marketing/brand name-related benefits, (c) financial innovation related economies, (d) benefits of diversification.

Information technology-related economies   The first source, information technology, is most likely of great importance. Recent developments in information technology facilitate a more efficient and effective utilization of data bases over ranges of services and customers. That is, client-specific information may allow for scope economies and facilitate a competitive advantage to financial institutions that can offer a range of services to their clientele. Similarly, possibilities for reusability of information across customers may have increased.

Information technology helps in identifying related client needs. Scope economies therefore apply to all products that could be sold to the same client group. Examples for bank–insurance conglomerates include life insurance features in mortgages, asset management/private banking services combined with life insurance, commercial credits in combination with industrial risk insurance, and export financing together with export credit insurance.

This also indicates distribution network-related benefits. These benefits may be rooted in information technology developments. In particular, IT developments may facilitate scale economies in running a sizable distribution network. Simultaneously, scope economies may become much more visible. For example, information technology facilitates an increasing array of financial products and services to be offered through the same distribution network. Customers may attach value to 'one-stop shopping' which encourages some financial institutions to offer a broader package of financial services tailored to particular customer categories.

Observe also that the developments in information technology may affect the scope of control; information technology could facilitate the management of a bigger organization. This means that information technology could result in scale and scope economies. The implication is also that sizable investments in information technology are needed to truly benefit from scale and scope economies.

Reputation and brand name/marketing   The second source of scale and scope economies is linked to brand name/marketing and reputation. Scope benefits may be present in the joint marketing of products to customers. Brand image is partly marketing related but is also linked to the notions of 'trust', 'reputation' and 'confidence'. These notions play an important role in the financial services industry. Increasingly, financial service providers offer services that crucially depend on their reputation. For example, the growing importance of off-balance sheet claims puts great emphasis on the ability of financial institutions to honor these contingent liabilities. But also the success of modern 'virtual' distribution channels (Internet) may depend crucially on reputation. Under certain conditions, increasing scale and scope allows financial institutions to capitalize more on their reputation. That is, a wider scope (and/or scale) may help a financial institution to put its reputational capital at work (see Boot *et al.*, 1993).

A concrete example here is the Dutch bank–insurance conglomerate ING that offers direct banking services in Spain, for example. The name ING is linked in advertisements explicitly to the Nationale Nederlanden brand name, its insurance subsidiary, a well-known and respected institution in Spain. This type of branding 'externality' is also used by players entering the financial services arena from other industries (for example supermarkets leveraging their brand name for financial services offerings).[31]

Financial innovation   The next source of potential scale and scope economies is financial innovation related economies. Financial innovation as a source of scope and scale economies is a two-edged sword. Some suggest that larger institutions are less likely to innovate because of the inherent bureaucracy.

This might be true but that is a governance issue. *Ceteris paribus*, larger institutions could better recoup the fixed costs of financial innovations. Innovations could be marketed to a larger customer base and/or introduced in a wider set of activities. For financial innovations scale and scope might be particularly important given the rapid imitation by competitors. Only for a short period of time does a true competitive advantage exist. A wider scope and larger scale may help recoup the fixed costs in this short period of time. Financial innovation-related economies could also be directly related to product/client data bases (see also the first two sources of economies). Wider product and client data bases can provide superior information for the design of financial innovations.

Bank–insurance combinations could be successful in leveraging each other's product skills. For example, insurance subsidiaries could benefit from derivative innovations coming from the banking arm. Similarly, securitization skills developed in banking are heavily used elsewhere and, more recently, several securitization innovations have been motivated by particular needs in the insurance operation.

Diversification   The fourth potential source of scale and scope economies is the benefit of diversification. Several products might be close substitutes, for example pension, life insurance and saving products. Combining these products and services within one organization mitigates the effects of demand substitution over these products/activities. This could be interpreted as a diversification benefit, but may also indicate cross-selling benefits (see above).

From a corporate finance perspective, diversification is a controversial argument. After all, investors (shareholders) could diversify, and why would a financial institution itself need to do this (unless of course there are synergies, and thus scope benefits)? However, various frictions may explain the value of diversification. For example, diversification facilitates an internal capital market where cash flow-generating businesses could help other activities that need funding. If raising external funds is costly, this may add value. Nevertheless, this might be a mixed blessing. Often the presence of internal capital markets invites cross-subsidization of marginal or loss-making activities that could wipe out potential benefits. This is also the finding of Berger and Ofek (1995) who find an average diversification discount of 13–15 per cent. Having said this, it is true that a low volatility of returns is considered very important in banking. This points to some benefit of diversification.

A link can also be made to the proliferation of off-balance sheet banking; see, for example, the analysis of securitization in Section 2.4. These activities involve all kinds of guarantees that lead to contingent liabilities. For such activities, the credibility of the bank in being able to honor such guarantees is crucially important. One measure of this is a bank's credit rating. With the proliferation of off-balance sheet banking, ratings have become more important. If diversification helps in getting a better rating, a stronger argument for diversification can be made.

3.6 Further observations and conclusions

The various sources that I have discussed point to potential *revenue* (output) and *cost* (input) synergies. In Table 5.3, I have summarized the discussion so far.

Table 5.3 Revenue and cost synergies

Source	Type of synergy	Example(s)
Information technology-related economies	Revenue	Cross-selling potential
	Cost	Fixed cost of IT
		Reusability of information: cross-sectional and intertemporal
		Scale economies in running distribution network
Reputation and marketing/brand name related benefits	Revenue	Acceptance of new distribution channels (Internet)
		Cross-selling potential
	Cost	Fixed cost of marketing, branding
Financial innovation-related benefits	Revenue	Superior innovations based on broader information set
		Better rent extraction due to bigger network
	Cost	Fixed cost of innovation
Benefits of diversification	Revenue	Avoiding loss of turnover to substitutes
		Benefits linked to off-balance sheet activities
	Cost	Internal capital market

Looking at Table 5.3, we see that most potential sources of economies of scale and scope are related to distribution. The importance of the distribution network is clear and should be considered a primary source of scope and scale benefits.

The possibility for scope economies is generally present. For example, on the demand side, the proliferation of saving products and their link to pensions, mutual funds and life insurance clearly urges joint distribution, and thereby facilitates economies of scope. However, a word of caution is warranted. Consider, for example, IT investments. IT developments may have made it possible to exploit potential scope economies better with multiple product offerings to a particular customer group, using new direct distribution channels with relatively easy access to (formerly) distant customers. However, the IT developments offer very good possibilities for focused single-product players as well. Also interfaces (may) come up that help bundle the product offerings of specialized providers, thereby becoming a substitute for an integrated provider. Only very well managed financial services firms may realize positive scope economies. The execution (X-efficiency) is probably more crucial than ever before, since inefficiencies will be exploited by single-product players. What this means is that it is very unlikely that (ultimately) a single strategy will dominate in the financial services sector.

The same arguments apply for vertical disintegration of the value chain. Specializing in one segment of the value chain might for now be too risky a strategy. Banking is too much in turmoil and specialization within the value chain may lead to an overly vulnerable dependence on the other players. But, ultimately, it does not seem unrealistic to expect the emergence of, for example, product specialists without a distribution network (see also McKinsey & Co, 2002). This would fit a situation where financial intermediaries become supermarkets that sell products from a variety of suppliers.[32] The scale economies and benefits coming from focus could be substantial.

In the particular context of bank–insurer mergers, several other comments can be made. An important issue is the potential benefits coming from asset management. Some argue that the income stream from asset management is relatively stable, and hence a welcome addition to the otherwise erratic revenue stream of financial institutions. There might be some truth in this, but this benefit, at least from a corporate finance perspective, cannot be really big. That is, diversification for purely financial reasons could also be accomplished by investors individually in the financial market. Thus, unless the synergies with other business lines are substantial (and possibly they are, see below), an independent asset management operation is a credible alternative.

Similarly, people argue that bank–insurance combinations have a distinct benefit on the funding side. Diversification may allow for a more effective use of equity capital. Also direct funding synergies may apply. The mismatch between assets and liability on the bank's balance sheet (short-term funding, long on the asset side) might be the reverse of that of an insurer (long-term obligations). Again corporate finance theory is skeptical about the validity of these arguments.

Another argument for combining life insurance and banking is that it could augment the total asset management pool, and thus offer scale economies. While this might be true, more recently banks and insurers have learned that the asset management operation requires distinct skills and is not 'automatically' profitable as passive spin-off from other (feeding) activities. Thus synergies are present, but not necessarily dominant. This is not to say that combining banking and insurance with an appropriate customer focus could not be value-enhancing. As stated earlier, combining banking and insurance could offer synergies in distribution. This builds on the distribution network-related benefits discussed earlier.

However, as discussed in Section 3.4, other factors may undermine the possibility of realizing scope benefits. For example, owing to national tax regulations, life insurance needs to be tailored to each specific country. Also other differences exist between countries in terms of (corporate) culture, law, etc. These complications make it important to have well-focused operations outside the home market and to abstain from scope-expanding strategies that would complicate the operation even more. In some cases this also means that one should abstain from broad cross-border acquisitions and only choose to go cross-border where the specific activity at hand requires this.

These observations help us to understand the reconfiguration of many European financial institutions. In particular, it becomes increasingly questionable to rationalize a universal banking strategy based on some company-wide synergy argument. Scope economies need to be carefully examined, and linked directly to specific market segments across clients, products and geographic areas of operation (see also Smith and Walter, 1997).

4   Scope as a strategic advantage

4.1   Introduction
The analysis so far has focused solely on scope and scale economies. This in itself is inadequate for predicting or explaining the positioning of financial institutions. The actual positioning will depend on quite a few other factors as well. In particular, a financial institution that has to position itself today will take the following factors into account:

- What are my core competencies? And what is my current position and financial strength?

- How do I expect the market for financial services to develop? Can I distinguish various scenarios?
- What market structure do I expect in the various scenarios? In particular, what do I expect the competition will do?

And only at this stage, the potential for scope and scale economies enters:

- What are the scope and scale economies in the delivery of financial services?

What this implies is that scope and scale economies are just one input, albeit an important one, for the positioning today. It is also worth noting that the decision about scale and scope (involving choices about clients, products and geographic presence) is not final. For example, the choices being made today could seek to keep options open anticipating further restructuring once more information becomes available. This is important for interpreting the restructuring that we observe. The current restructuring is motivated by strategic considerations (for example positioning) and may not give a good indication of what the future structure of the financial services sector will be. Current decisions might be 'posturing' vis-à-vis competitors that might be undone in the future. In the following section, I develop this strategic rationale for the restructuring in the financial services sector.

4.2   General framework

The explanation developed in this section is that strategic uncertainty about future exploitable core competencies may dictate broadening of scope. The basic idea is as follows. Suppose a financial institution knows that – perhaps because of deregulation – it can participate in another market at some time in the future. The problem is that this is a new market, so the financial institution is highly uncertain about whether it has the skills to compete effectively in that market.[33] It has two choices. It can wait until that future time to find out whether it has the capabilities and 'core competencies' (as defined by Hamel and Prahalad, 1990) for this new market. Or it can enter the market 'early' and discover what its skills are prior to making costly resource allocation decisions. The advantage of the second approach is that it permits the institution to 'experiment' with a new business and learn whether it has the skills to compete in that business. This learning permits better decisions when competition commences. In particular, having better knowledge about its own skills allows the institution to be more aggressive in its output decisions, to gain market share when it knows that its skills are superior to those of its competitors and to leave the market when its skills are inferior.

One could explain scope expansion as the financial institution reserving the right to play in a variety of 'new' activities. By making incremental investment today, the institution puts itself in a privileged position through the acquisition of superior information by learning. This allows it to wait until the environment becomes less uncertain before determining whether to compete in the new market and, if so, how aggressively.[34] In a recent paper (see Boot *et al.*, 2002) a formal model has been developed that formalizes these ideas and incorporates scope as a potential competitive advantage. The framework in that paper is as follows. It starts out with a financial services sector with narrowly defined existing activities and asks whether financial institutions should expand into a 'new' activity. A key feature of the analysis is that there is strategic future uncertainty about the demand for this new activity; that is the activity has prospects only in the long run and demand may not materialize. The institution must decide whether or not to expand in this activity and, if so, whether to enter early or late. Early entry is costly because the activity becomes important only later. Demand may not materialize, and entering early requires investments to be made prior to the resolution of demand uncertainty. Moreover, the scope expansion associated with investing in strategic options could reduce the competitiveness of existing operations (say owing to loss of focus). However, early entry offers potential strategic advantages. In particular, early entry could lead to the discovery of skills that would allow for a more efficient delivery of the new activity and hence make the financial institution a more credible competitor once the prospects of this activity become clear.

The question is: when will the benefits of early entry outweigh the costs? The uncertainty about skills plays a key role here. If this uncertainty is substantial, early entry may be beneficial. The other key factor is the competitive environment of the financial services sector, and the anticipated competition for the new activity. Suppose that the new activity can also be offered by a specialized provider (a 'boutique' specializing in this activity). If the financial institution enters (early or late), one could consider the market for this activity as a Cournot duopoly game. Early entry is beneficial because the institution would then learn its skills in the new activity. This allows the institution to compete more aggressively when it has favorable information about its skills and more cautiously when it has poor information about its skills. The benefits of early entry also depend on how likely it is that a specialized provider will come along. Whether early entry is optimal will thus crucially depend on the competitive environment.

4.3 Importance of the competitive environment
The competitive environment of the existing activities also enters the analysis because of the investment and risk associated with early entry

in the new activity. If the existing activities face 'too much' competition, financial institutions will be unable to absorb the investment and risk that come with early entry in the new activity. An immediate implication is that investments in strategic options and thus the adoption of broader, less focused strategies will be observed in less competitive industries, whereas firms in competitive industries will embrace more focused strategies. This could explain why continental European financial institutions generally follow broad strategies. Their local market power allows them to afford the 'widening of scope' strategy and benefit from its potential future strategic advantages.

Moreover, as stated earlier, the anticipated future competitive environment for the new activity matters as well. If the financial institution anticipates facing little or no competition in this activity in the future, early entry – with its accompanying cost and dilution of focus – is unnecessary because a competitively unchallenged institution can operate successfully in this market without the benefit of early entry. At the other extreme, when the anticipated competition for the new activity is very intense (perhaps owing to many potential future competitors), early entry is not an attractive proposition and is once again suboptimal. The analysis thus leads to the prediction that moderate anticipated competition in the new activity together with not too much competition in the existing activities facilitates early entry. Table 5.4 summarizes the main insights.

Table 5.4   Optimal scope as function of the competitive environment

Anticipated competitive environment in the strategic option (new activity)	Current competitive environment in existing financial services activities	
	Little competition	High competition
Little competition	Narrow	Narrow
Medium competition	Broad	Narrow
High competition	Narrow	Narrow

Note: Narrow: no early investment in new activity; broad: early investment in new activity.

The analysis shows that, starting from a situation with strategic uncertainty, the competition the financial institution faces in its current activities, together with the competition it anticipates in the future, in the new activity leads to predictions about early entry and hence optimal scope. Scope expansion is seen to be optimal when there is high strategic uncertainty, moderate competition expected in the new activity, and low-to-moderate competition in the existing activity.

In this context also the benefits of consolidation could be explored. Now assume that there are multiple competing institutions at the outset. Consider two of these contemplating a merger. The question before them is whether consolidation (merging) today gives them a competitive advantage in undertaking the new activity tomorrow. The answer is affirmative. Merging helps create 'deep pockets' and possibly also reduces the degree of competition, making investments in strategic options more affordable. It should be clear that these effects have little significance in an environment without strategic uncertainty. The analysis thus predicts greater consolidation in industries with more strategic uncertainty.

4.4 Is strategic uncertainty special to financial services?
Why does this model of strategic uncertainty fit financial institutions so well? There are at least three reasons. First, deregulation in the financial services sector is opening doors to new activities at a rate unprecedented since the Great Depression. Second, the swirling tides of technological and regulatory changes are generating a level of uncertainty about the skills needed to operate successfully in the future that is perhaps greater in the financial services sector than in any other industry. Lastly, banks and to some extent insurers have traditionally faced limited competition in their home markets. This has created 'deep pockets' across the industry, and serves to support the broad strategies observed particularly in banking. The combined validity of these arguments makes the model especially suited for the financial services industry.

The precise interpretation of the model of strategic uncertainty could be amended to fit financial institutions even better. In particular, one could interpret the institution's problem as its not knowing what combination of activities will give it a competitive edge in the future. In this interpretation, a financial institution is contemplating entering, not new activities, but possibly 'old' activities that it traditionally chose to abstain from. Early entry or, better, choosing a wider set of activities, would let the institution discover what activities optimally fit together.

4.5 Summary
Strategic considerations play an important role in the restructuring of the financial services industry. The arguments developed in this section help to identify where scope and (to some extent) scale become important from a strategic perspective.

What activities are most readily subjected to these considerations? The primary deciding factor is strategic uncertainty, with the degree of competitiveness as a complementary factor. In my view the development of alternative distribution channels (for example the Internet) is a primary source of strategic uncertainty. Also the developments in IT may have substantially broadened the feasible scope of control. This has induced uncertainty about the desirable scale and scope of operations. For the moment, 'bigger and broader' seems the safest option.

'Deep pockets' are important for the broad scope strategy. Here the competitive environment comes in. In particular, 'too much' competition would dilute the deep pockets and prevent or limit scope expansion. Until recently, however, the relative protected position of institutions in their home markets has allowed institutions to choose a broad positioning. As markets become more open, both to foreign competitors and to inter-sector entry, this choice will be reconsidered; actually we have, in my view, now entered that phase. More focus is rapidly becoming inevitable.

5   Competition, fragility and public policy

Regulators are ambivalent about truly promoting competition in the financial sector. Prudential regulators in particular think in terms of trade-offs between competition and stability. In this popular view, restrictions on competition would improve banks' profitability, reduce failure rates and hence safeguard stability (Keeley, 1990; Demsetz, Saidenberg and Strahan, 1996). The argument is that market power enhances the charter value of the bank and that this would curtail risk-taking because by taking risks the charter value might be lost. As such, it punishes deviant behavior more.

In my view, the real trade-off between competition and stability is, however, much more complex. Recently several authors have argued that the trade-off might go the other way, or is at best ambiguous (Cruickshank, 2000; FSA, 2000). In any case, the available evidence does not give clear prescriptions; it very much depends on the particular situation at hand (OECD, 1998; Riksbank, 2000; Group of Ten, 2001).[35]

On market power increasing mergers, one may conclude that national regulatory and supervisory authorities have generally been lenient, with several 'national champions' as a result. Apart from the question whether the creation of such national champions leaves enough competition,[36] I have three reservations. First, banks are rather opaque institutions that combine many activities with, as a result, very limited market discipline. If facilitating a competitive financial system is an objective, and it should be, market discipline is in my view indispensable. The burden falling on regulation and supervision would otherwise be excessive. Improving market discipline should then be a key public policy objective. Market power enhancing mergers create more rather than less opaqueness and as such are undesirable. Second, the efficiency of large institutions with considerable market power is questionable. While this is not a public policy concern by itself, the ultimate survival of such a large institution is. Policymakers often refer to desirable diversification effects that could be captured in larger institutions. This should, however, not be taken for granted. Such institutions might be encouraged to take more risks which, together with the inefficiencies, could put that survival at risk. This could add substantial risk to the financial system.[37] Third, many European financial institutions are considered too-big-to-fail. This reduces market discipline even further. The dominant 'national' champion attitude clearly does not help.

As a caveat, note that the regulatory design has been mostly scrutinized in a precisely reversed causality, that is, how to continue to maintain some grip on a rapidly changing (and globalizing) sector in light of the rapid changes in the sector. The historic predictability of banking and the strong control of national governments on this sector facilitated and allowed for stringent regulation. This however is no longer feasible; issues related to regulatory arbitrage have directly undermined the effectiveness of regulation and level playing field concerns now also need to be taken into account.[38] The competitive effects of prudential regulation have a direct bearing on the latter.[39]

The consequence is such that competition policy in the financial sector has been somewhat obscure. The true motivations for the scale and scope expansion, and also the strategic rationale that I have highlighted, often involve a substantial softening of competition. In line with the more recent research that questions that validity of the trade-off view between competiton and stability, great care should be taken in safe guarding adequate competiton in the industry. This is a particular concern to the clientele that is primarily dependent on banking institutions (for example small and medium-sized businesses).

6   Value of alliances

A potentially important alternative to consolidation is the concept of an alliance. This concept is underdeveloped in the context of banking. This is to some extent surprising. Banks did, and still do, engage in correspondent banking, particularly in the context of cross-border payment services. But correspondent banking is losing its importance. In particular, with the advent of information technology, international payment and settlement systems have become available (for example the emergence of TARGET and settlement systems like Cedel and Euroclear). These developments reduce the need for correspondent banking. More importantly, correspondent banks may have become competitors in the areas they were cooperating in before. For example, some banks seek to gain a competitive edge by offering proprietary cross-border payment facilities. This points to an important consideration for the feasibility of correspondent banking, or alliances for that matter: it only works if the interests of the participating institutions are sufficiently aligned.[40] But why may alliances become important?

The fundamental reason I see is that vertical disintegration in the value chain will gain in importance (see also Berlin, 2001). This allows for greater specialization and hence focus, with potential scale economies as well. Alliances could play an important role in this process. They may introduce more durable, yet flexible, cooperative structures facilitating interactions between the different parties in the value chain. An example is the opening up of a bank's distribution network to products from others. In that way, institutions could exploit their local presence by capitalizing on their distribution network, and simultaneously product specialists may emerge that feed products into these distribution networks.

The applicability of this idea is broader. Financial institutions rooted in strong local relationships may gain access to more 'distant' asset management services that are scale intensive and globally, rather than locally, oriented. It may well be possible to offer some of these services in an alliance (that is to join forces) and still capitalize on customer-related synergies. While some will argue that a merger with these institutions would allow for a smoother operation of these services, I would like to take issue with this point of view.

First, for several reasons, cross-border mergers may not (yet) be feasible. A focused alliance would create valuable linkages between institutions with immediate synergy benefits (see above), but could also allow the possibly nationally rooted partners to get to know each other. In that sense, it would be an intermediate phase. As a second argument, the alliance model based on asset management and/or specific investment banking activities may, if properly designed, combine the benefits of an integrated universal banking structure and a stand-alone type of organization of those activities. For example, the alliance partners all have a limited exposure to these activities, which helps them maintain focus. In particular, cultural conflicts and distractions associated with trying to build up (or buy) an investment bank next to running the relationship-rooted regional bank are prevented.[41] Obviously, the alliance model does not come without cost. The important task is to define a clearly defined portfolio of activities that would become part of the alliance. This will not be investment banking in the broadest sense of the word. Similarly, in the case of asset management, the alliance partners would each maintain their own proprietary access to the customers but join forces in the asset management operations including research and back office activities. This would facilitate the information technology investments that allow the partners to capitalize on scale economies.

Maintaining proprietary access by the individual alliance partners preserves customer-related scope economies.

The same arguments could be made for bank–insurance combinations. That is, banks could choose to engage in an alliance with an insurer rather than merge. The alliance model is indeed seen (for example Crédit Suisse–Winterthur before the merger). It is possible to distribute insurance products via a bank's distribution network based on a license agreement.[42] However, at least until recently, the perception in the market was that the integration of IT is only assured with an outright merger. Thus the desired synergy in distribution (and also the complementary feeding of asset management operations) would seem to favor integration.

A key question is whether this will remain the case. I tend to believe that joint ventures and alliances will gain importance in the future. It will also help if the level of uncertainty in the industry comes down a little. Vertical disintegration now may create an unpredictable dependence on other parties in the value chain. Developments in IT actually help provide smooth transitions between the different parties in the value chain. Economies of scale and benefits from focus could be obtained in this way (see also Section 3.6).

In the end, alliances only seem feasible if the activities that are part of them can be run as a more or less separate (jointly-owned) business unit with considerable independence from the mother institutions. This is at present probably most likely with (smaller) regionally specialized financial institutions that may want to join forces in, for example, investment banking and asset management. For bigger institutions, alliances are at present, less common, but when these institutions (finally) choose to focus, alliances will mushroom.

Let me first focus on the European experience as it may relate to the USA. Europe and the USA share some similar dynamics. In particular, the relaxation of constraints on inter-state banking in the USA is reminiscent of the European Union banking directives liberating cross-border banking. However, a fundamental difference between the USA and Europe immediately surfaces. The domestic banks in Europe were, and are, protected as domestic flagships. A fundamental belief that foreigners should not control financial institutions has (so far) prevented all but a few cross-border mergers.

The political dimension is at the root of this. Even in countries that do not have any direct interference by governments in banking operations and where banks are considered truly commercial enterprises (and have generally been successful, for example ABN AMRO and ING in The Netherlands), the political dimension is important. Central banks, ministries of finance and the banks operate in close concert. This is not very surprising, a very homogeneous group of executives is in charge of the financial sector, central bank and government ministries guaranteeing a clear national identity of domestic institutions. In countries with explicit government involvement (for example France and Italy), foreign control over domestic institutions is even more unlikely unless banks become so inefficient and weak that involvement of foreigners becomes almost inevitable. To some extent this is already happening. For example, in the bidding war for the French bank CIC, ABN AMRO was favored by some because of its excellent track record vis-à-vis competing French bidders, and the UK bank HSBC recently succeeded in buying up Crédit Commercial de France.

The primary response to the liberating EU directives has so far been defensive: domestic mergers are generally encouraged to protect national interests, and indeed create national flagships (see e.g. The Netherlands, France, Spain and Switzerland). A case in point is also Germany. Many have observed that banking in that country is surprisingly dispersed despite the (traditionally!) powerful images of Deutsche Bank, Commerzbank and Dresdner Bank (now part of Allianz). Public policy definitely aims at protecting the interests of these powerful institutions, but the consolidation is played out mainly on the Länder-level (the separate states): indeed, precisely at the level where the political dimension is at work. This is an important explanation for the regional and not national consolidation in German banking.

I would conclude that the national flagship dimension has been of primary importance in Europe. Cross-border expansion is rare and consolidation is primarily observed within national borders. For the USA this development in Europe has all but weak implications. Inter-state expansion has been a driving force behind the consolidation in US banking. Politics now seems to interfere little with inter-state expansion. The political dimension in the USA seems focused on the demarcations between commercial banking, investment banking and insurance. Powerful lobbies are successful in mobilizing (local) politicians and in this way have been able to obstruct major banking reform in the US Congress, at least up to the passing of the Gramm–Leach–Bliley Act of 1999.

In other words, in both the USA and Europe vested interests are at work. In Europe there are national authorities preserving their national flagships, in the USA, powerful lobbies that seek to preserve traditional demarcations between financial institutions. These observations do not yet answer the question whether national (European) authorities are serving the interests of their constituencies when advocating national flagships. This is a different issue, and may have to be looked at in a game-theoretic context. If other countries are following these policies, an individual country may be well advised to follow the same policy. However, all would possibly be better off if none followed a national flagship policy.

7   Concluding remarks

The consolidation and restructuring in the financial sector will continue for many years to come. There are powerful forces behind consolidation. The regional expansion that characterizes much of the US merger wave will also carry over to Europe. Cross-border acquisitions are coming, particularly with the arrival of the Euro and the European Monetary Union (EMU). The Euro and EMU are catalysts that will accelerate the integration of national financial markets and induce a more pan-European view on financial services.

Strategic considerations, as highlighted in this study, have created broad powerhouses. But this will change. Competitive pressures will force financial institutions to discover their true competitive advantages, and choose an optimal configuration of services and activities. What will be the new demarcations between financial institutions? Which activities will ultimately be combined in one institution and offer economies of scope? Where is focus more important? Many questions and few answers. The process of restructuring will be a fascinating one for sure. For public policy, and competition policy in particular, the challenges will be enormous.

Notes

1. This paper is adapted and updated from Boot (2003).
2. For example the acquisition of the Belgian Bank BBL by the Dutch financial conglomerate ING.
3. Several European banks – for example ING in the Netherlands and the Belgium–Dutch conglomerate Fortis – already engage in *bancassurance*, that is, combining banking and insurance activities. Similarly, Credit Suisse expanded into insurance by acquiring the insurance corporation Winterthur. But in the USA until the passing of the Gramm–Leach–Bliley Act of 1999, many restrictions remained on combining banking, securities underwriting and insurance.
4. See for example a recent report by Oliver Wyman & Company in collaboration with Morgan-Stanley (2002) that has the illuminating title, 'The Need to Differentiate'.
5. See Canoy, Rey and van Damme (Chapter 7, this volume) on the power to 'act independently' from rivals.
6. See Martin (Chapter 1, this volume) on a general discussion on the nature of competition.
7. From this perspective it is not surprising that several European banks are currently integrating their debt capital market activities with their corporate lending operations. Previously, they had the debt capital market activities typically linked to equity capital market operations (within their investment banking divisions). The commitment to equity-linked IB activities is being reduced or even dismantled by many players in the industry.
8. Diamond (1984) introduces intermediaries as delegated monitors. See Chan *et al.* (1986) for a discussion on information reusability, and James (1987) and Lummer and McConnell (1989) for empirical evidence. For a nice illustration supporting the special role of banks, see Berlin (1996).
9. See for example Simon (1936) and Boot *et al.* (1993).
10. Mayer (1988) and Hellwig (1991) discuss the commitment nature of bank funding. Boot *et al.* (1991) address the *credibility* of commitments. Schmeits (2002) formally considers the impact of discretion (flexibility) in bank loan contracts on investment efficiency.

11. See Dewatripont and Maskin (1995) on the issues of soft-budget constraints. Diamond (1993), Berglöf and Von Thadden (1994), and Gorton and Kahn (1993) address the priority structure.
12. One could ask whether bondholders could be given priority and allocated the task of timely intervention. Note that bondholders are subject to more severe information asymmetries and are generally more dispersed (that is have smaller stakes). Both characteristics make them ill-suited for an 'early' intervention task.
13. The bondholders will obviously ask to be compensated for their subordinated status. This, ignoring the timely intervention effect, the priority (seniority) or subordination features can be priced out. That is, as much as senior debt may *appear* cheaper (it is less risky), junior or subordinated debt will appear more expensive.
14. Empirical evidence provided by James (1987) and Slovin, Sushka and Hudson (1988) supports the certification role of banks. Other evidence can be found in Houston and James (1996).
15. See for example Petersen and Rajan (1994) and Houston and James (1996) for empirical evidence.
16. The relationship feature of (primarily commercial) banking also has drawbacks. There are two primary costs to relationship banking: the soft-budget constraint problem and the hold-up problem. The soft-budget constraint problem has to do with the potential lack of toughness on the bank's part in enforcing credit contracts that may come with relationship banking proximity. The problem is that borrowers who realize that they can renegotiate their contracts ex post like this may have perverse incentives ex ante (Bolton and Scharfstein, 1996; Dewatripont and Maskin, 1995). The seniority structure of bank loans, as discussed above, may mitigate this. The hold-up problem has to do with the information monopoly the bank generates in the course of lending that may allow it to make loans at non-competitive terms in the future to the borrower. More specifically, the proprietary information about borrowers that banks obtain as part of their relationships may give them an information monopoly. In this way, banks could charge (ex post) high loan interest rates (see Sharpe, 1990; Rajan, 1992). The threat of being 'locked in', or informationally captured by the bank, may make the borrower reluctant to borrow from the bank. Potentially valuable investment opportunities may then be lost. Alternatively, firms may opt for multiple bank relationships. This may reduce the information monopoly of any one bank, but possibly at a cost. Ongena and Smith (2000) show that multiple bank relationships indeed reduce the hold-up problem, but worsen the availability of credit.
17. Gorton and Penachi (1995) provide an economic rationale for bank loan sales and securitization. See also Stone and Zissu (2000).
18. The reputation of the originating bank will be equally important. Moreover, accreditation by credit rating agencies could also add to the marketability of the securitized claims.
19. See also Boyd and Gertler (1994). They argue that a substitution from on-balance sheet to off-balance sheet banking may have (falsely) suggested a shrinking role for banks. As in the description of securitization in the text, much of the bank's value added in the primal activities would be preserved.
20. As a caveat, some of this activity in securitization is undoubtedly induced by capital arbitrage, and the new Basle II capital requirements may mitigate this somewhat.
21. A second trend is the better dissemination of information. This, by itself, could reduce the value of (previously) proprietary information in the hands of banks, and possibly reduce the value of relationship banking.
22. Berlin and Mester (1998) provide a related, albeit different argument. Their analysis suggests that competition forces banks to pay market rates on deposits, which may complicate the potentially value-enhancing smoothing of lending rates.
23. An extensive empirical literature focuses on the effect of consolidation in the banking sector on small business lending. This consolidation may in part be a response to competitive pressures. The effects on small business lending are, however, not clear-cut (see Berger *et al.*, 1998).

24. Boot and Thakor (2000) distinguish generic (information-extensive) transaction lending by banks from relationship lending. Transaction lending is most similar to direct funding in the financial market. Boot and Thakor's analysis attaches two dimensions to relationship lending: volume and intensity or quality. That is, banks can choose to offer more relationship loans (at the expense of transaction loans) but also have to decide on the *intensity* of their relationship loans. Intensity points at, for example, sector specialization: how much does a bank invest in specific knowledge of a firm or industry? The more the bank invests, the better it can fine-tune its services to the needs of its relationship borrowers. Boot and Thakor's main finding is that competition induces banks to make more relationship loans at the expense of (generic) transaction loans. However, the quality (or intensity) of the relationship loans is lower when inter-bank competition heats up.

25. See also Shaffer and David (1991), Cornett and Tehranian (1992), Mester (1992), Mitchell and Onvural (1996) and Clark (1996).

26. This is not really surprising. US banks faced substantial regulatory constraints on their activities concerning both the type of their activities (for example banks could engage in commercial banking or investment banking, not both) and their location (for example limits on inter-state banking). More recently, however, regulatory constraints have become less binding. This undoubtedly partially explains the surge in mergers and acquisitions.

27. An important issue is whether this only points to market-power benefits or whether true efficiency gains could also be at work.

28. Surprisingly, this type of research is still hard to find. A lot of research has been done on potential conflicts of interest in universal banking. To some extent, this is activity-specific (investment banking versus commercial banking). However, this research is of very limited interest for this study because it ignores the question of complementarity between activities. This is not really surprising because the literature is solely motivated by the obscure Glass–Steagall regulation in the USA (see Kroszner and Rajan, 1994; Puri, 1996). See Ramirez (2002) for some evidence on the scope economies in pre-Glass–Steagall Act US banking.

29. Geographical expansion in the USA often involves buying up neighboring (focused) retail banks which allow for economies on IT systems, management processes and product offerings. Relative to the European scene, where geographical expansion often implies buying up big universal banks across the border, fewer barriers to an effective integration exist. This may explain the more favorable US evidence.

30. In an interesting recent paper, Focarelli *et al.* (2002) contrast the motivation for mergers to that of acquisitions. They conclude, using Italian data, that mergers often have a strategic, revenues-enhancing objective (cross selling) while acquisitions often aim at improving the credit policy (and thus the loan book quality) of the target.

31. The ING example also shows the possible sharing of marketing expertise between insurance and banking subsidiaries. Banking subsidiaries have generally benefited from the extensive direct marketing expertise of the insurance arm. In the case of ING, the Postbank (an ING subsidiary) skills in direct banking were also relevant.

32. On the benefits of vertical (dis)integration in the financial services industry there is little empirical work. An interesting exception is a recent paper by Berger *et al.* (2000) who look at profit scope economies in combining life and non-life in the insurance industry. They find that conglomeration (and hence scope) *might* be optimal for larger institutions that are primarily retail/consumer-focused and have vertically integrated distribution systems.

33. Note that these are strategic investments in activities that are 'uncertain'. What I mean by this is that the investment is in an activity with uncertain profit potential, or that the fit between the new activity and the existing activities is uncertain. In both interpretations, the profit potential is 'uncertain'.

34. See also Courtney *et al.* (1997) for the link between strategy and uncertainty.

35. Some have argued that competition undermines a bank's incentives to invest in relationships and that this increases risk as well. What is meant is that when customers switch too often, such investments are no longer worthwhile. Monitoring may then become less effective and risks may increase. This argument is, however, incomplete. Boot and Thakor (2000)

show that competition could elevate investments in relationships. In a related work, Koskela and Stenbecka (2000) provide an example where more competitiveness does not lead to more asset risk. Boyd, De Nicoló and Smith (2003) show that competition *could* be good for financial stability. In particular, they show that a monopoly bank will economize on its holdings of cash reserves. This elevates the crisis probability. Countering this effect is the lower deposit rate that it can choose to offer. Boyd and De Nicoló (2003) identify two more effects countering the conventional wisdom that competition is bad for stability (that is, moral hazard with the borrower and fixed costs of bankruptcy). See also Caminal and Matutes (2002) and surveys by Carletti and Hartmann (2002), Bikker and Wesseling (2003) and De Mooij *et al.* (2001).

36. An important issue to assess this is how to define the 'relevant market' (see Geroski and Griffith, Chapter 8, this volume). For many services at the retail and SME level these are local and do not encompass the whole of the EU.

37. On a more theoretical level one could envision large, yet efficient, fully diversified financial institutions competing in many (all) product and geographical markets but facing perfect competition. If this would be possible, distinct value would be created (that is, such institutions face smaller expected dissipative default cost). While some, see Vives (2001), seem to believe in the feasibility of such an industry structure, my view is that that is highly unlikely. Nevertheless, in some activities a global diversified playing field might definitely be feasible for some (for example, a few top-tier investment banks).

38. Boot, Milbourn and Dezelan (2001) emphasize that bank regulation should move in the direction of certification requirements because only then can competitive distortions be mitigated. See also Bhattacharya, Boot and Thakor (1998).

39. As I indicated, it is probably justified to characterize the current state of the banking industry as one with a high degree of strategic uncertainty. In my view, we are in a period of transition; what is unclear is what the exact new steady state will be and when it will be reached. In such a transitory situation stability concerns are paramount and the challenges for prudential regulation are enormous.

40. Observe that traditionally correspondent banks could not enter each other's markets. Interests were therefore more readily aligned.

41. The experience of some Western banks is that top management gets fully distracted by the investment banking activities and spends disproportionably little time on the often more profitable non-investment banking activities.

42. Very recently, ABN AMRO announced that it would put its (limited) insurance operations into a joint venture with Delta Lloyd. It hopes that the alliance will promote a more effective cross-selling of insurance products via its own distribution networks.

Bibliography

Allen, F. (1993): 'Stock markets and resource allocation', in C. Mayer and X. Vives (eds), *Capital Markets and Financia Intermediation*, Cambridge, UK: Cambridge University Press.

Allen, F. and D. Gale (1995): 'A welfare comparison of the German and US financial systems', *European Economic Review* 39, 179–209.

Beitel, P. and D. Schiereck (2001): 'Value creation and the ongoing consolidation of the European banking market', Working paper no. 05/01, Institute for Mergers and Acquisitions, University of Witten/Herdecke.

Berger, A.N. (1997): 'The efficiency effects of bank mergers and acquisition: a preliminary look at the 1990s data', in Y. Amihud and G. Miller (eds) *Bank Mergers and Acquisitions*, Boston: Kluwer Academic Publishers.

Berger, A.N. (2000), 'Efficiency in banking: professional perspectives, in A. Saunders (ed.), *Financial Institutions Management*, New York: McGraw-Hill, pp. 300–301.

Berger, A.N. and D.B. Humphrey (1997): 'Efficiency of financial institutions: international survey and directions for future research', *European Journal of Operational Research* 98, 175–212.

Berger, A.N. and L. Mester (1997): 'Inside the black box: what explains differences in the efficiencies of financial institutions?', *Journal of Banking and Finance* 21, 895–947.

Berger, A.N., A. Saunders, J.M. Scalise and G.F. Udell (1998): 'The effects of bank mergers and acquisitions on small business lending', *Journal of Financial Economics* 50, 187–230.

Berger, A.N., G.A. Hanweck and D. Humphrey (1987): 'Competitive viability in banking: scale, scope and product-mix economies', *Journal of Monetary Economics* 20, 501–20.

Berger, A.N., W.C. Hunter and S.G. Timme (1993): 'The efficiency of financial institutions: a review and preview of research past, present and future', *Journal of Banking and Finance* 17 (special issue on *The Efficiency of Financial Institutions*), 221–49.

Berger, A.N., A.K. Kashyap and J.M. Scalise (1995): 'The transformation of the US banking industry: what a long, strange trip it's been', *Brookings Papers on Economic Activity* 2, 55–218.

Berger, A.N., D.B. Humphrey and L. Pulley (1996): 'Do consumers pay for one-stop banking? Evidence from an alternative revenue function', *Journal of Banking and Finance* 20, 1601–21.

Berger, A.N., R.S. Demsetz and P.E. Strahan (1999), 'The consolidation of the financial services industry: causes, consequences and implications for the future', *Journal of Banking and Finance* 23, 135–94.

Berger, A.N., J.D. Cummins, M.A. Weiss and H. Zi (2000), 'Conglomeration versus strategic focus: evidence from the insurance industry', *Journal of Financial Intermediation* 9, 322–62.

Berger, P.G. and E. Ofek (1995): 'Diversification's effect on firm value', *Journal of Financial Economics* 37, 39–65.

Berglöf, E. and E.L. von Thadden (1994): 'Short-term versus long-term interests: capital structure with multiple investors', *Quarterly Journal of Economics* 109, 1055–84.

Berlin, M. (1996): 'For better and for worse: three lending relationships', *Business Review Federal Reserve Bank of Philadelphia*, December, 3–12.

Berlin, M. (2001): 'We control the vertical: three theories of the firm', *Business Review*, Federal Reserve Bank of Philadelphia, Q3, 13–22.

Berlin, M. and L.J. Mester (1992): 'Debt covenants and renegotiation', *Journal of Financial Intermediation* 2, 95–133.

Berlin. M. and L.J. Mester (1998): 'On the profitability and cost of relationship lending', *Journal of Banking and Finance* 22, 873–98.

Bhattacharaya, S. and G. Chiesa (1995): 'Proprietary information, financial intermediation, and research incentives', *Journal of Financial Intermediation* 4, 328–57.

Bhattacharya, S., A.W.A. Boot and A. Thakor (1998), 'The economics of bank regulation', *Journal of Money, Credit and Banking* 30, 745–70.

Bikker, J.A. and A.A.T. Wesseling (2003), 'Intermediation, integration and industrialization: a survey on banking in Europe', working paper, DNB (Dutch Central Bank).

Bolton, P. and D.S. Scharfstein (1996): 'Optimal debt structure and the number of creditors', *Journal of Political Economy* 104, 1–25.

Boot, A.W.A. (2000): 'Relationship banking: what do we know?', *Journal of Financial Intermediation* 9, 7–25.

Boot, A.W.A. (2003), 'Consolidation and strategic positioning in banking with implications for Europe', in R.E. Litan and R. Herring (eds), *Brooking-Wharton Papers on Financial Services*, pp. 37–84.

Boot, A.W.A. and A.V. Thakor (1997): 'Financial system architecture', *Review of Financial Studies* 10, 693–733.

Boot, A.W.A. and A.V. Thakor (2000): 'Can relationship banking survive competition?', *Journal of Finance* 55, 679–713.

Boot, A.W.A., S.I. Greenbaum and A.V. Thakor (1993): 'Reputation and discretion in financial contracting', *American Economic Review* 83, 1165–83.

Boot, A.W.A., T. Milbourn and S. Dezelan (2001), 'Regulation and the evolution of the financial services industry', in *Challenges for Central Banking*, A.M. Santomero, S. Viotti and A. Vredin (eds), Massachussetts: Kluwer, pp. 39–58.

Boot, A.W.A., T. Milbourn and A.V. Thakor (2002), 'Evolution of organizational scale and scope: does it ever pay to get bigger and less focused?', Working paper, University of Amsterdam.

Boot, A.W.A., A.V. Thakor and G. Udell (1991): 'Credible commitments, contract enforcement problems and banks: intermediation as credibility assurance', *Journal of Banking and Finance* 15, 605–32.

Boyd, J.H. and G. De Nicoló (2003), 'Bank risk and competition revisited', IMF working paper, May.

Boyd, J.H., G. De Nicoló and B.D. Smith (2003), 'Crises in competitive versus monopolistic banking systems', IMF working paper, September.

Boyd, J.H. and M. Gertler (1994): 'Are banks dead, or are the reports greatly exaggerated?', working paper, Federal Reserve Bank of Minneapolis.

Calomiris, C.W. and J. Karceski (1998): 'Is the bank merger wave of the 90's efficient? Lessons from nine case studies', working paper, Columbia University.

Caminal, R. and C. Matutes (2002), 'Market power and banking failures', *International Journal of Industrial Organization* 20, 1341–61.

Canals, J. (1994): *Competitive Strategies in European Banking*, Oxford: Clarendon Press.

Carletti, E. and P. Hartmann (2002), 'Competition and stability: what is special about banking?', working paper, European Central Bank.

Chan, Y., S.I. Greenbaum and A.V. Thakor (1986): 'Information reusability, competition and bank asset quality', *Journal of Banking and Finance* 10, 255–76.

Chemmanur, T.J. and P. Fulghieri (1994): 'Reputation, renegotiation and the choice between bank loans and publicly traded debt', *Review of Financial Studies* 7, 475–506.

Clark, J.A. (1996): 'Economic cost, scale efficiency, and competitive viability in banking', *Journal of Money, Credit and Banking* 28, 342–64.

Comment, R. and G.A. Jarrell (1995): 'Corporate focus and stock returns', *Journal of Financial Economics* 37, 67–87.

Cornett, M.M. and H. Tehranian (1992): 'Changes in corporate performance associated with bank acquisitions', *Journal of Financial Economics* 31, 211–34.

Courtney, H., J. Kirkland and P. Viguerie (1997): 'Strategy under uncertainty', *Harvard Business Review*, November–December, 67–79.

Cruickshank, D. (2000), *Competition in UK Banking: A Report to the Chancellor of the Exchequer*, (339 pages), March.

Cybo-Ottone, A. and M. Murgia (2000): 'Mergers and shareholder wealth in European banking', *Journal of Banking and Finance* 24, 831–59.

Degryse, H. and P. Van Cayseele (2000): 'Relationship lending within a bank-based system: evidence from European small business data', *Journal of Financial Intermediation* 9, 90–109.

Demsetz, R.S., M.R. Saidenberg and P.E. Strahan (1996), 'Banks with something to lose: the disciplinary role of franchise value', *Federal Reserve Bank of New York Economic Policy Review 2*, 1–14.

De Mooij, R., M. Canoy, J. Lemmen, M. van Dijk and J. Weigand (2001), 'Competition and stability in banking', CPB Special Study, Den Haag: CPB, November.

Dennis, S.A. and D.J. Mullineaux (1999): 'Syndicated loans, working paper', University of Kentucky.

Dewatripont, M. and E. Maskin (1995), 'Credit and efficiency in centralized and decentralized economies', *Review of Economic Studies* 62, 541–55.

Dewatripont, M. and J. Tirole (1995): *The Prudential Regulation of Banks*, Cambridge, MA: MIT Press.

Diamond, D. (1984): 'Financial intermediation and delegated monitoring', *Review of Economic Studies* 51, 393–414.

Diamond, D. (1991): 'Monitoring and reputation: the choice between bank loans and directly placed debt', *Journal of Political Economy* 99, 689–721.

Diamond, D. (1993): 'Seniority and maturity of debt contracts', *Journal of Financial Economics* 33, 341–68.

Diamond, D. and R. Rajan, (2001), 'Liquidity risk, liquidity creation and financial fragility: a theory of banking', *Journal of Political Economy* 109, 287–327.

Ferrier, G., S. Grosskopf, K. Hayes and S. Yaisawarng (1993): 'Economies of diversification in the banking industry: a frontier approach', *Journal of Monetary Economics* 31, 229–49.

Flannery, M. (1999): 'Comment on Milbourn, Boot and Thakor', *Journal of Banking and Finance* 23, 215–20.

Focarelli, D., F. Panetta and C. Salleo (2002): 'Why do banks merge?', *Journal of Money, Credit and Banking* 34, 1047–66.

FSA (2000), *Response by the Financial Services Authority to the Cruickshank Report on Competition in UK Banking*, (32 pages), July.

Gorton, G. and J. Kahn (1993): 'The design of bank loan contracts, collateral, and renegotiation', NBER working paper 4273.

Gorton, G. and G. Pennacchi (1995): 'Banks and loan sales: marketing nonmarketable assets', *Journal of Monetary Economics* 35, 389–411.

Greenbaum, S.I. and A.V. Thakor (1995): *Contemporary Financial Intermediation*, New York: Dryden Press.

Grossman, S.J. and O. Hart (1986): 'The costs and benefits of ownership: a theory of vertical and lateral integration', *Journal of Political Economy* 94, 691–719.

Group of Ten (2001), 'Report on consolidation in the financial sector', www.bis.org.

Hamel, G. and C.K. Prahalad (1990): 'The core competence of the corporation', *Harvard Business Review*, May–June, 79–91.

Hellwig, M. (1991): 'Banking, financial intermediation and corporate finance', in A. Giovanni and C. Mayer (eds), *European Financial Integration*, Cambridge, UK: Cambridge University Press.

Hoshi, T., A. Kashyap and D. Scharfstein (1993): 'The role between public and private debt: an analysis of post-deregulation corporate financing in Japan', NBER Working Paper 4421.

Houston, J. and C.M. James (1996): 'Bank information monopolies and the mix of private and public debt choices', *Journal of Finance* 51, 1863–89.

James, C. (1987): 'Some evidence on the uniqueness of bank loans', *Journal of Financial Economics* 19, 217–35.

John, K. and E. Ofek (1995): 'Asset sales and increase in focus', *Journal of Financial Economics* 37, 105–26.

Kashyap, A., R. Rajan and J. Stein (1999): 'Banks as liquidity providers: an explanation for the co-existence of lending and deposit-taking', working paper, University of Chicago.

Keeley, M.C. (1990), 'Deposit insurance, risk and market power in banking', *American Economic Review 80*, 1183–201.

Koskela, E. and R Stenbecka (2000), 'Is there a trade-off between bank competition and financial fragility?', *Journal of Banking and Finance*, 1853–73.

Kroszner, R.S. and R. Rajan (1994): 'Is the Glass–Steagall Act justified? A study of the US experience with universal banking before 1933', *American Economic Review* 84, 810–32.

Long, G.L. (2001): 'Stockholder gains from focusing versus diversifying bank mergers', *Journal of Financial Economies* 59, 221–52.

Lummer, S. and J. McConnell (1989): 'Further evidence on the bank lending process and the reaction of the capital market to bank loan agreements', *Journal of Financial Economics* 25, 99–122.

Mayer, C. (1988): 'New issues in corporate finance', *European Economic Review* 32, 1167–83.

McKinsey & Co. (2002): 'Europe's banks: verging on merging', *McKinsey Quarterly* 3.

Merton, R.C. (1993): 'Operation and regulation in financial intermediation: a functional perspective', in P. Englund (ed.), *Operation and Regulation of Financial Markets*, Stockholm: Economic Council.

Mester, L.J. (1992): 'Traditional and nontraditional banking: an information-theoretic approach', *Journal of Banking and Finance* 16, 545–66.

Mitchell, K. and N.M. Onvural (1996): 'Economies of scale and scope at large commercial banks: evidence from the Fourier flexible functional form', *Journal of Money, Credit and Banking* 28, 178–99.

OECD (1998), *Enhancing the Role of Competition in the Regulation of Banks,* Committee on Competition Law and Policy, (428 pages), September.

Oliver Wyman & Co (2002): 'The future of European corporate & institutional banking', in collaboration with Morgan-Stanley, March.

Ongena S. and D.C. Smith (2000): 'What determines the number of bank relationships? Cross-country evidence', *Journal of Financial Intermediation*, 9, 26–56.

Petersen, M. and R. Rajan (1994): 'The benefits of lending relationships: evidence from small business data', *Journal of Finance* 49, 1367–1400.

Petersen, M. and R. Rajan (1995): 'The effect of credit market competition on lending relationships', *Quarterly Journal of Economics* 110, 407–43.

Pulley, L. and D. Humphrey (1993): 'The role of fixed costs and cost complementarities in determining scope economies and the cost of narrow bank proposals', *Journal of Business* 66, 437–62.

Puri, M. (1996): 'Commercial banks in investment banking: conflict of interest or certification role?', *Journal of Financial Economics* 40, 373–401.

Rajan, R. (1992): 'Insiders and outsiders: the choice between informed and arm's length debt', *Journal of Finance* 47, 1367–1400.

Rajan, R.G. and A. Winton (1995): 'Covenants and collateral as incentives to monitor', *Journal of Finance* 50, 1113–46.

Ramirez, C.D. (2002): 'Did banks' security affiliates add value? evidence from the commercial banking industry during the 1920s', *Journal of Money, Credit and Banking* 34, 391–411.

Riksbank (Central Bank of Sweden) (2000), 'The Banking Law Committee's main and final report', *Economic Review* 3.

Saunders, A. and I. Walter (1994): *Universal Banking in the United States*, Oxford: Oxford University Press.

Saunders, A. and L. Schumacher (2000): 'The determinants of bank interest margins: an international study', *Journal of International Money and Finance* 19, 765–941.

Schmeits, A. (2002): 'Discretion in bank contracts and the firm's funding source choice between bank and financial market financing', working paper, Washington University.

Shaffer, S. and E. David (1991): 'Economies of superscale in commercial banking', *Applied Economics* 23, 283–93.

Sharpe, S. (1990): 'Asymmetric Information, bank lending, and implicit contracts: a stylized model of customer relationships', *Journal of Finance* 45, 1069–87.

Siconolfi, M. (1998): 'Big umbrella: Travelers and Citicorp agree to join forces in $83 billion merger', *Wall Street Journal*, 7 April.

Simon, H.C. (1936): 'Rules versus authorities in monetary policy', *Journal of Political Economy* 44, 1–30.

Slovin, M.B., M.E. Sushka and C.D. Hudson (1988): 'Corporate commercial paper, note issuance facilities, and stakeholder wealth', *Journal of International Money and Finance* 7, 289–302.

Smith, R.C. and I. Walter (1997): *Global Banking*, Oxford: Oxford University Press.

Stone, C.A. and A. Zissu (2000): 'Securitization: the transformation of illiquid financial assets into liquid capital market securities', *Financial Markets, Institutions & Instruments*, New York University, Salomon Center, Boston: Blackwell Publishers.

Vander Vennet, R. (2002): 'Cost and profit efficiency of financial conglomerates and universal banks in Europe', *Journal of Money, Credit and Banking* 34, 254–82.

Vives, X. (2001), 'Competition in the changing world of banking', working paper, INSEAD.

Walter, I. and R. Smith (2000): *High Finance in the Euro-Zone*, London: Financial Times, Prentice-Hall.

6 Political economy of antitrust

Charles Rowley and Anne Rathbone

1 Introduction

The concept of market power is of central importance to any discussion of antitrust economics. In essence, market power exists when a specific firm, or a group of firms acting in combination, has sufficient control over a particular commodity to determine significantly the terms on which other firms, or individual consumers, shall have access to it.

The polar models of perfect competition and pure monopoly provide useful insights into the nature of market power, however unrepresentative these models may seem to be of the real world. For these models provide a level of generality that the intermediate models – monopolistic competition and oligopoly – just cannot match.

Four principal assumptions form the basis for the perfectly competitive model. The first assumption is that each firm is sufficiently small, relative to the total market for the commodity, not to be able to influence price by changes in its own rate of output. The second assumption is that the commodity of any one firm is identical, from the perception of the consumer, to that of any other firm supplying that market. The third assumption implies that all resources are perfectly mobile, implying that firms can move costlessly into and out of markets (perfect contestability) in response to relevant economic signals. The fourth assumption is that both consumers and producers are perfectly informed about the present market situation. The model is motivated by the core behavioral assumption of profit maximization.

If all relevant markets are perfectly competitive, a Pareto optimal solution occurs in which all relevant prices, both in factor and in commodity markets, are equated with marginal cost. In the long run, equilibrium occurs with price equated to the average cost of production for each surviving firm. In such an economy, there is simply no need for antitrust policy to enhance economic efficiency.

The assumptions that define pure monopoly are significantly different. First, in pure monopoly, a single firm alone supplies a clearly defined market as a consequence of increasing returns to scale (natural monopoly), of innovation, and/or of the application of restrictive market strategies.

Second, the commodity supplied may be homogeneous or heterogeneous, depending on the economic opportunities to discriminate among consumers. Third, resources, typically, are relatively immobile, impeded by natural and unnatural barriers both to entry into and to exit from the market (non-contestability). Fourth, consumers are assumed to be less well informed than the producer with respect to current market conditions (asymmetric information). Fifth, profit maximization governs the behavior of the pure monopolist.

Where pure monopoly exists, the necessary conditions for Pareto optimality do not hold. Long-run equilibrium occurs with marginal cost equated with marginal revenue (and less than price), with average cost equal to or less than average revenue, and with output less and price higher than required for economic efficiency. Such circumstances, superficially, appear to support an activist antitrust policy, though, as we shall demonstrate in this chapter, the case is by no means clear-cut, even by reference to the criteria of neoclassical welfare economics and, most especially, from the perspective of public choice.

2   The perspective of neoclassical welfare economics
Neoclassical welfare economists assess the efficacy of antitrust policy from the perspective of welfare maximization, where economic efficiency is the posited criterion of the public interest (Rowley, 1973). Because the Pareto criterion offers only a quasi-social ordering, as a consequence both of the ordinal nature of utility and of the prohibition on making internal personal utility comparisons, neoclassical economists rely instead on the more expansive Kaldor–Hicks–Scitovsky potential compensation test to determine whether or not a policy change is or is not welfare-improving.

The potential compensation test suppresses the Pareto restriction on making interpersonal utility comparisons, relies on money income as a cardinal surrogate for ordinal utility and treats the distributional consequences of any change in resource allocation as irrelevant or ethically neutral. The outcome is a social welfare function that typically takes the form:

$$\text{Maximize } W = TR + S - (TC - R), \qquad (6.1)$$

where W = net economic benefit, TR = total revenue, S = consumers' surplus, TC = total cost and R = inframarginal rent.

Economists who deploy this social welfare function rely, more or less implicitly, on three important postulates (Harberger, 1971):

1. The competitive demand price for a given unit measures the value of that unit to the demander.
2. The competitive supply price for a given unit measures the value of that unit to the supplier.
3. When evaluating the net benefits of a given action, the costs and benefits accruing to each member should normally be added without regard to the particular individuals to whom they accrue.

2.1 The basic Harberger model

The tradition of analyzing the welfare implications of market power, in terms of the concept of economic surplus defined in (1) above, is quite lengthy, encompassing Dupuit (1844) and Alfred Marshall (1890). This method was first deployed formally by Arnold Harberger in 1954 as a method of quantifying the social cost of monopoly in the United States. In terms of the social welfare defined above, Harberger (1954) established a (relatively small) case in favor of antitrust policy, in terms of the deadweight cost of consumers' surplus, initially referred to as the Marshallian deadweight loss triangle, but subsequently characterized as the Harberger triangle. Figure 6.1 illustrates this outcome.

In Figure 6.1, AC represents constant per unit and marginal costs, presumed to be identical both for the single-firm monopolist and (in aggregate) for the competitive industry. DD' represents the demand curve for the output both of the monopolist and of the competitive industry. The equilibrium output rate for the monopolist is OQ_m, where marginal cost equals marginal revenue. The equilibrium output rate for the competitive industry is OQ_c, where marginal cost equals price.

The loss of consumers' surplus attributable to monopoly is measured (approximately) by the area $P_m ACP_c$, against which must be offset the producer's surplus, measured approximately by the area $ABP_c P_m$. This leaves a net loss of surplus that can be measured (approximately) by the area of the Harberger triangle, ABC, that constitutes the deadweight loss attributable to monopoly under the conditions posited by Figure 6.1.

Assuming that the point elasticity of demand for each industry's product was unity throughout the relevant output range, Harberger (1954) estimated the magnitude of the annual net welfare losses from monopoly in manufacturing industries for the United States in the mid-1920s. He calculated that this loss was positive, but trivial, amounting to little more than one-tenth of one per cent of US gross domestic product.

Statistics for the 1920s admittedly are very sketchy by modern standards, and Harberger's assumptions of constant costs and unit demand elasticity are open to question. Nevertheless, a variety of later studies, calculating the welfare loss to monopoly and tariffs across a range of countries on the

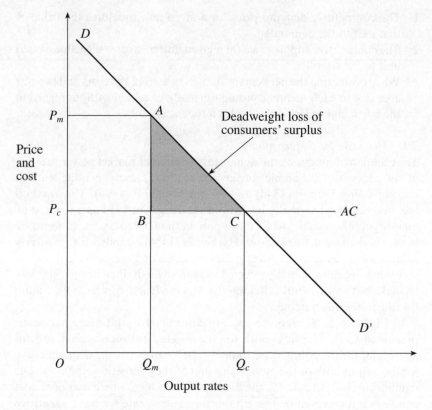

Figure 6.1   The deadweight loss from monopoly

basis of the Harberger model, all came up with relatively trivial magnitudes (for example, Schwartzman, 1960).

   This is not at all surprising. Following Leibenstein (1966), let us play around with some numbers. Suppose that 50 per cent of a country's national output is produced in monopolized industries, that the price differential is 20 per cent, and that the average demand elasticity is 1.5. In such circumstances, the welfare loss to monopoly turns out to be only 1.5 per cent of total product. Yet these still relatively small welfare losses are based on enormous numbers by comparison with the reality of any advanced economy.

2.2   Scale economies and the Williamson trade-off model
Economists have long recognized that the constant cost assumptions of perfect competition are not always reflected in the real world. In particular, economists suspected, long before formal cost studies became available, that increasing returns to scale might be a major stimulus to monopoly.

The profession had to wait until 1968, however, for the development of a formal model incorporating scale economies into the neoclassical analysis of the case for and against antitrust policy (Williamson, 1968a).

Williamson focused attention exclusively on mergers that simultaneously provide cost savings though the exploitation of scale economies and price increases through monopolization. He could easily have generalized his analysis, however, to cases where firms achieve monopoly power through internal expansion or through collusion. Williamson (1968a) demonstrated that taking account of scale economies renders the efficiency case for antitrust policy ambiguous, and requires a trade-off analysis between the gains from cost savings and the loss of consumers' surplus. Figure 6.2 illustrates this outcome.

Figure 6.2 depicts the case of a proposed merger that would introduce market power into a previously competitive market. In the pre-merger market, firms produce an identical and constant average and marginal cost

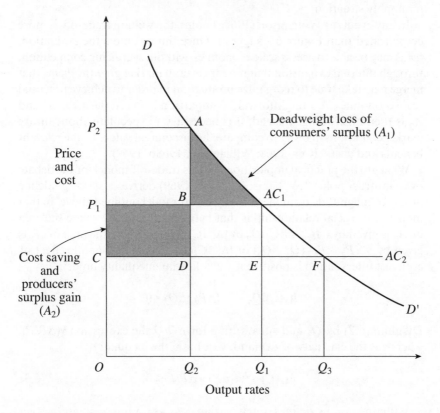

Figure 6.2   Economics of scale and antitrust welfare trade-off

curves, represented in aggregate by AC_1. The competitive output rate is OQ_1, at competitive price, OP_1. By contrast, the post-merger monopolist produces on a lower, and constant, short-run average and marginal cost curve, depicted by AC_2. The monopoly output rate is OQ_2, at price OP_2.

In such circumstances, economic efficiency depends on a trade-off between the loss of consumers' surplus indicated by the triangle $ABAC_1$ (the shaded area A_1 in Figure 6.2) and the cost-savings achieved by the firm, indicated by the rectangle P_1BDC (the shaded area A_2). In naïve terms, only if A_1 exceeds A_2 is there a case for antitrust intervention.

Suppose that $A_2 > A_1$ and that the merger is allowed. The necessary conditions for a welfare optimum are not satisfied, since potential consumers' surplus, depicted by the triangle ADF, is sacrificed. Neverthless, there is a net social benefit achieved by comparison with any feasible competitive solution. The trapezoid, P_1CFAC_1 is simply unavailable to a competitive industry, as is output rate OQ_3, where marginal cost equals price in the monopoly situation.

In any event, as Williamson (1968a) notes, the welfare trade-off is more complicated than Figure 6.2 suggests. Once timing enters the evaluation, firms may be able to access scale economies, without sacrificing competition, through internal expansion that mirrors overall market growth. Firms that merge may take time to reorganize production in order to achieve potential scale economies. A straightforward comparison between the areas A_1 and A_2 is then misleading. Instead, it is necessary to speculate about future market conditions in order to compare the discounted values of the relevant benefits and costs (Ross, 1968; Williamson, 1968b, 1969).

What are the practical implications of this trade-off model for the debate over antitrust policy? Williamson (1968b, 1969) derives a set of guideline orders of magnitude from the naïve trade-off model outlined above. In that model, the crucial relationship is that between A_2 and A_1, where the area of A_2 is given by $(AC_2 - AC_1)Q_2$ or $[\Delta(AC)Q_2]$ and where the area of A_1 is given by $1/2(P_2 - P_1)(Q_1 - Q_2)$ or $[\Delta(AC)Q_2]$. The net economic effect of antitrust intervention is positive if the following inequality holds:

$$[(AC)]Q_2 - 1/2(\Delta P)(\Delta Q) < 0. \qquad (6.2)$$

Dividing (6.2) by Q_2 and substituting for $\Delta Q/Q$ the expression $\gamma(\Delta P/P)$, where γ is the elasticity of demand, we obtain the inequality:

$$\Delta(AC) - 1/2(\Delta P)\, \gamma\, \Delta P/P < 0. \qquad (6.3)$$

Williamson now defines a new variable, k, as an index of pre-merger market power. This variable takes on values equal to, or greater than, unity with a value of unity indicating a fully competitive market. The pre-merger price is equal to $k(AC_1)$. Where $k = 1$, we divide (6.3) by $P_1 = k(AC_1)$ to obtain:

$$\Delta(AC)/AC - k/2\,\gamma\,(\Delta P/P)^2 < 0 \qquad (6.4)$$

Williamson suggests that, typically, pre-merger values of k will lie in the neighborhood of 1, although values as high as 1.05 would occasionally be encountered. On this basis, he calculated the percentage savings in cost, through scale economies, sufficient to offset a range of percentage price increases for a selected range of demand elasticities. Table 6.1 outlines some relevant orders of magnitude.

Table 6.1   Percentage cost reductions required to offset percentage price increases

$\Delta P/P_1$ x 100	$\gamma=2$		$\gamma=1$		$\gamma=1.05$	
	$k=1$	$k=1.05$	$k=1$	$k=1.05$	$k=1$	$k=1.05$
5	0.26	0.78	0.12	0.38	0.06	0.19
10	1.05	2.15	0.50	1.03	0.24	0.50
20	4.40	6.82	2.00	3.10	0.95	1.45
30	10.35	14.28	4.50	6.21	2.10	2.90

Source: Williamson (1969, p. 975, adapted).

Table 6.1 clearly indicates that the efficiency effects of even relatively small cost savings overwhelm the negative efficiency effects of significant price hikes in markets characterized by economies of scale. Williamson's model appears to turn the tables decisively against any presumption in favor of antitrust intervention in modern capitalist economies. However, the neoclassical story has not yet ended, as we shall proceed to indicate.

2.3   The relevance of X-inefficiency

Textbook economic theory, until the mid-1960s, for the most part assumed that firms combine factor inputs efficiently, and thereby minimize production and distribution costs for any selected rate of output. This assumption seems to follow quite naturally, even in non-contestable monopolistic markets, from the basic postulate that firms seek to maximize profit. It holds by implication in competitive markets where each firm's survivorship depends on efficiency in production.

In 1966, Harvey Leibenstein challenged the generality of this assumption with respect to non-competitive markets. He suggested that in imperfectly competitive markets production costs would tend in practice to be higher than the minimum level that efficient production could achieve, largely because management and workers would substitute their own objectives (a desire for the quiet life) for those of the equity interests (profit maximization). Leibenstein defined the gap between the actually obtained and the minimum attainable production costs as *X-inefficiency*.

Although Leibenstein (1966) asserted that a positive relationship exists between the degree of market power and the extent of X-inefficiency, he failed to formalize the nature of this relationship. In 1971, Crew, Rowley and Jones-Lee developed an X-theory of the firm, within the general framework of Leibenstein's contribution, in order to explain the co-existence of X-inefficiency and profit maximization in imperfectly competitive markets. A brief review of this theory is helpful prior to a discussion of the welfare economics implications of X-inefficiency for antitrust policy.

Crew *et al.* (1971) retain profit maximization as the central objective in the X-theory of the firm on the supposition that this is the motive of the equity shareholders in whom the property rights are vested. However, the separation between ownership and control in the large corporation predictably gives rise to a clash between those who own the equity and those employed within the organization (management as well as shopfloor labor) whose utility functions do not coincide with those of the owners, but encompass such arguments as a desire for leisure in the workplace and other non-profit-related accoutrements of office

Under competitive conditions, the threat of bankruptcy pressures management and labor, however reluctantly, into full cooperation with the profit maximization objective. This does not imply necessarily that competition is capable of improving the quality of low-grade personnel. However, it does imply that personnel of whatever quality will work as effectively as possible.

Once competitive forces weaken, however, the scope for management and labor non-cooperation increases, and X-inefficiency will result in the absence of active policing. Management itself is somewhat motivated to police shopfloor labor in order to maximize the discretion available to itself. It may do so by the use of monetary incentives such as piece-rate systems and annual bonuses, or by resort to control devices, such as work study experts, foremen, gatekeepers, watchmen and timekeepers. Equity interests may also attempt to police management by such monetary incentives as stock option schemes and profit-related bonuses, or by such control devices as management consultant exercises and budgetary control systems. To the extent that it is not prevented from doing so by regulations, the stock market will also police X-inefficiency through the threat of takeover acquisitions of poorly performing by better performing corporations.

Policing measures such as those outlined above absorb economic resources. The cost of such resources is incorporated into the cost functions of firms operating in imperfectly competitive markets. Moreover, policing outlays rationally will be expended only to the point where marginal policing costs equal the marginal cost savings due to policing. In such circumstances, residual X-inefficiency is predictable, and will also be incorporated into the cost functions of such firms. Thus the cost functions of profit-maximizing firms predictably will be higher, *ceteris paribus*, for firms operating under conditions of monopoly than for those operating under conditions of competition.

Let us now complicate the Williamson trade-off model by assuming that the cost curves of a monopolist are lowered, by scale economies, but elevated by the presence of policing costs and residual X-inefficiency. Figure 6.3 (Comanor and Leibenstein, 1969; Crew and Rowley, 1971) illustrates two

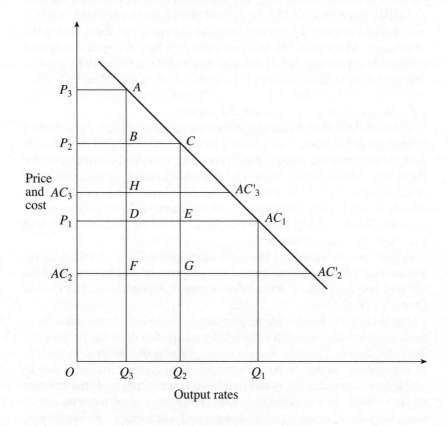

Figure 6.3   The welfare implications of X-inefficiency

alternative outcomes, (1) where scale economies dominate cost elevations and (2) where the reverse applies.

In Figure 6.3, the competitive industry is assumed to produce at constant average (and marginal) cost on the cost curve AC_1, and to operate at output rate OQ_1 and at price OP_1. The single firm monopoly, by contrast, is assumed to benefit from scale economies but to suffer from cost elevation. On the one hand, where X-inefficiency and its policing do not swallow up all available economies, the firm produces on the cost curve AC_2 ($<AC_1$) and operates at output rate OQ_2 and price OP_2. The relevant efficiency trade-off is that between the area of cost savings, P_1EGAC_2 and the area of the Harberger triangle, $CEAC_1$.

On the other hand, where X-inefficiency and policing costs exceed the magnitude of potential scale economies, the monopolist produces on the cost curve AC_3 ($>AC_1$), operating at output rate OQ_3 and at price OP_3. No trade-off is then required, since the additional cost, measured by the area AC_3HDP_1 must be added to the area of the Harberger triangle, $ADAC_1$, in order to compute the welfare loss due to monopoly. Even within the companies themselves, the computations involved are speculative and complex. From outside, they constitute a major obstacle to the adoption of an efficient policy towards monopoly (see also Cowling and Mueller, 1978).

2.4   The significance of invention and innovation

Invention is defined as the process whereby conventional inputs and general knowledge are combined to produce technical knowledge. Innovation is defined as the process through which invention is applied commercially for the first time (Nordhaus, 1969). The close relationship between these two processes does not imply necessarily that neoclassical economics should treat them jointly from the perspective of framing an efficient policy towards antitrust (Rowley, 1973). However, in the forthcoming discussion, we shall treat them in a unified manner.

Let us start by analyzing the most appropriate form of organization for successful invention and innovation in terms of an important debate between two neoclassical economists, Kenneth Arrow (1962) and Harold Demsetz (1969).

Arrow (1962) examines the relative incentives to invent and innovate in monopolistic and competitive markets by comparing potential profit. In so doing, he centers attention on an inherent property of information, namely its indivisibility in use. In Arrow's model, a competitive market is one in which the market affected by an invention is competitive, while the inventor sets the royalty for use of his invention. The monopoly situation is one in which only the monopolist itself invents, and where entry barriers prevent invasion by other would-be inventors. On this basis, Arrow (1962) centers attention on cost-reducing inventions and develops two hypotheses, (1) that competitive markets provide a less than efficient incentive to invent and (2) that the incentive to invent is less under monopoly than under competition. Figure 6.4 explains why these outcomes are predictable.

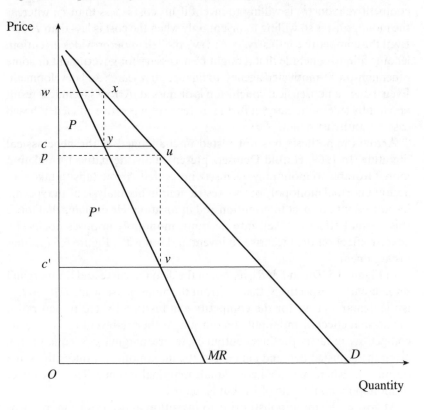

Figure 6.4   Arrow's model of the incentive to invent

In Figure 6.4, unit costs are constant at *c* before and at *c'* after the invention, with *c'* < *c*. The competitive price before the invention is also *c*. The inventor sets the per unit royalty at *r* to maximize the size of the rectangle *c'puv*, designated by Arrow as *P'*. The potential investor will invest in invention as long as the cost of invention is less than *P'*. If he does so, the market price for the competitive industry falls from *c* to *p*.

By contrast, the monopolist, before the invention, would set price at *w* to maintain the rate of output at which *c* (marginal cost) equals marginal revenue. Profit is given by the size of the rectangle *cwxy*, designated by Arrow as *P*. Following the invention, unit costs would fall from *c* to *c'*, and the new profit-maximizing price would fall to p, yielding a new profit rectangle of P' as defined above.

On this basis, Arrow concludes that the incentive to invent is lower under monopoly than under competition since the inventor selling to a competitive industry is willing to invent if his cost is less than P', whereas the monopolist is so willing to invent only when the cost is less than $P' - P$. Even the competitive industry, in Arrow's model, underprovides invention, leading him to conclude that it might be necessary for government or some other non-profit-motivated agency, to finance all research and development. Even if such a nonsensical conclusion is dismissed, Arrow's technical result apparently stacks the case yet further in favor of a positive efficiency-based case for antitrust policy.

Arrow's hypothesis has not rested unchallenged in the neoclassical literature. In 1969, Harold Demsetz presented an alternative formulation more favorable to monopoly. Demsetz notes that Arrow fails to take into account normal monopoly output restrictions in his analysis of the specific incentives with respect to invention and innovation. He explains that, once this normal effect is taken into account, monopoly imposes no *special* adverse effect on the incentive to invent and innovate. Figure 6.5 outlines his argument.

In Figure 6.5, D_m and MR_m represent the demand curve and the marginal revenue curve, respectively, that confront the monopolist, while $D_c (=MR_m)$ is the demand curve for the competitive industry adjusted to neutralize the normal effect of monopoly on output. At the pre-invention cost c, the competitive industry produces output cu, where marginal cost equals price, given the adjusted demand curve, and the monopolist produces the same output, cu, where marginal cost equals marginal revenue. Thus the effect of monopoly on the rate of output is removed.

At cost c, the monopolist, prior to invention and innovation, receives profit $P = cptu$. Following invention and innovation, the monopoly profit is $P'' - c'p'yx$. Thus the incentive for monopoly invention and innovation is $P'' - P$. The best that the inventor can do, if he sells his invention to an equal size competitive industry, is to charge a royalty equal to $p' - c'$, causing the industry to produce at the rate of output $p'v$, thereby maximizing the inventor's royalty at $c'p'vw$. The question at issue is whether the incentive to invention offered by the competitive industry, $c'p'vw (=P')$ is greater or smaller than $P'' - P$.

In Figure 6.5, $P'' - P$ is clearly greater than P, suggesting that the monopolist has a greater incentive to invent and innovate, once its normal output restriction is ignored. On this basis, Demsetz concludes that, where patent protection exists, antitrust in the product market should be pursued less

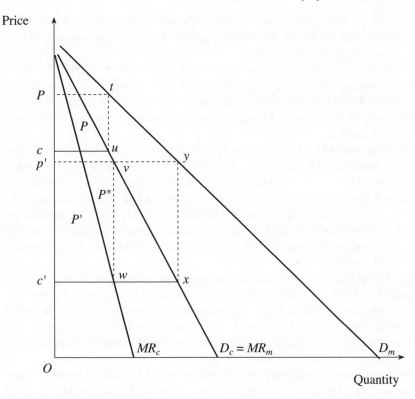

Figure 6.5   Demsetz's model of the inventive to invent

diligently than considerations of output restriction alone would suggest, in order to take account of the differential incentive to invent and innovate.

Neoclassical economics raises other important issues that are not addressed by this specific debate. It is argued that specific peculiarities in the information market, namely lumpiness of inventive inputs and the low degree of appropriability of knowledge, threaten failure in the market for invention and innovation.

Lumpiness in the process of invention and innovation occurs because knowledge is expensive to produce but cheap to reproduce. In this sense, marginal cost is low relative to average cost. Lumpiness is not entirely analogous to the case of increasing returns, but rather reflects a strong asymmetry between the original discoverers and the subsequent rediscoverers of knowledge. This asymmetry may favor quasi-monopoly over competition as a means to overcome potential market failure and to ensure that appropriate incentives exist for the market in invention and innovation to operate efficiently.

The second (and closely related) feature of the market in invention and innovation is the problem of spillovers or of non-appropriability, characterized by the inability of first-movers to capture the full fruits of their successes. In such circumstances, a policy tension exists between, on the one hand, protecting first-movers from fast-seconds in order to preserve incentives and, on the other hand, encouraging solutions that allow fast-seconds to lower prices in response to low marginal costs of information dissemination.

Economists like Arrow (1962) allow such potential problems to strengthen their support for a government monopoly over all research and investment. We infer that such scholars allow a pathological dislike of capitalism to cloud their judgments. A regulated private market solution, far superior on efficiency grounds to that of socialism, is readily available, in the form of patent legislation that strikes a balance between supporting the first-mover's quasi-monopoly with the longer-term erosion of his quasi-rents as the patent expires.

The evidence is still out on the question whether monopoly retards invention and innovation. Therefore, in principle, it is appropriate to adopt a neutral or, at worst, only a slightly adverse position on this issue. In any event, the impact of monopoly on technical progress (be it positive or negative) can readily be incorporated into the Williamson-type trade-off model outlined above. Following Williamson (1968a), let us illustrate with the case where monopoly is expected to retard technical progress. Let us denote by θ the ratio of immediate post-merger to pre-merger average costs, by g_1 the rate of productivity increase in the absence of the merger, by g_2 the rate should the merger be approved, by $Q(t)$ output in period t and by r the social rate of discount. In such circumstances, the loss of technical progress would just offset scale economies when the following equality holds:

$$\int_0^\infty \left[(AC)Q(t)e^{-g_1 t} \right] e^{-rt} dt = \int_0^\infty \left[(AC)Q(t)e^{g_2 t} \right] e^{-rt} dt \tag{6.5}$$

Assuming that output increases exponentially at the rate α, the critical value of g_2 is given by:

$$g_2 = \theta g_1 - (1 - \theta)(r - \alpha). \tag{6.6}$$

2.5   Overall implications for antitrust policy

Evidently, economists cannot confidently rely on deadweight cost arguments to justify on efficiency grounds a per se policy of antitrust intervention such as that initially advanced in the United States 1890 Sherman Act. In principle, it is clear that a very detailed case-by-case study is required to determine whether specific instances of monopoly, whether induced by conspiracy, by merger or by internal expansion, are justified in terms of economic criteria. Of course, economists may argue that the transaction costs of investigation outweigh any benefits that may arise from the case-by-case approach. In such latter circumstances, we would suggest that, even in terms of welfare economics alone, the presumption should be in favor of the unregulated market process, justified in terms of the Hippocratic oath: '*first, avoid doing harm*': Jasay, 1996). This presumption becomes much more pronounced, as we shall demonstrate, once public choice influences are taken into account. Yet leading scholars from the University of Chicago, widely (though perhaps mistakenly) regarded as a leading pro-market school of economics worldwide, reverse this presumption specifically and exclusively when dealing with antitrust policy.

3 The University of Chicago perspective on antitrust policy

Antitrust is clearly a form of economic regulation, with non-trivial, and arguably harmful, implications for the allocation of resources in any predominantly market economy. Chicago political economy, starting with the seminal 1971 paper by George Stigler, and supplemented by the 1976 paper by Sam Peltzman and the 1983 paper by Gary Becker, provides a powerful positive analysis of regulation – the economic theory of regulation – that underpins a normative view that regulation is generally economically inefficient.

For several decades, a number of economists known collectively as 'the Chicago School' have defined the intellectual agenda of antitrust (McChesney, 1991, p.775). Among the best known are Aaron Director, George Stigler, Richard Posner, Robert Bork, Yale Brozen, Harold Demsetz and Frank Easterbrook. Together they have led an extremely successful revolution in antitrust, focusing attention on the efficiency or otherwise of antitrust legislation and of court antitrust decisions.

One might expect that Chicagoans, so well-versed in the economic theory of regulation, would exhibit an equally skeptical and even adverse stance regarding the efficacy of antitrust policy. This expectation is incorrect (McChesney, 1991). Chicago economists, almost without exception, view antitrust as a desirable public interest intervention designed to correct market failures implicit in monopoly. Perhaps George Stigler (1982) best summarizes the Chicago position regarding antitrust policy:

> If you propose an antitrust law, the only people who should be opposed to it are those who hope to become monopolists, and that's a very small set of any society. So it is a sort of public-interest law in the same sense in which I think

having private property, enforcement of contracts, and suppression of crime are public-interest phenomena.

Stigler is not at all alone in this Polyannish view of antitrust policy. Let us briefly review the Chicago high command, starting with the most puzzling case of all, Richard (now Judge) Posner. Posner has made significant contributions to the economic theory of regulation, a theory that explains regulation as being driven by well-organized interest groups and their political representatives, and not by government officials who act altruistically to protect the public at large from market failures (see especially Posner, 1975, and Landes and Posner, 1975).

Throughout several editions of his textbook, *Economic Analysis of Law*, Posner has never deviated from his fundamental hypothesis that the common law is economically efficient, whereas the statutory law is not. Yet Posner explicitly excludes the antitrust statutes from this criticism. His widely cited 1976 book, *Antitrust Law: An Economic Perspective*, unequivocally endorses antitrust intervention as socially beneficial:

> economic theory provides a firm basis for the belief that monopoly pricing, which results when firms create an artificial scarcity of their product and thereby drive above its price under competition, is inefficient. Since efficiency is an important, although not the only social value, this conclusion establishes a prima facie cased for having an antitrust policy. (Posner, 1976, p. 4)

Posner fully recognizes that antitrust policy, as it has developed in the United States, is poorly suited to promoting competition and economic efficiency. This evident failure, however, does not lead Posner to question the fundamental case for antitrust policy. Rather, he optimistically concludes that 'The endeavor has failed; the system is in disarray. The time has come to rethink antitrust with the aid of economics' (ibid., p. 236).

In 1978, in his widely regarded book, *The Antitrust Paradox: A Policy at War with Itself*, Robert (sometime Judge) Bork also strongly supports antitrust policy, specifically in terms of its potential contribution to consumer welfare. Bork takes the reader carefully and accurately through the myriad ways in which the evolution of antitrust law has deviated from its original promise to protect consumers. He recognizes that political influences have played an important role in this deviance. Yet, ultimately, he remains wedded to the notion that the promulgation of sound economic arguments will return antitrust to its original role (as he views that role):

> This book attempts to supply the theory necessary to guide antitrust reform. Such an attempt assumes that reasonable certainty concerning basis issues is possible. I believe that it is. Basic microeconomic theory is of course a science, though like

many other sciences it is by no means complete in all its branches. Were it not a science, rational antitrust policy would be impossible. (Bork, 1978, p. 8)

More recent Chicago scholarship, also ignoring the public choice revolution, continues to advocate antitrust policy in public interest terms. For example, Frank (now Judge) Easterbrook claims that 'The goal of antitrust is to perfect the operation of competitive markets' (Easterbrook, 1984, p. 1). Likewise, Harold Demsetz expresses the hope that 'our antitrust laws can be marshaled to attack government-sponsored protectionism' (Demsetz, 1989, p. 27).

Every one of these Chicago scholars explicitly recognizes that antitrust in the United States has failed to achieve its public interest goals. Each explains away observed inefficiencies in terms of mistaken theories that (hopefully) will be corrected (McChesney, 1991, p. 783). In so doing, each promulgates a theory of antitrust policy predicated on error, an intellectual approach that Stigler himself castigates elsewhere as 'profoundly anti-intellectual' (Stigler, 1982, p. 10). Indeed, in an earlier attack on the public interest theory of regulation, Stigler hints at a devastating truth that he is evidently prepared to ignore when dealing with antitrust:

> Policies may of course be adopted in error, and error is an inherent trait of the behavior of men. But errors are not what men live by or on. If an economic policy has been adopted by many communities, or if it is persistently pursued by a society over a long span of time, it is fruitful to assume that the real effects were known and desired. Indeed, an explanation of a policy in terms of error or confusion is no explanation at all – anything and everything is compatible with that 'explanation'. (Stigler, 1975, p. 140)

We now turn to an approach that is fully capable of explaining the evolution of antitrust policy, both in the United States and elsewhere, an approach that Stigler and other Chicagoans are eager to embrace with respect to economic regulation but that they inexplicably reject when dealing with antitrust policy. The approach is that subfield of public choice characterized as the theory of interest group politics.

4 The perspective of the theory of interest group politics

The interest group theory of government rests on two basic premises (Shughart, 1990, p. 37). The first premise is that the same behavioral model used to explain decision making in ordinary markets also applies to decision making in the public sector. Public policymakers are not benevolent maximizers of social welfare. Instead, their own interests motivate them. Firms seek to maximize profits, and consumers seek to maximize utility; interest groups seek to maximize the returns to their members, policymakers seek to maximize political support, bureaucrats seek to maximize the size or the rate of growth of their discretionary budgets, and judges seek to maximize the size of legislative appropriations relevant to their remuneration and to their office staffing and other valued perquisites of office (Rowley, 2003).

The second premise of the interest group theory is that, while policy errors are possible, it is not at all helpful to rely on error or ignorance as a basis for explaining policy outcomes. In particular, when a policy has persisted over an extended period, it must be assumed that the intended effects of that policy can be deduced from the actual effects. In this sense, the interest group theory of government is a positive theory, an application of well-honed tools of positive economic science to the analysis of political choices.

The interest group theory of government does not ignore the potential for the political process to contribute to the wealth of a nation. However, its primary focus is on the potential for the political process to serve as a vehicle for facilitating wealth transfers (Shughart, 1990, p. 37; Rowley, 2003). In this regard, the principal distinction between the market for private goods and the market for wealth transfers consists of differences in the constraints that confront self-interested actors. Outcomes differ in political markets from outcomes in private markets because the institutions through which individuals pursue their own gain in the two markets differ.

The interest group model applies to any situation in which one group of individuals is able to mobilize the monopoly power of the state to transfer wealth from other groups or individuals. Suppose (following Shughart, 1990, pp. 38–9) that we are able to order the n individuals in the economy into all possible coalitions, running from n coalitions of size 1 to one coalition of size n. There are $2^n - 1$ such possible groups. We then rank these possible coalitions in descending order, in terms of their demand for wealth transfers of \$1. Each group determines its bid price by netting out from one dollar its costs of organization (including overcoming the free-rider problem identified in 1965 by Mancur Olson). Proceeding in this manner identifies the downward-sloping demand curve for wealth transfers, D, outlined in Figure 6.6.

In Figure 6.6, groups located closer to the origin have lower costs, and hence, higher net demand prices for transfers. At the point where D crosses the horizontal axis, the relevant coalition has a net demand price of zero. Beyond that point, groups have a negative net demand for transfers. The net supply curve for transfers is the mirror image of D, determined by netting out from one dollar each group's costs of collective action. Groups located near the origin consist of coalitions least resistant to expropriation. The upward-sloping curve, $S-f$, where f represents the fee extracted by political brokers, depicts the supply curve for wealth transfers.

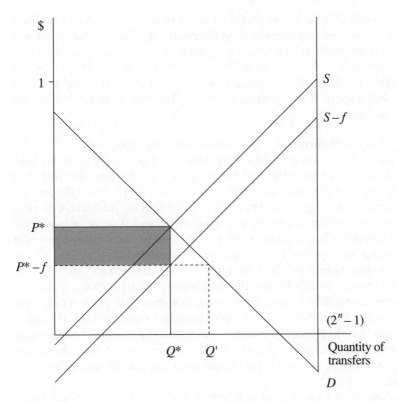

Source: Adapted from Robert E. McCormick and Robert D. Tollison, *Politicians, Legislation, and the Economy: An Inquiry into the Interest-Group Theory of Government* (Boston: Martinus Nijhoff, 1981), p. 20.

Figure 6.6   The demand for and supply of wealth transfers

The role of political representatives is to identify the characteristics of this figure in order to broker wealth transfers from suppliers to demanders. The market-clearing price is P^* and the market-clearing quantity of transfers is Q^*. Groups with demand prices below P^*, but above $P^* - f$, are unaffected by the wealth transfer process because the cost of transacting makes it uneconomic to segment these coalitions into demanders and suppliers.

The process of transferring wealth through the political process is not costless. Resources equal to the area of the shaded rectangle in Figure 6.6 are wasted in clearing the market. There are no offsetting gains since such activities do not create new wealth. In general, small cohesive groups tend to enjoy a comparative advantage in seeking transfers, both because each member has a larger financial stake in the outcome and because organization costs are relatively low. Successful politicians therefore broker wealth transfers from large dispersed groups in favor of small concentrated groups, much in the same manner as depicted by Stigler (1971) and by Peltzman (1976) in the economic theory of regulation. It is important to note that 'supply' in this context denotes 'willingness to be coerced' rather than 'willingness to pay'.

4.1   Testable implications for the enactment of antitrust laws

Neoclassical welfare economics predicts that a country's antitrust laws are enacted by a benevolent and public-spirited government that responds to the legitimate concerns of the consuming public about the loss of consumers' surplus generated by price-gouging (pricing products or services unreasonably high in the presence of unusual demand, disaster, or monopoly status), by X-inefficiency and by delayed innovations on the part of powerful trusts and monopolies. Despite the public choice revolution, this view is still dominant in the political economy of antitrust.

The interest group theory of government predicts that a country's antitrust laws will be a brokered response to lobbying on the part of groups that pursue the self-interest of their respective memberships. It further suggests that the legislative outcome will tend to favor small, concentrated groups at the expense of more dispersed, larger groups of individuals who confront significant free-rider obstacles to organizing themselves into effective lobbies.

Section 5 of this chapter will briefly review available United States evidence on the forces that led to the enactment of key antitrust statutes in an attempt to determine which of these alternative hypotheses is the more convincing.

4.2   Testable implications for the enforcement of antitrust laws

Neoclassical welfare economics predicts that the antitrust authorities will focus attention on reining in the power and/or the activities of firms whose monopoly power inflicts the largest burden on the economy as measured in terms of the aggregate loss of consumers' and producers' surplus over cost. In this perspective, antitrust suits should be brought primarily against existing monopolists, potential mergers and existing price conspiracies that operate in markets with exceptionally low demand elasticity, whose price–cost margins are exceptionally high, whose production costs appear to reflect significant X-inefficiency, and whose record of invention and innovation appears to be below average for the economy as a whole. Evidence that such characteristics are supported by business practices unavailable to firms operating under conditions of competition should further attract antitrust investigation into such companies. Confronted with evidence of significant scale economies, the antitrust authorities should significantly loosen their vigilance with respect both to single firm monopolies and to mergers likely to give rise to market power.

The interest group theory of government predicts that the antitrust laws will be deployed only incidentally in response to evidence of efficiency losses. Instead, they will be deployed in response to political pressures and by media attention induced by lobbying on the part of firms whose livelihood is threatened by the superior cost efficiency, marketing expertise and innovative skills of their larger competitors. In particular, the direction of the antitrust authorities will be governed by lobbying outlays on the part of companies whose stock market performance is significantly below average and will be directed against companies whose stock market performance is well above average and whose defensive lobbying outlays are low or non-existent. Fundamentally, antitrust enforcement will reflect the forces of rent seeking (Tullock, 1967), rent protection (Rowley and Tollison, 1986) and rent extraction (McChesney, 1987, 1991) in an explicitly political equilibrium.

Section 5 of this chapter will review available United States evidence on the application of the antitrust laws in an attempt to determine which of these alternative hypotheses is the more convincing.

4.3   Testable implications for the behavior of the antitrust bureaucracy
Neoclassical welfare economics predicts that the antitrust bureaucracy will pursue the expressed intent of the antitrust statutes impartially and efficiently, regardless of outside pressures either from interested private parties, from the legislative branch or from the executive branch. The antitrust bureaus will conserve economic resources by securing the maximum social return at a minimum budgetary cost. They will not deploy antitrust resources in pursuit of personal economic advantage (Weber, 1947).

The interest group theory of government predicts that the antitrust bureaucracy will actively pursue antitrust outcomes designed (1) to maximize the size of its budget (Niskanen, 1971, 1975), (2) to enhance the short-term career prospects of its senior bureaucrats and to pander to the political wishes of its political oversight and appropriations committees (Weingast and Moran, 1983). In so doing, it will willingly flout the explicit intent of the antitrust statutes.

Section 5 of this chapter will review available United States evidence concerning the behavior of the antitrust bureaucracy in an attempt to determine which of these alternative hypotheses is the more convincing.

4.4   Testable implications for the behavior of the courts
Neoclassical welfare economics predicts that the appellate judges assigned to significant antitrust cases will be well trained both in the relevant law and

in the relevant economics and will be dedicated to upholding the explicit intent of the antitrust statutes.

The interest group theory of government predicts that the appellate judges will be appointed for political rather than for economic and legal skills. Further, they will be more concerned with pandering to prevailing political and media pressures in order to enhance their personal career prospects, to maximize the size of their salaries and to enhance appropriations for staff and other office perquisites, than with upholding the explicit intent of the antitrust statutes (Rowley, 1989).

Section 5 of this chapter will review available United States evidence concerning the behavior of the appellate courts in an attempt to determine which of these alternative hypotheses is the more convincing.

5   The evidence
In this section, we summarize the small but growing body of United States literature that pursues a positive approach to the analysis of antitrust policy (Shughart and Tollison, 1985). Our task in this chapter is not to undertake additional empirical analysis, but rather to evaluate existing evidence as a means of comparing the approach of neoclassical welfare economics with that of the interest group theory of government.

5.1   The origins of key United States antitrust statutes
We shall evaluate the origins and the contents of three important United States antitrust statutes, namely the Sherman antitrust Act of 1890, the Clayton Act of 1914 and the Federal Trade Commission Act of 1914. In so doing, we shall test the hypothesis that each of these statutes was, for the most part, a response by the United States legislature to interest group lobbying.

The Sherman Act of 1890   Prior to the enactment of the Sherman Act in 1890, antitrust policy was the responsibility of individual states and not of the federal government. The states relied on precedents, handed down at common law by individual judges under the judicial authority of *stare decisis*, to constrain restraints of trade and to control the behavior of monopolies. These common law rules were part of the English heritage honored following the successful War of Revolution, and indeed adhered to, for the most part, more rigorously in the United States than in England and Wales throughout the 19th century. Indeed, one interpretation, in our view unjustified, is that the Sherman Act was simply a codification of the existing common law, introduced to deal with infringements that affected inter-state commerce.

The first systematic political–economic investigation of the origins and legislative intent of the Sherman Act of 1890 is the widely cited 1966 paper by Robert Bork. Writing well before the public choice revolution had invaded mainstream political economy, Bork focuses attention exclusively on the content of the Congressional Record and the specific wording of the statute, and ignores any impact of lobbying by interest groups.

On the basis of evidence from the Congressional Record, Bork unequivocally concludes that 'Congress intended the courts to implement (that is, to take into account in the decision of cases) only that value that we would today call consumer welfare' (Bork, 1966, p. 7). This intent 'requires courts to distinguish between agreements or activities that increase wealth through efficiency and those that decrease it through restriction of output' (ibid., p. 7). Bork acknowledges that alternative motives for antitrust legislation were advanced during the legislative debates, but concludes that, with only trivial exceptions, 'It is impossible to find even colorable language suggesting most of the other broad social or political purposes that have occasionally been suggested as relevant to the application of the Sherman Act' (ibid., p. 42).

In this judgment, Bork relies significantly on the recorded testimony of Senator Sherman (Republican, Ohio) who introduced the Bill in December 1889, and whose name was attached to the statute itself. In itself, this reliance is far from conclusive in justifying Bork's hypothesis, since Senator Sherman completely lost control of the Bill during the congressional debates, where it was amended into incoherence. The Judiciary Committee ultimately salvaged the Bill by completely rewriting it into its final form. Moreover, Sherman was a major supporter of the McKinley Tariff Act of 1890, one of the most protectionist trade statutes in the history of the United States (Hazlett, 1992, p. 265).

As Hazlett (1992) clearly demonstrates, the thrust of the debate in the Judiciary Committee was far removed from the pursuit of consumer welfare. The sentiment that surfaced in support of the Sherman Act, without objection, and indeed with some support, from the original backers of the Bill, was overtly protectionist. Typical of this was the statement of Judiciary Committee member, Senator George (Republican, Mississippi) who supported the bill by attacking the 'trusts' in the following anti-consumer terms: 'By use of this organized force of wealth and money the small men engaged in competition with them are crushed out, and that is the great evil at which all this legislation ought to be directed.' (21 Cong. Rec. 3147).

In a similar vein, Congressman Mason praised the Sherman Act for its role in restricting competition:

Some say that the trusts have made products cheaper, have reduced prices; but if the price of oil, for instance, were reduced by one cent a barrel, it would not right the wrong done to the people of this country by the trusts which have destroyed legitimate competition and driven honest men from legitimate business enterprises. (21 Cong.Rec. 4100)

It is worthy of note that every Republican member of the Judiciary Committee responsible for rewriting the Sherman Act also voted in favor of the protectionist McKinley Tariff Act of 1890. Each of the Republican senators on the Judiciary Committee represented a protectionist state. Only Senator Evarts (Republican, New York), at 57 per cent protectionist, fell below 83 per cent protectionist in his voting record (Hazlett, 1992, p. 268).

The Senate promptly passed the rewritten Sherman Antitrust Bill 52 to 1, whereas it divided closely on strict party lines to pass the McKinley Tariff Act. Electoral pressures over the issue of protectionism, however, are clearly discernible in the House of Representatives. The final House vote on the amended Sherman Act was 242 in favor and none opposed. However, 85 House members abstained from the vote. Of the 62 House Democrats who abstained in the final vote on the Sherman Antitrust Act, none voted subsequently in favor of the McKinley Tariff Act. Conversely, of the 117 House Republicans who voted in favor of the Sherman Antitrust Act, none voted against the McKinley Tariff Act.

The electoral significance of these voting records is unmistakable. Its Republican supporters certainly viewed the Sherman Act, not primarily as pro-competitive, but rather as protectionist of otherwise uncompetitive small businesses. These lawmakers deflected the natural antagonism of large US corporations to such protectionist legislation by promising to protect them from foreign competition by the forthcoming McKinley Tariff Act.

If Bork (1966) is incorrect in his interpretation of legislative intent, as the evidence suggests, and if the legislation was primarily designed to protect small businesses from competition to the long-term detriment of consumers, what were the forces that drove that latter outcome? To answer this question, we offer an explicit public choice analysis. Let us begin with the 1985 paper on the origins of the Sherman Act by George Stigler.

Because the notion that the Sherman Act was a cynical attempt by the Republican Party to head off the agrarian (Granger and Populist) movements, does not square with his initial hypothesis that the statute was based on public-interest motivations, Stigler (1985) is especially concerned to challenge that viewpoint empirically. He notes, correctly, that for the farmers to attack the railroads would amount to perverse behavior, since the railroad expansion had benefited farmers immensely. Moreover, as

Stigler (1975) demonstrates, railroad prices and profits declined throughout the period 1880 to 1900, and thus antitrust regulation provided negligible potential gains to farm profits.

In order to test the hypothesis that the Sherman Act was supported by small business interests against the opposition of monopolies, Stigler (1985) analyzed the pattern of state antitrust laws prior to 1890. A comparison of states that did and did not pass antitrust laws prior to 1890 supported this hypothesis with a Chi square measure of 5.06 and a probability of only 0.02 of arising by chance. Nevertheless, Stigler (1985) concludes with only lukewarm support for the public choice explanation of the Sherman Act. His heart was not in the analysis.

In 1985, Thomas DiLorenzo offered a much more convincing public choice analysis of the origins of the Sherman Act. Unlike Stigler (1985), he analyses in some detail the composition of the Grangers and the Farmers' Alliance, and determines that the primary goal of those interest groups was the promotion and protection of relatively small farms that were experiencing difficulty during the late 19th century in competing with 'giant' wheat farms.

These small farm interest groups' targets, in particular, were the alleged jute bagging and binder twine 'trusts' that were encroaching on the market in cotton cloth, and also the railroads, primarily to eliminate efficiency-based, quantity transportation discounts provided to the larger farms. In both fields, small farm businesses sought to protect themselves from more efficient large-scale farmers (DiLorenzo, 1985, pp. 75–6).

DiLorenzo also demonstrates that the 51st Congress either lied to the public or was fooled by progressive journalists in basing its case for antitrust legislation on the growth of monopoly in the United States. The essence of monopoly is that it restricts output in order to raise prices in excess of marginal cost. Of the industries identified by Congress as being monopolies, data exist for 17. DiLorenzo (1985) analyzes those data and shows that, in all but two relatively unimportant industries (matches and castor oil), output grew much more rapidly than output in all other industries during the ten years preceding the Sherman Act. Data for these industries also shows that prices were generally falling, not rising, even when compared to the declining general price level. Consumers were far better of with these so-called 'trusts' than without them.

In conclusion, the Sherman Act should be viewed as nothing more than the response of Congress to lobbying by both small farms and small businesses incapable of competing effectively on the one side and as a smokescreen to provide Congress with cover for the highly protectionist tariff legislation enacted in order to raise taxes from a largely unsuspecting public on the other.

The Clayton Act and the Federal Trade Commission Act of 1914   The trusts issue, which remained politically alive during the progressive era, culminated in the passage of the Clayton Act and the Federal Trade Commission Act in 1914. Conventional wisdom holds that Congress enacted these closely interrelated laws as a response to the perceived ineffectiveness of the Sherman Act of 1890. This perception is based on a number of events occurring between 1890 and 1914, notably the greatest merger movement in American history, allegations that powerful investment bankers and financiers were creating monopolies among the largest railroad and industrial corporations, and the recurrent financial crises believed to have been caused by banking interests.

In a detailed public choice analysis, Ramirez and Eigen-Zucchi (2001) challenge this conventional wisdom and suggest that both 1914 Acts were the product, not of a populist concern for the public interest, but of interest group politics. The primary focus of their investigation concerns the Clayton Act.

The Clayton Act prohibited four specific types of monopolistic practices: (a) price discrimination, (b) exclusive dealing contracts, (c) the acquisition of competing companies through stock purchases, and (d) interlocking directorates among companies within the same industries. However, Section 6 of the Act provided exemptions for agricultural organizations and labor organizations. These exemptions were not accidental oversights. They were political responses to lobbying outlays, designed to provide wealth transfers to agriculture and labor at the expense of consumers and stockholders in the manufacturing and industrial sectors (Benson *et al.*, 1987).

Section 7 of the Act exempted mergers and acquisitions accomplished through the purchase of physical assets, such as plant and equipment. Once again, these exemptions were not accidental oversights, but were designed to affect companies of different size disproportionately. In particular, large dominant firms can expand more easily than small firms by purchasing physical assets (Ekelund *et al.*, 1995).

Ramirez and Eigen-Zucchi (2001) identify three major groups at play in the 1914 legislation: agriculture, large corporations with dominant market shares and small manufacturing companies with limited market shares. The wealth transfers provided to agriculture are clear. Farmers benefit from the legislation since they are allowed to cartelize the industry. Large companies with dominant market shares may be disadvantaged since they face a higher probability of being sued for violations of the Act, although they are partially exempt from Section 7 provisions (Ekelund *et al.*, 1995). Small companies with limited market shares are mostly advantaged since they are protected from the growth of more efficient rivals.

Ramirez and Eigen-Zucchi (2001) use stock market data to determine the relative impact of the Clayton Act on large dominant and small, less dominant companies. They compare the cumulative stock returns (adjusted for market returns), over the period March 1912 to January 1914, of two constructed portfolios, one composed of large companies with dominant market shares and the other that includes a control group of small manufacturing companies. They find that the returns on the portfolio of companies with dominant market shares suffered significantly through this gestation period of the Clayton Act. By contrast, the cumulative return on the portfolio of the control sample gained significantly. These results suggest that small firms predictably would lobby strongly in favor of the Clayton bill and that large dominant firms would behave more ambiguously, depending on the particular relevance of the Section 7 exemption for their strategic plans.

Ramirez and Eigen-Zucchi (2001) find supportive evidence for this hypothesis in the pattern of voting in the Senate. The Clayton bill passed in the Senate on 2 September 1914 by a vote of 46 to 16 with 34 abstentions. The senators representing southern states, characterized by agricultural and small business constituents, voted predominantly in favor of the bill. The senators representing northern, and especially New England, states, characterized by large manufacturing businesses, voted predominantly against the bill. However, because the southern states were disproportionately Democratic and the Clayton bill was sponsored by the Democratic party and supported by the Democratic president, Woodrow Wilson, this interest group test is not decisive.

Therefore, Ramirez and Eigen-Zucchi (2001) reinforced the test with a careful regression analysis, using the Theil multinomial logit as well as the ordered logit models, regressing a senator's vote and abstention choice on variables designed to represent ideology, political party other senator-specific variables and several carefully chosen economic variables to represent constituency interest groups. Both regression models performed well. Each interest group variable was positive and significant. Importantly, the size of the coefficient on the small business group variable was significantly higher than that for medium-sized businesses, which in turn was significantly higher than that for large businesses with dominant market shares. These results provide strong support for the interest group hypothesis.

Of course, these results do not determine whether the Clayton Act serves the public interest. They do offer strong support, however, for the public choice hypothesis that the Clayton Act, whatever its ultimate policy impact, was driven by interest group pressures, and not by populism, at least within the Senate of the United States.

5.2   Enforcement of the US antitrust laws

The literature on the welfare costs of monopoly, and the estimated consumer gains from its elimination, provides an implicit basis for formulating antitrust policy in cost–benefit terms (Long *et al.*, 1973). If the antitrust agencies (in the United States, the Antitrust Division of the Department of Justice and the Federal Trade Commission) are motivated by efficiency objectives, they will deploy antitrust resources optimally to this end.

Drawing on a detailed statistical analysis of US antitrust enforcement over the period 1947 to 1970, by Richard Posner (1970), Long *et al.* (1973) test the efficiency hypothesis with respect to the enforcement behavior of the Antitrust Division of the Department of Justice by reference to the cases brought against two-digit SIC manufacturing industries over the period 1945 to 1970. To this end Long *et al.* collected data on average profits and sales over the same period and computed excess profits from rates of return on capital in different industries, using total assets in 1956 as a base.

The authors ran a regression equation of cases brought on the Harberger welfare loss measure and another of cases brought on the Kamerschen welfare loss measure. In both cases, the relevant regression coefficient is positive. In both cases, the R^2 is very small. They ran a third regression equation of cases brought on the level of concentration within an industry, and found no statistically significant relationship between those variables. Further empirical analysis suggested that industry size, as measured by sales, was the most important determinant of antitrust suits over the period under investigation. These results do not support the efficiency hypothesis.

Asch (1975) and Siegfried (1975) separately presented further evidence that enforcement efforts by the US antitrust bureaucracy do not follow the welfare-loss model. Asch regressed the number of cases brought per year by industry on average annual industry sales, the number of firms as of 1967 and average annual sales per firm. On the basis of the separate results for both the Antitrust Division and the Federal Trade Commission, he concluded that 'case-bringing activity cannot be characterized as predominantly "rational" or predominantly "random"' (Asch, 1975, 580–81). Siegfried (1975) used a sample of industries significantly less aggregated than that used by Long *et al.* (1973) but also concluded that 'economic variables have little influence on the Antitrust Division' (Siegfried 1975, 573).

In sum, the available evidence suggests that the US antitrust bureaucracy does not select cases on the basis of the potential net benefit to society as measured in terms of economic efficiency.

5.3   The behavior of the US antitrust bureaucracy

To the extent that the antitrust bureaus are not motivated by economic efficiency in the selection of their cases, a major lacuna exists in the neoclassical model. This gap is readily and effectively filled by relevant public choice analysis. Three separate but overlapping public choice models are well supported by empirical evidence.

The first such is the antitrust pork-barrel model, first advanced by Richard Posner (1969) and later tested by Faith *et al.* (1982). This model focuses primarily on the relationship between the US Congress and the Federal Trade Commission (FTC). Each member of Congress is obligated for electoral reasons to protect and to further the provincial interests, not least the business interests, of the jurisdiction that he represents. The power to control the FTC lies primarily in the hands of the members of the relevant congressional committees and subcommittees responsible for its behavior and for its financial appropriations. The model hypothesizes that FTC behavior will favor geographically the interests of these members.

Faith *et al.* (1982) tested this hypothesis for the period 1961–79, splitting their data into two sets, the first covering the period 1961–9, widely considered as reflecting a period of grave FTC economic inefficiency, and the second covering the period 1970–79, following the reforms of 1970 that were put in place allegedly in order to improve the economic efficiency of FTC interventions. Both tests provide support for the antitrust pork-barrel hypothesis.

Over the period covered by the investigation, congressional jurisdiction over the FTC was shared by two Senate committees and one Senate subcommittee (The Committee on Interior and Insular Affairs, The Committee on Commerce, Science, and Transportation, and the Subcommittee on Antitrust and Monopoly of the Senate Judiciary Committee). It was also shared by five House subcommittees (the House Subcommittees on Independent Offices, and the Department of Housing and Urban Development, on Agriculture and Related Agencies, and on State, Justice, Commerce and the Judiciary and related agencies – (all of the House Committee of Appropriations) – the Subcommittee on Oversight and Investigations of the House Committee on Interstate and Foreign Commerce, and the Subcommittee on Monopolies and Commercial Law of the House Judiciary Committee. This suggests that there might be many pork-lovers effectively milling around the FTC trough.

The evidence compiled by Faith *et al.* (1982) supports this latter hypothesis. FTC action against businesses can take place in various forms. Although the FTC can initiate cases on its own, some 90 per cent of investigations are begun in response to complaints by the public. Following a staff review, a case may be closed for lack of evidence or a formal complaint may be filed. This complaint may be withdrawn if the respondent agrees to a consent order to cease and desist. If the complaint is issued, the case goes before an administrative judge who either dismisses the case for lack of evidence or issues a cease and desist order.

Faith *et al.* (1982) compiled statistics of all such cases, together with the headquarter addresses of all respondents. These respondent addresses were categorized by congressional districts and Senate states throughout the United States and were plotted against maps showing the congressional districts and the Senate states of the members of the eight committees and subcommittees outlined above. The pork-barrel hypothesis was then tested on two sets of such data separately for 1961–69 and for 1970–79.

In the first data set, the base is cases brought (dismissals, cease and desist orders and consent decrees). In the second set, the base is complaints (dismissals and cease and desist orders). In the latter case, the authors focus exclusively on the pattern of formal FTC decision making. The authors compile ratios of dismissals to cases brought and dismissals to complaints for the jurisdictions represented by each committee's members and for the remaining congressional jurisdictions. According to the null hypothesis, the difference between these ratios should not be significantly different from zero. They test for this in terms of z-statistics.

For the period 1960–69, membership of the Senate subcommittee on Antitrust and Monopoly is significantly related to favorable rulings on both data sets. This is an important result since that subcommittee, on average, encompassed only eight states. The pork-barrel hypothesis is also strongly supported for the House subcommittees as a group, especially with respect to the second data set. The authors conclude that 'The House subcommittees, taken as an observational unit, appear to have been a ripe arena for antitrust pork barrels in the 1960s' (Faith *et al.*, 1982, 209).

For the period 1970–79, the authors find some support for the view that the 1970 FTC reforms influenced the Senate away from pork barrel politics. There is no statistically significant relationship over that period between membership of any Senate committee and FTC decision making. The House, however, is another matter. The results for all five subcommittees taken as a unit continue to bear out the pork barrel hypothesis for both sets of data. If anything, the pork-barrel process became more pronounced and apparent in the data.

One interesting result of the 1970 reforms is a significant reduction in the number of cases brought (dropping from 2475 to 1840) and the fall in the number of formal actions by the FTC (dropping from 579 to 196). The leverage of the House subcommittees over this reduced number of formal actions becomes much more important.

The second public choice model, also used to evaluate the relationship between the US Congress and the FTC, is the principal–agent model outlined and tested by Barry Weingast and Mark Moran (1983). In this model, the members of the relevant congressional oversight committees are viewed explicitly as the principals whose preferences control the behavior of the FTC.

Using a sample of cases considered by the FTC between 1964 and 1976, Weingast and Moran (1983) report results showing that the enforcement activities of the FTC in four areas (mergers, credit reporting, textile labeling and Robinson–Patman cases) were related significantly to the scores assigned by the Americans for Democratic Action (ADA) to the voting records of committee members. Higher ADA scores, which indicate more 'liberal' voting records, clearly imply greater preferences for FTC activism. The FTC faithfully reflected changes in these preferences over the period of the study.

Of course, the ADA ratings may simply reflect the preferences of each member's constituency, rather than his own personal ideology. Nevertheless, however those preferences are derived, as they change, so does the policy of the FTC. In this respect, FTC policy is determined by influences that may extend beyond the narrow geographical constituency of each committee member.

The third public choice model, directed equally at explaining the behavior of the Antitrust Division and the FTC, focuses attention on the opportunities for agency discretion provided by the multiplicity of principals and the transaction costs of monitoring agency behavior (Rowley and Vachris, 1995). This model analyzes the internal incentive structure of the antitrust agencies in order to predict typical bureaucratic behavior under conditions of agency discretion.

The first such study is the interview-based study of the Antitrust Division by Suzanne Weaver (1977). Based on the results of interviews during 1971 with 100 staff members, private attorneys and other observers of the Division, Weaver concluded that events during the early 1950s (passage of the Celler–Kevauver Act, and the indictment of electrical equipment manufacturers for price conspiracy) made 'antitrust expertise a more valuable commodity to the business community and to law firms serving it' (Weaver, 1977). In turn, lawyers benefited financially from experience in the Antitrust Division and, in particular, from trial experience in the federal courts. Therefore, at the margin, getting a case to trial was more important than winning a case on its merits.

In 1980, Katzman reached conclusions similar to those of Weaver (1977) with respect to the FTC. Katzman (1980) determined that most legal staff members at the FTC coveted jobs with prestigious law firms. For this reason, staffers disliked investigations directed at broad structural issues and industry-wide cases because they involved years of tedious study before reaching the trial stage. Instead, upper-level FTC executives tended to support 'the opening of a number of easily prosecuted matters, which may have little value to the consumer … in an effort to satisfy the staff's perceived needs' (Katzman, 1980, p. 83).

In 1981, Clarkson and Muris focused attention on internal organizational conflicts, staff incentives and external constraints in explaining FTC behavior. For example, they suggest that the FTC substituted cases employing the market concentration doctrine for Robinson–Patman cases largely as a means of resolving internal conflicts between FTC lawyers and economists and because the greater complexity of the former cases provided human capital benefits to FTC attorneys. The FTC was also reluctant to initiate price-fixing cases (arguably the most promising from the standpoint of consumer welfare) in deference to the desire of its attorneys to differentiate their product from their Justice Department counterparts.

Finally, in presenting a public choice explanation of the behavior of the antitrust bureaucracy, it is instructive to review evidence concerning dual enforcement of the antitrust statutes. For antitrust is unique among US federal government policy programs in terms of the degree to which it is administered by autonomous bureaus (Shughart, 1990, p. 94). Dual enforcement may lead to wasteful duplication of resources on the one hand or to more (competition-induced) efficiency on the other. It is possible to investigate these alternative hypotheses because, from 1914 to 1948, the Antitrust Division and the FTC competed for case loads and, thereafter, by agreement, they divided areas of responsibility between themselves.

In 1987, Higgins, Shughart and Tollison evaluated dual enforcement empirically, deploying a model that assumed that the Antitrust Division and the FTC each sought to maximize their own budgets while behaving according to Cournot output conjectures. Their hypothesis was that independent dual enforcement should lead to greater output, and to greater output per budget dollar, than collusive joint enforcement.

The evidence is startling. Mean annual case output, real budgets and output per thousand budget dollars were collected for two time-periods, 1932–48 and for 1949–81. Although total antitrust activity remained roughly the same over the two periods (239 cases a year for the former period and 249 cases per year for the latter period) the average number of cases per real budget dollars fell dramatically during the latter period. The liaison agreement halved antitrust output per thousand budget dollars. In essence, following the 1948 accord, the Antitrust Division and the FTC employed double the resources per case than they did prior to 1948. The implications for bureaucratic waste are obvious.

Research into the bureaucracy of antitrust is still in its infancy and much more work remains to be done before definitive judgments can be made. However, the small sample of studies outlined above clearly indicates that conventional public interest explanations are in trouble, and that public choice explanations cannot be ignored.

5.4 The behavior of the US courts

Most observers of the Constitution of the United States view the federal judiciary as the branch most removed from the political process. Many such observers continue to view the judicial branch as the protector of the Constitution and of the laws enacted within the framework of that Constitution, against political or bureaucratic invasion. Inevitably, this interpretation spills over into the conventional analysis of the enforcement of US antitrust laws. Fundamentally, those who by now are disenchanted with notions of impartial and benevolent legislatures continue to place their faith in notions of an impartial and benevolent judiciary. How well does such a latter notion stand up to public choice scrutiny?

In answering this question, we shall focus attention on the nature and behavior of the US federal court system, most notably on that of the United States Supreme Court. US federal judges (and Supreme Court justices) are granted life tenure, have salaries that cannot be reduced in nominal terms, and can be removed from the bench only through the difficult mechanism of impeachment. These benefits, in principle, seem to place the federal judiciary above the fray of interest group politics (Shughart, 1990, p. 121). The reality is actually more complex (Rowley, 1989).

All US federal judges are appointed and promoted through an explicitly political process, which involves nomination by the President as well as advice and consent by the Senate. In such circumstances, where the ideology of the President and the Senate majority coincide, it can be predicted that the appointed judges will carry that ideology onto the bench. Where the respective ideologies diverge, this prediction is less clear.

For the most part, judges appointed through such a fractured political process are likely to be judicial nonentities who have failed to leave any significant judicial footmarks in the sand. The independence granted to appointed judges, therefore, provides discretionary power for them either to pursue their own respective ideologies or to flounder in their own respective inadequacies. Predictably, federal judges will manifest such patterns of behavior in the field of antitrust policy, conditioned by any recognition that their judgments may affect positively or negatively the magnitude of their budget appropriations by Congress. It is by no means obvious that the judiciary will typically supply efficient antitrust judgments under such circumstances.

We cannot explore this public choice hypothesis adequately in this chapter. In any event, there remains a great deal of work to be done. However,

Paul Rubin (1995) provides telling evidence against the null hypothesis that the US federal courts pursue economic efficiency in their antitrust policy judgments. Rubin surveys published economic scholarship on 23 important US antitrust cases to determine which are viewed as economically justified in terms of economic efficiency. The criteria that he employs are approximately consistent with the efficiency criteria that we set out in Section 2.

On this basis, Rubin (1995) concludes that 14 cases (61 per cent of the sample) were economically justified and that nine cases were unjustified. Of the 14 justified cases, the plaintiff won nine, or 64 per cent. Of the nine unjustified cases, the plaintiffs won seven, or 78 per cent. Using a differences-in-proportions test, the difference in these proportions is statistically significant, despite the small numbers, at the 10 per cent level. Plaintiffs are less likely to win a justified case. Moreover, of the nine justified cases that the plaintiff won, in four the victory is viewed as having had no economic effect.

Based on this sample, Rubin (1995) concludes that, if antitrust judgments perform a deterrent function, they are at least as likely to deter efficient as inefficient behavior. This may explain, at least in part, the reduction in support among economists for 'vigorous' antitrust enforcement over the period 1976 to 1990. If factors other than economic efficiency are indeed driving judicial judgments in the antitrust arena, public choice impulses may well provide an effective alternative explanation.

6 Conclusions

We have argued in this chapter that the primary objective of US antitrust policy never was, and is not now, the achievement of economic efficiency. In this sense, accumulating evidence of the failure of the antitrust authorities to pursue and/or to achieve economic efficiency is not evidence of policy failure; nor should antitrust policy be viewed as the product of a long series of errors that conceivably could be corrected by yet more economic research. Rather, the US antitrust laws should be viewed as the highly successful application of policy in response to the politically effective preferences of individuals who coalesce into powerful interest groups that dominate the market place in regulatory policy.

Of course, the grip exercised by interest groups over US antitrust policy does not preclude the possibility that some antitrust interventions may provide widespread efficiency benefits. The law of unintended consequences applies across the entire range of legislative activity, not only to that undertaken for public interest reasons. Nevertheless, antitrust policy should be viewed, not as an outstanding exception to the political economy of regulation, but rather as one of its most compelling examples.

Bibliography

Arrow, K.J. (1962): 'Economic welfare and the allocation of resources for invention', in National Bureau for Economic Research (ed.), *The Rate and Direction of Inventive Activity*, Princeton: NJ, Princeton University Press, pp. 609–26.

Asch, P. (1975): 'The determinants and effects of antitrust activity', *Journal of Law and Economics* 17, 575–81.

Becker, G.S. (1983): 'A theory of competition among pressure groups for political influence', *Quarterly Journal of Economics* 98, 371–400.

Benson, B.L., M.L. Greenhut and R.G. Holcombe (1987): 'Interest groups and the antitrust paradox', *Cato Journal* 6, 801–17.

Bork, R.H. (1966): 'Legislative intent and the policy of the Sherman Act', *Journal of Law and Economics* 9, 7–48.

Bork, R.H. (1978): *The Antitrust Paradox: A Policy at War with Itself*, New York: Basic Books.

Clarkson, K.W. and T.J. Muris (eds) (1981): *The Federal Trade Commission since 1970*, Cambridge, UK: Cambridge University Press.

Comanor, W.S. and H. Leibenstein (1969): 'Allocative efficiency, X-efficiency and the measurement of welfare losses', *Economica* 36, 304–9.

Cowling, K. and D.C. Mueller (1978): 'The social costs of monopoly power', *Economic Journal* 88, 727–48.

Crew, M.A. and C.K. Rowley (1971): 'On allocative efficiency, X-efficiency and the measurement of welfare loss', *Economica* 38, 199–203.

Crew, M.A., C.K. Rowley, and M. Jones-Lee (1971): 'X-theory versus management discretion theory', *Southern Economic Journal* 38, 173–84.

Demsetz, H. (1969): 'Information and efficiency: another viewpoint', *Journal of Law and Economics* 12, 1–22.

Demsetz, H. (1982): *Economic, Legal and Political Dimensions of Competition*, Amsterdam: North-Holland.

Demsetz, H. (1989): *Efficiency, Competition and Policy: Organization of Economic Activity*, Oxford: Blackwell.

DiLorenzo, T.J. (1985): 'The origins of antitrust: an interest-group perspective', *International Review of Law and Economics* 5, 73–90.

DiLorenzo, T.J. (1990): 'The Origins of antitrust: rhetoric versus reality', *Regulation* 13, 26–34.

Dupuit, A-J-E. (1844): 'On the measurement of the utlity of public works', trans. by R.H. Barback from the *Annales des Ponts et Chaussées* in *International Economic Papers*, 2, London: Macmillan.

Easterbrook, F. H. (1984): 'The limits of antitrust', *University of Texas Law Review* 63, 1–40.

Ekelund, R.B., M.J. McDonald and R.D. Tollison (1995): 'Business restraints and the Clayton act of 1914: public or private-interest legislation?', in F.S. McChesney and W.F. Shughart (eds), *The Causes and Consequences of Antitrust*, Chicago: University of Chicago Press, pp. 271–86.

Faith, R.L., D.R. Leavens and R.D. Tollison (1982): 'Antitrust porkbarrel', *Journal of Law and Economics* 25, 32–42.

Harberger, A.C. (1954): 'Monopoly and resource allocation', *American Economic Review* 44, 77–87.

Harberger, A.C. (1971): 'Three postulates for applied welfare economics: an interpretative essay', *Journal of Economic Literature* 9, 781–97.

Hazlett, T.W. (1992): 'The legislative history of the Sherman Act re-examined', *Economic Inquiry* 30, 263–76.

Higgins, R.S., W.F. Shughart and R.D. Tollison (1987): 'Dual enforcement of the antitrust laws', in R.J. Mackay, J.C. Miller and B. Yandle (eds), *Public Choice and Regulation: A View from inside the Federal Trade Commission*, Stanford: Hoover Institution Press.

Jasay, A. de (1996): *Before Resorting to Politics*, The Shaftesbury Papers 5, Cheltenham, UK and Brookfield, USA: Edward Elgar Publishing.

Katzman, R.A. (1980): *Regulatory Bureaucracy: The Federal Trade Commission and Antitrust Policy*, Cambridge: MIT Press.

Landes, W.M. and R.A. Posner (1975): 'The independent judiciary in an interest-group perspective', *Journal of Law and Economics* 18, 875–901.

Leibenstein, H. (1966): 'Allocative efficiency versus X-efficiency', *American Economic Review* 56, 392–415.

Long, W.F., R. Schramm and R.D. Tollison (1973): 'The economic determinants of antitrust activity', *Journal of Law and Economics* 16, 351–64.

Marshall, A. (1890): *Principles of Economics*, London: Macmillan.

McChesney, F.S. (1987): 'Rent extraction and rent creation in the economic theory of regulation', *Journal of Legal Studies* 12, 101–18.

McChesney, F.S. (1991): 'Be true to your school: Chicago's contradictory views of antitrust and regulation', *Cato Journal* 10, 775–98.

McChesney, F.S. and W.F. Shughart (eds): *The Causes and Consequences of Antitrust: The Public-Choice Perspective*, Chicago: University of Chicago Press.

Niskanen, W.A. (1971): *Bureaucracy and Representative Government*, Chicago: Aldine-Atherton.

Niskanen, W.A. (1975): 'Bureaucrats and politicians', *Journal of Law and Economics* 18, 617–43.

Nordhaus, W. (1969): *Invention, Growth and Welfare*, Cambridge: MIT Press.

Olson, M. (1965): *The Logic of Collective Action*, Cambridge: Harvard University Press.

Peltzman, S. (1976): 'Towards a more general theory of regulation', *Journal of Law and Economics* 19, 211–40.

Posner, R.A. (1969): 'The Federal Trade Commission', *University of Chicago Law Review* 37, 48–89.

Posner, R.A. (1970): 'A statistical study of antitrust enforcement', *Journal of Law and Economics* 13, 365–419.

Posner, R.A. (1973): *Economic Analysis of Law*, Boston: Little Brown & Co.

Posner, R.A. (1975): 'The social costs of monopoly and regulation', *Journal of Political Economy* 83, 807–27.

Posner, R.A. (1976): *Antitrust Law: An Economic Perspective*, Chicago: University of Chicago Press.

Posner, R.A. (1979): 'The Chicago School of antitrust analysis', *University of Pennsylvania Law Review* 127, 925–48.

Ramirez, C. and C. Eigen-Zucchi (2001): 'Understanding the Clayton Act of 1914: an analysis of the interest group hypothesis', *Public Choice* 106, 157–81.

Ross, P. (1968): 'Economies as an antitrust defense: comment', *American Economic Review* 58, 413–15.

Rowley, C.K. (1973): *Antitrust and Economic Efficiency*, London: Macmillan.

Rowley, C.K. (1989): 'The common law in public choice perspective', *Hamline Law Review* 12, 355–83.

Rowley, C.K. (2003): 'Public choice and constitutional political economy', in C.K. Rowley and F. Schneider (eds), *The Encyclopedia of Public Choice*. Boston: Kluwer Academic Publishers.

Rowley, C.K. and R.D. Tollison (1986): 'Rent-seeking and trade protection', *Swiss Journal of International Relations*, 141–66.

Rowley, C.K. and M.A. Vachris (1995): 'Why democracy does not necessarily produce efficient results', *Journal of Public Finance and Public Choice*, 95–111.

Rubin, P.H. (1995): 'What do economists think about antitrust?: A random walk down Pennsylvania Avenue', in F.S. McChesney and W.F. Shughart (eds),: *The Causes and Consequences of Antitrust*, Chicago: University of Chicago Press, pp. 33–62.

Schwartzman, D. (1960): 'The burden of monopoly', *Journal of Political Economy* 68, 727–30.

Shughart, W.F. (1990): *Antitrust Policy and Interest-Group Politics*, New York: Quorum Books.

Shughart, W.F. and R.D. Tollison (1985): 'The positive economics of antitrust policy: a survey', *International Review of Law and Economics* 5: 39–57.

Siegfried, J.F. (1975): 'The determinants of antitrust activity', *Journal of Law and Economics* 17, 559–74.

Stigler, G.J. (1971): 'The theory of economic regulation', *Bell Journal of Economics and Management Science* 2, 3–21.

Stigler, G.J. (1975): 'Supplementary notes on economic theories of regulation', in G.J. Stigler (ed.), *The Citizen and the State*, Chicago: University of Chicago Press.

Stigler, G.J, (1982): 'The economists and the problem of monopoly', in G.J. Stigler (ed.), *The Economist as Preacher and Other Essays*, Chicago: University of Chicago Press.

Stigler, G.J. (1985): 'The origin of the Sherman Act', *Journal of Legal Studies* 14, 1–12.

Tullock, G. (1967): 'The welfare costs of tariffs, monopoly and theft', *Western Economic Journal*, 256–70.

Weaver, S. (1977): *The Decision to Prosecute: Organization and Public Policy in the Antitrust Division*, Cambridge: MIT Press.

Weber, M. (1947): *The Theory of Social and Economic Organization*, New York: The Free Press.

Weingast, B.R. and M.J. Moran (1983): 'Bureaucratic discretion or congressional control? Regulatory decision-making by the Federal Trade Commission', *Journal of Political Economy* 91, 765–800.

Williamson, O.E. (1968a): 'Economies as an antitrust defense: the welfare tradeoffs', *American Economic Review* 58, 18–36.

Williamson, O.E. (1968b): 'Economies as an antitrust defense: reply', *American Economic Review* 58, 18–36.

Williamson, O.E. (1969): 'Economies as an antitrust defense: a further reply', *American Economic Review* 59, 954–9.

7 Dominance and monopolization

Marcel Canoy, Patrick Rey and Eric van Damme

1 Dominance and competition policy

A firm is in a dominant position if it has the ability to behave independently of its competitors. Dominant firms attract public attention and often arouse mixed feelings. Consumers enjoy branding when it makes life predictable, but grumble when the price of their favorite brand is raised. Policymakers may be proud of their Heinekens, Microsofts or McDonalds, but become unhappy if they restrict choices. Rivals of dominant firms may be lucky if the dominant firm is a toothless giant, but a predatory tiger scares them off.

The mixed feelings can easily be explained. From a theoretical point of view, it is not clear whether dominant firms reduce or enhance welfare. There are many reasons for that. First, a dominant firm can be a successful innovator which is typically good for welfare. But it can also be a firm that emerged from an anti-competitive merger which is typically bad for welfare. Second, some ex post behavior may have adverse welfare consequences even when dominance stems from innovation. An innovator may engage in such abuses as predatory pricing that might well prevent or delay subsequent innovations. Third, when dominant firms engage in behavior that might reduce welfare (such as predatory pricing), how can such behavior be distinguished from normal efficiency-enhancing business practices (such as discounts)? Fourth, welfare reductions today might be traded off against welfare gains tomorrow (or vice versa), and who is going to determine which generation goes first?

When we assess the status and behavior of dominant firms using 'welfare' as the criterion, we do what most economists would seem to find 'normal'. Yet there are a number of subtle discussions behind this presumed 'normality'. Welfare is an often used notion in economic and legal texts, but there are several conflicting definitions. Welfare in the classical sense is used in the *first welfare theorem*, which states that a competitive equilibrium is Pareto optimal. The problem is that we are faced with real life markets that do not satisfy the nice properties that are required for the first welfare theorem to hold. Most notably, treating agents as price takers is simply not on in any real life market, let alone in markets where dominance is an issue. So we leave Pareto and general equilibrium aside, and move towards partial equilibrium analysis. The two most common welfare notions in industrial economics are consumer surplus and total surplus, that is, the sum of consumer and producer surplus.

Why would one look at consumer surplus rather than total surplus in welfare analysis? The deadweight loss argument is the most straightforward reason for looking at consumer surplus. In a simple monopoly setting, total welfare is maximized if consumer surplus is maximized and price equals marginal cost. The reason is that maximizing consumer surplus implies minimizing the deadweight loss (see, for example, Tirole, 1988). Yet there are more complex settings in which the two welfare notions diverge. A too simplistic application of the deadweight loss argument results in ignoring dynamic considerations which are also important for consumers. Consumers appreciate innovation and product choice, but they are not part of deadweight loss triangles. How does this compare with the goals of competition authorities?

It is not obvious that competition authorities (always) strive for maximization of (consumer) welfare. In the USA, antitrust policy was a reaction to the formation of trusts that concentrated economic power. Small firms and farmers complained about the economic power of these trusts and lobbied for protection.

After World War II, competition policy was imposed on Germany by the occupation authorities. Germany had known a Cartel Law since 1923, but cartels were not forbidden: they just had to be registered. In fact, the Nazis made participation in cartels compulsory, thereby coordinating economic decision making and concentrating economic power. Perhaps as a result of that, the German competition law (Act Against Restraints of Competition) stresses economic freedom, and maintaining economic freedom may be seen as one of the main goals of their competition law. A strict interpretation of maintaining freedom of action would conflict with the efficiency goal.

In the European Union, competition policy is an instrument to achieve the goals of the Community: (roughly) the creation of a single market area with a high standard of living for all those that live in it. Consequently, two goals are usually distinguished: market integration and economic efficiency. Note that these two goals may conflict: market integration, when interpreted as the prohibition of price discrimination across countries, may come at the expense of economic efficiency.

From the above it followed that there are various potential goals of competition law and that some goals can conflict. Two cases that are interesting in this respect are *UK Distillers* and *Ford/Volkswagen*. In *UK Distillers*, the Commission was upset by price discrimination by the Distillers Company for whisky between France and the UK. When ordered to end the practice, the company simply stopped supplying the French market, leaving prices in UK unchanged. In *Ford/Volkswagen*, the Commission allowed a joint venture of these two car makers to produce MPVs (Volkswagen Sharan and Ford Galaxy) in Portugal, with the argument that this created jobs in Portugal and would lead to better integration of Portugal in the Community.

Within the public interest domain, one may distinguish several objectives for competition policy: maintaining competition, maintaining economic freedom, achieving market integration, maximizing total welfare, and maximizing consumer surplus.

It is difficult to argue what the goal of a competition authority should be, although one may say that competition policy is guided by the objectives mentioned above. In the European Union, Article 81 of the Maastricht Treaty reveals an underlying ambiguity. Article 81 EU Treaty(1) prohibits all agreements between firms that restrict competition, but Article 81 EU Treaty(3) exempts from the prohibition agreements that are efficiency-enhancing, provided that consumers get a fair share of the resulting benefits. Hence, in Article 81 EU Treaty(1), the goals of maintaining competition and economic freedom feature (some even identify a restriction of competition with a restriction of freedom of action), while in Article 81 EU Treaty(3) the goals of maximising total welfare and consumer surplus feature. Therefore we can conclude that a criticism of a competition authority's decision would be justified only if that decision cannot be justified by any reasonable combination of the above criteria that could be adopted by the competition authority.

One may argue that consumer welfare should be the goal of competition policy. For example, Robert Bork (1978, p. 405) has stated, 'The only goal that should guide interpretation of the antitrust laws is the welfare of consumers.' What can be inferred from official documents?

In the UK, the Office of Fair Trading's (OFT) mission is 'to protect consumers and explain their rights' and 'to ensure that businesses compete and operate fairly'.[1]

The European Commission (2000, p. 4) puts it slightly differently:

> The Community's competition policy pursues a precise goal, which is to defend and develop effective competition in the common market. Competition is a basic mechanism of the market economy involving supply (producers, traders) and demand (intermediate customers, consumers). Suppliers offer goods or services on the market in an endeavor to meet demand. Demand seeks the best ratio between quality and price for the products it requires. The most efficient response emerges as a result of a contest between suppliers. Thus, competition leads everybody individually to seek out the means of striking this balance between quality and price in order to meet demand to the best possible extent.
>   Competition is therefore a simple and efficient means of guaranteeing consumers a level of excellence in terms of the quality and price of products and

services. It also forces firms to strive for competitiveness and economic efficiency. This consolidates the Community's industrial and commercial fabric so that it is able to confront the competitiveness of our main partners and to put Community firms in a position to succeed in markets around the world.

The US Federal Trade Commission, finally, puts it as follows:[2]

[competition] enforces a variety of federal antitrust and consumer protection laws. The Commission seeks to ensure that the nation's markets function competitively, and are vigorous, efficient, and free of undue restrictions. The Commission also works to enhance the smooth operation of the market-place by eliminating acts or practices that are unfair or deceptive. In general, the Commission's efforts are directed toward stopping actions that threaten consumers' opportunities to exercise informed choice. … In addition to carrying out its statutory enforcement responsibilities, the Commission advances the policies underlying Congressional mandates through cost-effective non-enforcement activities, such as consumer education.

The common element is that (apart from possible other goals) competition authorities protect consumers and assume that vigorous competition is the right tool for getting good deals for consumers. In theory it is possible to reconcile total surplus and consumer surplus. Consumer surplus in the long run comes closer to total surplus than just consumer surplus in the short run. Maximizing consumer surplus in the long run must involve producer surplus. Profits are necessary for investment and innovation, and are therefore also ingredients of consumer benefits in the long run. Of course, this is not hard evidence in favor of consumer surplus and nuancing is needed. Consumer surplus is only a reasonable approximation of welfare if long run effects are taken into account. It is not automatic that competition authorities do this.

The attention that scholars and policymakers dedicate to monopolies, oligopolies and dominant firms suggests that there are indeed lots of dominant firms around. It is not feasible (at least not at this moment) to test 'dominance' per se, but given the (statistical) correlation between size (market shares) and dominance, we use concentration tendencies as a rough approximation for dominance. This exercise is not to test a certain hypothesis, but to get a feeling for numbers and trends.

We start with a discussion of the older evidence. The international commodity market is dominated by a few multinational corporations (Cowling, 2002). Concentrated industries tend to be more profitable, also in the long run (Mueller, 1986). Of more recent significance is the concentration in the services industries, such as banking, communications, IT and media. In the USA, in 1985, there were 14 600 commercial banks. The 50 largest banks owned 45.7 per cent of all assets, the 100 largest held 57.4 per cent. In 1984, there were 272 037 active corporations in the manufacturing sector, 710 of which held 80.2 per cent of total assets. In the service sector 95 firms of the total of 899 369 owned 28 per cent of the sector's assets. In 1986, in agriculture, 29 000 large farms (1.3 per cent of all farms) accounted for one-third of total farm sales and 46 per cent of farm profits. In 1987, the top 50 firms accounted for 54.4 per cent of the total sales of the Fortune 500 largest industrial companies (Du Boff, 1989, p. 171).

Looking further, we find that in 1995 about 50 firms produced about 15 per cent of the manufactured goods in the industrialized world. There are about 150 firms in the worldwide motor vehicle industry, but the two largest firms, General Motors and Ford, together produce almost one-third of all vehicles. The five largest firms produce half of all output and the ten largest firms produce three-quarters. Four appliance firms manufacture 98 per cent of the washing machines made in the USA. In the US meatpacking industry, four firms account for over 85 per cent of the output of beef, while the other 1245 firms have less than 15 per cent of the market.

Another fact is that large companies tend to become more diversified as the concentration levels in individual industries increase. Tobacco companies are the masters of diversification. Jell-O products, Kool-Aid, Log Cabin syrup, Minute Rice, Miller beer, Oreos, Velveeta and Maxwell House coffee are all brands owned by Tobacco companies.

More recent evidence points in the same direction. Many European and US markets have been consolidating in a rapid fashion. However, most mergers tend to be unhappy marriages.[3] Does that mean that the large firms destroy welfare? Whether concentrations are as bad as some people believe is unclear. The mere fact that the merged parties are, on average, unhappy ex post does not mean welfare is reduced, since the source of unhappiness is unknown. Perhaps they are unhappy because competitors reacted more fiercely than anticipated. Perhaps welfare was reduced for the merged parties but not for their competitors or for the consumers. A priori, the tendencies can equally likely point at increased possibilities of exploiting scale and scope economies as at increased abuses of market power. It is the duty of competition authorities to make up their mind which of the two prevails.

We observe that oligopolies and (near) monopolies occupy large and important parts of the economy, yet there seems to be a widespread presumption among economists that dominant firms have a tendency to decline. It is important to check in how far this presumption is right, since rapidly declining dominant firms obviously affect optimal policy responses. Mueller (1986) and Geroski (1987) in seminal contributions have actually tested this hypothesis empirically.[4] Checking the actual decline of market leaders in the UK and the USA, Geroski finds no evidence of actual decline, defined as some mix of incumbent's erosion of profits and market shares over time. For example, based on the market shares result of the 108 observed dominant firms, 32 did not decline, between 46 and 51 declined by 6 per cent or less (Geroski). However difficult these results are to be interpreted, it shows that there is nothing like a systematic rapid decline of dominant firms. Mueller (1986) studied the largest 1000 firms in the USA in the period 1950–72 and concluded that the typical firm with persistently high earnings has a large market share and sells differentiated products.

Lacking stronger evidence, we will employ the working hypothesis in this chapter that alert dominant firms, when left untouched by competition authorities, have enough possibilities to maintain their position, at least in a non-trivial number of cases.

Most of what we have discussed so far is not altogether controversial. However, when we come to discuss policy responses to dominant firm behavior, there is more room for controversy. We distinguish two polar views. At one end of the spectrum is what we call the 'Schumpeter-visits-Chicago' position. This position takes a relaxed view towards dominant firms, arguing that they are in general good for consumers, create lots of jobs, innovate and exploit scale economies. It typically plays down potential adverse effects of dominant firms, suggesting that the adverse effects are temporary and cannot be detected at socially acceptable costs anyhow. In the words of Schmalensee (1987, p. 351):[5]

> Firms may achieve short-run dominance through merger or other actions that are not directly productive. But most dominant positions, particularly those created in the US after 'merger to monopoly' was ruled illegal in 1903, have their origins to an important extent in innovation, broadly defined. Firms that attain short-run dominance by merger or other means but have no advantages over actual and potential rivals and are badly managed tend to perform poorly and lose dominance in a matter of years. In other cases, dominant positions may take many decades to decay appreciably.

It comes as no surprise that the 'Schumpeter-visits-Chicago' position worries in particular about possible adverse effects of government intervention. The favorite quotation is 'The successful competitor, having been urged to compete, must not be turned upon when he wins' (Judge Hand in the *Alcoa* decision).[6]

At the other end of the spectrum is what some might be tempted to baptize 'Old Europe'. Here the aim is to 'chase the villains'. It finds supporters among a number of regulators, competition authorities, politicians, anti-globalists and some academic scholars. In the words of Cowling (2002):[7]

We can conclude at this point that oligopolistic structures generally prevail at some stage of the global production process: obviously, myriad small production units exist, but they exist within a system dominated by relatively few giants. The implication is that we can expect a general divergence of prices from the competitive level. We shall now assess theoretical grounds and empirical evidence for the significance of this divergence, the factors underlying it and the consequences for profits, and thus for the broad distribution of income between capital and labor.

At this end of the spectrum there is less worry about dynamic features and government failure. The favorite quotations here are from the *Michelin* case (57/1983) 'a finding that an undertaking has a dominant position is not in itself a recrimination but simply means that, irrespective of the reasons for which it has such a dominant position, the undertaking concerned has a special responsibility not to allow its conduct to impair genuine undistorted competition on the common market' and Hicks's 'The best of all monopoly profits is a quiet life' (1935, p. 8).

Differences between the two polar views can be explained by different weights that are attached to type I and type II errors. With Judge Hand's *Alcoa* quotation in mind, it is not surprising that the 'Schumpeter-visits-Chicago' position dislikes unjust convictions of innocent firms. This parallels American cultural habits of rewarding winners and ignoring losers. Equally so, Old Europeans tend to protect the poor and weak, and hence put more weight on type II errors. Both polar views seem to have some good arguments and some bad ones. Available empirical evidence also produces a mixed blessing.

Most economists would adopt arguments from both sides and we are no exceptions. First, we see no reason to take a relaxed attitude towards dominant firms. There are robust economic theories showing that dominant firms have all the incentive and ample possibilities to reduce welfare, however measured. There is no indication that dominant firms spontaneously fall apart (Mueller, Geroski) nor are there convincing arguments that (persistent) dominance is required to innovate.[8] Dominant firms also produce the major part of the GNP and occupy positions in vital sectors of the society such as telecom, banks, electricity, transport and so forth. This means that underperformance of dominant firms may also have adverse non-economic effects. So these are useful Old Europe arguments. Yet, dominant firms are often firms that heavily invest in infrastructure, assets or innovation. A government that decides to intervene in this type of market should be aware of the potential consequences of intervention, in particular, of the consequences of making mistakes. As Fisher (1991, p. 201) has put it in the context of monopolies:

Economists and others ought to approach the public policy problems involved in these areas with a certain humility. Real industries tend to be very complicated. One ought not to tinker with a well-performing industry on the basis of simplistic judgments. The diagnosis of the monopoly disease is sufficiently difficult that one ought not to proceed to surgery without thorough examination of the patient and a thorough understanding of the medical principles involved.

A mistake in a market with a lot of volatility, innovation and big stakes is not only more costly, the probability of a mistake being made is greater than in other markets. A lot of dynamics implies more uncertainty, therefore a higher probability of mistakes. Also the need for intervention reduces when markets tomorrow look different from markets today. As a consequence of this, government intervention should be proportionate to the problem, no more and no less.

Counteracting potential welfare reductions by dominant firms is typically the policy area of competition law. Competition law has been designed to prevent serious welfare reducing-actions by firms, such as cartel agreements, and to punish such actions when they occur. Competition law can also block mergers if the merged entity becomes too powerful. However, competition law has not been designed to counteract all possible welfare reducing actions. First of all, for reasons explained above, not all welfare reducing actions require countermeasures, and, secondly, legal solutions are not always the best solutions. Competition law bears similarities to criminal justice. Villains must be punished, but many deviations from optimal behavior by civilians (such as being rude) is best left untouched or counteracted by policy measures other than legal actions (such as education). Canoy and Onderstal (2003) show in a number of oligopoly cases that policy measures such as entry barrier reduction, increasing transparency or reducing switching costs are likely to be much more successful than going for collective dominance cases and the like. In terms of type I and type II mistakes, in the legal history of the Western world it is commonplace only to convict criminals if their guilt is proven beyond reasonable doubt. This puts all the eggs in the type I basket. The reason is by and large normative in nature: as explained above, it is felt that only serious cases should go to court. For less clear-cut cases other instruments are easier to use. Policymakers have much more leeway than judges to do what they think is best. Whether this leeway is always used in a welfare-enhancing way is of course a different matter.

This chapter further elaborates on the welfare consequences of dominance and monopolization and possible policy responses to that. Section 2 delves deeper into the two major policy responses towards dominance, regulation and antitrust. Section 3 then introduces single-firm dominance and different types of abuses of dominance. Section 4 discusses collective (or group) dominance. Section 5 compares legal approaches in the USA and Europe towards dominance and monopolization. Section 6 does the same with mergers. Section 7 concludes.

2   Regulation versus competition policy

Dominant firms are exposed to various types of supervision. In some cases, as for example in the telecommunications industry, they are subject to rather detailed, industry-specific regulation. In other cases, they are only subject to general antitrust supervision. It is therefore useful to start this section with a brief comparison of 'regulation' and 'antitrust'; several dimensions are relevant in this respect: timing of oversight, procedures and control rights, information and continued relationship.

An important difference between regulation and antitrust is that the former operates mainly ex ante and the latter ex post. Antitrust authorities assess conduct after the fact while regulators define the rules for price setting, investment and profit sharing ex ante. Some qualification is in order, however, since for example merger control often requires notification for large mergers and is a quasi-regulatory process.[9]

Relatedly, ex ante supervision must be more expedient. The necessity not to halt productive decisions often puts pressure on regulators and merger control authorities to converge on rapid decisions. In contrast, the ex post nature of antitrust intervention does not call for a similar expediency, except maybe for predatory cases, where interim provisions may be necessary to prevent irreversible damages.[10]

The uncertainty about the overseer's decision making differs between the two institutions. Ex ante intervention removes most of the uncertainty about this intervention (although not necessarily about its consequences); it may thus facilitate financing of new investment by alleviating the lender's potential informational handicap with respect to this intervention and by sharpening the measurement of the firm's performance.

Ex ante intervention also improves the supervisor's commitment to the firm. This commitment is desirable whenever the industry supervisor has the incentives and the opportunity to exploit the firm's efficiency or investment. To be sure, competition authorities can publish guidelines to announce their policy in advance. However, these guidelines may still leave some scope for interpretation, and moreover they need not be followed by the courts.

Finally, ex ante intervention may force the firm to disclose information that it would not disclose ex post. It is indeed often less risky for the firm to conceal or manipulate information ex post rather than ex ante; for instance, the firm may know ex post that a lie about information that conditioned some business decision will not be discovered, but it may have no such certainty ex ante. Relatedly, an ex ante regulator can ask the firm to collect and organize information in a given way; getting specific information ex post may prove difficult if it is not planned for in advance.

A drawback of ex ante intervention is that it may foster collusion between the industry and the supervisor. The industry knows whom it is facing while it is much more uncertain about whether it will be able to capture the (unknown) overseer in a context in which the oversight takes place ex post. This uncertainty about the possibility of capture increases the firm's cost of misbehaving.

A second benefit of ex post intervention is of course the opportunity to take advantage of information that arrives 'after the fact'. For example, it may over time become clearer what constitutes acceptable conduct. To be certain, ex ante decisions could in principle allow for ex post adjustments that embody the new information; but describing properly ex ante the information that will determine acceptability may be prohibitively difficult.

While antitrust authorities usually only assess the lawfulness of conduct, regulators have more extensive powers and engage in detailed regulation; they may set or put constraints on wholesale and retail prices, determine the extent of profit sharing between the firm and its customers (as under cost-of-service regulation or earnings-sharing schemes), oversee investment decisions and control entry into segments through licensing for new entrants and line-of-business restrictions for incumbents.[11]

Regulators' discretionary power is of course qualified by the many constraints they face in their decision making: procedural requirements, lack of long-term commitment, safeguards against regulatory takings, constraints on price fixing or cost reimbursement rules (cost-of-service regulation, price caps, and so on), cost-based determination of access prices, and so forth. Conversely, antitrust authorities and courts sometimes exercise regulatory authority by imposing line-of-business restrictions or forcing cost-of-service determination of access prices. A case in point is Judge Greene's becoming a 'regulator' of the American telecommunications industry. In Europe, where there has been a growing interest in essential facility and market access issues, the European Commission has tried to develop both antitrust and regulatory competences and methods.

There is some convergence of regulatory and competition policy procedures. For example, in the USA, regulatory hearings are quasi-judicial processes in which a wide array of interested parties can expose their viewpoints. The enlisting of 'advocates' is prominent in both institutions and contributes to reducing the informational handicap of the industry overseer.[12]

There are also a couple of differences, however. Private parties tend to play a bigger role in antitrust enforcement than in a regulatory process. Indeed, while competition authorities occasionally conduct independent industry studies, the vast majority of cases are brought forward by private parties.

Another difference is that interest groups are motivated to intervene in the regulatory process solely by the prospect of modifying policy while they urge competition authorities or courts either to modify industry conduct (through an injunction) or to obtain monetary compensation (for example, treble damages in the USA). Yet another difference comes from the fact that competition authorities have less control over the agenda than regulators; the activities of courts and, to a lesser extent, competition authorities are somewhat conditioned by the cases put forward.

Another distinction between the two institutions is the possible separation of investigation and prosecution in antitrust. Regulators conduct regulatory hearings and adjudicate on their basis, while at least in some countries competition authorities may have to win their case in court.[13] For example, in the USA the decisions of the Federal Communications Commission (FCC) take effect directly (except if appealed); in contrast, the Antitrust Division of the Department of Justice must not only go to court but it also bears the initial burden of proof. Regulatory decisions may, however, be appealed in court, in the same way as a court decision may be overruled by a higher court.[14]

Eventually, while regulators and competition authorities are both required to apply consistent reasoning, regulators are mainly bound to be fairly consistent with their previous decisions for the industry they oversee. In contrast, competition authorities and courts must also refer to decisions pertaining to other industries and, moreover, in common law systems, they must take into account other court decisions.[15]

Regulatory decisions tend to rely on superior expertise. While antitrust enforcers have a fairly universal mandate, regulatory agencies usually specialize on a specific industry on a long-term basis. In addition, regulators usually have larger staffs and monitor the firms' accounts on a continuous basis rather than on an occasional one; they can also insist on specific accounting principles (such as accounting separation) as well as disclosure rules.

Superior expertise allows better-informed decision making. For example, regulators may use cost-based rules for retail and wholesale prices in spite of the difficulty in assessing costs, while antitrust enforcers are more at ease with cases based on qualitative evidence (price discrimination, price fixing, vertical restraints and so on) than with cases that require quantitative evidence (predation, tacit collusion or access pricing).

Superior expertise may, however, be a handicap when regulators have limited commitment powers. When a firm invests to improve its technology, regulators (or politicians) may wish to confiscate the efficiency gains, for example, through lower prices. The regulator's access to information exacerbates this 'ratchet effect', which impedes efficiency. Similarly, an excessive attention may inhibit the firm's initiative. In contrast, an arm's length relationship may entail more commitment power and help provide better incentives.[16]

The regulatory agencies' expertise stems in part from their long-term relationship with the industry. But, as is well-known, long-term relationships are, in any organization, conducive to collusion. In addition, the need for industry-focused expertise imposes constraints on the recruitment of regulators, and natural career evolutions are more likely to involve close links with this industry; as a result, the regulators' expertise may reinforce 'revolving doors' problems.

This brief overview of the analogies and differences involved in the two types of supervision suggests that antitrust supervision by a 'generalist' competition agency is best suited when detailed regulation is not crucial; in contrast, oversight by an industry-specific regulatory agency may be warranted when detailed ex ante regulation is needed, as may for example be the case with access policies.

We now turn to competition policy regarding single and collective dominance.

3   Single-firm dominance and monopolization

3.1   Introduction

Throughout the world, competition authorities ask the question: how do firms with (substantial) market power behave? Or, more specifically, how can firms with (substantial) market power exploit this power? The economics literature can help answer these questions. Indeed, for decades monopolies and oligopolies have filled economic textbooks and governments have longstanding traditions in using these theories to design policy responses to counter adverse effects of powerful firms. Yet real-life markets do not always behave according to textbook predictions. Assessing monopolistic and oligopolistic behavior is complex and cannot be solely based on textbook predictions.

Over the last decade an increasing number of scholars have stressed the importance of finding a neat balance between unfettered competition and intervention. As explained earlier, the laissez-faire 'Schumpeter-visits-Chicago' view stresses the importance of free markets and innovation, while the 'Old Europe' view indicates what can go wrong in free markets. Using arguments from both sides, it is perhaps best to scrutinize abuses of a dominant position while realizing the potential downsides of government intervention. Against this background, this section describes what market power amounts to, and how firms can abuse market power.

According to the European Commission's official documents, dominance is defined as follows:[17] 'A firm is in a dominant position if it has the ability to behave independently of its competitors, customers, suppliers and, ultimately, the final consumer.' The crucial part in this definition is 'to behave independently'. By behaving independently firms can mimic monopoly behavior and thereby reduce welfare: 'A dominant firm holding such market power would have the ability to set prices above the competitive level, to sell products of an inferior quality or to reduce its rate of innovation below the level that would exist in a competitive market.' Crucial here is to 'have the ability'. A dominant position is thus a status, not an action:

> Under EU competition law, it is not illegal to hold a dominant position, since a dominant position can be obtained by legitimate means of competition, for example, by inventing and selling a better product. Instead, competition rules do not allow companies to abuse their dominant position. The European merger control system differs from this principle, in so far as it prohibits merged entities from obtaining or strengthening a dominant position by way of the merger.

To punish a dominant firm, one has to show that the firm actually exploits 'the ability to behave independently of its competitors'. To show that the probability of abuse after a merger has increased significantly creates a high burden of proof for merger analysis, which is by nature ex ante. That is why it is enough to show that a dominant position is sufficiently likely to emerge after a merger.

The USA has a longer tradition of dealing with firms with market power, starting with the Sherman Act in 1890, the Clayton Act in 1914 and the Federal Trade Commission Act in 1914. The motivation of these acts (in particular the Sherman Act) was not to enhance efficiency. Rather they were motivated primarily to protect small and medium sized businesses (see for example, Hovenkamp, 1999). Despite this motivation, the legal practice developed more and more in the direction of the 'efficiency doctrine'; for example, judges are unhappy to block a merger just to protect some small player in the market.

The general approach in the USA is to outlaw monopolization, attempts to monopolize or conspiracies to monopolize. Similar to the dominance doctrine, it requires firms to have market power. Many practices can be illegal (sabotage, mergers, refusal to deal, tying, price discrimination, raising rival's cost and so on), but all of them require firms to have 'sufficient market power'. Since an appropriate definition of market power is 'the power to raise prices above the competitive level without losing so many sales that the price increase is unprofitable',[18] having 'sufficient market power' is very similar to dominance. So we conclude that the general approach towards monopolization is not fundamentally different on the two sides of the Atlantic. That is not to say that there are no important differences, though.

The US approach is aimed at preventing monopoly situations. It is less worried about actual behavior once a monopoly has been established. By contrast, the European approach forbids various types of conduct by dominant firms. More detailed differences will be addressed shortly, as well as in Section 5.

There are basically two different economic models underlying single firm dominance. The first is the most straightforward one: the monopoly model. A monopolist obviously 'has the ability to behave independently of its competitors, customers, suppliers and, ultimately, the final consumer'. It is well known that monopolies have an incentive to raise price above the competitive level, at the expense of consumers, that is, giving rise to a deadweight loss. Indeed, in the most straightforward textbook model, monopolies have an incentive to produce less than is socially desirable. There are also more subtle ways in which welfare can be reduced by monopolists, such as rent seeking, lack of innovation incentives, X-inefficiencies and suboptimal product selection. These suboptimal effects need not occur. Counterforces include the exploitation of scale economies, the threat of potential entry, commitment problems[19] and innovation.

Which of these forces prevail is hard to say. Even in concrete cases such as the Microsoft case economists tend to disagree on the appropriate economic model and the welfare consequences. Nevertheless, some general conclusions can be drawn.

- Monopolies tend to select suboptimal levels of output and price in markets characterized by relatively modest scale economies, lack of fast innovation and entry barriers.
- Even in the presence of counterforces, such as innovation, monopolies can still reduce welfare.
- Even if monopolies do reduce welfare, it is neither straightforward nor costless to counteract such monopoly behavior.
- Whether counterforces do outweigh the welfare losses associated with monopolies is context dependent.

The second economic model underlying single-firm dominance is the oligopoly model. Casual observation suggests that oligopolies are covered by collective (or group) dominance rather than single-firm dominance, but this is not the case. Take an oligopoly that consists of one large player, say with a market share of 50 per cent, and three smaller players, with say 20 per cent, 15 per cent and 15 per cent. In such an oligopoly two things may happen that raise concern. The first concern is that the oligopolists manage to collude tacitly for example on price. Here we enter the world of collective dominance, to be discussed in Section 4. The second concern is that the large firm succeeds in abusing its position to 'behave independently of its competitors, customers, suppliers and, ultimately, the final consumer'. However, if that is the case, it is not clear which 'oligopoly' model should apply, since the firm in question apparently behaves as a monopolist. The fact that the market structure looks more like an oligopoly than a monopoly seems irrelevant. However, this observation denies the importance of strategic interactions.

What does it mean, in the context of an oligopoly, to behave 'independently' of its competitors? Section 3.2 provides economic examples of (abuse of) independent behavior, such as predation and foreclosure. These examples are characterized by the fact that a single firm punishes a (potential) competitor. It can only do so profitably if it faces relatively little competition. Competitive forces will make (anti-competitive) price discrimination unattractive, which will prevent predation as well as foreclosure. This does not mean that the monopoly model applies. Oligopoly theory teaches us how firms interact strategically (see, for example, Tirole, 1988). A dominant firm that attempts to eliminate a rival by predatory pricing has to predict how the prey will react to the pricing as well as likely responses by future rivals. Hence strategic interaction and oligopoly theory are as vital for understanding single-firm dominance as monopoly theory.

The use of oligopoly models becomes clear when studying attempts to deter entry. Firms with market power who want to deter entry have to play a strategic oligopoly game with (potential) rivals. The outcome of such a game determines whether deterring entry is a profitable strategy. The outcome of the game is influenced by the parameters of the game. In a stylized two-period, two-firm model the incumbent firm chooses some variable X (for example capacity) in period 1. Firm 2 (the potential entrant) observes X and decides to enter or not. In period 2 some strategic variable (for example price) is set. The parameters that influence the Nash equilibrium of such a game are whether the strategies are substitutes (quantities) or complements (prices), the level of asymmetry, the level of product differentiation, the switching costs and so on.[20] So what appears to be 'monopoly behavior' could easily be sustained as a Nash equilibrium in an oligopoly game. It becomes clear that oligopoly models are vital tools for understanding incentives for powerful firms to deter entry. The same applies for other types of behavior such as raising rivals' costs or predation (see, further, subsection 3.2).

There is also another important category of so-called 'independent behavior'. It is best explained in the context of a potential merger in a Cournot-type setting. First, in the words of the Commission:

Under certain circumstances, a merger weakens competition by removing important competitive constraints on one or more sellers, who consequently find it profitable to increase prices or reduce output post merger. The most direct effect will be the elimination of the competitive constraints that the merging firms exerted on each other. Before the merger, the merging parties may have exercised a competitive constraint on each other. If one of the merging firms had raised its price or reduced then it would have lost customers to the other merging firm, making it unprofitable. The merger would thus eliminate this particular constraint. In addition, non-merging firms can also benefit from the reduction of competitive pressure that results from the merger since the merging firms' price increase or output reduction may switch some demand to the rival firms, which, in turn, may find it optimal to increase prices. The elimination of these competitive constraints could lead to a significant price increase or output reduction in the relevant market.[21]

Put differently, if there are four players playing Cournot, a merger between two of them will, *ceteris paribus*, reduce output and increase price. It is questionable whether this particular interpretation of 'independent behavior' should fall under the heading of dominance. In economic terms this type of oligopoly behavior can hardly be called 'independent' since it depends, inter alia, on conjectures on behavior of other players. It is also not related to market shares. The same arguments can be used whether or not we are facing a 50–20–15–15 split of the market or a 25–25–25–25 split.

It is noteworthy that the Cournot-type unilateral effects in oligopolies mentioned above are not part of the 'old' dominance definition in Article 82 EU Treaty cases. For the purposes of this chapter, we prefer to keep the old definition of single-firm dominance (with a possible exception for mergers), that is interpreting 'independent behavior' in a rather strict sense, that is excluding Cournot-type behavior.

Concluding, we may say that the monopoly model is important for its focus on behavior by a firm that faces little (or no) competition. The oligopoly model is important for its focus on strategic interaction. Even if a firm faces little competition, its behavior can easily be based on strategic motives, for example attempts to deter entry.

As it is not clear a priori under which circumstances firms are able to 'behave independently', there is need for further clarification. The most common legal tool to test whether or not a firm is dominant is the market share test. If a firm has a 40–50 per cent market share, then it is assumed to have sufficient market power to be called dominant. While being practical, measurable and legally accepted, from an economic perspective the market share test is too simplistic, for two reasons. First, even large players need not be dominant. In the case where innovation is taking place at a rapid pace, in the case of fierce competition between large players, or strong disciplining by potential entrants, firms cannot 'behave independently'. Second, there can be cases where firms have lower shares, say 25 per cent, but are still dominant. This can occur if entry barriers are high and market power is reflected through other channels than just market share. Arguably, such cases are statistically less significant,[22] but should not be neglected.

Arguably the most extreme position towards market power was taken by Judge Wyzanski in *United States* v. *United Shoe Machinery Corp* (1953).[23] He claimed that a firm with sufficient market power monopolizes 'whenever it does business'. This position has not been followed on either side of the Atlantic.[24] Instead, firms have to be in a dominant position and abuse the position. Why is this needed? There are basically two reasons. First, a firm can owe its dominant position to superior past performance, for example, in the form of an innovation. The sheer fact that a firm is in such a position does not seem to be worrying and does not warrant intervention. Second, in the case of a natural monopoly, it is cost-inefficient to have more players in the market, so it is hard to see the justification for punishing efficiency.

To cater to the various degrees of market power, legal practice in the USA has developed a difference between 'a lot of market power' and 'a smaller amount of market power'. If the evidence suggests substantial market power then the courts have identified a certain set of practices that will find the defendant guilty of illegal monopolization. If the evidence suggests less market power, then the courts tend to go for 'attempt to monopolize', which carries stricter conduct requirements (cf. Hovenkamp, 1999). In Europe, such a 'sliding scale' of market power does not exist, at least not in a legally formal way. In the USA, (sufficient) market power and abuse of market power are not treated separately. In Europe, however, there is a rather strict distinction between dominance and abuse of dominance. The advantage of the European approach is that it starts with a 'dominance test', which is relatively straightforward compared to abuse. If there is no dominance, there is no case. This simple rule creates clarity for firms within a relatively short time period. The disadvantage is that it creates a somewhat artificial split between a 'problem' area and a 'no-problem' area, largely based on a market share criterion.[25]

From economic theory we know, however, that there is not such a clear-cut split. It is not so difficult to envisage a heterogeneous goods market with high switching costs, minor innovative activity and large reputation effects failing the dominance test, and yet posing a potential problem, in a welfare sense.[26] At the other end of the spectrum, firms that are labeled 'dominant' face the restriction that certain types of behavior per se are almost forbidden. These types of behavior are not related to the seriousness of the effects of possible abuse; that is, certain behavior that might be abusive is forbidden in a perhaps too mechanistic way. As a consequence, if there are competition authorities or regulators who have a tendency to overregulate, labeling a firm as dominant gives opportunities to impose unnecessary restrictions.

The integrated approach in the USA gives more possibilities for taking the seriousness of effects into account, yet the USA, in response to fears that expansive applications of antitrust may reduce innovation, is becoming more and more reluctant to pursue monopolization cases. It is also rather odd to be strict on preventing monopolization (under the assumption that monopolies are bad) and yet be relaxed about actual monopolies.

In conclusion, the current EU system, while being practical, bears a risk of running into type I and type II errors, that is some dominant firms may escape attention while some welfare-enhancing behavior by dominant firms may be punished. The US system is not likely to produce many type I errors, but may be too lenient towards monopolization practices.[27]

Let us discuss an option that might improve the European situation. There are two problems. The first is that the dominance test relies too much on market shares. The second one is that possible abusive behavior is treated too mechanistically. A way to solve the first problem is to put more economics into the dominance test, which implies less weight being put on market shares and more on other economic variables, in particular entry barriers. Competition authorities can have dominance cases with lower market shares but high entry barriers and other problems. On the other hand, market players with high market shares (say 60 per cent or so) will have the opportunity to argue why they are not dominant despite their high market share. The disadvantage of that approach is that it is less predictable and that it may take more time.

To tackle the second problem, also more economics should be put into the abuse of dominance. When a firm is labeled 'dominant', more economic analysis is needed to underpin a ban on certain types of behavior (see subsection 3.2). The reason is that many types of behavior that can be called abusive have plausible welfare-enhancing interpretations as well. Think of price discrimination. It is not clear a priori whether or not price discrimination by a dominant firm is good or bad. A recent case in Europe, *Virgin /British Airways*, clarifies this point. In 1998, Virgin complained about British Airways' Performance Reward Scheme (PRS) as infringing Article 82 EU Treaty. The Commission criticized the PRS for travel agents as 'being abusive of a dominant position' (IV/D-2/34.780, p. 12). While the Commission analyzed the scheme at length, it did not make an explicit attempt to show that the scheme was actually anti-competitive and that the effects were welfare reducing.

Putting more economics into the dominance test without doing the same with abuse runs the risk of overregulation. Applying more economics in both areas creates a better balance between market and government failure so that type I and type II errors will be reduced.

3.2   *Abuse of a dominant position and monopolization*

As explained in Section 2, for merger cases it is sufficient to demonstrate that a merger creates or strengthens a dominant position. For Article 82 EU Treaty cases it is *not* sufficient to demonstrate that a firm has a dominant position. In the words of the EC, abuse of a dominant position is defined as:

> anti-competitive business practices (including improper exploitation of customers or exclusion of competitors) which a dominant firm may use in order to maintain or increase its position in the market. Competition law prohibits such behaviour, as it damages true competition between firms, exploits consumers, and makes it unnecessary for the dominant undertaking to compete with other firms on merit. Article 82 EU Treaty lists some examples of abuse, namely unfair pricing, restriction of production output and imposing discriminatory or unnecessary terms in dealings with trading partners.[28]

The USA has a list in similar vein (sabotage, mergers, refusal to deal, tying, price discrimination, raising rival's cost etc). This section tries to shed some economic light on a number of these potential abuses.

Firms with a dominant position can employ a wide range of strategies that fall under the heading of abuse. The strategies may be grouped in three categories.

1. *Strategies aimed at deterring entry.* The most common examples are strategic barriers, such as pre-emptive and retaliatory action by incumbents, for example strategic price discounts, excess capacity and advertising.
2. *Strategies aimed at forcing exit of a rival.* Most studied examples of pushing a rival out are foreclosure and predation.
3. *Strategies aimed at raising rivals' costs.* Think for example of exclusive deals. Notice that the last two sets of strategies can also deter entry in addition to harming rivals.

There is a large literature on each group of strategies, including some general purpose articles such as Ordover and Saloner (1989). While much that has been said in Ordover and Saloner is still valid today, there are also a number of new developments in various areas. This section will focus on some of these new developments.

Before we do that, we reiterate that each of the strategies discussed is not an automatic abuse, or should not be an automatic abuse. Price cutting, advertising, vertical relationships and so on are all part of normal business strategies. What has to be shown *economically* is that welfare is reduced by employing a certain strategy. Because welfare is not easily measurable, in particular since long-run effects have to be taken into account as well, welfare does not necessarily yield a practical *legal* tool to distinguish anti-competitive practices from normal business strategies.[29] We will come back to this question when discussing various anti-competitive practices.

Strategies aimed at deterring entry   Firms can abuse a dominant position (or indeed create a dominant position) by deterring entry. While the analysis of entry barriers is crucial for understanding the effectiveness and persistence of market power, it is not so easy to isolate entry-deterring strategies as a single source of abuse. Many types of abuse, such as predation, are based on the notion that future entry is discouraged. In fact, it is often a condition to make abusive strategies profitable. Eliminating a potential entrant or a rival today is of no use if there will be a fresh rival tomorrow. Still, there are some examples of (strategic) entry deterrence that can constitute an abuse by themselves.

Strategic entry barriers are defined as incumbency actions that are designed to influence the behavior of potential rivals. They are effective if potential rivals consider current strategies as indications of future market conditions (see Gilbert, 1989). Examples of strategic entry barriers are strategic output expansion, pre-emptive innovation, shelving, excessive investment in advertising, R&D or product differentiation. These actions have in common that firms need to have market power to make them an effective strategy. How does such a strategy work? Take the example of shelving. It can pay off for a dominant firm to wait with the introduction of an innovation and 'milk' its cash-generating established product until entry is an immediate threat. The dominant firm has to be prepared to counter innovative entry immediately, as it takes place; that is, it has to have the innovation 'on the shelf'. If entry indeed occurs, the firm puts his new product on the market to take away demand from the entrant.

This strategy is in its effect similar to predatory pricing. Hakfoort and Weigand Bijl (2000) provide an example in the Dutch consumer magazines market.[30] New magazines are often aimed at creating a new market segment. The launch can therefore be seen as an attempt to differentiate products. For a dominant firm, launching a new magazine can be less attractive if, in the face of stagnant advertising budgets and consumer demand for magazines, it dilutes its circulation and advertising revenues. However, if a new firm enters the market with a 'new format' magazine, it may be rational for the established publisher to bring a similar magazine to the market and drive the rival out of the market.

In contrast to predatory pricing, 'predatory product imitation' need not be based on charging a price that is lower than, in the extreme, the entrant's marginal cost. It is sufficient to launch the imitating and thus substituting product, charge the same price, and steal demand away from the new entrant to make entry unprofitable. In addition, there is also a long-run effect. The publisher can build a reputation for retaliating whenever an entrant attempts to establish a new magazine. The threat of retaliation may discourage potential future entrants.

As said above, it is quite rare to prove abuse of a dominant position without actually harming a rival. In *Berkey Photo* v. *Eastman Kodak* (1979),[31] the monopolist's failure to disclose information about a new product was seen as anti-competitive.[32] It is however, far from easy to prove a convincing case. Some practices are easier to use to deter entry than to harm rivals. Rivals have invested in sunk costs and are less likely to divert assets to other areas (or even leave the market) than potential entrants. It follows that one is expected to find lots of possibilities for anti-competitive entry deterrence. Whether this also implies lots of legal cases is a different matter. Potential entrants have very bad track records as plaintiffs: 'Most are denied standing. The practices are also generally subtle and hard to identify, and the public enforcement agencies are generally reluctant to spend vast amounts of money in litigating them' (Hovenkamp, 1999, p. 281).

Another example from the economic literature is 'banked advertising', where firms engage in (large amounts of) advertising to scare off entrants (Pepsi and Coke come to mind). In practice, it turns out to be virtually impossible to distinguish anti-competitive advertising from normal advertising practices. This problem is endemic to strategic entry barriers and also holds for other types of strategies, such as strategic product differentiation.

To summarize, while there seem to be ample possibilities for anti-competitive entry deterring strategies, filing suits against them as a single source of abuse is problematic.

Strategies aimed at forcing the exit of a rival   This category of abusive behavior is the most common, and the most studied in the economic and legal literature. Notice that the words 'forcing exit' are in fact a little too extreme. Strategies that are aimed at 'hurting a rival', with exit as its ultimate consequence, are perhaps a more appropriate description. The reason why exit is not a *sine qua non* is that profits can be increased if one hurts a rival to the extent that it becomes a less effective rival. However, the strategies discussed in this section should not be confused with 'raising rivals' costs', discussed below. Although the difference between the two types of strategies may not be that great, there is one clear distinction. Strategies that aim at forcing a rival out require the incumbent to incur upfront costs, while raising rivals' costs does not.

There are two main ways of forcing a rival out, predation and foreclosure. Other varieties, such as price discrimination, can best be grouped under predation, since discrimination is only anti-competitive if it is predatory in nature. Both on predation and on foreclosure there is a bulky literature which we will not consider here. Instead, we will point at some new developments in both areas.

The historical case on predatory pricing is *Standard Oil* (1911, 221 US 1); the company attained a 90 per cent market share, in part through price warfare. While the *Standard Oil* case stoked up the debate on predation, and many predation cases were won between 1940 and 1975, the debate was considerably cooled down after the publication of the Areeda and Turner (1975) article. The article, which suggested a standard check on predation based on average variable costs, made so much impression on judges that plaintiffs have virtually gone empty-handed ever since. Combined with the Areeda–Turner logic there have been two other developments, one economic and one legal. The economic development is the Chicago School logic which argued 'forcefully' that predation was not rational and therefore it did not make sense to make a lot of fuss about it. The notion of irrationality of predation remains the dominant legal paradigm in the USA until today. The legal development was the famous *Brooke* case in 1993 (*Brooke Group* v. *Brown & Williamson Tobacco Corporation*, 509 US 209), which boiled down to a heavier burden of proof on the part of the plaintiff because, unlike the earlier days of predation, the Supreme Court upheld the lower court's view that the plaintiff had to show that recoupment of predation losses was sufficiently likely.

As advanced by Bolton *et al.* (2000), economic theory has moved considerably beyond the simplistic irrationality paradigm and also provides new strategic recoupment possibilities neglected in earlier economic theory. These new insights, if adopted by the judges as the current state of the art, could very well lead to a renewed interest in the subject.

Let us start by defining predatory pricing. Various causes can result in prices being 'too low'. On the one hand, prices might be too low because firms want to attract customers, creating a demand for a new or updated product. On the other hand, low prices can also be the result of an attempt by the incumbent to force a rival out of the market. The incumbent opts for a short-term loss in order to make long-term extra profits thanks to a dominant position.

Predatory pricing implies that there is a price reduction which is profitable only because of the added market power the predator gains from eliminating, disciplining or otherwise inhibiting the competitive conduct of a rival or potential rival. In the short term customers may benefit from lower prices, but over a longer period weakened competition will lead to higher prices, lower quality or less choice. The fact that an activity is being run at a loss is not sufficient to establish a case of predatory pricing. The question is whether it has an anti-competitive effect. In order to prove the anti-competitive effect of predatory pricing, Bolton *et al.* (2000) propose a five-criteria rule: a facilitating market structure, a scheme of predation and supporting evidence, probable recoupment, price below cost and the absence of efficiencies or business justification defense.

The market structure must make predation a feasible strategy. A company must have the power to raise prices (or otherwise exploit consumers or suppliers) over some significant period of time (dominant firm or small group of jointly acting firms, entry and re-entry barriers).

Predation pricing and recoupment require that predation be plausible ex ante (that is, based on prediction and extrapolation) and probable ex post (that is, retrospectively). This means that there must be a predatory scheme ex ante under which the predator can expect to recoup its initial losses. Using the tools of applied game theory can help to identify economic conditions under which predation is rational profit-seeking conduct by a dominant firm. Ex post probability is shown by the subsequent exclusion of rivals and post-predation market conditions that make future recoupment likely.

At the very least, the losses incurred from a predation strategy must be recouped somehow. Should the operator be unable to recoup the losses, because of competition from existing or potential competitors, the predation strategy is not viable. Recoupment is only possible if there is an exclusionary effect on (potential) rivals, or through the disciplining of the rival's competitive conduct. The most common and straightforward recoupment occurs when prices in the predatory market rise above the competitive level. In more complex settings, recoupment can occur through other channels, for example, by raising the prices of complementary or closely related services. It is essential that these latter price increases should unambiguously be explained by the earlier predatory pricing (see also Cabral and Riordan, 1997).

In the predatory period, prices should be below average variable cost, although also prices which are above average variable cost but below average total cost might be predatory and injure competition. The most commonly used cost standards are average total cost (ATC) and average variable cost (AVC) or long-run average incremental cost (LRAIC) as a substitute for ATC and average avoidable cost as a substitute for AVC (Bolton *et al.*, 2000). If prices are above ATC, there is no problem. If prices are below AVC, predation can be assumed. A price between ATC and AVC is either presumptively or conclusively legal. If the price is presumptively legal, there is a need for evidence that the operator intends to eliminate or to discipline a competitor.

Finally, cases can arise where below-cost pricing by a dominant operator might be efficiency-enhancing rather than predatory. However, in such cases one has to examine very closely whether the efficiency enhancement is also to the benefit of the consumers in the long term. Otherwise the argument could be abused to foreclose a market on the grounds that it is 'efficient' to do so.

The five criteria rule provides a clear procedure for handling a potential predatory pricing case. However, predatory pricing might be hard to prove, particularly the recoupment aspect. Bolton *et al.* (2000) provide new economic underpinning for predation to be rational and to distinguish it from normal business practices. To sort out the differences between the two they suggest checking whether there are indeed plausible efficiency gains as a result of the below-cost pricing, whether there are alternative means to achieve those efficiency gains and whether the efficiency gains materialize in for example higher quality (instead of just higher profits).

Bolton *et al.* then continue to develop plausible ways in which predation can occur, using new insights from economic theory. We may mention two examples.

- *Financial predation.* The argument here depends on capital market imperfections. Investors faced with moral hazard and selection problems, tend to favor large firms at the expense of smaller ones. This incumbency advantage can be exploited. When start-ups need cash flow to pay back their debts, predators may have an easy target. Cutting prices reduces cash flow and the capital market imperfection stimulates predation. Bolton *et al.* (2000) show how financial predation could be used in a recent cable TV case in Sacramento.
- *Signaling and reputation.* The predator can also lower its price in order to mislead the prey into believing that market conditions are unfavorable. The incumbent exploits its superior knowledge on cost and demand to deter entry or eliminate a rival. Bolton *et al.* illustrate this possibility with the old *Bell* case (1879).

Bolton *et al.* (2000) conclude by asserting that courts should use modern economic insight to assess the plausibility of predation strategies. However, their insights were not uncontested. Elzinga and Mills (2001) criticize Bolton *et al.* for being too simplistic and too model specific. Without going into the details of this discussion (there was also a lengthy reply by Bolton *et al.*), we conclude the following:

- Predation can be rational in a variety of settings, and more than previously assumed (in particular by US courts), mostly hinging on incomplete information arguments.
- It is not clear how serious predation is in practice. Ultimately, this is an empirical question.
- Applying the five-step procedure by Bolton *et al.* seems a sensible thing to do, no matter how strongly one feels about the applicability of economic theory or the empirical relevance of predation strategies.

When we look at the European practice, we observe a difference in views again. The US law on predatory pricing has been reasonably clear at least since the *Brooke Group* v. *Brown & Williamson* case in 1993. There the court held that, to be found predatory, conduct must satisfy a two-part test: (i) the allegedly predatory price must be below an appropriate measure of cost, and (ii) there must be a 'dangerous probability' that the alleged predator will be able to recoup its losses through monopoly prices once its rivals leave the market. The European Court of Justice (ECJ) has adopted the first part of the Brooke Group test, but has declined to adopt the second part, holding that recoupment is not a necessary element of predation under Article 82 EU Treaty.[33] Recoupment seems an essential element of the test because cutting prices in order to increase business often is the very essence of competition.'[34]

The marked difference in approaches between the USA and the EU again reflects differences in the view on treating behavior of powerful firms (see, further, Section 5). In addition to the recoupment debate there is a second difference. Whereas most US courts have held that the appropriate measure of cost is average variable cost, the European Court of Justice left open the possibility of finding prices above average variable cost but below average total cost predatory if they are 'part of a plan for eliminating a competitor'.[35]

The most recent advance in the literature on cost rules is Elhauge (2003), who argued that, recently, European and US officials have made moves toward restricting firms from using above-cost price cuts to drive out entrants. The legal developments most likely reflect legitimate critiques of cost-based tests of predatory pricing. Elhauge argues that costs should be defined in a pragmatic way, as a measure that assures that prices above 'costs' cannot deter or drive out equally efficient rivals. Elhauge shows that price cuts do not necessarily indicate an undesirable protection of market power, but rather can be an efficient response to deviations from a price discrimination schedule in competitive markets, and warns against harmful restrictions on reactive above-cost price cuts.

Concluding, while the US practice could gain from acknowledging the potential rationality of predation, the European practice could gain by acknowledging the potential irrationality of setting low prices without the possibility of future recoupment.

Another way of eliminating a rival is by foreclosing a market. The standard example is a vertically integrated firm with an upstream bottleneck facility and downstream competition. The downstream competitors need input from the upstream monopolist to do business. The integrated firm may have an incentive to provide the input on such unfavorable terms that it effectively forecloses the market. In a less extreme case we have an example of raising rivals' costs here. The downstream competitor may not be eliminated but faces a competitive disadvantage. Think of telecommunications. An upstream incumbent owns the network and provides downstream services as well. Downstream competitors need the network to offer services. The incumbent can put its downstream competitors at a disadvantage by offering higher network access charges than it charges itself. The competitors may survive if the charge is not too high to run them out of business.[36]

Besides the access example there are other forms of foreclosure. Firms can refuse to cooperate, grant exclusivity or price discriminate. Similar to other types of abuses, one needs incomplete information arguments to make foreclosure a rational strategy. In the absence of informational asymmetries the Chicago School tells us that it is not obvious how an upstream monopolist could gain by foreclosing a (possibly profitable) downstream market.

The argument to back up rationality of foreclosure is not unlike the Coasian durable goods dilemma, in which a monopolist has an incentive to charge high prices early on to attract the customers with a high willingness to pay, but then wants to reduce price to attract additional customers who are less willing to pay but still profitable to have. A dilemma exists when willing to pay customers anticipate a price drop. An upstream monopolist faces a similar commitment problem. It wants to make money on access, but it also wants to protect its downstream profits. Each additional 'customer' adds to its access profits but also increases downstream competition.

There are several policy responses to foreclosure. Rey and Tirole (2003) mention: (i) structural policies (divestiture); (ii) access pricing; (iii) access quantity control; (iv) disclosure requirements and (v) so-called 'common carrier policies'.

We will not repeat the pros and cons of each of these responses in different settings, but the last type of policy requires further explanation. Suppose that 'upstream' and 'downstream' are not based on fundamental technological constraints but on historical coincidences. If an upstream monopolist is 'worse' (in terms of welfare) than a downstream monopolist (or vice versa), a policy option is to change the vertical structure of the market so that the 'best monopoly variant' prevails. Such policies are called 'common carrier policies' by Rey and Tirole. An example of such a policy is the US gas market reform.[37]

The broad implications of the Rey and Tirole (2003) analysis are as follows. First it does matter whether the competitive segment is upstream or downstream. Downstream monopolies are worse because they do not have the commitment problem described above. Henceforth, in the absence of other counterforces, downstream monopolies will behave as textbook welfare reducers. Since the same does not apply to upstream monopolies, this has consequences for the effectiveness of the above-mentioned common carrier policy: policy can ensure that consumers do not have to deal directly with a monopolist.

Second, forbidding discrimination by an upstream monopolist can be counterproductive, since it bypasses the commitment problem (upstream firms not being allowed to lower their prices to attract further customers).

Another area where foreclosure plays a role is in the adjacent markets literature. In contrast to the literature on direct market power, it is much less clear under which circumstances firms can inflict damage in adjacent markets.

Rey *et al.* (2001) discuss adjacent market foreclosure. In many respects the adjacent markets situation resembles the discussion on conglomerate mergers. In both cases it should be clear that there are fewer concerns a priori about welfare-reducing behavior. This is so because firms often have less ability as well as less incentive to foreclose adjacent market (or to leverage market power) than they would have in more direct situations. Firms have less ability because it is more complicated to foreclose an adjacent market, and – more importantly – they have less incentive because foreclosing adjacent markets is often costly. It can be costly because it can reduce business opportunities or reduce economies of scale and scope.

Nevertheless, there remain situations where welfare concerns are legitimate. Firms may leverage their market power to adjacent markets if the adjacent markets are somehow related to the market in which the firm has market power. Think of Microsoft having market power in the operating systems market. It may use (or may have used) this power to take control of the adjacent browser market. It can leverage market power by refusing to deal, by making products incompatible, by denying access, and so on.

From an economic point of view, it is important to focus the analysis on the entire market arena (Canoy and Onderstal, 2003), that is including all relevant markets that are related. In the current practice of European competition law, the European Commission always starts a merger case or a case related to the abuse of a dominant position by delineating the relevant market. When assessing market performance on the relevant market, all markets that (strongly) influence behavior on the relevant market have to be taken into consideration in order to get a complete picture. For instance, the relevant scale of entry may not coincide with the relevant market. In some situations, a firm needs to enter several markets before being able to realize sufficient economies of scale. If too much emphasis is put on *the* relevant market, one may falsely conclude that entry barriers are low. The market arena consists of markets that are connected by important links, such as supply-side relationships (for example, by operating both markets, firms can accomplish economies of scale or scope), demand-side relationships (for example, a firm sells complementary goods, such as hardware and software) or vertical relationships (a firm's conduct in the upstream market has influence on the performance of the downstream market).[38] Assessing possible abuse of a dominant position by leveraging is more easily understood in a context of connected markets.

In which case is foreclosure by leveraging a profitable strategy for a dominant firm? In Whinston's (1990) paper the dominant firm ties its product of market A (where it is dominant) to market B (where it is not dominant), so as to make the firm more aggressive in market B and thereby scares off its rivals.[39] The most important insight in Rey *et al.* (2001) is that foreclosing adjacent markets can protect monopoly profits on the 'home' market. Recent literature provides a synthesis of the older leveraging theories and the Chicago critique. The Chicago critique emphasizes that it does not make sense to extend monopoly power to adjacent markets unless the adjacent market belongs to the home market, in which case it is misleading to call it adjacent. The new insights work from the hypothesis that the monopoly profits on the home market are somehow insecure, for example because there is a permanent threat of innovation. Think of software or pharmaceutical markets. The arguments are similar to the Coasian durable goods dilemma mentioned above, albeit in a different way. In the case of an upstream monopolist, the durable goods dilemma means that the upstream monopolist has less incentive to foreclose the downstream market. In the adjacent markets case, the durable goods dilemma can be bypassed by foreclosing the adjacent market.

To conclude, assessing foreclosure requires close inspection of the incentives of powerful firms. If powerful firms have the incentive and ability to foreclose a market, an attractive policy response is changing the market structure so that the incentives are lowered, for example by changing the vertical structure.

Strategies aimed at raising rivals' costs   Raising the costs of a rival (RRC) has the advantage over the forcing strategies discussed above, in that it often requires fewer upfront costs for the dominant firm. A predator must incur substantial losses with uncertain future returns. A firm that succeeds in raising its rivals' costs often incurs fewer costs and may yield immediate returns. Clearly, also the legal rules governing RRC should differ from those for predation, since cost-based rules and recoupment do not apply. Another interesting difference between strategies aimed at exit, such as foreclosure and predation, and RRC is that the Chicago critique does apply to RRC. Clearly, if RRC is not costly it must be rational, also in the absence of incomplete information. Still the differences between RRC and strategies aimed at exit should not be overstated, since RRC often requires firms to incur costs as well. Many antitrust violations can be interpreted as RRC (tying, bundling, exclusive dealing and so on). In legal practice it is often not explicitly addressed as such, although there are ample legal examples of condemning practices that raise rivals' costs (see Hovenkamp, 1999).

The economic research on this set of strategies was initiated by Salop and Scheffman in a number of papers. Salop and Scheffman (1983, 1987) identify a variety of RRC strategies, such as refusals to deal, advertising and R&D. Scheffman (1992) showed that RRC strategies may be much more widespread than initially thought and are not restricted to dominant firms. Coate and Kleit (1994), however, argue that the transactions costs of RRC are often neglected in the literature and may well offset its benefits. The most straightforward example of RRC is refusal to deal. In the 1927 *Kodak* case, a monopoly manufacturer of camera film attempted to integrate forward into retail.[40] Accordingly, it refused to wholesale its supplies to other retailers. The court ruled that Kodak leveraged its market power to the detriment of competitors, and repeated this in a later (1992) *Kodak* case. From these cases and the other legal practices in the USA one can infer that convincing RRC cases are rare. While the rationality of RRC is beyond discussion, the mechanisms are often subtle, much more subtle than refusal to deal. As a consequence, it turns out to be very hard to distinguish RRC from normal business practices.

Arguably the most important RRC case was Microsoft, which might also have been discussed in the section on foreclosure or predation. In fact Microsoft was alleged to have eliminated a competitor by a combination of predatory and cost-raising actions. Obviously, space is too limited to repeat all the discussions on the Microsoft case here.[41] The case was interesting for many reasons. From an economist perspective it provides a good test for competition policy in the 'new economy' and it shows how thin the line is between anti-competitive behavior and normal business practices.

Microsoft has integrated Internet Explorer with Windows Explorer and made it part of the operating system Windows which it monopolizes. It has been alleged that, by not allowing competitors in the browser market,

Microsoft is essentially providing a lower-quality operating system when used with other browsers than when used with Internet Explorer. Even when Internet Explorer is not integrated in the operating system, the exclusive installation of it on a new computer by the manufacturer may increase the cost of a rival browser if there is some cost (or time or expertise) required for other browsers to be installed by the user.

The first discussion point concerned the actual level of market power. Traditional tools point at Microsoft having monopoly power in the market for operating systems, but Microsoft (through Richard Schmalensee) argued that the relevant scale of competition is the one for platforms, not operating systems. Microsoft felt that traditional methods of calculating market shares fell short in high-tech industries, where competition for the market was as important as competition on the market. In contrast to the government, Microsoft claimed that competition for the market, that is potential competition from innovators, was vigorous.

Although many economists would agree that network effects and entry barriers provide Microsoft with substantial market power, however measured, there is less agreement on the question whether Microsoft has actually used this power to the detriment of consumers. The central role in answering this question is played by so-called 'Middleware'. Obviously, a competitor to Microsoft's operating system cannot offer the full Office product line without incurring a prohibitively large amount of sunk costs. Middleware is written on top of Windows and does not suffer from this problem. A widescale adoption of Middleware would imply that Microsoft cannot exploit its market power which it derives from its operating system.

Focusing on Microsofts potential RRC strategies, the government charged that Microsoft used contractual arrangements to exclude competitors (*US* v. *Microsoft*, 1998, para. 75–102). An example of such a contractual arrangement is an arrangement between Microsoft and an Internet service provider (ISP), in which the ISP was granted favorable terms. In return the ISP agreed to deny its subscribers access to competing browsers. The reason why subscribers buy such an 'unfavorable contract' is that there exists an external effect; that is, individual buyers do not feel the reduction of competition effect, since their individual purchases contribute in a negligible way to that.[42] Clearly, without counterforces, such practices are harmful for consumers. What are the possible counterforces? They are three in number. The first one is that Microsoft may have raised the cost of an inefficient rival, which could be welfare-enhancing. The second is that exclusive deals can enhance efficiency. In particular, in potential hold-up situations, exclusive deals can increase relation-specific investments. The third counterforce is innovation. An exclusive arrangement with a content provider can spur innovation since it can trigger complementary investments by those providers.[43]

Since theory provides ambiguous welfare consequences of exclusive deals, the antitrust authority has to verify the specific details of the Microsoft case to come to an assessment. The complication in the Microsoft case is that long-run effects have to be taken into account. The introduction to this chapter revealed the importance of long-run effects in general, but, in an innovation-driven market, the long-run effects are even more important than they are otherwise. The difficulties of making accurate long-term predictions in the Microsoft case are that (i) long-term predictions in innovation-driven markets are notoriously difficult and (ii) the theoretical linkages between competition and innovation and between innovation and welfare are ambiguous. Clearly, delving deeper into the details of the case reveals that there are a number of welfare enhancing features (free browsers, single standard, some welfare-enhancing innovation spurs) but also some welfare reductions (lack of choice, higher prices for Windows, reputation effects on aggressive conduct). How should one add these welfare effects? To quantify them is a tall order indeed, involves among other things weighing short-term and long-term effects and quantifying highly complex uncertainty issues. It is therefore unsurprising to find legal and economic scholars on both sides. In sum, the Microsoft case neatly showed the difficulty of abuse of dominance (or monopolization) cases. Elements of subjective judgment will always play a part.

Reviewing the literature on RRC reveals similarities to the previous abuse cases. There are many convincing economic examples of profitable ways of raising rivals' costs, as there are of predation or foreclosure. New economic insights reveal an enlarged set of possibilities for a firm to raise its rivals' costs profitably, yet the mechanisms are often rather subtle and cannot be easily distinguished from normal business practices. Therefore, the legal successes of abuse cases based on RRC are modest.

3.3   Conclusion

There is one fundamental difference between EU and US approaches towards monopolization. While competition authorities on both sides of the Atlantic are concerned with anti-competitive practices by firms with large market power, the USA is mainly concerned with preventing a market structure where such practices are likely, while the EU also fights the practices themselves.

The main forms of abuse are grouped into three categories: (i) strategies aimed at deterring entry; the most common examples are strategic sources of barriers, such as pre-emptive and retaliatory action by incumbents; (ii) strategies aimed at forcing the exit of a rival, with the main examples being foreclosure and predation; (iii) strategies aimed at raising rivals' costs, for example of exclusive deals.

All categories share the fact that it is hard to distinguish anti-competitive strategies from normal business strategies. Since intervention in abuse cases is associated with social costs as well (time, government failure), some caution is needed. On the other hand, anti-competitive practices such as predatory pricing can be socially very costly, also in the long run.

4   Dominance through collusion[44]

Even when no single firm enjoys a dominant position, firms may collectively exert market power similar to that of a dominant firm. This will in particular be the case when firms coordinate their decisions through some form of collusion.

There is a rather general consensus – at least in practice – that naked collusion, be it in the form of horizontal price fixing or of market-sharing agreements, should be forbidden.[45] Unfortunately, it does not suffice to 'forbid' collusion, since it can be implicit rather than explicit. Explicit collusion, where firms engage in written or oral agreements, organize meetings to design and implement collusive mechanisms, and so forth, is indeed caught by Article 81 EU Treaty in the EU and by Section 1 of the Sherman Act in the USA provided that the appropriate evidence is recovered. But implicit collusion does not involve any explicit agreement; it arises instead from the mere repetition of competitive interactions. In the EU, however, the concept of collective dominance provides a basis for antitrust intervention in such cases; similarly, in the USA, collusion is accounted for through the concept of 'coordinated effects' in the context of merger control.

This section discusses the scope for antitrust intervention against such tacit collusion. We first study the circumstances in which collusion can arise, and the forms it can take, before discussing the alternative courses of action available to competition authorities.

4.1   Relevant factors for tacit collusion

Tacit collusion may arise when the same firms repeatedly compete in the same markets. A firm may then have an incentive to maintain high prices if it expects that, if it does not do so, the rivals will lower their own prices in the future. Whether firms can in fact maintain high prices depends on four main factors.

First, how much does each firm gain from undercutting its rivals? Tacit collusion is clearly easier to sustain when the gains from undercutting are low. This puts limits on the level of collusive prices that can be sustained, since the gains from undercutting depend, among other things, on the price–

cost margin and the elasticity of the firm demand.[46] The degree of product differentiation may thus matter, as well as the nature of competition: for example, the benefits from undercutting are typically smaller when firms compete in quantities than when they compete in prices.

Second, how much will the deviating firm lose in the future if its rivals retaliate? The long-term profit loss from a deviation is the difference between the long-run collusive profit that the firm would obtain by sticking to collusion and the long-run profit it obtains under the market conditions that may prevail if undercutting occurs. The reaction of firms to perceived undercutting of the collusive price is often referred to as 'retaliation', although it need not always take the form of aggressive actions against the firm.

Indeed, a simple form of retaliation consists in the breakdown of collusion and the restoration of 'normal' competition and profits. Firms then anticipate that collusive prices will be maintained as long as none of them deviates, but if one attempts to reap short-term profits by undercutting prices, there will be no more collusion in the future, at least for some time. Firms may then abide by the current collusive prices in order to keep the collusion going, in which case collusion is self-sustaining. This form of collusion has a simple interpretation: firms trust each other to maintain collusive prices but, if one of them deviates, trust vanishes and all firms start acting in their short-term interest.

However, more sophisticated forms of retaliation may inflict tougher punishments and thereby allow sustaining higher collusive prices. For example, retaliation may include temporary price wars, leading to profits below 'normal' levels for some period of time.[47] It may also include actions that are specifically aimed at reducing the profits of the deviant firm.[48] Alternatively, firms may refuse to cooperate on other joint policies (such as joint ventures or joint distribution arrangements) or in standard setting processes. The retaliatory power of rivals thus depends on market specificity and determines to a large extent the ability of all parties to maintain tacit collusion.

Third, how likely is undercutting by the firm to lead to such retaliation? Clearly, if there is little chance that undercutting triggers retaliation, the fear of losing the collusive profit will be an ineffective deterrent. The probability that undercutting by one firm triggers retaliation depends mostly on firms' ability to monitor each other's behavior, and thus on market transparency. The extent of publicly available information on prices and quantities is thus highly relevant, but other dimensions such as market stability (demand and cost volatility, frequency of innovation and so forth) or the degree of similarity in cost and demand conditions matter as well.

Finally, how much does the firm discount future profit losses relative to today's gains?[49] If firms care mostly about current profits, they tend to focus on the short term and thus 'ignore' the consequences of retaliation. They thus have a strong incentive to undercut and collusion is difficult to sustain. The relative weight of current and future profits in the firm's objectives depends among other things on the market real interest rate. Future profits matter more with low interest rates, which facilitates collusion. Another key determinant is the delay before competitors react, which depends on monitoring and structural factors such as adjustment costs, long-term contractual arrangements, and so forth.

These four factors, which determine the sustainability of tacit collusion, in turn depend on market characteristics, which can be grouped into three categories. The first category includes necessary ingredients for collusion. The second category covers important characteristics that determine whether collusion can be sustained. The last category corresponds to characteristics that are relevant, although to a lesser extent.

Some characteristics have a decisive impact on firms' ability to sustain tacit collusion. These include entry barriers, the frequency of interaction and the role of innovation.

- *Entry barriers*. Collusion cannot be sustained in the absence of entry barriers and it is more difficult to sustain the lower the entry barriers. In the absence of entry barriers any attempt to maintain supracompetitive prices would trigger entry (for example, short-term or 'hit-and-run' entry strategies), which would erode the profitability of collusion. In addition, the prospect of future entry tends to reduce the scope for retaliation, since firms have less to lose from future retaliation if entry occurs anyway.
- *The frequency of interaction*. Frequent interaction and frequent price adjustments facilitate collusion. As already noted, firms could not tacitly collude if they did not anticipate interacting again in the future. Similarly, collusion is unlikely when firms interact only infrequently, since the short-term gains from undercutting a collusive price could then be 'punished' only in a far-off future.[50] Collusion is instead easier when firms interact more frequently, since they can then react more quickly to deviations and retaliation can thus come sooner.[51]
- *Innovation*. Collusion is easier to sustain in mature markets where innovation plays a small part than in innovation-driven markets. The reason is that innovation, particularly if it is drastic, may allow one firm to gain a significant advantage over its rivals. This prospect reduces both the value of future collusion and the amount of harm that rivals will be able to inflict if the need arises. If, for example,

the probability of drastic innovation is substantial, the incumbents anticipate that their market position will be short-lived; they thus put less emphasis on future retaliation and are more tempted to cheat on collusion.

Clearly, there is little scope for collusion in the absence of entry barriers, or if firms interact very infrequently, or else in innovation-driven markets. Therefore, whenever an industry presents one of these features, collusion is unlikely to constitute a significant concern. In practice, unfortunately, many industries may not be so clearly exempted. It is therefore useful to consider now the key factors that may affect the scope for collusion. In addition, in the context of merger control, the above industry features are less likely than others to be affected by a proposed merger; it is therefore also useful to see how a merger may affect these key factors.

The second group of market characteristics includes key determinants of the scope for collusion. These factors include of course the number of market participants, but also the degree of symmetry among those participants, the existence of maverick firms, of structural links or of cooperative agreements.

* *Number of participants.* Collusion is more difficult when there are more competitors. For one thing, coordination is more difficult, the larger the number of parties involved, in particular when coordination is only based on a tacit common understanding of the collusive market conduct. For example, identifying a 'focal point' in terms of prices and market shares becomes less and less obvious, particularly when firms are not symmetric.[52]

   There is another reason that makes it difficult to collude with many competitors. Since firms must share the collusive profit, as the number of firms increases each firm gets a smaller share of the pie. This has two implications. First, the gain from deviating increases for each firm since, by undercutting the collusive price, a firm can steal market shares from all its competitors; that is, having a smaller share, each firm would gain more from capturing the entire market. Second, for each firm the long-term benefit of maintaining collusion is reduced, precisely because it gets a smaller share of the collusive profit. Thus the short-run gain from deviation increases, while at the same time the long-run benefit of maintaining collusion is reduced. It is thus more difficult to prevent firms from deviating.[53] This impact of the number of competitors is likely to be particularly important when there are few competitors.[54]

• *Symmetry*. It is easier to collude among equals, that is, among firms that have similar cost structures, similar production capacities or which offer similar ranges of products. Suppose, for example, that firms have different marginal costs. The presence of such cost asymmetry has several implications.[55]

First, firms may find it difficult to agree to a common pricing policy, since firms with a lower marginal cost will insist on lower prices than what the other firms would wish to sustain.[56] More generally, the diversity of cost structures may rule out 'focal points' for pricing policies and so exacerbate coordination problems. In addition, technical efficiency would require allocating market share to low-cost firms, but this would clearly be difficult to sustain in the absence of explicit agreements and side-transfers.[57]

Second, even if firms agree on a given collusive price, low-cost firms will be more difficult to discipline, both because they might gain more from undercutting their rivals and because they have less to fear from a possible retaliation from high-cost firms.[58] Retaliation is indeed less effective when exerted by an inefficient firm against an efficient one, since the ability of the former to compete against the latter is limited.

A similar reasoning applies when one firm has a superior product quality, since such a firm has less to fear from retaliation. The argument also extends to other types of cost differences, such as asymmetric production capacities. Capacity constraints potentially affect the sustainability of collusion in two ways. They limit the gain from undercutting rivals but also limit firms' retaliatory power. At first glance, capacity constraints may thus appear to have an ambiguous effect on collusion, since they reduce both the incentives to deviate and the ability to punish such deviations. And indeed, studies that have focused on symmetric capacities[59] have confirmed this apparent ambiguity.[60] The impact of asymmetric capacities is, however, less ambiguous since, compared with a situation where all firms would face the same capacity constraints, increasing the capacity of one firm at the expense of the others both increases the first firm's incentive to undercut the others and limits these other firms' retaliatory power. Overall, therefore, introducing such asymmetry hinders collusion.[61]

The most effective collusive conducts usually involve asymmetric market shares, reflecting firms' costs or capacities;[62] thus, while market shares are highly endogenous variables, *market share asymmetry* may provide indirect evidence of a more profound asymmetry that tends to hinder collusion.

The intuition that 'it is easier to collude among equals' also explains the role of so-called 'mavericks'. A maverick firm can be interpreted as a firm with a drastically different cost structure, which is thus unwilling to participate in collusion.[63] Consider, for example, a firm that has a drastically different cost structure or production capacity, or that is affected by different factors than those of the other market participants.[64] Very often such a firm will exhibit market conduct that differs from others', reflecting its different supply conditions. This firm may then be unwilling to be part of collusive conduct or willing to do so only under terms that would not be acceptable or sustainable for the other firms. Similarly, a firm may have a stronger preference for the short term and be therefore more tempted to undercut rivals.[65]

- *Structural links* can facilitate collusion among firms. For example, cross-ownership reduces the gains derived from undercutting the other firm. Joint venture agreements can also enlarge the scope for retaliation: for example, a firm can then punish a deviating partner by investing less in the venture.[66] For these reasons, collusion is more likely to appear in markets where competitors are tied through structural links.

In the absence of structural links, simple *cooperation agreements* can also contribute to foster collusion. As in the case of joint ventures, these cooperation agreements can for example enlarge the scope for retaliation, thereby enhancing the ability to punish deviating partners. This may be particularly relevant for industries such as the telecommunications industry, where competitors need to reach interconnection agreements in order to offer good services. These agreements not only enlarge the scope for retaliation, they also have a direct impact on the operators' pricing strategies. Competitors may then design these interconnection agreements so as to facilitate collusion.

More generally, firms may alter their contractual agreements, either between themselves or with third parties, so as to facilitate collusion. Marketing agreements can constitute good tools to that effect. Jullien and Rey (2002) show for example that producers of consumer goods can resort to Resale Price Maintenance to impose more uniform prices across local retail markets, thereby making it easier to detect deviations from a collusive price. Record companies have been accused of marketing their disks according to simple pricing grids (with only a few categories, instead of personalized prices for each author or composition) for a similar purpose.

Other factors can have an influence on the sustainability of collusion, although possibly to a lesser extent or in a more ambiguous way. Among these, the degree of market transparency appears to be a key factor. Other factors include product differentiation, the characteristics of demand (demand trend and fluctuations, as well as demand elasticity and buying power), multi-market contact, club effects or the organization of particular markets such as bidding markets. These dimensions are relevant to assessing the plausibility of collusion, particularly when the factors of the first two groups do not suffice to send a clear signal.

- *Market transparency*. Collusion is easier when firms observe each other's prices and quantities. Frequent price adjustments give firms the physical possibility to retaliate quickly when one market participant undercuts the others, but such deviation must first be identified by the other participants. As a result, collusion can be difficult to sustain when individual prices are not readily observable and cannot be easily inferred from readily available market data. This, in turn, supposes that some uncertainty affects the market: otherwise any deviation would be detected by the rivals, who would perceive a reduction in their market share.

This observability problem was first stressed by Stigler's (1964) classic paper, and formally analyzed by Green and Porter (1984) and Abreu *et al.* (1986) the lack of transparency on prices and sales does not necessarily prevent collusion completely, but makes it both more difficult to sustain and more limited in scope.

What matters here, however, is not what is directly observed by the firms, but what information firms can infer from the available market data. For example, inferring deviations from collusive conduct is easier and requires less market data[67] when the market is stable rather than unstable. Moreover, the delay necessary to obtain reliable data on prices and quantities matters, as well as its nature. For example, professional associations sometimes publish information on prices, output or capacity utilization rates. It first matters whether this information is about aggregate or individual data, since in the latter case it is easier to identify a deviant firm.[68] The time lag elapsed between the pricing period and the publication period is also important. Even detailed information may not help to sustain collusion if it is available only after a long delay.

- *Demand growth*. Collusion is easier to sustain in growing markets, where today's profits are small compared with tomorrow's. Conversely, collusion is more difficult to sustain in declining markets, where tomorrow's profits (with or without retaliation) will be small anyway: in the limiting case where the market is on the verge of collapsing, there is almost no 'future' and therefore no possibility to induce firms to abide with a collusive conduct.

- *Business cycles and demand fluctuations* hinder collusion. This is a corollary of the above impact of demand growth or decline. The idea, formally captured by Rotemberg and Saloner (1986) and Haltiwanger and Harrington (1991), is that, when the market is at a peak, short-term gains from a deviation are maximal while the potential cost of retaliation is at a minimum. Hence collusion is more difficult to sustain at such times. To see this, suppose that demand fluctuates from one period to another and, to fix ideas, assume for the moment that demand shocks are independent and identically distributed across periods. In this hypothetical scenario, firms know that they face an uncertain future, but in each period the prospects are the same; the probability of benefiting from a good shock is for example the same in each future period, and likewise for the probability of bad shocks. This in turn implies that the amount of future retaliation to which a firm exposes itself in each period remains the same over time. However, in periods where demand is higher than average, the short-term benefits from a deviation are themselves higher than average. Therefore, in such a period, the firm must trade off higher than average gains from deviation against a constant (and thus 'average') level of punishment. Clearly, deviations are more tempting in such a period and, by the same token, collusion is more difficult to sustain than in the absence of demand fluctuations, where both the short-term gains from deviations and retaliation possibility would always remain at an average level.

  As fluctuations gain in scale, collusion becomes more and more difficult to sustain, at least in those states where demand is especially high. Firms are then obliged to collude 'less' (by lowering the collusive price) or even to abandon any collusion when demand is high. A similar analysis applies to more deterministic fluctuations, as for example in the case of seasonal or business cycles. There again, undercutting rivals is more tempting when demand is high, and the perceived cost of future price wars is lower when the cycle is currently at its peak, since retaliation will only occur later, thus in periods of lower demand.

- *Product differentiation.* This factor can have a more ambiguous impact on collusion, since it affects both the incentives to undercut rivals and their ability to retaliate. This is particularly the case when product differentiation consists of offering different combinations of characteristics, possibly at comparable prices but aimed at different types of customers; this corresponds to what economists refer to as 'horizontal differentiation'. Such differentiation aims at segmenting customers, in order to gain market power over specific segments by creating customer loyalty: a customer may then be reluctant to switch away from a favorite brand, even if he or she would benefit from a small price reduction by turning to an alternative brand. This segmentation strategy affects the scope for collusion in two ways. First, it limits the short-term gains from undercutting rivals, since it becomes more difficult to attract their customers. Second, it also limits the severity of price wars and thus the firms' ability to punish a potential deviation. Overall, therefore, the impact of horizontal differentiation appears quite ambiguous.

Indeed, the economic work on this issue has shown that collusion may become easier or more difficult, depending on the exact nature of the competitive situation (for example, competition in prices versus competition in quantity).[69] Raith (1996) notes, however, that *product differentiation may exacerbate informational problems in non-transparent markets.* That is, even if firms do not observe their rivals' prices or quantities, they may still be able to infer the relevant information from their own prices and quantities. But such inference may be easier to achieve when all firms offer the same goods than when they offer highly differentiated products. This may be one reason why antitrust authorities usually interpret product homogeneity as facilitating collusion.[70]

It is often perceived that low demand elasticity should exacerbate collusion concerns. The elasticity of the demand has in fact no clear impact on the sustainability of collusive prices. For example, in the case of an oligopolistic industry where n identical firms produce the same good and repeatedly face the same demand, collusion is sustainable when the discount factor of the firms lies above a threshold equal to $1 - 1/n$ whatever the shape of the demand, which is therefore irrelevant. This comes from the fact that demand elasticity (and, more generally, the shape of consumer demand) affects in the same way both the short-term gains from undercutting rivals and the long-term cost of forgoing future collusion.

Collusion is, however, more profitable when demand elasticity is low. When picking a collusive price, the firms must trade off the increased margins generated by higher prices against the reduction in sales that these higher prices would trigger. The industry's ideal collusive price is the monopoly price, p^M, which maximizes the joint profit of the firms and is higher when the demand elasticity is lower.[71] Therefore, for a given market size, the firms have more to gain from sustaining the monopoly price when demand elasticity is low. In that sense, demand elasticity may constitute a relevant factor, although of a different nature than the factors listed above.[72] In addition, collusion is a greater concern for consumers when demand is inelastic than when it is elastic. This is both because the potential for a large profitable increase in prices above the 'normal' level decreases when demand becomes less elastic, and because consumers suffer more from a given price increase when they have few alternatives.[73]

A related factor concerns the countervailing buying power of the customers. If buyers are powerful, even a complete monopolist may find it difficult to impose high prices. The profitability of collusion is similarly reduced. In addition, Snyder (1996) notes that large buyers can successfully break collusion by concentrating their orders in order to make firms' interaction less frequent and to increase the short-term gains from undercutting rivals; more generally, large buyers can design procurement schemes that reduce the scope for collusion.

• *Multi-market contact*. It is well recognized that firms can sustain collusion more easily when they are present on several markets. First, multi-market contact increases the frequency of the interaction between the firms. Second, it may allow easing asymmetries that arise in individual markets. For example, one firm may have a competitive advantage in one market and its rival can have its own competitive advantage in another market. While a market-level analysis may then suggest that collusion is difficult to sustain, multi-market contact restores in such a case an overall symmetry that facilitates collusion. Third, multi-market contact may allow the firms to sustain collusion in markets where the industry characteristics alone would not allow such collusion.[74]

The principles reviewed above apply as well to *bidding markets*. For example, collusion is easier when there are fewer bidders that repeatedly participate in the same bidding markets, when the frequency of these markets is high (for example, daily markets) and so forth. In addition, however, bidding markets can be designed in ways that either hinder or facilitate collusion. For example, sealed bid auctions generate less information (that is, unless the auctioneer reveals the details of all the bids afterwards) than public descending procurement auctions, where sellers observe at each moment who is still bidding at the current price. Therefore, a close look at the organization of the bidding markets may be necessary to assess the likelihood of collusion.[75]

Some markets are subject to club or network effects, where consumers benefit from being in the same 'club' by using the same software or the same keyboard layout, subscribing to the same operator, and so forth.[76] Club effects have several implications. They tilt the market in favor of a single participant, thereby creating a 'winner-takes-all' type of competition which is not prone to collusion. In addition, club effects create lock-in effects that reinforce the position of the market leader and thus increase the benefits derived from such a position. By undercutting its rivals, a firm can trigger snowballing effects that could easily tilt the market in its favor and thus obtain a durable leadership position. Club effects therefore exacerbate the gains from undercutting rivals and, at the same time, lock-in effects limit retaliation possibilities. Both factors contribute to making collusion less likely.

The above discussion applies as well to other forms of competition. Where, for example, firms compete in quantity or production capacity, collusion consists in reducing the production levels below competitive levels and retaliation can either take the simple form of reverting to 'normal' competition, with higher output levels, or involve temporary large increases of competitors outputs, in order to further depress prices to punish the deviating firm. While the nature of competition is different and often less intense under quantity competition than under price competition, it does not follow that the scope for collusion is larger or smaller, since retaliation possibilities are affected as well as the short-run gains of deviations from collusion: increasing one's production level is less profitable, since prices will adjust to sell out the competitors' output, but at the same time, retaliation is somewhat more difficult since the firm can always adapt its output level.

4.2   What can competition authorities do?

The above analysis underlines relevant factors but does not allow concluding when or whether collusion actually takes place. For one thing, there is a multiplicity of equilibrium issues. In particular, even if collusion is indeed sustainable, firms may well end-up 'competing' in each and every period as if it was the last.[77] While there is a good understanding of the factors that facilitate collusion, this is not the case for the conditions under which coordination emerges.[78]

Even assessing the likelihood of collusion is tricky. As we have seen, the sustainability of tacit collusion depends on many factors, and only some of them can be quantified with a reasonable degree of precision. In addition, these factors may go in opposite directions in a given industry. Having said this, how can antitrust fight collusion? There are several possible courses of action.

Ex ante, competition authorities can prevent the emergence of an industry structure that is prone to collusion by taking into account this concern when examining proposed mergers or joint venture agreements. They can also ban facilitating practices.

Ex post, competition authorities can take steps to fight collusion per se, for example, by uncovering evidence of explicit coordination or by attacking specific agreements that again facilitate collusion. We discuss these approaches in turn.

As mentioned, a given market situation can generate multiple equilibria. It is thus impossible to rely on theory alone to determine whether collusion is actually taking place. While the analysis of the history of the industry may help determine whether collusion occurred in the past, it provides limited help for evaluating whether it will occur in the future, and even more limited if a merger takes place.[79]

Thus it will not be possible to reach a definite conclusion from available market data on whether tacit collusion will actually occur as a consequence of the merger or not. However, the merger control authority can address a different and yet relevant question: will the merger create a situation where collusion becomes more likely; that is, will collusion be significantly easier to sustain in the post-merger situation?

A merger often affects many of the factors that are relevant for the sustainability of collusion and it can affect them in ways that tend to offset each other. The impact of the merger on collusion can thus involve a difficult assessment of possibly conflicting effects. Ideally, this could be done by building a 'meta-model' encompassing all relevant characteristics, but such a global model would probably not be tractable and thus would be quite useless.

The above discussion provides a basis for prioritizing the relevant factors, however, with an emphasis on the necessary ingredients (high entry barriers, frequent interactions and a minor role for innovation) and on the most important factors (number of market participants, their degree of symmetry, and so forth). Understanding the respective role of each factor also facilitates an overall assessment when several factors have a role and push in different directions.

Evaluating the impact of a merger on collusion will, however, remain by nature more difficult than the analysis of single dominance. This is also reflected in the more limited help offered by quantitative or econometric approaches. In particular, while some successful efforts have been made to evaluate ex post the likelihood of collusion in a particular industry, predicting the impact of a merger on the future likelihood of collusion appears substantially more challenging. If firms were not tacitly colluding in the pre-merger phase, past market data and econometric studies can help in assessing key structural parameters but will not provide direct information on potential collusive behavior. But even if there is some evidence on past collusive conduct, one has to account for the fact that firms will adapt their conduct to accommodate the new environment created by the merger, which again requires some prospective analysis.

Antitrust authorities can attack explicit forms of collusion where, say, managers meet, exchange information and conclude agreements on prices or market shares. The main difficulty in that case is to establish the existence of such explicit agreements and get hard evidence that would stand in court. Antitrust enforcement can launch detailed investigations and dawn-raids, and rely on indirect or informal evidence to focus on likely suspects.

Another possibility is to encourage informed parties to come and provide the needed evidence. The interest of this approach is exemplified by the development of leniency programs which have already encountered substantial successes, first in the USA and then in Europe.[80] Leniency programs vary in design and scope: they may apply to companies or individuals, provide full or limited protection, concern first informants or be extended to later ones as well, and so forth. The performance of these leniency programs also varies,[81] which provides some ground for enhancing and fine-tuning their design.[82]

In the absence of any hard evidence of explicit agreements, which could be caught in the EU under Article 81 EU Treaty and in the USA under Section 1 of the Sherman Act, it is difficult if not impossible to fight collusion itself directly. There might actually be a debate as to whether antitrust authorities should take action against purely tacit collusion, where by definition firms set prices non-cooperatively. Such actions would come close to regulating prices, something that competition authorities and courts are generally reluctant to do. In the USA, Section 2 of the Sherman Act condemns for example monopolization but not the exploitation of market power through high prices. In the EU, charging an excessive price can constitute an abuse of a dominant position. Article 82 EU Treaty thus provides a basis under which tacit collusion could be attacked. However, building a case on the abuse of a dominant position requires establishing dominance, which in this case would amount to proving that collusion indeed occurred and, as noted, raises large difficulties on both legal and economic grounds.[83] Overall, it is unlikely that an abuse of collective dominance case could rely solely on the past realization of prices or market shares.[84]

Short of fighting collusion directly, competition authorities can attack those practices that facilitate collusion. Thus, for example, antitrust authorities may want to block Resale Price Maintenance when it facilitates collusion by generating more uniform prices. In the same vein, competition agencies may want to have a close look at marketing practices that tend to make the market more 'transparent', in the sense that they allow the market participants to infer more easily the pricing strategies of their competitors.

5   Dominance versus monopolization: a legal overview

Throughout the world, antitrust authorities aim to maintain effective competition on markets by fighting cartels, by constraining the behavior of firms that are insufficiently disciplined by the competitive process itself, and by controlling mergers. In this section and the next we look at two jurisdictions, the USA and the EU, and at two of these policy domains; that is we do not look at issues related to agreements and cartels. Although phrased in different terms, superficially, the US Antitrust Laws and the EU Competition Laws in these domains appear very similar, but here we will focus more on the differences between the two systems. This section focuses on the policies with respect to dominance and monopolization, while the next section compares policy towards mergers in these two jurisdictions.

5.1   The rules of the game

The Sherman Act, which dates from 1890, constitutes the core of the US competition regime. Section 1 of that Act prescribes agreements on restraint of trade. It is very much like Article 81 EU Treaty, and will not be dealt with here. Section 2 of the Sherman Act prohibits monopoly abuse. It states:

> Every person who shall monopolize, or attempt to monopolize, or combine or conspire with any other person or persons, to monopolize any part of the trade or commerce among the several States, or with foreign nations, shall be deemed guilty of a felony. (15 USC 2)

Note that the offense is monopolization, not monopoly itself, and that two types of abuse are distinguished: attempted monopolization and monopolization. Attempted monopolization is the use of improper business strategies to attain monopoly status; monopolization is the use of improper methods to attain or maintain a monopoly, or to extend it still further. Here monopoly should not be taken literally; the use of improper tactics is also forbidden for firms that do not have 100 per cent market share. What matters is whether the firm has considerable market power, that is, the ability to control price.

In Europe, 'dominance' is the key concept in the two areas of competition policy on which we focus. Article 82 EU Treaty (formerly Article 86), which was signed in 1958, aims to constrain the behavior of firms that are not constrained by other competitors on the market; it forbids firms to abuse a dominant position. The article states:

> Any abuse by one or more undertakings of a dominant position within the common market or in a substantial part of it shall be prohibited as incompatible with the common market in so far as it may affect trade between Member States. Such abuse may, in particular, consist in:

a)   directly or indirectly imposing unfair purchase or selling prices or other unfair trading conditions;
b)   limiting production, markets or technological development to the prejudice of consumers;
c)   applying dissimilar conditions to equivalent transactions with other trading parties, thereby placing them at a competitive disadvantage;
d)   making the conclusion of contracts subject to acceptance by the other parties of supplementary obligations which, by their nature or according to commercial usage, have no connection with the subject of such contracts.

These articles raise the questions whether a dominant position should be interpreted as a (near) monopoly, whether monopolization should be interpreted similarly to abuse of a dominant position, and how to deal with combined monopolization (joint dominance). We will discuss these issues in turn.

Before going into differences, let us, however, stress the similarity in procedures that are used in both jurisdictions. In the USA, as well as in Europe, antitrust analysis starts with the identification of the relevant market and the competitive situation on that market: both dominance and monopoly refer to a certain relevant market. The European Commission's *Notice on the Definition of the Relevant Market* gives a good description of the way that market is identified. It also shows how economic thinking, as represented by the SSNIP test,[85] which originated in US antitrust practice, influences policy making. In this respect, it is interesting to note that both the authorities in the USA and those in Europe have been criticized for having identified an aftermarket (that is the market for complementary services associated with a durable product) as a separate relevant market, even in cases where the durable product itself is offered on a market with effective competition. It will be clear that the issue of whether 'locked-in' consumers should receive special protection is a controversial issue. In Europe, the next step in the procedure is to see whether there is a position of dominance on that market, after which it is studied whether that position has been abused by a certain business strategy. In the USA, the procedure is roughly similar, but there is somewhat less emphasis on the second step, as we will explain below. In any case, the tests and economic theories that are used in the third step are similar, although different weights may be attached to them.

5.2   *Dominance, monopoly and market power*
In cases that come under Section 2 of the Sherman Act, having identified the relevant market, the authorities next investigate whether the firm in question has attained monopoly status. Typically, if the market share is about 75 per cent or more, that is said to be the case. In the third step, the

behavior in question is investigated. Here, the distinction between 'attempt to monopolize' and 'monopolization' is relevant. As in actual antitrust practice, emphasis is on the behavior and not on the status of the firm. We defer discussion of this to Section 6.2.

In contrast, in Europe relatively great importance is attached to the status of the firm: is it dominant or not? In one of the early cases arising out of Article 82 EU Treaty, *United Brands*, the ECJ (the European Court of Justice) gave a definition of dominance that it has frequently relied upon since. One year later, in *Hoffmann-La Roche*, the ECJ somewhat refined that earlier definition. It still stands today:

> 38. The dominant position thus referred to relates to a position of economic strength enjoyed by an undertaking which enables it to prevent effective competition being maintained on the relevant market by affording it the power to behave to an appreciable extent independently of its competitors, its customers and ultimately of its consumers.
> 39. Such a position does not preclude some competition, which it does where there is a monopoly or a quasi-monopoly, but enables the undertaking which profits by it, if not to determine, at least to have an appreciable influence on the conditions under which that competition will develop, and in any case to act largely in disregard of it so long as such conduct does not operate to its detriment.

The reader notices that this definition has two elements to it. First, the dominant firm is able to behave (to an appreciable extent) independently of others; secondly, the dominant firm is able (to an appreciable extent) to influence how competition on the market will develop. While the definition is not one that one finds in economics textbooks, the second element should make it clear that dominance is a broader concept than 'uncontested monopoly': a firm that is able to influence the 'parameters of competition' may be found to be in a dominant position. An economist is inclined to think that a dominant firm is one that has considerable market power; that is, it is able profitably to set price considerably above (marginal) cost. Of course, market power is a matter of degree and there is no clear dividing line between monopoly and perfect competition. Also note that, in contrast to the SMP (significant market power) framework known from the European telecommunications sector, dominance is not a label that a firm carries with it and that brings special obligations. In the telecommunications sector, there is asymmetric regulation and firms that are classified as having SMP do have special obligations imposed upon them. Furthermore, the label 'SMP operator' is assigned in advance, and is withdrawn only by a decision of the regulator in charge. In competition policy, a firm is found dominant (or not) in the course of an investigation and also a dominant operator 'just' has to follow the law. Nevertheless, as we will see below, there is some asymmetry: some types of behavior that would be considered 'unproblematic' for non-dominant firms are considered to be violations of the law for dominant firms.

In assessing whether a firm is dominant, the European Commission and the European Court of Justice place great emphasis on the market share of the firm. Already in *Hoffmann-La Roche*, the court held that very large market shares are in themselves indicative of dominance:

> 41. Furthermore, although the importance of market shares may vary from one market to another the view may legitimately be taken that very large market shares are in themselves, and save in exceptional circumstances, evidence of the existence of a dominant position.

In the case in question, several markets were investigated. When market shares were above 75 per cent, the court did not look beyond the market shares; where the share was lower (around 50 per cent), the court looked at other factors, such as the market shares of the competitors, and in one market (that for Vitamin B3), the court annulled the Commission's finding of dominance since the Commission had not looked at these other factors. Later, in *AKZO*, the court ruled that a share of 50 per cent was a very high market share. We may conclude that, if the market share is above 50 per cent, there is essentially a presumption of dominance. In *United Brands*, UBC was found to be dominant with a market share of 45 per cent. To date, there have been no cases where a firm with a market share of 40 per cent or less was found to be dominant, although the Commission has not excluded that possibility.

In both the USA and Europe, the antitrust authorities have frequently been criticized for attaching too much weight to market shares and for paying relatively little attention to entry barriers. Of course, economists are well aware (for example through the theory of contestable markets) that high market shares are, in themselves, no indication of market power. In the absence of entry barriers, firms with very high market shares need not have much market power. Conversely, firms with relatively small overall market shares may nevertheless enjoy high market power in special circumstances. Here one may think of electricity markets, where the ability to influence price is also related to the flexibility of the production technology that is employed. If the market is tight and large-scale base-load facilities are operating at full capacity, a small-scale producer that has the opportunity to turn units on or off may be able to drive up the price considerably by withholding capacity from the market. In other words, market share is a very imperfect indicator of market power and it should not be looked upon in isolation. Other factors, such as entry barriers and flexibility, and the time it takes to adjust competition variables, play an equally important role.

For sure, it is true that the European Commission and the court do take into account a variety of other factors to assess dominance. In addition to the market share of the firm concerned, one looks at the relationship between the market share of this firm and those of its competitors, at entry barriers, and at whether the firm has a superior technology, or better access to financial markets or to other key inputs than its competitors, and so on. The current thinking of the European Commission on the relevance of market shares and other factors for assessing dominance is well described in the recent *Draft Commission Notice* on the appraisal of horizontal mergers, to which we refer the interested reader for further details.

Article 82 EU Treaty forbids 'any abuse by one or more undertakings of a dominant position', a formulation that leaves room for the possibility that several firms collectively hold a dominant position, and that such a position might be abused either collectively or by at least one of the firms involved. The question under what conditions firms can be considered collectively dominant, that is, whether Article 82 EU Treaty can be used to restrain behavior in (tight) oligopolies, has been extensively discussed in the literature. In a couple of relatively recent judgments (*Flat Glass*, *Almelo* and *Compagnie Maritime Belge*) the Court of First Instance (CFI) has provided some clarity on this issue. In the latter, most recent case, the CFI wrote:

> 36. (...) a dominant position may be held by two or more economic entities legally independent of each other, provided that from an economic point of view they present themselves or act together on a particular market as a collective entity. That is how the expression 'collective dominant position', as used in the remainder of this judgment, should be understood.

To an economist, 'independent firms acting together as a collective entity' is very much like the definition of collusion; hence, an economist is tempted to interpret the above as 'firms, in a tight oligopoly, that tacitly collude, may be found to be collectively dominant'. While this may clarify the definition of collective dominance, it is not clear that this is of much help. For one thing, having a dominant position is not forbidden, only abusing it is. Secondly, since (tacit) collusion constitutes a violation of Article 81 EU Treaty, the question is, what is the 'added value' of being able to classify firms in an oligopolistic industry as being collectively dominant? For sure, even if one could perhaps agree that tight oligopolies need special scrutiny, it seems that one would not want to classify non-cooperative oligopolies as holding a dominant position. We will return to these issues in Section 6, where we will discuss mergers. As we will see there, the concept of collective dominance also plays a role when evaluating mergers, and the term (collective) dominance has the same interpretation under the European Community Merger Regulation (ECMR) as under Article 82 EU Treaty.

5.3 Abuse and monopolization

The essence of the US system is that honest, tough competition is never forbidden. In other words, whether a business strategy is proper or not does not depend on the position that the firm occupies. In this respect, there is a difference from Europe, where dominant firms have a special responsibility towards competition on the market. Hence, in Europe, some strategies that are legal when pursued by non-dominant firms are no longer so when employed by dominant firms. Of course, in the USA, whether the antitrust authorities scrutinize a firm may depend on that firm's position, but (in theory at least) the classification of the strategy adopted does not depend on the status of the firm. Whatever the situation of the firm, conduct is improper if it is other than competition on the merits, and such improper conduct may be declared illegal if it could lead to monopolization.

Somewhat more formally, in the USA, unfair business tactics that attempt monopolization are illegal whenever, in the view of the court handling the case, there is a 'dangerous probability' that the attempt could be successful. Most courts would look at the market power of the firm in question to gauge that probability and market shares of around 40–50 per cent might be indicative of the probability being dangerous; hence, in such cases, the behavior will be scrutinized more closely. The court will then investigate whether there is 'monopolistic intent'; that is, whether there is evidence that the firm wanted to destroy competition and create a monopoly. The evidence can be direct, in the form of company documents, or indirect, in the form of business strategies that are only rational as part of a plan to eliminate competition.

What about a firm that already has acquired a monopoly position? We note that, although having a monopoly is not illegal, neither in the USA, nor in Europe, there is an essential difference in treatment in the two jurisdictions. In the USA, a monopoly may exploit its monopoly position, but such 'monopolistic exploitation' is not allowed in Europe. While Section 2 of the Sherman act aims (only) at preventing 'monopolization' of markets, Article 82 EU Treaty primarily seems to focus on constraining monopolies. Historical factors may explain this difference in emphasis. In the USA, the main goal of policy was to prevent dominant firms coming into existence. In Europe, at one time it was (and, in some circles, it perhaps still is) thought that large European firms are necessary to exploit scale advantages to compete successfully on world markets. According to this view, competition policy should not stand in the way of firms trying to become dominant. In this respect we may also note that, in Europe, merger control became an instrument of competition policy only in 1990, 32 years after the signing of the Treaty of Rome, which included provisions for cartels and dominant positions, and that, even at present, the policy with respect to mergers is more lenient than the policy with respect to cartels.

In the USA, just as any other firm, a monopoly simply may not use improper methods to suppress competition on the merits, but it is not forbidden to maximize its profits through any regular means. This is not to say that regulation of dominant firms does not play a role in the USA, it certainly does, but it is not done by the competition authorities, but by sector-specific regulators. In these cases, the monopoly usually does not result from superior entrepreneurship, but rather is the natural consequence of technology or the outcome of political privilege; hence, in such cases, no special reward is necessary. In Europe, when the competition laws were established, there were few such regulators, and perhaps this is another reason why more regulatory powers were given to the European Commission.

In Article 82 EU Treaty, four examples of possible abusive behavior are given. One notices that the examples all deal with the relation between the dominant firm and its customers or the final consumers. All of these examples, therefore, deal with straightforward monopolistic exploitation. In fact, there has been a discussion about whether Article 82 EU Treaty only aimed to deal with exploitative behavior, or whether, like Section 2 of the Sherman act, it could also catch 'monopolization', that is anti-competitive behavior directed at competitors of the dominant firm. This discussion was at least in part fuelled by the fact that the French and German texts of Article 82 EU Treaty speak of 'abusive exploitation'. The French competition lawyer Joliet, at one time a judge in the ECJ, has argued that Article 82 EU Treaty was only intended to deal with monopolistic exploitation, and not with preservation of the competitive process; hence, in his view, the only aim of the article was to regulate monopolistic market power. In *Continental Can*, the ECJ made it clear for the first time that Article 82 EU Treaty does not apply only to exploitative behavior but also to anti-competitive conduct which further weakens competition that is already weak:

> 20 (...) The question is whether the word 'abuse' in Article [82] refers only to practices of undertakings which may directly affect the market and are detrimental to production or sales, to purchasers or consumers, or whether this word also refers to changes in the structure of a market, which lead to competition being seriously disturbed in a substantial part of the Common Market.
> 26 (...) the provision is not only aimed at practices which may cause damage to consumers directly, but also at those which are detrimental to them through their impact on an effective competition structure, such as is mentioned in Article [3(1)9] of the Treaty. Abuse may therefore occur if an undertaking in a dominant position strengthens such position in such a way that the degree of dominance

reached substantially fetters competition; that is that only undertakings remain in the market whose behavior depends on the dominant one.

Since *Continental Can*, the ECJ has confirmed on various occasions that Article 82 EU Treaty may apply to anti-competitive conduct. A particularly clear statement is found in *Hoffman-La Roche*, where the ECJ used a wording that it has frequently used since:

> 91 (...) The concept of abuse is an objective concept relating to the behavior of an undertaking in a dominant position which is such as to influence the structure of the market where, as a result of the very presence of the undertaking in question, the degree of competition is weakened and which, through recourse of methods different from these which condition normal competition in products or services on the basis of the transactions of commercial operators, has the effect of hindering the maintenance of the degree of competition still existing in the market or the growth of that competition.

The conclusion thus is that Article 82 EU Treaty does not deal only with exploitative behavior but also with anti-competitive behavior that aims to weaken competition on a market where competitive pressure is already weak. In fact, since the Commission has dealt with only very few cases of monopolistic exploitation, the European Commission has been unwilling to act as a price regulator, the emphasis in Article 82 EU Treaty cases has been on anti-competitive behavior and the difference from US law thus appears not to be so great.

The reason for the fact that the Commission has dealt with few cases of 'excessive pricing' is probably that the Commission burnt its fingers in *United Brands*, the leading case of this type. The ECJ annulled that decision and since then the Commission has been careful not to burn its fingers again. Of course, it may be very difficult to decide which prices are fair and which prices are excessive. Furthermore, if it is found that prices are excessive, the only remedy may be price regulation and this may not be something for which a competition authority is well-equipped: it may require relatively many resources, and may not yield benefits proportional to the importance of the case (see the discussion in Section 2.)

Whether a price is excessive may (perhaps) be determined by comparing the price in question with prices of comparable products in comparable markets, but, of course, the question is: what is comparable? In *United Brands*, the Commission adopted this methodology and, while the ECJ accepted it as a valid one, the ECJ did not accept the data presented by the Commission. Even if the Commission claimed price differences of about 100 per cent, the ECJ annulled the decision on this point. The ECJ also accepted that prices that do not bear a relation to the product's economic value could be excessive, and that a high price–cost margin, or high profits, might be signals of excessive pricing, but it did not want to commit itself to levels. Consequently, there is even now quite some ambiguity about when prices should or could be classified as being excessive.

Undeterred by this state of affairs, competition authorities that are new entrants to this game, such as the Dutch NMa, which came into existence only in 1997, have shown a willingness to investigate claims of excessive prices, with an equal willingness to perform detailed cost studies. The methodology used in some of these cases is the usual one adopted by regulators in capital-intensive industries, such as telecoms: a price is 'reasonable' if the return on the assets invested is not (much) higher than the return on capital that investors demand, as measured by the weighted average cost of capital (WACC) of the company. Competition authorities should only behave like regulators and do detailed cost studies if the dominant position has been clearly established and there are substantial entry barriers. After all, absent entry barriers, high prices will invite entry; hence it is unlikely that prices could be excessive.

Moving from exploitative behavior to anti-competitive behavior, we note that, in contrast to Joliet's views referred to above, European policy with respect to 'anti-competitive behavior' appears to have been more hostile and more interventionist than policy in the USA. The above quotation from *Hoffmann-La Roche* raises the question about how to differentiate 'normal competition' from 'anti-competitive actions' and here it seems that the EU authorities are inclined to label actions readily as being 'anti-competitive'. In this regard, the European Commission and the European Court of Justice frequently refer to the fact that dominant firms have a special responsibility towards their competitors and the competitive process. For example, in *Michelin*, the court stated

> 57. (...) A finding that an undertaking has a dominant position is not in itself a recrimination but simply means that, irrespective of the reasons for which it has such a dominant position, the undertaking concerned has a special responsibility not to allow its conduct to impair genuine undistorted competition on the common market.

The court returned to this phrasing in later important decisions such as *Irish Sugar* and *Compagnie Maritime Belge*. Note that this quotation suggests that even a firm that has obtained its dominant position as a result of its own economic strength will have special responsibilities and may not be able to use business strategies that would, under situations of non-dominance, be unobjectionable. US authorities would not be willing to go that far: one may scrutinize dominant firms, but why should one deny them the use of usual business practices? Not surprisingly, then, the

EC policy has been criticized in this respect (for example, see Jebsen and Stevens, 1996).

It is in cases where a dominant firm refuses to supply an existing customer or a potential competitor on the output market that the difference between EU and US policy most probably traditionally is largest. Ordering the dominant firm to supply is a strong interference with business freedom; hence, authorities should be most reserved in adopting such measures. In the USA, the antitrust authorities have always shown considerable restraint, but, in Europe, policy has typically been much more interventionist. It is here that the special responsibility towards competition that a dominant firm is said to have is playing an important role. Leading cases of this type (*Commercial Solvents, United Brands, Hugin*) all referred to already above illustrate this very clearly.

In *Commercial Solvents*, a pharmaceutical company cancelled orders for a certain raw material, presumably expecting to be able to buy more cheaply elsewhere. When the alternative supplies did not prove satisfactory, it turned to the original supplier again, but the latter did not want to supply any more, as it wanted to expand vertically into the end product market itself. The ECJ ruled that the dominant producer of the raw material had abused its dominant position as its strategy could eliminate all competition from the market. *Hugin* is essentially similar: a manufacturer no longer wanted to supply spare parts to a retailer as it wanted to build up its own spare parts business. In *United Brands*, UBC wanted to punish a distributor for the fact that it had participated in a promotional campaign of a competitor of UBC. According to the ECJ, the countermeasure of no longer supplying this distributor was not proportional and, hence, was abusive. It is remarkable that, in all these cases, there is little attention to efficiency arguments: the dominant firm is simply said to have a responsibility to keep competition alive.

In some of the refusal to supply cases discussed above, a competitor could not compete on the market for some final product if it did not have access to some raw material that is produced by the dominant firm. In the case of essential facilities, the situation is similar, but now a competitor needs access to the production facilities of the dominant firm. The question now is under what conditions, and against which terms, the dominant firm should be forced to share its facilities.

The first essential facility cases that the Commission considered were related to physical infrastructure, harbors in particular. In these cases, a vertically integrated company that owned the facilities at harbor A, also offered a ferry service between this harbor and harbor B. A competitor also wanted to offer ferry services between A and B, but, in order to do so, it needed access to the facilities at harbor A. Should the incumbent be forced to offer harbor services? If so, at what price? Cases that the Commission dealt with include, among others, *Sealink/B&I Holyhead* and *Sea Containers Ltd. v. Stena*, and in these it established the position that the integrated company was not allowed to discriminate between its own ferries and that of the competitor; hence, it should offer access. The first, non-infrastructure, case in this domain was *Magill*. In this case, broadcasting stations were not willing to hand over their programming data to a publisher who wanted to publish a complete programming guide. The ECJ argued that the refusal to supply prevented a new product, for which there was apparent demand, from coming on the market. Hence the refusal to supply constituted an abuse according to Article 82 EU Treaty(b).

These decisions have been criticized for being too interventionist and for eliminating firms' incentives to invest. Quite interestingly, in these cases, the European Commission has made use of the so-called 'essential facilities doctrine' which originated in the USA, and which also has been extensively criticized there, mainly for the fact that it deters investment both in existing and in competing infrastructure and, hence, prevents infrastructure from coming into existence (see Areeda, 1989).

In a recent important essential facilities case, *Bronner*, the ECJ has, however, taken a very different attitude. In this case, the ECJ shows its awareness of the investment issue and it shows restraint in granting a competitor access to the facilities of a dominant firm. *Bronner* deals with a small newspaper company, with low circulation, that wants to get access to the nationwide distribution system of a larger competitor. Bronner argues that its circulation is too small for it to have its own viable system, hence that it should get access to the unique nationwide distribution system, that of its competitor. The ECJ, in essence, argues that, given the current market shares, the claim might be true, but that this fact does not justify getting access. If Bronner had an equal market share as the leading firm, then a nationwide distribution system would be viable for Bronner itself; hence the competitor should not be forced to share. It has been argued in Bergman (2000) that this 'Bronner test' constitutes a formidable hurdle for new entrants: it may simply not be feasible to reach a comparable market share within a reasonable time frame. It has also been argued (see Hancher, 1999) that, if the Commission had adopted this stringent test in earlier cases, it would not have been able to come to the conclusion that access should be granted, as was the conclusion at the time.

6   Dominance versus substantial lessening of competition

Both the USA and the EU know a system of merger control. Remarkably, in both jurisdictions, this instrument of structural control over the market was introduced only some 20 years after the first behavioral controls over business were introduced. While the Sherman Act dates from 1890, merger control was introduced in the USA only in 1914. The EU came much later: laws prohibiting cartels and 'regulating' dominant firms were introduced in 1958, while the European Community Merger Regulation (ECMR) came into effect only in 1980. Already in 1966, the European Commission had remarked that, as both Article 81 and Article 82 EU Treaty deal with behavior, it did not have a strong instrument to control essential changes in the structure of the market, and that a full system of merger control was needed to maintain effective competition in the common market and to reach the goals of the EU Treaty. As the change required unanimous approval by the council and since different member states had different views on what the goals of merger policy should be (and, in particular, about the role of industrial policy), it took 23 years until the ECMR was finally adopted.

Indeed, it is an interesting question what the goals of merger policy should be. Two broad goals may be distinguished. Given the difficulties involved in constraining the behavior of dominant firms, the main purpose of EC merger control seems to be preventing dominant firms from coming into existence. In the USA, the main goal seems to be to prevent 'anti-competitive' market structures. The difference in emphasis leads to a different test: while the US authorities check whether a merger would lead to a significant lessening of competition, the European Commission verifies whether it would lead to a dominant position. In the following section, we investigate the consequences of these different substantive tests, and we also briefly touch upon differences in procedures.

6.1 Rules and procedures

In the USA, Section 7 of the Clayton Act, first enacted in 1914, controls mergers. It states that forbidden are acquisitions 'where in any line of commerce or in any activity affecting commerce, in any section of the country, the effect of such acquisition may be substantially to lessen competition, or to tend to create a monopoly' (15 USC 18). The EC Merger Regulation, which was adopted in 1989 and which came into force on 21 September 1990, states in Article 2(3): 'A concentration which creates or strengthens a dominant position as a result of which effective competition would be significantly impeded in the common market or in a substantial part of it shall be declared incompatible with the common market.'

We note that, in the ECMR, dominance has the same meaning as in Article 82 EU Treaty; hence the definition was provided in the previous section. Of course, one important difference is that merger analysis is prospective, whereas Article 82 EU Treaty looks at the firm's past behavior. Also note that the substantive test in merger appraisal is a two-part test: the merger should create or strengthen a dominant position and, as a result of that, effective competition should be significantly impeded. It is thus possible that a merger creates or strengthens a dominant position, but is nevertheless allowed, since it does not significantly impede competition. Furthermore, according to this test, mergers that significantly impede competition without creating or strengthening a dominant position should be allowed as well. The EU test thus appears permissive: both conditions have to be satisfied for merger to be forbidden. In contrast, the Clayton Act states that mergers that substantially lessen competition or tend to create a monopoly are forbidden. In practice, since competition will usually be lessened already before monopoly is reached, cases in the USA focus on 'significant lessening of competition', while in Europe the focus is on 'dominance'.

Firms that want to merge have to notify this to the agencies that are responsible for those jurisdictions where the merger has effect. There are important procedural differences in the way merger notifications are handled in the USA and in Europe. In the USA, one has to notify both the Federal Trade Commission and the Antitrust Division of the Department of Justice. One of these agencies will handle the merger and will decide whether there is no anticompetitive effect and it can go through, or whether to file suit to prevent the merger from taking place. The US system is an adversarial system. If the Antitrust Division wants to block a merger, it has to bring a court case, and the court will weigh the arguments of the merging parties against those of the Department of Justice. In Europe, parties notify the European Commission, which investigates the case, which negotiates with parties to get remedies to relieve competition concerns, and which decides to block the merger in the case where the latter is judged to be unsatisfactory. Consequently, the European Commission has a rather large discretionary power.

In Europe, parties can appeal the Decision of the Commission, with the Court of First Instance (CFI), but it takes a long time before that court will decide. For example, in *Airtours/First Choice*, the Commission blocked the merger in 1999, and it took three years before the CFI annulled that decision. Of course, the industry might have changed considerably during such a long period, and it is, hence, not too surprising that relatively few cases have been appealed, although recently, there has been more activity, with also more cases being annulled by the CFI. It has been argued that, as a consequence of these procedural differences, the European Commission faces less effective checks and balances and, therefore, as Patterson and Shapiro (2001) argue, has more room to fall prey to 'demonstrably erroneous economic theory, and speculation contrary to the weight of the evidence', this leading to a larger probability of mistaken decisions.

Patterson and Shapiro (2001) also point to the notable fact that, until recently, the European Commission has not been willing to commit itself by issuing guidelines on how it will evaluate mergers. In the USA, the first merger guidelines were published in 1968; in Europe it took until the end of 2002 before the Commission published its first draft of the guidelines for horizontal mergers. Remarkably, this draft shows a close resemblance to the US Merger Guidelines.

The US Merger Guidelines describe the analytical framework and methodology used by the Antitrust Division and the Federal Trade Commission to determine whether a horizontal merger is likely substantially to lessen competition and, hence, should be challenged. The unifying theme of the guidelines is that mergers should not be permitted to create or enhance market power. They specify a five-step procedure to answer the ultimate inquiry in US merger analysis: is the merger likely to create or enhance market power or to facilitate its exercise?

In the first step, the relevant (affected) markets and the players on these markets are identified, and it is assessed whether the merger would significantly increase concentration. The Herfindahl–Hirschman Index (HHI) is used to measure market concentration and three broad regions are distinguished: unconcentrated markets (HHI below 1000), moderately concentrated markets (HHI between 1000 and 1800) and highly concentrated markets (HHI above 1800). In evaluating a merger, both the post-merger market concentration and the increase in concentration resulting from the merger are considered. If the post-merger market is moderately concentrated (highly concentrated) and the merger increases the HHI by more than 100 (more than 50) points, then the merger potentially raises competitive concerns, and should be investigated. In highly concentrated markets, it is presumed that mergers that increase the HHI by 100 points or more are likely to enhance market power. In all other cases, the antitrust authority (the one that is handling a case, either the FTC or the Antitrust Division of the DOJ) regards the merger as unlikely to have adverse competitive effects and ordinarily to require no further analysis. The authorities consider that market share and market concentration data may either understate or overstate market power, hence the rule cannot be mechanical. A variety of other market characteristics (such as volatility of market shares and the importance of innovation) are therefore considered.

In the second step, it is studied whether the merger could have adverse competitive effects. Two channels through which a merger may harm competition are distinguished. First, a merger may diminish competition by making it easier for firms to coordinate their actions, hence to collude either tacitly or overtly. To check whether this possibility is real, the authorities go over a checklist of market factors ('facilitating circumstances') as in

Section 4, in order to check whether it is possible for firms to coordinate and to discipline potential deviators. Here also factors that would make such coordination more difficult, such as the existence of 'maverick firms' are investigated. Secondly, as a merger eliminates one competitor from the market, it loosens a competitive constraint, and this may enable the merged firm (and indeed, in response also its competitors) to raise prices. This is the second channel through which a merger may diminish competition, the so-called 'unilateral effects': the merging firms may find it profitable to alter their behavior unilaterally following the acquisition by elevating price and suppressing output. Of course, if competitors could easily replace the offerings that, as a result of the merger, are withdrawn from the market, the competitive constraint would not be much loosened and there would not be much reason for concern.

It is realized that a merger is not likely to create or enhance market power or to facilitate its exercise if entry into the market is so easy that existing market participants could not profitably maintain a price increase above pre-merger levels. Such entry will likely deter an anti-competitive merger at birth, or deter or counteract the competitive effects of concern. The third step of the analysis thus involves checking whether new market entry could counteract the competitive effects of concern. The antitrust authority investigates whether entry is possible and probably, whether it would be timely and would be sufficient to return competition and market prices to their pre-merger levels.

In the fourth step, the antitrust authority assesses any efficiency gains that cannot reasonably be achieved by the parties through other means than the merger. Here it is realized that efficiencies generated through merger can enhance the merged firm's ability and incentive to compete (for example, two high-cost producers may join forces and obtain cost savings, making them a more effective competitor), which may result in lower prices, hence, higher consumer surplus. The antitrust authority will thus investigate whether such efficiencies are likely to be achieved, and whether they are merger-specific. Cognizable efficiencies are defined as merger-specific efficiencies that have been verified and do not arise from anti-competitive reductions in output or service. If such cognizable efficiencies likely would be sufficient to reverse the merger's potential to harm consumers in the relevant market, for example, by preventing price increases in that market, then the antitrust authority will not challenge the merger.

Finally, the antitrust authority assesses whether, but for the merger, either party to the transaction would be likely to fail, causing its assets to leave the market. In such cases, the merger will have no effect on competition in the market, it is not likely to create or enhance market power or to facilitate its exercise, and can be allowed.

Broadly speaking, the European Commission follows a similar procedure to that outlined in the US guidelines, but there are important differences in the second and fourth step. Before turning to these differences, let us briefly consider the elements of communality. In the first step, there is not much difference, certainly not in the way the relevant market is identified. The Commission also looks at ease of entry. Furthermore, the 'failing firm defense' is also allowed in Europe. Recall that the ECMR specifies a two-part test: proscribed are mergers that create a dominant position as a result of which competition is significantly impeded. It is possible that a merger will create or strengthen a dominant position, but is nevertheless allowed. *Kali and Salz* or, more generally, any case in which a failing firm is taken over by a dominant firm, provides a real life example of this possibility: dominance is strengthened, but there is no significant effect on competition. For example, in *Kali and Salz*, the court remarked:

124. It follows from the foregoing that the absence of a causal link between the concentration and the deterioration of the competitive structure of the German market has not been effectively called into question. Accordingly, it must be held that, so far as that market is concerned, the concentration appears to satisfy the criterion referred to in Article 2(2) of the Regulation, and could thus be declared compatible with the common market without being amended.

The two-part test implies that, in Europe, mergers that significantly impede competition without creating or strengthening a dominant position should be allowed. As such mergers may well have negative consequences for welfare or consumer surplus, this may be considered undesirable. As a theoretical example of this possibility, think of a merger between the numbers two and three in a triopoly where the leader has 51 per cent of the market: competition is impeded, but no individually dominant firm is created or strengthened. It should thus not be surprising that the Commission has attempted to stretch its powers. In the specific case covered by this example, and indeed more generally, the Commission has done this by invoking the concept of 'collective dominance'.

In the remainder of this section, we first discuss this concept of collective dominance. Our discussion will lead to the conclusion, as also drawn by the Commission, that stretching 'dominance' to 'collective dominance' is not the way to go and that an alternative way is to be preferred. Already at this stage we can remark that there are two obvious ways by means of which the substantive merger test in the EU could be strengthened: first, by dropping the reference to dominance, in which case the test would become very much like the SLC (significant lessening of competition) test that is used in the USA and, recently, in the UK, and second, by dropping the reference to 'competition being impeded', in which case one would have a pure dominance test.

Having discussed 'collective dominance', we will see that the Commission has recently proposed a third, and different, way to strengthen (or at least to clarify) the merger test from the ECMR.

6.2   Collective dominance

We have already encountered this concept in the previous section. Note, however, that, while Article 82 EU Treaty explicitly refers to a dominance position that may be held by one or more undertakings, there is no such reference in the European Commission merger test, hence the question has arisen whether mergers that would create or strengthen situations of joint (or collective, or oligopolistic) dominance could be blocked: can mergers that produce tight oligopolies be forbidden?

While the European Commission had already argued, in 1986, that, in its view, mergers creating collective dominant positions were forbidden by the regulation, it took until 1998 before the ECJ clarified in *Kali and Salz* that collective dominance was caught by the Merger Regulation: '178. It follows from the foregoing that collective dominant positions do not fall outside the scope of the Regulation.'

This decision, however, left unclear what situations would be classified under the label of collective dominance; in particular, what links (structural or economic) between the firms were needed for these to be able to adopt a common policy on the market. This is the issue that we have already visited in the previous section. Clarity was provided in *Gencor*, a decision in which the CFI also referred to *Flat Glass*, and used similar terms to those in that case, making it clear that collective dominance has the same meaning in merger cases as in abuse cases. In particular, in *Gencor*, the CFI held that contractual links between firms are not necessary for these to be collectively dominant: it is sufficient for there to be a tight oligopoly in which tacit collusion is a possibility:

> 276. Furthermore, there is no reason whatsoever in legal or economic terms to exclude from the notion of economic links the relationship of interdependence existing between the parties to a tight oligopoly within which, in a market with the appropriate characteristics, in particular in terms of market concentration, transparency and product homogeneity, those parties are in a position to anticipate one another's behavior and are therefore strongly encouraged to align their conduct in the market, in particular in such a way as to maximize joint profits by restricting production with a view to increasing prices. In such a context, each trader is aware that highly competitive action on its part designed to increase its market share (for example a price cut) would provoke identical action by the others, so that it would derive no benefits from its initiative. All the traders would thus be affected by the reduction in price levels.

Just as in the previous section, we can conclude that situations of tight oligopoly in which tacit collusion is feasible can carry the label 'collective dominance'. Indeed, in paragraph 277 of *Gencor*, the CFI explicitly states that the Commission should be able to control mergers in 'market structures of an oligopolistic kind where each undertaking may become aware of common interests and, in particular, cause prices to increase without having to enter into an agreement or resort to a concerted practice'.

The above description allows us to conclude that the coordinated effects that we encountered in the US Merger Guidelines are also covered by the ECMR; therefore in this domain, the policies on the two continents should not be different, and the 'checklist' from Section 4 applies to both jurisdictions. The model (theorem) that underpins this checklist is the Folk Theorem from the theory of repeated games. Here we wish to stress, however, that the Folk Theorem only tells us that, in tight oligopolies, tacit collusion may be an equilibrium outcome; it does not tell us that firms will necessarily collude. The question, therefore, remains how to assess the likelihood of tacit collusion and whether, in situations where mergers might produce market structure that could be conducive to tacit collusion, it would not be preferable to be more permissive and to rely more on monitoring ex post and intervention through Article 82 EU Treaty. Given the fact that tacit collusion can be caught by Article 81 EU Treaty, is the mere fear that a merger possibly might lead to tacit collusion sufficient to block a merger?

In 1999, the British tour operator and supplier of package holidays *Airtours* wanted to acquire its competitor *First Choice*. It notified the transaction to the Commission, which decided to block the acquisition, as it would lead to a position of collective dominance on the UK market for package holidays. In its decision, the Commission tried to stretch the notion of collective dominance:

54. (...) it is not a necessary condition of collective dominance for the oligopolists always to behave as if there were one or more explicit agreements (e.g. to fix prices or capacity, or share the market) between them. It is sufficient that the merger makes it rational for the oligopolists, in adapting themselves to market conditions to act – individually – in ways which will substantially reduce competition between them, and as a result of which they may act, to an appreciable extent, independently of competitors, customers and consumers.

What is suggested in this passage (in particular, by using the word 'individually') is that the ECMR could also be used to catch non-cooperative adaptation to the changed market conditions. The decision itself was, however, not completely clear on this, as it also went over the checklist from Section 4 of facilitating factors for tacit collusion. Hence, in

Airtours / First Choice, the Commission added confusion to the meaning of collective dominance.

Airtours appealed the Commission's decision, arguing both that the Commission had applied a new and incorrect definition of collective dominance and that it had erred in its assessment that the merger would create a collective dominant position on the UK market for short-haul package holidays. In 2002, the CFI annulled the decision of the Commission, arguing that the Commission had not proved to the requisite legal standard that the concentration would give rise to a collective dominance position that would significantly impede effective competition. In essence, the CFI argued that the characteristics of this market were such that tacit collusion was not very likely, or at least that the Commission had not argued convincingly that it was likely. The CFI, however, did not make any comments on the more fundamental point of whether 'tight non-cooperative oligopolies' could be caught by the ECMR: 'the Decision must be annulled, without it being necessary to examine the other complaints and pleas put forward by the applicant' (para. 295).

While there is not enough space here to discuss the case in detail, it is worthwhile to mention some relevant aspects, so that the reader can form an opinion. In *Airtours / First Choice*, the European Commission distinguishes two types of players on the relevant market, which is the market for short-haul package holidays: major tour operators that have market shares exceeding 10 per cent and that are integrated both upstream (operation of charter airlines) and downstream (travel agencies), and secondary operators that have smaller market shares and that typically do not have their own charter airlines or travel agencies. The major companies account for about 80 per cent of the market, divided as follows: Thomson 27 per cent, Airtours 21 per cent, Thomas Cook 20 per cent, First Choice 11 per cent. Note that, with an HHI of over 1800 and an increase in HHI of over 400, the US authorities would start the analysis of this case with a presumption of market power being enhanced. The post-merger market share of 32 per cent would not lead one to conclude that *Airtours/First Choice* would be dominant. Indeed, the Commission did not argue the case on single firm dominance, but on grounds of collective dominance (para. 58 of the Decision).

Let us go over the checklist of factors facilitating tacit collusion, as mentioned in Section 4: how likely is tacit collusion? In the words of the CFI 'Is it possible for the three major companies that remain after the merger to adopt a common policy on the market?'. In para. 62, the CFI writes:

> three conditions are necessary for a finding of collective dominance as defined: first, each member of the dominant oligopoly must have the ability to know

how the other members are behaving in order to monitor whether or not they are adopting the common policy ... There must, therefore, be sufficient market transparency for all members of the dominant oligopoly to be aware, sufficiently precisely and quickly, of the way in which the other member's market conduct is evolving; second, the situation of tacit coordination must be sustainable over time, that is to say, there must be an incentive not to depart from the common policy on the market ... The notion of retaliation in respect of conduct deviating from the common policy is thus inherent in this condition ... for a situation of collective dominance to be viable, there must be adequate deterrents to ensure that there is a long-term incentive in not departing from the common policy ...; third, to prove the existence of a collective dominant position to the requisite legal standard, the Commission must also establish that the foreseeable reaction of current and future competitors, as well as of consumers, would not jeopardize the results expected from the common policy.

These conditions are broadly in line with the checklist from Section 4: tacit collusion requires that the players can monitor each other's actions, so that they can detect deviations from the common policy; that they can punish deviations, so that deviating is not profitable; and that there are entry barriers, so that outsiders cannot make tacit coordination unprofitable by undercutting.

In its plea, *Airtours* argued that, in this specific market, none of these conditions was satisfied. First of all, while the Commission argued that the market involved a relatively homogeneous product, *Airtours* argued that there is a lot of product heterogeneity; for example, there are 50 holiday destinations and 20 airports of departure in the UK, hence 1000 combinations (and even many more different hotels) and these have different characteristics. The product heterogeneity makes coordination difficult and the market non-transparent. Secondly, demand for holiday trips is volatile and demand is difficult to forecast at the point in time when capacity is planned, which is 18 months in advance of the season; hence this also contributes to lack of transparency and makes monitoring difficult. Thirdly, because capacity is planned well in advance, retaliation cannot be quick and, as a consequence, it is unlikely that deviation from the common policy can be deterred. Finally, *Airtours* argued that barriers to entry and barriers to expansion for smaller players were low. If the dominant players tacitly colluded and restricted hotel capacity, the smaller players could easily expand, by making more bookings and by making more seat reservations with competing airlines. As a result, tacit collusion could not succeed.

The CFI reviewed these arguments and concluded that the Commission made various errors in its assessment of the market (predictability and volatility of demand, and the degree of market transparency), that it wrongly concluded firms could easily coordinate, that it erred in finding that there was a sufficient incentive for a member of the dominant oligopoly not to depart from the common policy, and that the Commission exaggerated the importance of entry barriers. As a result of these findings, the CFI was forced to annul the Commission's decision.

6.3   SLC or dominance: does it make a difference?

The above discussion has made clear that the ECMR catches mergers that create situations of single or collective dominance. However, these situations are not the only ones in which effective competition may be significantly impeded. In an oligopolistic situation, a merger may considerably reduce consumer surplus also if it does not lead to coordinated behavior. It seems that, thus far, the Merger Regulation has not caught such mergers and it might be argued that this is undesirable. In 2000, the European Commission published a green paper in which it examined, among other things, whether and how the substantive test of the ECMR should be strengthened to deal with such situations. In particular, the question was posed whether the European Commission should switch and also adopt the SLC (substantial lessening of competition) test that is being used in the USA. Following this consultation, on 11 December 2002, the European Commission proposed a far-reaching reform of its merger control regime in which, among other things, it proposes a new regulation in order to strengthen its substantive merger test. Before discussing the test proposed by the Commission, we now discuss whether the test would make a difference.

European Commissioner Monti has suggested that the exact substantive test, or at least the wording of it, does not make much difference. As illustrative evidence, he has pointed to the fact that there have been very few cases of conflict between the USA and the EU, and that even in cases such as *GE/Honeywell*, the conflict was not the result of the tests being different, but of the facts of the case being interpreted in a different way on the two sides of the Atlantic. We would like to argue that the tests are very different and that the EC test is really too weak. Of course, this value judgment relates to the goal one assigns to merger control. In our view, the goal of merger control should not simply be to prevent dominant positions being attained, but rather to prevent market structures in which competitive forces are too weak. The essence of merger control is to prevent mergers that would result in market structures in which competition would be significantly impeded. We remark that this is also the position taken by the European CFI. In *Gencor*, the Court writes:

> 106. (...) while the elimination of the risk of future abuses may be a legitimate concern of any competent competition authority, the main objective in exercising control over concentrations at Community level is to ensure that the restructuring of undertakings does not result in the creation of positions of economic power which may significantly impede effective competition in the common market.

Community jurisdiction is therefore founded, first and foremost, on the need to avoid the establishment of market structures which may create or strengthen a dominant position, and not on the need to control directly possible abuses of a dominant position.

In our view, the dominance test is too weak to deal adequately with 'non-cooperative tight oligopolies' and, for this reason, changing to the SLC-test would be desirable. At the same time, however, we note that the European Commission has a great deal of discretionary power, and that implementation of policy is already imperfect at the moment. The vagueness of the SLC test, and the associated possible loss of some relevant (constraining) case law, would give the European Commission greater power to intervene than it currently has, hence switching to the SLC test might exacerbate the problems resulting from a too interventionist Commission. In fact, one might say that this is an argument for retaining the current test. After all, the current test asks for both the creation or strengthening of a dominant position and, as a consequence of it, a significant impediment to competition. It thus imposes a strict standard.

If, as we argue here, the essence of merger control is to prevent market structures in which competition would be significantly impeded and if the current ECMR is insufficiently powerful for this purpose, there seems an easy fix to the problem: it then suffices simply to eliminate the reference to dominance in Article 2 of the current Merger Regulation; thus the text would become:

3. A concentration as a result of which effective competition would be significantly impeded in the common market or in a substantial part of it shall be declared incompatible with the common market.

In the proposal for a new ECMR, the Commission has not taken this route, although stresses, just as we do, that it should also be able to tackle 'non-cooperative mergers' in oligopolistic settings. Instead of deleting the word 'dominance' from the ECRM, the Commission proposes to redefine the term. Specifically, the Commission proposes to add a new Article 2 to the Regulation, in which 'dominance' is redefined as follows:

2. For the purpose of this Regulation, one or more undertakings shall be deemed to be in a dominant position if, with or without coordinating, they hold the economic power to influence appreciably and sustainably the parameters of competition, in particular, prices, production, quality of output, distribution or innovation, or appreciably to foreclose competition.

Although the Commission remarks, in recital 56 of the proposed Regulation, that this proposed definition closely follows the characterization of a dominant position given by the court, we are not entirely convinced by this. It seems to us that, since the concept is stretched to include also situations in which oligopolists do not coordinate their behavior, adopting this proposal by the European Commission would have the consequence of dominance coming to mean something different in merger cases than it does in abuse cases, unless, of course, the concept of 'oligopolistic dominance' was stretched in these cases as well. However, as our discussion in the previous section has shown, such a strengthening would be both unnecessary and undesirable. Given the decisions of the Court in cases such as *Airtours*, we also believe that the European CFI would be unwilling to stretch the definition in that direction.

Given that the Commission thus proposes in effect to adopt a different definition in merger cases than in abuse cases, we prefer to do away with dominance in merger cases altogether. In order to deal with the problem of discretion referred to above, we advocate using merger guidelines, just as is done in the USA, and we are pleased that, as part of its comprehensive reform process, the European Commission has indeed published draft guidelines for the appraisal of horizontal mergers. This notice is structured around the same five steps that we have encountered in the US guidelines, with the additional element that buyer power is explicitly taken into account. While there are certain differences between the EU guidelines and the US guidelines (for example, the Commission states that it is unlikely that it will challenge mergers with an HHI below 1000, where the 'safe haven' in the USA is somewhat more generous), in broad terms, with the exception possibly of the treatment of efficiencies, one may state that there is agreement between the two, at least as far as methods of analysis are concerned. Consequently, the Draft Commission Notice in effect declares that the Commission will be performing an SLC test.

Perhaps this is not that surprising, as it has been claimed that the Commission may also in the past have been using this test. Whish (2001), for example, notes that, in *Carrefour/Promodes*, the combined market share of the merging firms share stood at less than 30 per cent and that still the merger was prohibited. Consequently, it is possible that in some past merger cases the Commission would have found dominance where it would not so have concluded, had the case been one under Article 82 EU Treaty.

6.4   Efficiencies

The second substantive issue on which the Commission's green paper invited views was the treatment of efficiencies in merger control. The Commission has frequently been criticized for not having a transparent policy with respect to this issue and, in the present consultation process, many respondents have argued in favor of treating efficiency claims more explicitly. The

European Commission, however, decided not to honor these requests. In the proposal for the new ECMR, it writes that it is legally possible to deal with efficiency issues under Article 2(1)(*b*) of the ECMR and, consequently, the proposal is to leave this aspect unchanged. Article 2(1)(*b*), however, gives some rather general observations; it states, among other things, that, in making the merger appraisal, the Commission shall take into account 'the development of technical and economic progress provided that it is to consumers' advantage and does not form an obstacle to competition'. In reaction to the proposal, several commentators have therefore argued that Article 2(1)(*b*) of the ECMR is not the proper place to incorporate efficiencies and that these should be taken into account in the substantive test, that is in Articles 2(3) and 2(4) of the Regulation. We are of the same opinion, but, if our analysis in the previous section is correct, the issue is more semantic than one of substance. This reading is also supported by the chapter on efficiencies in the Draft Commission Notice on the appraisal of horizontal mergers. There we read, in paragraph 88:

> The Commission considers any substantiated efficiency claim in the overall assessment of the merger. It may decide that, as a consequence of the efficiencies that the merger brings about, this merger does not create or strengthen a dominant position as a result of which effective competition would be significantly impeded. This will be the case when the Commission is in a position to conclude on the basis of sufficient evidence that the efficiencies generated by the merger are likely to enhance the incentive of the merged entity to act pro-competitively for the benefit of consumers, by counteracting the effects on competition which the merger might otherwise have.

On the face of it, this does not seem to be different from the way efficiencies are handled in the USA and one would hope that the Commission would adopt a similar position also in mergers that are not purely horizontal (see below). Of course, the Commission is right to insist, as it does in the Draft Commission Notice, that the efficiencies that the merging parties claim are verifiable, substantial, timely, merger-specific and of direct benefit to the consumers, but this is not different from the situation in the USA.

We conclude from the above that, on paper, it appears that in the future EU merger policy will be very much like the policy in the USA, hence that there will be little scope for conflict. In the past, however, there has been conflict: in 2001, the US and EU competition authorities reached diametrically opposed conclusions in the proposed merger of General Electric with Honeywell. While this merger was unproblematic for the US authorities, it was blocked by the European Commission. We conclude this section by briefly discussing this important case: how to explain that different conclusions were reached?

The essence of the European Commission's argument for blocking the merger was that, through packaged offers, the merged entity would be able to charge lower prices and, hence, to foreclose competitors from the market. At the same time, the US authorities viewed these efficiencies that the merged company was able to obtain as being pro-competitive. To appreciate these arguments, some background information on the players involved and the markets on which they are active is needed.

General Electric is a widely diversified industrial corporation, with revenues exceeding $125 billion in 2001. In the area of aviation, with which this case is concerned, it produces aircraft engines and it holds a dominant position on several of such engine markets. Through a joint venture with the French company CFMI, for example, it exclusively supplies engines for Boeing's B737. Competitors on this market are Pratt & Whitney (P&W) and Rolls Royce (RR). Honeywell is a leading avionics and technology firm, with revenues of about $23 billion in 2001, of which half came from its aerospace division. Given the breadth of activities of both of these companies there was a remarkable lack of overlap in their aircraft activities. Consequently, the usual horizontal market power issues (elimination of a competitor, thereby relaxing the competitive constraints and allowing increase in price) in this case were not of major concern. Instead, the focus was on 'conglomerate effects'.

The European Commission claimed that, by combining the dominant position of GE in the aircraft engines markets with the leading position of Honeywell in several avionics markets, the merged company would be able to offer product packages at discount prices that rivals would not be able to match, and that, as a consequence, these rivals would exit, thus leading to a strengthening of GE's dominant position. In making this argument, the Commission also gave an important role to the financial strength of GE, as derived from its financial arm, GE Capital and, in particular, its important role in the purchasing, leasing and financing of aircraft. The following excerpts from the Decision illustrate the Commission's concerns (see paragraphs 351–5 of the Decision):

> 353. As a result of the proposed merger, the merged entity will be able to price its packaged deals in such a way as to induce customers to buy GE engines and Honeywell BFE and SFE-option products over those of competitors, thus increasing the combined share of GE and Honeywell on both markets. ...
> 355. (...) the merged entity's packaged offers will manifest their effects after the merger goes through. Because of their lack of ability to match the bundle offer, these [that is the competing, VCR v. D] component suppliers will lose market shares to the benefit of the merged entity and experience an immediate damaging profit shrinkage. As a result, the merger is likely to lead to market foreclosure on those existing aircraft platforms and subsequently to the elimination of competition in these areas.

To an economist, these arguments definitely do not suffice to block the merger: the goal of merger control is not to protect (inefficient) competitors. In fact, in this case, the Commission itself acknowledges that the customers will benefit from the discount, but it is also worried that, by engaging in short-term cost cutting, these customers will ultimately harm themselves:

> 449. Airlines generally welcome the financial incentives that come with bundled offers. Given the very nature of their competitive environment, airlines are under great pressure in the short term to keep their costs under control. Therefore, while airlines are likely to understand that their long-term interests would be better served through the preservation of competition among suppliers, each individual airline also has, and is likely to pursue, a short-term interest in achieving costs savings through bundled offerings.

What is at issue here is the really fundamental question of the extent to which one can rely on markets as being self-correcting: the more one is a market believer, the less one will be inclined to think that there will be a conflict between the short term and the long term. Related to that, should one act on the assumption that government officials are better able to take the long-term interests of customers into account than these customers themselves? Interestingly, in this case, the customers were not opposed to the merger, but the competitors (RR in particular) forcefully made the above point. Why would one block a merger from which consumers do benefit? As pointed out earlier, in the USA there is, generally, a stronger belief in the market than there is in the EU and, indeed, in the USA, the same arguments led to the conclusion that the merger should be allowed, since it would lead to lower prices, and, hence, benefit consumers. In other words, in the USA, the efficiencies obtained through the merger were considered as advantageous, while in Europe they were considered as disadvantageous.

The economist's comparative advantage lies in his knowledge of the functioning of markets. He is trained not to believe in markets, but to evaluate them on their merits. While an antitrust economist may not have detailed knowledge of the markets relevant in this specific case, he may bring to bear models that allow one to get a better feeling for the forces that play a role. What are we to make of the above arguments? Can the fears of the European Commission be substantiated?

As is known already from theoretical work dating back to Cournot, a merger of firms that are active in complementary product lines may allow them to reduce price, since, after the merger, they internalize externalities. Given price competition, competitors will follow by also reducing price, therefore overall prices will fall and consumers will benefit in the short run. What about the long run? Theory here is less developed and one has to rely more on intuition, aided by stylized ad hoc models that capture some relevant aspects of this case. If the merged entity is much more efficient than its competitors, it might drive them from the market, and, theoretically, one could imagine that the firm might engage in foreclosure practices in order to speed up this process. Consequently, strengthening of dominance seems possible, but even in those cases the welfare effects are ambiguous: the merger confers short-term benefits on consumers, while the long-term effects are ambiguous; that is they depend on the model that is adopted. From an economic point of view, is that sufficient to block a merger? It hardly seems so.

In this specific case, a model was constructed in support of the argument of the competitors and the relevance of that model to the case at hand and for the decision to be taken was discussed extensively. In the Decision, the European Commission summarizes the role of economic analysis as follows:

> 352. (...) The Commission has evaluated the theoretical premises of mixed bundling as presented to it in the economic analyses submitted by the parties and third parties. The various economic analyses have been subject to theoretical controversy, in particular, as far as the economic model of mixed bundling, prepared by one of the third parties, is concerned. However, the Commission does not consider the reliance on one or the other model necessary for the conclusion that packaged deals that the merged entity will be in a position to offer will foreclose competition from the engines and avionics/non-avionics markets.

In our view, the fact that one cannot rely on one or the other model does not imply that one should not take the lessons of these models to heart and that one can base one's decision on one's instincts.

7 Research agenda

This section sums up the discussion of this chapter. It does so by identifying research gaps in the various fields of interest.

The most striking and important research gap lies in empirical work on dominance. There is substantial empirical work on mergers, that is, the determinants and consequences of mergers, but much more useful empirical work which is needed is lacking. In the light of the fact that judges require strong empirical foundation, the economics profession falls short of providing competition authorities with sufficient tools and research. Just to mention a number of fields where empirical contributions will be helpful:

Importance of entry barriers. Entry barriers play a vital role in dominance issues, but there is hardly any clue on how to assess the importance of entry barriers in a quantitative way.

Factors driving collective dominance (tacit collusion). Section 4 introduced a classification of market structure characteristics (necessary ingredients, important factors and other factors). The practical usefulness of this classification can be enhanced if it can be backed up with empirical work.

Assessment of government failure. From economic theory we know that government intervention is associated with social costs. It would be good to have empirical studies conducted that assess the importance of government failure under various market structural characteristics.

Role of experiments. One of the reasons for empirical studies not yet having generated strong detailed conclusions about the functioning of markets is that they need to measure a wealth of variables. Some of these variables, such as firms' cost structures and demand conditions, may be hard to measure. Moreover, economists hardly have control over the relevant variables. An environment in which the researcher does not face these problems is the research laboratory. In the laboratory, subjects are confronted with oligopoly games of which the researcher knows the characteristics. Even better, the researcher can fully control these characteristics. Therefore laboratory experiments can help gain insights in the functioning of markets. This is useful in particular for assessing the importance of certain market structural characteristics, such as symmetry, transparency, the number of firms, pre-game communication and the like. There is already some experimental work being done on some of these issues,[86] but clearly more work is needed.

Implementation. This chapter focused on economic analysis of dominance and government responses to anti-competitive conduct and mergers. Economists often ignore the practical problems that governments have when implementing policies. While there is a growing literature on implementation issues, such as pricing rules, leniency programs, agency problems and fighting facilitating practices, the development of (applicable) theory is in its early stages and much more can be done.

Applied theory on abuse. There are recent developments in the literature on predation, foreclosure, raising rivals' costs and essential facilities, but much more can be done here as well. It would be particularly useful to study the relationship between certain market structural characteristics and the potential for the various types of abuse.

Ex ante versus ex post. There are a number of overview articles discussing the relative merits of ex ante versus ex post intervention. Indeed, Section 2 of this chapter also provides some general insights on this discussion. What is still lacking, though, is more concrete studies on this issue. One can think of international comparisons between markets which are regulated in one country but left to the competition law in another. One can think of markets that face a regime shift (typically from sector-specific regulation to competition law). Another idea is to analyze the role of regulation on investment decisions and innovation.[87]

Notes

1. http://www.oft.gov.uk/default.htm.
2. See FTC mission statement, http://www.ftc.gov/ftc/mission.htm.
3. See, for example Tichy (2001), Mueller (2001, and in the present volume), Schenk (forthcoming 2005).
4. See also Geroski and Jacquemin (1988) for a European cross-country study, the country-specific studies in Mueller (1990) as well as Odagiri and Maruyama (2002) for a recent study on Japanese manufacturing.
5. Schmalensee is in fact more moderate than the polar position suggests.
6. *United States* v. *Aluminum Co. of America*, 148 F.2d 416 (1945).
7. Cowling is in fact more moderate than the polar position suggests.
8. Reviewing the literature on competition and innovation, Bennett *et al.* (2001) conclude: 'It is generally true to say that the rate of innovation per firm will increase with competition when the degree of competition is not already too severe. ... However, increasing the number of firms when the underlying industry structure is already monopolistic generally increases the rate of innovation both at the firm level and at the industry level.'
9. See Neven *et al.* (1993) for a relevant discussion of institutions in the context of merger control. In the EU, inter-firm agreements that would fall under Article 81 EU Treaty must also be notified in order to benefit from an exemption; however, following a recent reform, these agreements will be dealt with 'ex post' from Spring 2004 on. Berges-Sennou *et al.* (2001) formally compare the prior notification regime with the ex post audit regime and stress that the balance tilts in favor of the latter as the competition agency's scrutiny becomes more precise.
10. In particular, ex post intervention may serve as a deterrent but come too late to act as a corrective device.
11. For example, in the USA the Federal Communications Commission has imposed price caps to limit the exercise of market power, while such behavior would not be an antitrust offence. In the EU, excessive prices could constitute an abuse of a dominant position under Article 82 EU Treaty, but so far the European Commission has rarely used this possibility.
12. See Dewatripont and Tirole (1999) for a formal analysis.
13. This is for example the case in the USA; in contrast, in the EU the European Commission both investigates and decides. It is, however, currently devising ways to disentangle these two aspects, in line with what has been adopted in European countries such as France, where the Competition Council (a jurisdictional entity with decision powers) has different bodies in charge of investigations and decisions.
14. In the case of the FCC, however, federal courts limit themselves to ensuring only that the Commission acts in a 'reasonable' manner and does not engage in 'arbitrary and capricious' behavior. In contrast, the Antitrust Division is not entitled to substantial deference.
15. The interaction between the two sets of case law is also interesting. The new European regulatory framework for telecommunications fosters a convergence of the two worlds and emphasizes, for example, that regulators must use available competition principles.
16. See, for example, Crémer (1995) and Aghion and Tirole (1997).
17. http://europa.eu.int/comm/competition/general_info/glossary_en.html.
18. *Graphic Products Dist., Inc.* v. *Itek. Corp.* 717 F 2d 1560, 1570 (11th Cir. 1983).
19. Such as in a Coasian-type durable goods monopoly; see subsection 3.2.
20. Fudenberg and Tirole (1984) provide a taxonomy of entry deterring strategies.
21. http://europa.eu.int/comm/competition/mergers/review/final_draft_en.pdf.
22. The bulk of empirical evidence reveals that one is most likely to find dominant firms under the larger ones (see, e.g., Scherer and Ross, 1990; Church and Ware, 2000).

23. 110 F.Supp. 295 (D. Mass. 1953).
24. Except, of course, in merger cases where the creation of dominance is enough to block a merger.
25. In practice, the discussion is not as black-and-white as suggested here. Antitrust authorities do look at other issues as well.
26. It is not clear, though, whether the competition law is the best way to deal with these types of markets; see Canoy and Onderstal (2003).
27. This point only holds for unregulated markets.
28. http://europa.eu.int/comm/competition/general_info/glossary_en.html.
29. This difficulty even frustrated a Nobel prize laureate: Ronald [Coase] said he had gotten tired of antitrust because when the prices went up the judges said it was monopoly, when the prices went down they said it was predatory pricing, and when they stayed the same they said it was tacit collusion. (William Landes, in Kitch 1983, p.193).
30. See also Hakfoort and Weigand (2003).
31. 603 F.2d 263 (2nd Cir. 1979).
32. The court returned to the rule of reason by holding that monopoly is not per se illegal; rather, the behavior of the monopolist must be considered.
33. See *Tetra Pak Rausing SA* v. *Comm'n*, Case C-333/94P, [1996] ECR I-5951.
34. See W. Kolasky, http://www.usdoj.gov/atr/public/speeches/11153.htm#N_17.
35. See *AKZO Chemie BV* v. *Comm'n*, Case C-62/86, [1991] ECR I-3359. 'The European Court has stated that, where prices are below the average variable cost of production (variable costs are costs which vary with the amount of output produced), predation should be presumed. The Court held also that, if prices are above average variable costs but below average total costs, conduct is to be regarded as predatory where it can be established that the purpose of the conduct was to eliminate a competitor. In these cases a key issue was whether the dominant undertakings were covering their costs, but evidence on the undertakings intentions was also relevant' (OFT website).
36. Rey and Tirole (2003) provide an overview on foreclosure.
37. Before the reform, pipelines (the bottleneck) sold gas to customers (distribution companies, large industrial customers) and purchased their gas internally or from independent producers who had no direct access to customers. Since the reform, producers can purchase access from pipelines and intereact directly with customers.
38. The link should be rooted in the firm's business operations or in the market's demand side. Without this condition almost all markets are connected.
39. A similar argument can be made in an oligopoly context with the weaker result that price competition is relaxed.
40. *Eastman Kodak Co.* v. *Southern Photo Materials Co.*
41. See for example Rey *et al.* (2001), Hogan (2001), Economides (2001), Gilbert and Katz (2001).
42. See Rasmusen *et al.* (1991), Segal and Whinston (2000).
43. Indeed, Judge Jackson concluded that these types of arrangements were not anti-competitive.
44. This section borrows from joint work with M. Ivaldi, B. Jullien, P. Seabright and J. Tirole; see, for example, Ivaldi *et al.* (2003).
45. Selten (1984) points out that tough price competition may discourage entry; fighting collusion may thus 'backfire' by reducing the number of market participants; a similar observation applies to investments and other endogenous sunk costs, as emphasized by Sutton (1991, 1998). As noted by D'Aspremont and Motta (1994), intensifying competition selects the most efficient competitors. Using a panel of UK manufacturing industries, Symeonidis (2000) finds that the UK cartel laws from the late 1950s triggered tougher price competition and had a strong effect on the structure of previously cartelized markets, but little impact on firm profits. See also Symeonidis (2003).
46. At a given demand level, the benefits from a small price cut increase as the price–cost margin or the own-price elasticity of demand increase.
47. See, for instance, the work of Porter (1983) on the Joint Executive Committee for the railroads industry in the 1880s.

48. For example, in *Compagnie Maritime Belge* (case C-395/96P) shipping companies allegedly chartered 'fighting ships' specifically designed to compete head-to-head against the ships of a target company.

49. A discount rate R means that the firm weights the profits in period T with a multiplicative discount factor $\delta = 1/(1+R)^T$. If the firm faces no risk and can freely access the credit market, the discount rate corresponds to the market interest rate.

50. Of course, other industry characteristics such as market transparency, which is discussed below, also affect the length of time before retaliation effectively occurs. But the point here is that retaliation will not even be feasible in the absence of frequent interaction.

51. A similar idea applies to the frequency of price adjustments, since retaliation can come sooner when prices adjust more frequently. Thus the more frequent price adjustments are, the easier it is to sustain collusion.

52. The idea that coordination is more difficult in larger groups is intuitive, but there is little economic literature on this issue. See, for example, Compte and Jehiel (2002).

53. This insight is valid when holding all other factors constant. The number of firms, however, is endogenous and reflects other structural factors such as barriers to entry and product differentiation.

54. For example, in the case of an oligopolistic industry where n identical firms produce the same good, it can be shown that collusion is sustainable when the discount factor of the firms lies above a threshold equal to $1 - 1/n$. This threshold increases by 33 per cent (from 1/2 to 2/3) when adding a third competitor to a duopoly, whereas it increases by only 12.5 per cent (from 2/3 to 3/4) when adding a fourth competitor.

55. See Bain (1948) for an early discussion. Gertner (1994) validates this insight for environments with 'immediate responses' where collusion is otherwise straightforward to achieve through simple price-matching strategies, even in the absence of repeated interaction.

56. It is, for example, well-known that the monopoly price is an increasing function of the industry's marginal cost.

57. Side-transfers need not be monetary, however. They may, for example, consist of in-kind compensation or, when the same firms are active in several markets, of concessions made in one of these other markets. Still, such collusion schemes are not very plausible in the absence of any explicit agreement, and thus go beyond the scope of this report. For a discussion of these issues, see Osborne and Pitchik (1983) and Schmalensee (1987).

58. Mason *et al.* (1992) note in experimental duopoly games that cooperation is more likely when players face symmetric production costs.

59. See, for example, Abreu (1986) for a symmetric Cournot context and Brock and Scheinkman (1985) for a first analysis of a symmetric Bertrand context, later extended by Lambson (1987).

60. Brock and Scheinkman (1985) show, for example, in a linear model that, with exogenously given symmetric capacity constraints, the highest sustainable per capita profit varies non-monotonically with the number of firms.

61. This insight had been hinted at by several studies: Lambson (1994) provides a first partial characterization of optimal collusion schemes in this context. Lambson (1995) shows further that introducing a slight asymmetry in capacities hinders tacit collusion; and Davidson and Deneckere (1984, 1990) and Pénard (1997) show that asymmetric capacities make collusion more difficult in duopolies, using particular forms of collusive strategies. This insight has recently been formally confirmed by Compte *et al.* (2002), who show that asymmetric capacities indeed make collusion more difficult to sustain when the aggregate capacity is itself quite limited.

62. A more efficient firm will be more willing to collude if it gets a larger share of the collusive profits, but this also affects the incentives of the less efficient firms. There is thus a limit to the possible reallocation of market shares and, while this may help collusion, it does not in general restore the same collusive possibilities as if firms were equally efficient. The same remark applies to asymmetric capacities: Compte *et al.* (2002) show that giving larger market shares to the larger firms alleviates somewhat the tension generated by the

asymmetry, but it does not remove it entirely, so that the scope for collusion is nonetheless reduced.

63. A new entrant can also appear to destabilize a pre-entry collusive structure during a transition period, until a new collusive situation is reached. This is a rather different scenario, where the temporary absence of collusion simply reflects a tâtonnement process for reaching a new focal point.

64. A firm that uses a different production technology than others will be affected by the price of different inputs, or the labor cost may fluctuate in a different manner.

65. See Harrington (1989) for an analysis of collusion between firms that have different discount factors.

66. Martin (1995) provides a detailed analysis of this issue.

67. For example, in the above hypothetical industry, in the absence of any demand shock, firms could perfectly detect any deviation by their rivals by simply looking at their own sales.

68. See, for example, Kühn (2001).

69. See for example Ross (1992) and Martin (1993).

70. Product differentiation also impairs collusion when one firm has a 'better product' than the others (what economists refer to as 'vertical differentiation'). In essence, the analysis is then similar to that of asymmetric costs. A firm that has a better quality (possibly adjusted for the cost) is in a situation somewhat reminiscent of that of a firm that would offer the same quality as the others, but at a lower cost.

71. More precisely, the monopoly price is such that the Lerner index is inversely proportional to the demand elasticity: $L = (p-c)/p = 1/\varepsilon(p)$, where the elasticity is given by $\varepsilon(p) = pD'(p)/D(p)$.

72. The profitability of collusion can in turn influence the firms' willingness to design and carry out practices that facilitate the implementation of a collusive action. It can also induce firms to engage in more explicit collusion, at the risk of being caught by antitrust enforcement.

73. The potential harm to consumers is thus larger, the less elastic is the demand. The impact on total welfare, however, is more ambiguous. The reason is that price increases generate fewer distortions when demand is inelastic (see, for example, Tirole, 1988, for a discussion of this issue).

74. Suppose that two firms compete in one market and face one more competitor in another market. The firms could sustain collusion in the first market if their discount factor is higher than 1/2, but could not a priori collude in the second market if their discount factor is below 2/3. Yet they can actually sustain collusion in both markets if their discount factor is close enough to 2/3, by giving a higher market share to the competitor in the second market, in order to induce that competitor to collude, and using the first market to discipline themselves.

75. See, for example, Klemperer (2002).

76. One important issue concerns the *compatibility* of rival clubs or networks. Club effects are fully internalized (and thus become irrelevant) when rival networks are fully compatible. This is, for example, the case in the telecommunications industry, where all operators are interconnected, so that subscribing to one or the other network does not affect who someone can communicate with. However, compatibility can be imperfect (for example, some services can be proprietary) and pricing policies can also induce indirect club effects (for example, when it is cheaper to call subscribers of the same operator).

77. The mere repetition of the 'static' or 'non-collusive' equilibrium is always an equilibrium (and even a subgame-perfect one) of the repeated game.

78. In this context, it is not surprising that courts are reluctant to tackle collusion cases in the absence of a 'smoking gun' (see the discussion below).

79. Past behavior can, however, provide some information about specific characteristics of the market participants, which can, for example, be useful for identifying whether firms are prone to collusion or are of a 'maverick' type.

80. In the USA, firms bringing information before an investigation is opened benefit from such a leniency program since 1978. The EU adopted a leniency program in 1996, which

allows firms that bring information to benefit from reduced fines. The Office of Fair Trading in the UK and the recent competition bill in France have also introduced leniency programs.

81. In the USA for example, it is only since the reform of 1993 extending leniency to firms that bring information after the investigation has been opened (as long as the Department of Justice has not yet been able to prove collusion), that the leniency programs have become effective. Thanks to this reform, on average two cartels are now disclosed every month, and the fines often exceed $100 million (not to mention jail for some managers). In 1999, the Antitrust Division alone secured more than $1 billion in fines, which is more than the total sum of fines imposed under the Sherman Act since its adoption more than a century ago. The EU has also recently amended its leniency program to improve its performance.

82. These programs have also triggered a body of theoretical work. See, for example, Spagnolo (2000a, 2000b) and Motta and Polo (2000).

83. While the past history of prices and market shares brings information, it will not in general provide a definite conclusion: even the most advanced econometric models only provide probability estimates. From a legal perspective, establishing collusion would involve a standard of proof similar to the high standard established by the European Court for Article 81 EU Treaty in its *Woodpulp* judgment (1993). The court basically required proof that no other behaviour than collusion could explain the observed realization of prices, a rather insurmountable task.

84. This suggests that a 'pure' Article 82 EU Treaty case is unlikely for collective dominance. However, cases could be built – and have already been so, see, for example, *Compagnie Maritime Belge* – on both Articles 81 and 82. Competition authorities can also use past behavior to alert industry 'supervisors' about abnormally high prices. They can, for example, provide such information to consumer associations, in order to increase customers' awareness of the problem. In regulated industries, competition authorities can also alert regulators or point to deficiencies in the regulatory environment.

85. See Geroski and Griffith in this volume.

86. See Canoy and Onderstal (2003, ch.3), for some recent references.

87. See Cave *et al.* (2002) for an example in the telecommunications sector.

Bibliography

Abreu, D. (1986): 'Extremal equilibria of oligopolistic supergames', *Journal of Economic Theory* 39, 191–225.

Abreu, D., D. Pearce and E. Stachetti (1986): 'Optimal cartel equilibria with imperfect monitoring', *Journal of Economic Theory* 39, 251–69.

Aghion, P. and J. Tirole (1997): 'Formal and real authority in organizations', *Journal of Political Economy* 105, 1–29.

Areeda, P. (1989): 'Essential facilities: an epithet in need of limiting principles', *Antitrust Law Journal* 58, 841.

Areeda, P. and D. Turner (1975): 'Predatory pricing and related practices under Section 2 of the Sherman Act', *Harvard Law Review* 88, 697–733.

Bain, J. (1948): 'Output quotas in imperfect cartels', *Quarterly Journal of Economics* 62, 617–22.

Bennett M., M. Canoy and P. de Bijl (2001): *Future Policy in Telecommunications: an Analytical Framework*, CPB Document, The Hague: CPB.

Berges-Sennou, F., F. Loss, E. Malavolti-Grimal and T. Vergé (2001): 'Competition policy and agreements between firms', University of Bristol CMPO Working Paper 01/034.

Bergman, M. (2000): 'The Bronner case: a turning-point for the essential facilities doctrine', *European Competition Law Review* 21, 59–63.

Bernheim, D. and M. Whinston (1990): 'Multimarket contact and collusive behavior', *Rand Journal of Economics* 21, 1–26.

Bolton, P., J. Brodley and M. Riordan (2000): 'Predatory pricing: strategic theory and legal policy', *The Georgetown Law Journal* 88, 2239–2330.

Bork, R.H. (1978): *The Antitrust Paradox: A Policy at War with Itself*, New York: Basic Books.

Brock, W.A. and J. Scheinkman (1985): 'Price setting supergames with capacity constraints', *Review of Economic Studies* 52, 371–82.

Cabral, L.M.B. and M.H. Riordan (1997): 'The learning curve, predation, antitrust and welfare', *Journal of Industrial Economics* 45, 155–69.

Canoy, M. and S. Onderstal (2003): *Tight Oligopolies: In Search of Proportionate Remedies*, CPB Document 29, The Hague: CPB.

Cave, M., S. Majumdar and I. Vogelsang (2002): *Handbook of Telecommunication Economics*, vol. 1, Amsterdam: Elsevier.

Church, J.R. and R. Ware (2000): *Industrial Organization. A Strategic Approach*, Boston: Irwin McGraw Hill.

Coate M. and S. Kleit (1994): 'Exclusion, collusion, or confusion?: the underpinnings of raising rivals' costs', *Research in Law and Economics* 16, 73–93.

Compte, O. and P. Jehiel (2002): 'Multi-party negotiations', mimeo, CERAS.

Compte, O., F. Jenny and P. Rey (2002): 'Capacity constraints, mergers and collusion', *European Economic Review* 46, 1–29.

Cowling, K. (2002): 'Globalization and corporate power', keynote speech, EUNIP Conference, Turku Finland, http://www.abo.fi/fc/eunip/.

Crémer, J. (1995): 'Arm's-length relationships', *Quarterly Journal of Economics* 2, 275–95.

D'Aspremont, C. and M. Motta (1994): 'Tougher price competition or lower concentration: a trade-off for antitrust authorities', Université Catholique de Louvain, discussion paper no. 9415.

Davidson, C. and R.J. Deneckere (1984): 'Horizontal mergers and collusive behavior', *International Journal of Industrial Organization* 2, 117–32.

Davidson, C. and R.J. Deneckere (1990): 'Excess capacity and collusion', *International Economic Review* 31, 521–41.

Dewatripont, M. and J. Tirole (1999): 'Advocates', *Journal of Political Economy* 107, 1–39.

Du Boff, R. (1989): *Accumulation & Power: An Economic History of the United States*, Armonk, NY: M.E. Sharpe.

Economides, N. (2001): 'The Microsoft antitrust case', *Journal of Industry, Competition and Trade: From Theory to Policy* 1, 7–39.

Elhauge, E. (2003): 'Why above-cost price cuts to drive out entrants do not signal predation or even market power – and the implications for defining costs', *Yale Law Journal* 112, 681–827.

Elzinga, K.E. and D.E. Mills (2001): 'Predatory pricing and strategic theory', *Georgetown Law Journal* 89, 2475–2528.

European Commission (2000): *Competition Policy in Europe and the Citizen*, Luxembourg: Office for Official Publications of the European Communities.

Evans, W.N. and I.N. Kessides (1994): 'Living by the "Golden Rule": multimarket contact in the US airline industry', *Quarterly Journal of Economics* 109, 341–66.

Fisher, F.M. (1991): 'Organizing industrial organization: reflections on the Handbook of Industrial Organization', *Brookings Papers on Economics: Microeconomics*, 201–40.

Fudenberg, D. and J. Tirole (1984): 'The fat-cat effect, the puppy-dog ploy, and the lean and hungry look', *American Economic Review* 74, 361–6.

Geroski, P. (1987): 'Do dominant firms decline?', in D. Hay and J. Vickers (eds), *The Economics of Market Dominance*, Oxford: Basil Blackwell.

Geroski, P. and A. Jacquemin (1988): 'The persistence of profits: a European Comparison', *Economic Journal* 98, 375–89.

Gertner, R. (1994): 'Tacit collusion with immediate responses: the role of asymmetries', mimeo, University of Chicago.

Gilbert, R. (1989): 'Mobility barriers and the value of incumbency', in R. Schmalensee and R. Willig (eds), *Handbook of Industrial Organization*, Amsterdam: North-Holland.

Gilbert, R. and M. Katz (2001): 'An economist's guide to *US* v. *Microsoft*', *Journal of Economic Perspectives* 15, 25–44.

Green, E. and R. Porter (1984): 'Non-cooperative collusion under imperfect price information', *Econometrica* 52, 87–100.

Hakfoort, J. and J. Weigand (2000): *Magazine Publishing: a Quiet Life? The Dutch Market for Consumer Magazines*, The Hague: CPB.

Hakfoort, J. and J. Weigand (2003): 'Strategic interaction in the Dutch market for consumer magazines', *De Economist* 154, 205–24.

Haltiwanger, J. and J. Harrington (1991): 'The impact of cyclical demand movements on collusive behavior', *Rand Journal of Economics* 22, 89–106.

Hancher, L. (1999): 'Casenote: *Oscar Bronner* v. *Mediaprint* 26.11.1998, Rs. C-7/97', *Common Market Law Review* 36, 1289.

Harrington, J. (1989): 'Collusion Among asymmetric firms: the case of different discount factors', *International Journal of Industrial Organization* 7, 289–307.

Hicks, J.R. (1935): 'Annual survey of economic theory: the theory of monopoly', *Econometrica* 3, 1–20.

Hogan J. (2001): 'Competition policy for computer software markets', *The Journal of Information, Law and Technology (JILT)*, http://elj.warwick.ac.uk/jilt/01–2/hogan.html.

Hovenkamp, H. (1999): *Federal Antitrust Policy: The law of competition and its practice*, 2nd edn, St. Paul, Minn.: West Publishing Co.

Ivaldi, M., B. Jullien, P. Seabright, P. Rey and J. Tirole (2003), 'The economics of tacit collusion', Report for the European Commission.

Jebsen, P. and R. Stevens (1996): 'Assumptions, goals, and dominant undertakings: the regulation of competition under Article 86 of the European Union', *Antitrust Law Journal* 64, 443–516.

Jullien, B. and P. Rey (2002): 'Resale price maintenance and collusion', mimeo, University of Toulouse.

Kitch, E. (1983): 'The fire of truth: a remembrance of law and economics at Chicago, 1932–70', *Journal of Law and Economics* 26, 163–233.

Klemperer, P. (2002): 'How (not) to run auctions: the European 3G Telecom auctions', *European Economic Review* 46, 829–45.

Kühn, K.-U. (2001): 'Fighting collusion by regulating communication between firms', *Economic Policy* 32, 169–204.

Lambson, V.E. (1987): 'Optimal penal codes in price-setting supergames with capacity constraints', *Review of Economic Studies* 54, 385–97.

Lambson, V.E. (1994): 'Some results on optimal penal codes in asymmetric Bertrand supergames', *Journal of Economic Theory* 62, 444–68.

Lambson, V.E. (1995): 'Optimal penal codes in nearly symmetric Bertrand supergames with capacity constraints', *Journal of Mathematical Economics* 24, 1–22.

Martin, S. (1993): 'Endogenous firm efficiency in a Cournot principal–agent model', *Journal of Economic Theory* 59, 445–50.

Martin, S. (1995): 'R&D joint ventures and tacit product market collusion', *European Journal of Political Economy* 24, 357–79.

Mason, C.F., O.R. Phillips and C. Nowell (1992): 'Duopoly behavior in asymmetric markets: an experimental evaluation', *Review of Economics and Statistics* 74, 662–70.

Motta, M. and M. Polo (2000): 'Leniency programs and cartel prosecution', mimeo, available at http://www.iue.it/Personal/Motta/.

Mueller, D. (1986): *Profits in the Long Run*, Cambridge, UK: Cambridge University Press.

Mueller, D. (1990) (eds): *The Dynamics of Company Profits*, Cambridge, UK: Cambridge University Press.

Mueller, D. (2001): 'Delusions regarding the proper role of markets and antitrust policy', *Review of Industrial Organization* 19, 27–36.

Neven, D., R. Nuttall and P. Seabright (1993): *Merger in Daylight*, London: CEPR.

Odagiri, H. and N. Maruyama (2002): 'Does the persistence of profits persist? A study of company profits in Japan, 1964–97', *International Journal of Industrial Organization* 20, 1513–33.

Ordover, J. and G. Saloner (1989): 'Predation, monopolization, and antitrust', in R. Schmalensee and R. Willig (eds), *The Handbook of Industrial Organization*, Amsterdam: North-Holland.

Osborne, M. and C. Pitchik (1983): 'Price competition in a capacity-constrained duopoly', *Journal of Economic Theory* 38, 238–60.

Parker, P.M. and L.-H. Röller (1997): 'Oligopoly and the incentive for horizontal merger', *American Economic Review* 75, 219–27.

Patterson, D.E. and C. Shapiro (2001): 'Trans-Atlantic divergence in *GE/Honeywell:* causes and lessons', *Antitrust Magazine* 16.

Pénard, T. (1997): 'Choix de capacites et comportements strategiques: une approche par les jeux repétés', *Annales d'Economie et de Statistique* 46, 203–24.

Porter, R. (1983): 'A study of cartel stability: the joint executive committee, 1880–1886', *Bell Journal of Economics* 14, 301–14.

Raith, M. (1996): 'Product differentiation, uncertainty and the stability of collusion', London School of Economics-STICERD Discussion Paper Series EI/1649.

Rasmusen, E., J. Ramseyer and J. Wiley (1991): 'Naked exclusion', *American Economic Review* 81, 1137–45.

Rey, P. and J. Tirole (2003): 'A primer on foreclosure', in M. Armstrong and R. Porter (eds), *Handbook of Industrial Organization*, vol. III Amsterdam: North-Holland, forthcoming 2005.

Rey, P., P. Seabright and J. Tirole (2001): 'The activities of a monopoly firm in adjacent competitive markets: economic consequences and implications for competition policy', working paper, IDEI, Toulouse.

Ross, T.W. (1992): 'Cartel stability and product differentiation', *International Journal of Industrial Organization* 10, 1–13.

Rotemberg, J., and G. Saloner (1986): 'A supergame-theoretic model of business cycles and price wars during booms', *American Economic Review* 76, 390–407.

Salop, S. and D. Scheffman (1983): 'Raising rivals' costs', *American Economic Review* 73, 267–71.

Salop, S. and D. Scheffman (1987): 'Cost-raising strategies', *Journal of Industrial Economics* 36, 19–34.

Scheffman, D. (1992): 'The application of raising rivals' costs theory to antitrust', *Antitrust Bulletin* 37, 187–206.

Schenk, H. (forthcoming 2005) *Mergers, Efficient Choice and International Competitiveness: Bandwagon behaviour and industrial policy implications*, Cheltenham, UK and Northampton, MA, USA: Edward Elgar.

Scherer, F.M. and D. Ross (1990): *Industrial Market Structure and Economic Performance*, Boston: Houghton/Mifflin.

Schmalensee, R. (1987): 'Competitive advantage and collusive optima', *International Journal of Industrial Organization* 5, 351–68.

Segal, I. and M. Whinston (2000): 'Naked exclusion: comment', *American Economic Review* 90, 296–309.

Selten, R. (1984): 'Are cartel laws bad for business?', in H. Hauptmann, W. Krelle and K.C. Mosler (eds), *Operations Research and Economic Theory*, Berlin: Springer-Verlag.

Snyder, D. (1996): 'A dynamic theory of countervailing power', *Rand Journal of Economics* 27, 747–69.

Spagnolo, G. (2000a): 'Optimal leniency programs', mimeo, Stockholm School of Economics.

Spagnolo, G. (2000b): 'Self-defeating antitrust laws: how leniency programs solve Bertrand's paradox and enforce collusion in auctions, mimeo', Stockholm School of Economics.

Stigler, G. (1964): 'A theory of oligopoly', *Journal of Political Economy* 72, 44–61.

Sutton, J. (1991): *Sunk Cost and Market Structure*, Cambridge, MA: MIT Press.

Sutton, J. (1998): *Technology and Market Structure*, Cambridge, MA: MIT Press.

Symeonidis, G. (2000): 'Price competition and market structure: the impact of cartel policy on concentration in the UK', *Journal of Industrial Economics* 48, 1–26.

Symeonidis, G. (2003): 'In which industries is collusion more likely? Evidence from the UK', *Journal of Industrial Economics* 51, 45–74.

Tichy, G. (2001): 'What do we know about success and failure of mergers?', *Journal of Industry, Competition and Trade* 1, 347–94.

Tirole, J. (1988), *The Theory of Industrial Organization*, Cambridge, MA: MIT Press.

Whinston, M. (1990): 'Tying, foreclosure and exclusion, *American Economic Review* 80, 837–60.

Whish, R. (2001): *Competition Law*, London: Butterworth.

8   Identifying antitrust markets

Paul Geroski and Rachel Griffith[*]

1   Why define markets?

The identification of markets is a standard feature of antitrust investigations, and the substantive decision in many cases stands or falls on the precise market definition selected. Market identification is important because the computation of market shares matters in antitrust cases, and this is so for at least two reasons. First, market shares are often used to help establish jurisdiction or, more generally, to sort out priorities for antitrust agencies. Merger regulations usually specify a threshold level of market share which triggers an investigation for mergers above a given size; investigations into various monopolistic abuses are usually centered on the leading firms in a market and, in most cases, the ability of an antitrust agency to initiate an investigation, or impose penalties at the end of it, depends on whether the (alleged) offending firm enjoys a position of market 'dominance'; that is enjoys a large market share. Second, market shares are sometimes used as an observable measure of market power, meaning that the fact of finding high market shares is sometimes taken to be tantamount to uncovering the existence of market power. Since, in practice, the important step in computing market shares is ascertaining the boundaries of the market, this practice tends to make the determination of market boundaries the substantively important decision in any attempt to identify pockets of market power.

The use of market shares to establish jurisdiction is a well established procedure. It is based on the relatively uncontroversial notion that firms with small market shares are unlikely to do much damage either to consumers or to their rivals if they behave non-competitively. However, the converse – that firms with large market shares will necessarily have the power to force through price rises or exclude rivals from the market – is not necessarily true (however plausible it might seem as a presumption). A firm with a large market share whose customers were (somehow) locked into purchasing from it come what may for a long period of time might well be deemed to have market power. If, on the other hand, its customers are mobile, if they can easily switch to rivals' products or can easily be poached by rival suppliers, it is likely that such power will evaporate in any attempt to use it. In this case, a firm might enjoy a high market share without enjoying much (if any) market power. To put the same point a different way, it is difficult to accept the proposition that market shares necessarily identify pockets of market power in the absence of an analysis of the full set of competitive forces that operate in the market. Since it is impossible to talk sensibly about 'the full set of competitive forces that operate in the market' without having a fairly clear definition of what that market is, it is clear that identifying market boundaries must be the first step taken in the assessment of competition. It cannot, however, be the final step.

Thus defining the market and identifying which firms operate within that market should be (and is) a central feature of antitrust investigations. There is, however, a second step which needs to follow any identification of market boundaries, and that is an assessment of how competitive that market actually is. This distinction is, of course, much easier to make conceptually than it is to do in practice: since identifying market boundaries effectively involves identifying the limits of substitution (on the demand and/or on the supply side) the process of evaluating competition and that of identifying market boundaries are, and will always be, inextricably intertwined. Nevertheless, the distinction is an important one, and we have organized what follows directly from it. In Sections 2 and 3 below, we discuss the standard method used by antitrust authorities to identify market boundaries (the so-called SSNIP test) and explore a number of the complications which arise when using it. In Section 4, we turn to the second step and briefly outline what is involved in assessing the competitiveness of a market. We conclude with a few final observations in Section 5.

2   The SSNIP test

The standard test used by most antitrust authorities to define markets is the SSNIP test (sometimes also called 'the hypothetical monopolist test'), which is designed to explore the consequences of a (hypothetical) *S*mall but *S*ignificant *N*on-transitory *I*ncrease in *P*rice on the profitability of the (hypothetical) firm that initiates it.[1] The test is effectively an iterative procedure, and works as follows.

We start with the narrowest group of products and geographical area that is reasonable;[2] we then suppose that these products sold in that area are wholly monopolized, and ask what would happen if that (hypothetical) monopolist were to raise its prices by 10 per cent. If that price rise is not profitable, we add the closest substitute product (or geographical area) to the (hypothetically) monopolized bundle, and repeat the procedure. The procedure stops when we find a collection of products sold in a particular area which, if monopolized, would sustain a price rise of 10 per cent by that monopolist.

Although it all seems simple enough, there are at least four aspects of this procedure that are worth a closer look. First, at the heart of this test is the question of what might make such a price rise unsustainable. Clearly, when the hypothetical monopolist raises its prices, it will lose some sales as at least some consumers choose not to purchase the product at all and drop out of the market. However, it will also lose sales for two other reasons: some consumers will switch to substitute products ('demand-side substitutability') and some firms operating 'near' to the (narrowly defined) candidate market will alter their production programs and supply similar products to other consumers in the market at lower prices ('supply-side substitutability'). If there are close demand or supply-side substitutes, the price increase initiated by the hypothetical monopolist will lead to a large reduction in its sales, and its profits will, as a consequence, fall.[3] The iterative procedure outlined above selects the closest of these supply or demand-side substitutes at each stage of the process and adds them to the candidate market definition being considered at that stage. The process ends when the addition of the marginal demand or supply-side substitute does not affect the ability of the hypothetical monopolist to profit from a price rise.

To understand how large the volume fall-off has to be to make the hypothesized price rise unsustainable, it is necessary to consider costs. If all costs were fixed, then a 10 per cent price rise that reduced volume sold by about 10 per cent would leave both revenue and costs unchanged and, therefore, it would have no effect on profits.[4] Hence, if all costs are fixed, any volume decrease larger than 10 per cent would necessarily reduce revenues and, therefore, profits. If some costs are variable, the decrease in volume caused by the hypothetical price rise will also lead to a reduction in costs and, hence, a volume fall of more than 10 per cent in volume may still be consistent with an increase in profits following the hypothesized price rise. It turns out that the critical volume decrease which separates a profitable from an unprofitable price rise depends on the prevailing price–marginal cost margin[5] that is being earned at the price from which the experiment starts (see the appendix for details): the smaller is that price–marginal cost margin (that is the closer to zero it is), the larger the volume fall-off has to be to make the hypothetical monopolist's price rise unsustainable. When all costs are fixed, the price–marginal cost margin is unity and, as we have just seen, a volume fall-off of just over 10 per cent will reduce profits.

Second, the starting point of the SSNIP test is 'the narrowest group of products and geographical area that is reasonable'. In practice, many firms involved in antitrust investigations operate in more than one market because they produce a wide range of goods. This usually means starting with a subset of the goods produced by the firm or firms whose behavior (or proposed merger) is the center of interest, and the process of adding the closest supply and demand side substitutes effectively identifies the most powerful competitive (that is demand or supply-side) constraints put on that firm (using the 10 per cent rule as a way of measuring how powerful they really are). The first bundle of activities added to the initial hypothetical monopoly are those most likely to undermine any attempt to exploit that monopoly; the second bundle are those next most likely, and so on. The importance of starting from a narrow initial definition is that the market boundaries eventually established by the procedure do not include products, geographical areas or suppliers who do not compete directly with each other. If this approach sins, it does so by omitting irrelevant products, areas and firms from the market. One consequence of this is that the SSNIP test almost always ends up with narrower market definitions than those in popular use, and many SSNIP markets populate sectors like 'telecommunications', 'pharmaceuticals' and so on. From the antitrust authorities' point of view this is probably the correct direction in which to err. If the market is defined too narrowly, so that market shares overstate a firm's market power, this will become apparent in the competition tests. On the other hand, if markets were defined too broadly, so that market shares were understated, this might lead to firms with potential market power not being investigated.

Third, one of the challenges of applying the SSNIP test is its hypothetical nature and gathering the information needed to put it into practice. It is almost always the case that one cannot directly observe an SSNIP test in operation. It is rare to find a 'natural experiment' in which a monopolist unilaterally pushes through a 10 per cent price rise to see what will happen. In practice, the sort of information that is used includes estimates of the parameters of a demand system (in particular the own and cross-price elasticities), information on product characteristics and consumer preferences (gathered either from industry sources or from consumer surveys), information on past price movements and information on product technologies and costs. As a consequence, calculating the outcome of applying the SSNIP test almost always involves making indirect inferences, and the answers which emerge almost always contain some degree of imprecision. There is a burgeoning literature which explores various methodologies (including econometric models and conjoint analysis) which might be used to help make these inferences.[6]

Finally, it is worth stepping back and putting all of this into perspective. The basic idea behind the SSNIP test is that a market is a collection of products and geographical areas which can be profitably monopolized. This is a natural way for antitrust authorities to think about market definitions, since what is of concern in antitrust cases is the incentives that firms have to create and exploit monopoly positions. However, it is not quite the same as the way of thinking about markets which features in the traditional approach to market definition entombed in first-year economics textbooks. That approach to identifying markets is often called the 'law of one price', and tests based on it attempt to identify an area in which arbitrage operates to eliminate price differences between identical products.[7] In a sense, it identifies what might be called 'a trading market', an area within which it will be impossible for a trader to sustain a price for the products of interest that is different from those prevailing elsewhere in the same area. The law of one price differs from the SSNIP test in at least two ways: it relies on the technology of arbitrage to set overall market boundaries and it typically concentrates only on demand side-substitution. In general, there is no obvious relationship between the market boundaries identified by using tests based on the law of one price and those identified by using the SSNIP test.[8]

3   Some complications
Identifying market boundaries is as much an art as it is a science, and it sometimes requires fairly finely tuned judgments to do the exercise properly. There are a number of areas where there is a need for such judgments, and we discuss four of these in what follows.

3.1   Intermediate goods markets
When a product is an intermediate good, and not sold direct to consumers, there are two transactions of interest: the retail transaction (between retailers and final consumers) and the wholesale transaction (between the manufacturer and the retailer).[9] If the market of interest is the wholesale market, then it is clear that the consequences of a 10 per cent increase in wholesale prices will depend, in part, on behavior in the downstream retail market. The two issues of importance here are the degree of pass-through (that is the extent to which retailers pass on the entire 10 per cent rise in wholesale prices to their customers) and the extent of consumer reaction to whatever percentage price rise actually is passed through. The responses of consumers will condition the action of retailers and, in effect, shape their demand at the wholesale level for the product.

The analysis becomes more complicated when the manufacturer is vertically integrated downstream, retailing (at least part of its output) direct to consumers. In this situation, it clearly competes with retailers and this observation is sometimes used to argue that the wholesale and retail markets are effectively one single market. The SSNIP test applied to such a market effectively asks what might happen to a vertically integrated monopolist who produces and sells all of the output produced in the candidate market. While this may be an interesting question to ask, it tells us nothing of substance about the wholesale market taken on its own (or, for that matter, the retail market). Further, it is (arguably) sloppy practice. The SSNIP test starts from the narrowest market definition, and in this case that must mean the wholesale market or the retail market taken on its own. Furthermore, it should not be the case that market definitions depend on how firms choose to organize their activities: that a firm chooses to integrate vertically forward does not necessarily mean that wholesale and retail markets are just one big market.

3.2   The cellophane fallacy

A monopolist will set prices at the point where consumers are just on the margin of switching to some other product or of dropping out of the market altogether. This is where profits are maximized. This means that, when monopoly prices prevail in the market, there will appear to be many substitutes for the monopolist's product. However, the fact that there appear to be many substitutes at this price does not mean that this is not a monopoly price; indeed, if there were no apparent substitutes at a particular market price, one would be tempted to conclude that that price was not being set at monopoly levels. The implication of this observation is that the appearance of substitutes at *prevailing* prices does not necessarily mean that they should be included in the same market. This observation has come to be known as the 'cellophane fallacy' after a famous US antitrust case against Du Pont.[10] Du Pont argued that cellophane was not a separate market, since at prevailing prices there appeared to be a high cross-elasticity of demand between cellophane and aluminum foil, wax paper and polyethylene. This meant that what seemed to be a near monopoly of 'the cellophane market' looked like a much more modest share of something that might be called 'the wrappings market' (or so the judge in the case thought).

The right way to avoid the cellophane fallacy depends on the kind of case that one is concerned with. In a merger case, one is typically concerned with whether the merger is going to enhance the firm's market position in a way which might be abused. The question of interest, then, is whether the firms involved in the merger are likely to be able to raise prices as a result of the merger and earn higher profits. To answer this question it seems natural to apply the SSNIP test to existing market prices: that is, to ask whether, as a consequence of the merger, a 10 per cent increase in prices above the current level can be sustained by the merged firm. If so, the merger will clearly enhance the firm's market power; if not, then the market that the merged firms operate in must include other products, areas and/or suppliers, and its competitiveness must be assessed when its exact boundaries have been ascertained (see Section 4 below). In a so-called 'monopoly inquiry', where one is exploring whether one or more firms have, or have abused, a monopoly position, it seems unwise to use prevailing market prices as the basis from which to consider a hypothetical 10 per cent price rise since there is at least a chance that those prices will already reflect an element of monopoly power. A better procedure is to start by ascertaining what level of prices might prevail were the market to be competitive, and then use that as the basis of the SSNIP test. If prevailing prices appeared to be sustainable and were 10 per cent or more higher than this level, then it would follow almost immediately that the firm(s) in question had at least some market power.

3.3   What is 'small but significant'?
It has become something of a convention to consider 10 per cent to be a 'small but significant' price rise. However, what is considered to be 'small but significant' will vary across markets and over time and will depend on product characteristics, past price increases, current inflation rates and a number of other factors. The 10 per cent convention was established at a time of rather high inflation, and many think it may be considered too high in times of lower inflation. These arguments usually result in the use of a test based on 5 per cent (for example see Competition Commission, 2002). One way to think about the reasonableness (or otherwise) of 10 per cent is as follows. Suppose that a competitive industry suddenly (somehow) becomes monopolized, and monopoly prices are set. If, prior to the monopolization, the market was competitive then prices would equal marginal costs; after monopolization, price–cost margins will rise and, for the sake of argument, let us suppose that they end up being 10 per cent higher.[11] Since the monopoly margin is equal to the reciprocal of the elasticity of demand, a 10 per cent margin implies that demand is quite elastic, and one might feel that, if a 10 per cent price rise is all the monopolist can engineer following his/her monopolization of the market, then that monopoly might be rather benign. If, however, the monopolist can engineer *at least* a 10 per cent rise, this must mean that demand is much more elastic than this – that buyers are, in a real sense, 'captive' in the market – and, therefore, that the monopoly might be rather less benign. Of course, one might make much the same argument in favor of a 5 per cent or a 15 per cent threshold level for SSNIP, so this argument does not really take us very far. What it suggests, however, is that, if at any stage of the iterative SSNIP procedure one finds a 10 per cent price rise to be sustainable, one ought to go on and ask the further question: 'in that case, just how high a price rise would be sustainable?'

'Small but significant' refers both to the size of the hypothesized price rise and also (at least implicitly) to how long it is maintained. It is clear that a 10 per cent price rise that is maintained for about two days is unlikely to induce much substitution one way or the other; on the other hand, a 10 per cent price rise maintained for two centuries is likely to paint quite a different picture of the market. There is no obvious rule to determine how long a price rise ought to be considered when applying the SSNIP test. In a sense, it depends on how long it will take consumers and suppliers to respond to the price rise (if, of course, they are actually minded to respond), and this will differ by type of product and type of consumer. The usual convention here is to suppose that the hypothetical price rise is maintained for a year. Again, it is hard to defend this practice except on the grounds of reasonableness: if it really takes more than a year for consumers to switch to alternative products, or for suppliers to re-engineer their product programs to produce a 'me too' substitute for the (hypothetically) monopolized product, the rewards for monopolization are likely to last longer than at least a year, and this seems, somehow, like a long time. The bottom line is that, if one finds at any stage of the iterative SSNIP procedure that a 10 per cent price rise maintained for at least a year is sustainable, one might want to go on and ask the further question: 'in that case, just how long would that price rise be sustainable?'.

3.4   Many markets, many market segments

All firms operate in many markets: labor markets, capital markets, raw material markets and, of course, downstream markets in which they sell their products to consumers. Further, any firm actively interested in increasing its profits is likely to try to segment its downstream markets, identifying different groups of consumers with different needs and a different willingness to pay, and serving each with a variant of the basic product that suits their needs and at a different price. The question that this raises is which market should the SSNIP test be applied to, and, in principle, the simple answer is 'all of them'. In practice, however, some of these markets are likely to be more interesting than others: some will seem to be inherently less likely to be competitive than others, or involve consumers or rival firms whose vulnerability might be a source of concern. Further, antitrust investigations are typically complaint-driven, and this naturally focuses attention on some markets rather than others. Finally, anti-competitive activity in one market (for example screwing down the prices of inputs paid to suppliers) might well be considered benign if the rents so gained were dissipated through competition in the other markets in which the firm in question operates, leaving consumers in these markets as the ultimate beneficiaries of whatever market power is exploited in the monopolized market. This suggests that any investigation into possible monopoly power in particular markets may require a complementary exploration of other markets.

Almost any market one might want to consider is likely to be divisible into a number of market segments, and it is almost always a moot question whether these segments ought to be regarded as markets in and of themselves, or as parts of a broader market. The SSNIP test starts from the narrowest market definition which seems reasonable in the circumstances, and this means that it is likely to lead one to the conclusion that particular segments are separate markets. The problem is that these separate segments are likely to be interdependent; activities which occur in one of them will almost certainly have effects on others. This should not cause a problem in defining the market (although the precise boundaries between segments that are 'near' to each other are likely to be difficult to fix with any certainty), but it will make the assessment of the degree of competition in any of them rather more tricky than would otherwise be the case. Thinking of different market segments as being different markets does, however, have one great virtue, and that is that it makes identifying the effects of anti-competitive behavior much more precise. If there are real differences between different groups of consumers, then a sensible monopolist will not treat them all the same: some will be more vulnerable than others and will, therefore, bear more of the burden of monopoly than others. Anything that addresses the effects of anti-competitive behavior – and, in doing so, identifies just who is adversely affected by it – makes the process of remedying such effects much easier and the design of remedies more effective.

4   Assessing competitiveness

The SSNIP test enables us to identify the relevant market for the purposes of analysis but, as we noted earlier, it is just the start of any antitrust inquiry. The real issue in every case is not what the market is, but how competitive it is (or how a merger affects competition). There are three features of the market, however defined, which determine its competitiveness: the degree of intra-market rivalry, the extent of buyer (or supplier) power, and the state of entry.[12] We consider each briefly in turn.

4.1   Intra-market rivalry

The SSNIP test identifies market boundaries by assessing the consequences of the actions of a hypothetical monopolist, but, in practice, the market so identified is unlikely to be completely monopolized. As a consequence, the firms who are at the center of antitrust interest in any particular case are likely to face potential competitive challenges from existing rivals producing similar products. Thus, in monopoly cases, whether this group of competitors is able to act collectively and behave as if they were a monopolist is the first and most natural question to ask; in merger cases one needs to ask whether competitors will effectively be able to constrain price increases in the enlarged post-merger firm.

Assessing intra-market rivalry is, of course, a very old chestnut, and there is not enough space to do it any kind of justice here.[13] The traditional approach to this question is structural, and involves computing market shares in search of 'high' levels of concentration or positions of market dominance. There has grown up a set of conventions, some of which have become embodied in statutes, built up around rules of thumb expressed in terms of market shares or levels of market concentration.[14] As we noted earlier, these rules of thumb, and this structural approach more generally, have much to recommend them as a way of prioritizing scarce antitrust resources or establishing jurisdiction. However, from the point of view of assessing the competitiveness of any particular market, it is probably too simple. It may be that a firm with a large market share will be able to act as a price leader, initiating, and then enforcing, high prices. It may also be, however, that the supposed power promised by a high market share will evaporate with use because of the actions of rivals, in which case high market shares identify no more than latent pockets of market power. To understand whether a firm really has market power, one needs to understand how independent of the leader the other firms in the market are, how strong their incentives are to try to take share away from the leader and whether they have the ability to do so. Clearly, this takes us beyond the use of simple structural measures of competition, and into an assessment of likely modes of market behavior.[15] Recent developments involve using richer structural models and evidence to suggest what equilibrium outcomes might be.

4.2 Buyer (or supplier) power

The SSNIP test examines buyer substitutability, asking (amongst other things) whether there is an attractive option (that is substitute product) open to buyers faced by a unilateral 10 per cent price rise initiated by a hypothetical monopolist. In fact, buyers not only have 'exit' options, they also have 'voice' options. In particular, when buyers are small in number and well organized, price setting becomes more like a bargaining process and less like a unilateral posting of prices. The power of buyers (or suppliers) to affect the methods by which prices are set is as important as their ability to exercise exit options. Further, well organized buyers are often in a position to affect the degree of intra-market rivalry, effectively setting one firm against another, or to encourage new entry.

Assessing the strength of buyers (or suppliers) is a delicate issue. The simplest (but still not wholly satisfactory) solution is structural, and involves computing the degree of buyer concentration. The principle here is just the obverse of high market share on the seller's side of the market: a buyer with a large market share swings a large purse, and that will almost certainly enable it to exert some countervailing power on would-be monopolists. More subtle analyses would almost certainly examine the strengths of buyers' 'exit' options by looking at switching costs and trying to ascertain the extent to which they are locked into a particular seller. More broadly, it is important to assess the degree to which buyers can act *strategically*: that is, to assess their ability to upset collusive arrangements, encourage entry, stimulate innovations which redefine the market and, in the limit, vertically integrate upstream (or downstream in the case of suppliers). As with intra-market rivalry, this takes us well beyond the computation of buyer market shares and into the murky area of behavior, potential and actual.

4.3   Entry

Rivals do not actually have to be present in a market to exert an effect on the degree of competition in that market. The threat of entry may, in some circumstances, discipline the behavior of firms who might otherwise enjoy monopoly power. Failing that, the fact of entry may soon correct any monopolistically induced distortions which might result from the exercise of market power.

To assess the likelihood of entry in any circumstance, one needs, in effect, to produce a business plan that a reasonably efficient entrant might use to commence operations. The comparison between this plan and the actual operations of the incumbent help to establish the margin that incumbents can raise price above costs without losing market share; that is without inducing entry. In effect, this is tantamount to measuring the height of entry barriers. In practice, however, an actual entrant is likely to incur a number of transitory costs which will fall away when it finally establishes itself in the market. This, in turn, means that one may have not only to compute the height of entry barriers but also to assess the ability of the entrant to finance its operations until it has managed to get control of the short-term or transitory costs incurred during the early phases of its entry into the market. Further, since entry is risky and often leads to exit, any exit barriers (like the need to incur large sunk costs) that a failed entrant may have to incur are likely to diminish his/her willingness to enter.

There are, perhaps, two observations worth making about assessing the competitive discipline imposed by entry into markets. The first is that entry and supply-side substitutability are very similar. The difference between a supply-side substitute (that is a rival producer producing a 'me too' product to compete with the hypothetical monopolist) and an entrant is that the former is able to enter and compete with the hypothetical monopolist within a year. That is, entry is in effect distinguished from intra-market rivalry by the time period in which it occurs. The second observation arises from the fact that entry does not actually need to occur to have an effect on incumbents' behavior. This, in turn, means that it is the perception of a threat of entry which matters as much, perhaps, as the actual fact of entry. Beauty, as they say, is in the eye of the beholder.

5   Some final reflections

There is nothing immutable about market boundaries and, as tastes and technology change over time, so do the contours of particular markets. Indeed, innovation blurs industrial boundaries, and it sometimes induces convergence between what were once seemingly quite independent markets.[16] As process innovations affect the supply side of a market, or product innovations affect demand, so the nature of substitution between particular products (that is, the 'how much' and 'how fast' response to a hypothetical 10 per cent price rise) also changes. And such changes also affect the competitiveness of markets, however they are defined. Changes in technology alter entry barriers, and affect the strategic position of particular buyers or suppliers. All of this makes the analysis of market boundaries much harder than it might otherwise be, but it changes relatively little in principle. The SSNIP test is still the right way to think about identifying market boundaries, even if the result of applying it to a particular market in one year is likely to differ from the results obtained by doing the same test in the same market a year or two later. Further, the same basic drivers of competition – intra-industry rivalry, buyers/suppliers and entry – all apply in principle, even if a new technology alters the particular effects that they have in practice.

The real complication comes because technological changes are not wholly exogenous. Firms make conscious decisions to invest in R&D, or to introduce new products or adopt new innovations introduced by other firms. Amongst other things, this means that the market boundaries that one is likely to observe in any one year will depend on decisions made by firms in past years. Firms that have favorable market positions in the past are likely to introduce those innovations which help to reinforce or protect those positions; innovations that disrupt existing market boundaries are more likely to be introduced by entrants or fringe players who have little to lose (and everything to gain) from a change in market boundaries. Again, this does not in principle affect how one ought to go about identifying market boundaries, but it does mean that forming expectations about how likely existing boundaries are to change, and in what direction, is more speculative than it might otherwise be.

Of course, firms that make investments in R&D compete with other firms who also choose to invest in R&D. Such investments affect costs as well as the product quality/diversity available to consumers. Indeed, some people believe that quality and diversity of choice are likely to be more important determinants of welfare than high prices, and, for those who think in this way, the important market whose competitiveness needs to be assessed is that in which R&D competition occurs (sometimes called 'the innovation market').[17] What makes this an interesting complement to normal product market analyses is that the forces of competition (and, indeed, the identity of the competitors) in the innovation markets that a firm compete in may well differ from those which are found in the product markets where it sells its products. At the end of the day, however, markets are the stage on which competition occurs, and the fact that firms compete in several interrelated markets, indeed, the fact that firms consciously try to shape the competitive structure of the markets that they operate in, does not in any way diminish the importance of trying to establish the exact contours of those markets, or of assessing their competitiveness.

Notes

* The views expressed in this paper are those of the authors alone and do not necessarily reflect those of the institutions – or any of the individuals in them – that they are affiliated with. We are obliged to Derek Morris and Geoffrey Sumner both for continuing discussions as well as for comments on an earlier draft. The usual disclaimer applies.

1. See USDOJ (1992), EC (1997), OFT (1999b, 2001), Competition Commission (2002).
2. In the case of a merger, for example, this is likely to include the principal products and areas of operation of the two firms – or at least those most directly affected by the merger. For geographical market definition, see for example Elzinga and Hogarty (1973).
3. That is, the existence of close demand or supply substitutes will make the demand curve facing the hypothetical monopolist, sometimes called its 'residual demand', more elastic than market demand. Clearly, the more elastic is its residual demand, the less likely it is that a price rise will be profitable.
4. Strictly speaking, the fall-off need only be 9.1 per cent. Initially, profits are $\pi_0 = p^*q$. When price rises to $1.1p$, profits become $\pi_1 = 1.1p^*(1 - x)q$ when quantity falls by x. Profits remain unchanged if $\pi_0 = \pi_1$; that is when $x = 0.91$.
5. The price–marginal cost margin is price minus marginal cost over price.
6. See, inter alia, Kovacic (1997), Baker and Rubinfeld (1999); the Competition Commission has begun to use consumer surveys to help quantify consumer reactions to a hypothetical price rise in particular markets.
7. There is a large literature on tests involving the law of one price. The most common approaches involve looking at price differences between different regions for the same or similar products, looking for correlations between price changes over time, or tracking trade flows. For further discussion, see Scheffman and Spiller (1987), Geroski (1998), Slade (1986), Baker and Bresnahan (1985), Fisher (1987), Hausman et al. (1996), Forni (2002) and others.
8. This said, price correlation tests have been used by antitrust bodies as evidence on market definition; see, inter alia, OFT (1999a), Steen and Salvanes (1999).
9. There may, in fact, be more transactions if one or more independent wholesalers is involved in the value chain.
10. *U.S.* v. *E.I. du Pont de Nemours & Co.*, 351 U.S. 377 (1956).
11. If marginal costs are rising, then a 10 per cent margin of price over marginal cost implies a rather higher margin of price over average cost, and thus a rather higher gross accounting margin.
12. Curiously enough, assessing competitiveness in this way is almost exactly how business strategists assess the 'attractiveness' of the market. In particular, Michael Porter's famous 'five forces' are: buyers, suppliers, entrants, rivals and substitutes; our classification above lumps buyers and suppliers, on the one hand, and rivals and substitutes, on the other, together; see Porter (1980).
13. For good overviews of how to assess intra-market rivalry – and more generally, of the economics of antitrust – see Neumann (2001), Harrington et al. (2000), and others.
14. One currently-used measure of market concentration is the Herfindahl–Hirschman Index (the HHI for short), which is defined as the sum of the squares of the market shares

of each supplier. For example, if there are five suppliers in a market, each with a share of 20 per cent, the HHI is equal to 2000 (that is 20^2, which equals 400 times five which equals 2000). The Department of Justice uses a rule of thumb which says that an HHI below 1000 is considered as indicating a low concentration, between 1000 and 1800 is considered a moderate level of concentration and over 1800 highly concentrated. The European Court presumes dominance (in the absence of contrary evidence) for market shares of 50 per cent and above (Case C62/86, *AKZO Chemie BV* v. *Commission* (1993) 5 CMLR 215) and the Director General of Fair Trading in the UK uses a threshold of 40 per cent (see OFT, 1999c).

15. See Canoy *et al.* (in this volume) for an extensive discussion.
16. See Geroksi (1998) for further discussion.
17. See Gilbert and Sunshine (1995) and Rapp (1995) for differing views on the usefulness of analyzing such 'innovation markets'.

References

Baker, J. and T. Bresnahan (1985): 'The gains from merger or collusion in product differentiated industries', *Journal of Industrial Economics* 33, 427–44.

Baker, J. and D. Rubinfeld (1999): 'Empirical methods in antitrust litigation: review and critique', *American Law and Economics Review* 1 (1/2), 386–425.

Competition Commission (2002): 'Economic guidance' (available from the website).

EC (1997): 'Notice on the definition of the relevant market for the purposes of community competition law', OJ C372, 09/12/97.

Elzinga, K. and T. Hogarty (1973): 'The problem of geographical market definition', *Antitrust Bulletin* 18: 45–81.

Fisher, F. (1987): 'Horizontal mergers: triage and treatment', *Journal of Economic Perspectives* 40, 23–40.

Forni, M (2002): 'Using stationarity tests in antitrust market definition', CEPR Working Paper 3236.

Geroski, P. (1998): 'Thinking creatively about markets', *International Journal of Industrial Organization* 16, 677–96.

Gilbert, R. and D. Sunshine (1995): 'Incorporating dynamic efficiency concerns in merger analysis', *Antitrust Law Journal* 63, 509–97.

Harrington, J., J.M. Vernon and W.K. Viscusi (2000): *Economics of Regulation and Antitrust*, Cambridge, MA: MIT Press.

Hausman, J., G. Leonard and C. Velturo (1996): 'Market definition under price discrimination', *Antitrust Law Journal* 64, 367–86.

Kovacic, W (1997): 'Administrative adjudication and the use of new economic approaches in antitrust analysis', *George Mason Legal Review* 5, 313–20.

Neumann, M. (2001): *Competition Policy*, Cheltenham, UK, and Northampton, MA, USA: Edward Elgar.

OFT (1999a): 'Quantitative techniques in competition analysis', OFT Research Paper 266.

OFT (1999b): 'Market definition', OFT Working Paper 403.

OFT (1999c): 'Assessment of market power', OFT Working Paper 415.

OFT (2001): 'The role of market definition in monopoly and dominance inquiries: a report prepared for the OFT by NERA', OFT Economic Discussion Paper 2.

Porter, M. (1980): *Competitive Strategy*, New York: Free Press.

Rapp, R. (1995): The 'misapplication of the innovation market approach to merger analysis', *Antitrust Law Journal* 64, 19–47.

Scheffman, D. and P. Spiller (1987): 'Geographical market definition under the USDOJ merger guidelines', *Journal of Law and Economics* 30, 123–47.

Slade, M. (1986): 'Exogeneity tests of market boundaries applied to petroleum products', *Journal of Industrial Economics* 34, 291–304.

Steen, F. and K.G. Salvanes (1999): 'Testing for market power using a dynamic oligopoly model', *International Journal of Industrial Organisation* 17, 147–77.

US DOJ (1992): 'Horizontal merger guidelines', www.ftc.gov/bc/docs/horizmer.htm

Appendix: the simple algebra of SSNIP

Profits beforehand (denoted with subscript 0) are equal to revenue (price, P, times quantity, Q) minus total costs (average cost, C, times quantity):

$$\Pi_0 = (P_0 - C_0)Q_0. \tag{A.1}$$

A change in price $\Delta P = P_1 - P_0$ leads to a change in quantity demanded $\Delta Q = Q_1 - Q_0$ and may also lead to a change in the average cost of production $\Delta C = C_1 - C_0$. This gives a new level of profits:

$$\Pi_1 = (P_1 - C_1)Q_1. \tag{A.2}$$

The change in profits is given by:

$$\begin{aligned} \Delta \Pi = \Pi_1 - \Pi_2 &= (P_1 - C_1)Q_1 - (P_0 - C_0)Q_0 \\ &= \Delta P Q_1 + (P_0 - C_0)\Delta Q - Q_1 \Delta C. \end{aligned} \tag{A.3}$$

Note that, when $\Delta P > 0$, we expect that $\Delta Q < 0$. We are interested in looking at when $\Delta \Pi$ will be less than zero. It is convenient to rewrite (A.3) by dividing through by P_0 (note that this does not change matters as $\Delta \Pi < 0$ if $\Delta \Pi / P_0 < 0$), yielding

$$\frac{\Delta \Pi}{P_0} = \frac{\Delta P}{P_0}Q_1 + \frac{P_0 - C_0}{P_0}\Delta Q - \frac{Q_1}{P_0}\Delta C. \tag{A.4}$$

Note that $\Delta P / P_0$ is the hypothetical price rise (usually considered to be 10 per cent).

Begin by considering the case where average cost is constant (it does not depend on the amount produced) so that $\Delta C = 0$. Then,

$$\frac{\Delta \Pi}{P_0} = \frac{\Delta P}{P_0}Q_1 + \frac{P_0 - C_0}{P_0}\Delta Q. \tag{A.5}$$

Thus a price rise will be profitable if

$$\frac{\Delta P}{P_0}Q_1 > \frac{P_0 - C_0}{P_0}\Delta Q; \tag{A.6}$$

that is, if the increased price charged on the new (lesser) quantity is greater than the lost margin on the decrease in quantity. If there are economies of scale, we also need to work out $(Q_1 / P_0)\, \Delta C$. If, for example, $\Delta C < 0$ when $\Delta Q < 0$, the increase in price on the new quantity needs to be greater than the lost margin on the decreased quantity plus the higher costs on the new quantity.

9 Competition policy vs. regulation: administration vs. judiciary

Christian Kirchner

1 Introduction

The relationship between competition policy and regulation has not always been clear. Conventional wisdom regards both activities as non-competing, or complementary. However, rivalry between competition policy and regulation shows up in certain phases during the deregulation of an industry or the transformation of former state monopolies into competitive markets. In practice, the conflict between competition policy and regulation often arises as one between competition authorities and sector-specific regulators.

In order to better understand the complex interdependence and substitution processes between competition policy and regulation, this chapter analyzes their relationship. We first look at the relationship between competition policy and regulation from an industrial organization perspective and then develop a new perspective resting on an institutional economics approach.

We define competition policy in the given context as the application and enforcement of competition law by competition authorities and law courts. Regulation will be understood as sector-specific regulation enforced by regulatory authorities and law courts. Whereas competition policy constitutes a branch of economic policy applicable to all sectors, regulation concerns specific industries.

We consider that administration plays a more prominent role in the case of regulation, while the judiciary is more decisive when it comes to the application and enforcement of competition law. Conclusions on the proper relationship between competition policy and regulation cannot be derived solely on grounds of different enforcement mechanisms.

2 Competition policy and regulation: non-competing or competing institutional devices?

2.1 Introduction

The widely accepted traditional view that competition policy and regulation are complementary, non-competing devices may serve as a starting point for the discussion (complementarity hypothesis). Both types of economic policy are directed towards influencing given market processes. But within this broad common framework they pursue different goals and ought to solve different problems.[1]

In order to better understand the relationship between competition policy and regulation it has to be clarified what solutions these institutional devices offer and what goals are to be attained. The take-off point for our analysis is the following four widely accepted propositions:

1. Competition in markets for goods and services gives rise to positive economic and social welfare effects. It is an important factor for the organization of society as based on individual freedom.
2. Competition exclusively left to market forces may be endangered by activities aimed at creating or strengthening market power (restrictive business practices).
3. Competition policy aims to protect freedom of competition by defining and enforcing measures preventing restraints of competition.
4. Markets in which competition would not produce the positive welfare effects industry should be regulated.

Position (4), widely accepted before the deregulation movement,[2] may be formulated differently: regulation is needed in certain cases of 'market failures' like 'natural monopolies' where competition policy is infeasible.

These propositions may be called summarily the *conventional* approach to 'competition', 'competition policy' and 'regulation'. It appears to be convincing at first sight but we will critically evaluate it, starting from the traditional framework of industrial organization analysis.

2.2   Competition, competition policy and regulation

Competition in a market means that market participants as customers have the choice between different suppliers and as suppliers the choice between different customers. The essence of competition is rivalry (Stigler, 1957, p. 235).[3] Rivalry on one side of the market means freedom of choice on the other side. Thus competition may be regarded as an instrument which simultaneously creates freedom and checks power, that is market power.

The relationship between market participants (either suppliers or buyers) may be characterized as a prisoner's dilemma. Cooperation (collusion) would make them better off but, if they cannot trust each other perfectly well and there is no punishment mechanism, the rational (Nash) strategy is to behave non-cooperatively; that is, to compete in order not to lose out. Market participants who gain market power can escape this prisoner's dilemma totally or to a certain degree. Market power may be the result of productive efficiency. However, as long as entry barriers are low or non-existent, this type of market power may be contested in a process of dynamic competition. In the absence of superior productive efficiency, market power may be the result of collusive activities which restrain competition, for example engaging in price fixing, elimination of competitors through mergers or other restrictive business practices, such as contractual and non-contractual restraints which raise entry barriers or predatory conduct which forces rivals to exit.[4] The result for market participants on the other side of the market is less freedom of choice and thus a deterioration of market conditions.

Competition policy can be defined as a public policy instrument to prevent constraints on competition. The goal of competition policy is to keep markets free from restrictive practices, that is, to safeguard freedom of choice against business practices which supposedly have negative welfare effects.[5]

The underlying assumption of competition policy defined in this way is that in the absence of such restrictive practices, effective competition will produce positive economic effects; that is, it will lead to an efficient use of scarce resources (allocative efficiency), thus serving economic welfare and protecting individual liberty as well.

Competition policy as such cannot create competition. It can only prevent or limit the effects of certain activities restricting freedom of competition. Competition is a dynamic search process which is dependent on various institutional prerequisites like private property and freedom of contract.[6] There cannot be any meaningful competition policy in the absence of such institutional devices.

There are limits to the effectiveness of competition policy. The assumption of positive welfare effects in the absence of restrictive business practices may not be satisfied because of the existence of public goods, externalities or so-called 'natural monopolies'. These imperfections of markets are often referred to as 'market inefficiencies' or 'market failures'. Competition under such circumstances is not feasible for technological or market reasons.

In the case of a 'natural monopoly', defined as the 'subadditivity of the cost function over the relevant range of output' (Berg and Tschirhart, 1988, p. 51), efficiency cannot be attained by competition between two or more firms in the market. Costs will be lower if only a single supplier exists. Thus, according to conventional wisdom, 'natural monopolies' should be subject to regulation in order to protect consumers and to attain the goal of allocative efficiency.[7]

2.3   The relationship between competition policy and regulation
According to the conventional wisdom competition policy and regulation are institutional devices which are not conflicting. They are applicable in

different settings and thus are complementary. There are markets in which competition policy will lead to satisfactory results, and other markets which need regulation in order to attain the efficiency goal.

The goals to be attained by both institutional devices are overlapping but not identical. Many scholars argue that competition policy should serve a broad catalogue of objectives.[8] Others focus on the efficiency goal.[9] Often the efficiency goal is combined with the consumer protection goal. In the case of regulation most authors stress the efficiency goal, but goals like consumer protection are being brought into play as well.[10,11]

If this (simple) analysis of competition policy and regulation is true, the following hypothesis may be formulated: competition policy and regulation are alternative, but complementary, institutional devices.

The answer to the question whether competition policy or regulation is the adequate institutional device to deal with issues of imperfect competition can, according to conventional wisdom, simply be derived from an analysis of market imperfections in a given market. When the market in question turns out to be a 'natural monopoly', the argument goes that regulation is the (only) feasible solution. In the case of public goods, the market mechanism may not be applicable or function properly, so that political decisions on the supply of these goods are in order and regulation may be required. In the case of externalities, institutional devices like property rights and/or civil liability should be applied. In all other cases, competition policy supposedly will produce satisfactory results.

The 'complementarity hypothesis', which has served in the United States of America as a justification for regulation of a number of industries, and which in Germany has been legitimizing the so-called exceptions from the German Law Against Restraints of Competition (see Emmerich, 1987), rests upon a questionable methodological fundament. This fundament has been challenged since the early 1960s by many scholars of economics.[12] In the light of this criticism the complementarity hypothesis may have to be given up or at least modified.

Competition policy and regulation may be competing institutional devices in situations in which regulation is being cut back or abolished (deregulation) or in which former state monopolies are being transformed into competitive markets (transformation). Deregulation can be viewed as a shift of regime, from regulation to competition policy. The essence of a normative theory of deregulation may be understood as the message that competition policy is the superior institutional device for the given markets, compared to regulation.

Transformation of state monopolies is a dynamic process where, in the initial stage, most scholars agree that (some sort of) regulation is necessary in order to open up markets. Whether, when and how in later stages of the process regulation should be replaced by competition policy will be discussed in Section 5.

If there are relevant cases in which competition policy and regulation are viable alternative institutional solutions, the choice between the options is an issue which needs to be based on economic theory more elaborated than the simple approaches just discussed. It is necessary to clarify the methodological approach first.

3   An institutional economics approach to competition policy and regulation

3.1   Competition policy
In a new institutional economics perspective competition policy may be understood as the design of an institutional framework (competition law) together with the enforcement of such legal rules (Kirchner, 1997).

Competition law in an institutional perspective is providing generally applicable rules which function as constraints for competitors when they determine strategies on how to maintain or improve their position in a market. Certain options, such as agreements to fix prices, split markets or abuse market power, are 'prohibited'. Such 'prohibition' means that competition law provides measure to sanction these activities. Such sanctions are perceived by the addressees as the price they have to pay for these activities. Thus competition law has the effect of a price system for certain activities which supposedly produce negative effects for the functioning of markets.

In an institutional perspective a distinction between public ordering and private ordering is relevant. The lawmaker is responsible for public ordering which provides an institutional framework for private actors, which engage in market transactions, organizing their business and contracting with others (private ordering). Both the lawmaker (or the lawmakers) and private actors are supposed to act rationally in their own interest. Rationality is not perfect, but 'bounded' (Herbert Simon) owing to systematic imperfections, such as incomplete and asymmetric information, which give rise to positive transaction costs. Public ordering thus may be understood as a learning process in which lawmakers design institutional devices by making use of the then existing information in a world of positive transaction costs.

Actors in the legislature, in administrative enforcement agencies and in law courts may be regarded as self-interested, rational actors, whose rationality is bounded and whose information is systematically imperfect. Their activities are interdependent, so that each group of actors may influence competition policy but is dependent on reactions from other players. One characteristic feature of competition policy in practice is its focus on lawmaking and law enforcement. Enforcement of legal rules of competition law takes place in an interplay between the competition authority and law courts when the latter have to find whether a decision of the competition authority on how to apply competition law in a concrete case is correct in the legal sense. Competition law, however, may also be enforced by law courts without the intervention of the competition authority. Law courts have to hear cases brought forward by actors claiming that they have been harmed by activities not in accordance with the existing competition law. Both enforcement devices are more or less controlled by the judiciary. It is the role of administrative authorities to pick such cases deemed to be important for the application and development of competition policy. These authorities enjoy a right of initiative: a powerful instrument thanks to the resources they can utilize in order to investigate. Nevertheless, the law courts have the final say, unless the lawmaker – after court decisions, which are supposedly not in line with the lawmaker's objectives – intervenes.

Competition policy in this new institutional economics perspective can be seen as a game between lawmakers, administrators, law courts and private actors. All actors in this game are boundedly rational and pursue their own interest.

According to the institutional economics approach there is no predefined public interest (Kirchner, 2002). Neither administrative authorities nor law courts are assumed to pursue a public interest, but individuals acting on behalf of these authorities can pursue their own objectives. These individuals however, are not free to pursue any objective subjectively perceived as advantageous for themselves. They act as agents for citizens (who are the principals); their activities are monitored and controlled by given political devices which define their responsibility and accountability vis-à-vis the principals. Because of the inbuilt weaknesses of existing governance structures there is a systematic deviation from the objectives actually pursued by the agents and those of the principals. This is true for political actors, for example at the level of lawmaking, and especially at the level of administrative authorities. In the case of competition law, where application of legal rules is enforced by law courts, the judges of these courts also may be viewed as agents acting on behalf of the citizens as principals. The feedback between the interests of the principals and the activities of law courts, that is judges, is more complicated than that between lawmakers, members of administrative authorities and the citizens. This is owing to the fact that one of the essential elements in a legal system is the independence of the judiciary. The feedback between judges and the interests of citizens thus cannot be one of direct accountability but is determined by the methods of applying the law in concrete cases. In the case of law systems, the relevant methodological tools define the binding force of precedents and the rules of distinguishing in fact and in law. In systems of statutory law, the relevant methodological tools are the methods of interpretation which have to be used by law courts.

Whereas administrators tend to legitimize their activities by stressing that they pursue positive goals (such as allocative efficiency and/or protection of consumers' interests), lawmakers tend to justify their activities by asserting that they serve the public interest (*bonum commune*). Owing to their constitutionally protected independence, law courts enjoy more discretionary power vis-à-vis the citizens as principals. In a system of statutory law they are bound by given statutory law (positive law). But statutory law is open to interpretation. Thus methods of interpretation are of utmost importance. In competition law, which translates economic rationale and terminology from economic theory (industrial organization theory) into legal terminology, the interpreters of statutory competition law tend to develop legal theories on competition law which relate to economic theory only to a certain degree. In order to defend this autonomy it makes sense for law courts not to translate economic objectives directly into legal concepts. This may be one of the reasons why in legal theory, even in the case of competition law, allocative efficiency as the ultimate goal of competition law is looked at with suspicion. Law courts rather tend to put competition law into the general legal framework, thus enabling them to emphasize other 'values' as well, such as 'freedom of contract' or 'social justice'.

An institutional approach necessarily makes a clear-cut distinction between a positive and a normative approach. Whereas the former analyzes the given effect of alternative institutional arrangements and/or the creation and change of such institutional arrangements, the latter provides arguments for choosing between competing institutional solutions. This institutional economics approach may be applied to regulation as well. Most elements of the institutional approach are the same whether applied to competition policy or to regulation. There are some specific features of an institutional economics approach to regulation which are worth discussing further.

3.2   Regulation
Applying the new institutional economics approach to regulation means at first a clear distinction between a *positive theory of regulation*, which explains why and how existing regulatory structures have been developed[13] and how the existing regulatory instruments work in practice (Kaserman and Mayo, 1995, pp. 432–57), and a *normative theory of regulation*, which discusses the justification of regulation and/or the merits of competing regulatory regimes and/or the rationale of a choice between regulation and application of competition law.[14]

As argued above, the assumption of self-interested (boundedly) rational behavior is combined with that of systematically incomplete information and positive transaction costs. As in competition policy, there is no predefined public interest in a new institutional economics approach. Regulation in an institutional economics perspective might be seen as an activity in which lawmakers, administrators and, to a certain degree, judges are engaged in public control of business activities. Market forces are totally or at least to a certain degree replaced by an administrative decision process.

Lawmakers, administrators and judges, as agents, have to justify their (costly) activities vis-à-vis the citizens, that is the principals, in the light of a positive balance between social benefits and social costs. Such a calculation has to take into account the cost of regulation as well. With regulation being justified by existing 'market failures', the problem arises that one cannot compare the existing market imperfections with perfect markets. Such perfect markets would be a good benchmark; but they do not exist. Such a comparison thus would lead to a nirvana approach. And it has to take into account that there are imperfections in state activities as well which may produce high, often invisible, costs. A cost–benefit analysis of the pros and cons of regulation in a specific market has to weigh benefits and costs, not just in a static model: it also has to take into account the impact of regulation on innovation as a driving force of future benefits as well. It has to be remembered that all the relevant decisions (at the level of lawmaking, administration and application of law by law courts) take place in a world of systematically incomplete information.

Such an institutional economics approach to regulation is far away from conventional welfare economics approaches to regulation focusing on efficiency implications of regulation and sometimes confusing the positive and the normative approaches. On the other side, an institutional economics approach cannot be reduced to a simple positive analysis of the relevant factors of existing regulatory structures. A normative analysis of alternative institutional devices is necessary in which regulation and competition policy are analysed in a comparative setting. This type of normative comparative institutional approach then may serve as a basis for choosing between competition policy and regulation in given market situations.

4   Competition policy and regulation during deregulation

A deregulation process can be understood as an attempt to replace (sector-specific) regulation by the application of general rules of competition law. In some cases that process just leads to a mitigation of existing regulation. Deregulation then means a change in the institutional framework for a given industry. The players in the market are confronted by a different set of rules and by different enforcement procedures.

As has been mentioned, deregulation may be justified in the light of deficiencies of existing regulation. The positive theory of regulation[15] has formulated many of these arguments which have then been turned into political activities. However, a deregulation process may be driven by legal changes beyond the reach of the national lawmaker and regulator. In the case of regulated industries in member states of the European Union which had been exempted from national competition law, the competition law of the European Community does not contain such exemptions and is pre-empting national competition law when restrictive practices affect the trade between member states (art. 81 para. 1 EC). While more and more markets have thus been covered by Community competition law rather than by national law: existing national regulation which was compatible with national competition law was not in accordance with European competition law. This legal change forced the member states to adjust drastically national regulation to fit the new supranational legal framework or to abandon regulation and replace it with the application of general competition law.

If a member state has opted for deregulation, national and European competition law may both be applicable to the deregulated industry. European competition law is confined to transactions which are of European concern, that is which affect trade between member states, whereas national competition law remains applicable to purely national cases. Replacement of (national) regulation is thus a complicated process. The relevant actors in the field of public ordering are lawmakers, competition authorities and the judiciary at the national and the European level. At the national level law courts play a decisive role in the enforcement of competition law; at the European level it has been the Commission shaping the enforcement of competition law. This role of the Commission derives from the specific structure of art. 81 EC, which contains two tests. According to paragraph 1, certain restrictions of competition are being prohibited, whereas according to paragraph 3 the provisions of paragraph 1 may be declared inapplicable under certain conditions (exemptions). The power to grant exemptions has been vested in the Commission between 1962 and May 2004. Exemptions under the very broad and vague wording of art. 81 para. 3 EC have rarely been challenged by the affected market participants before the law courts.

The implication is that a change from (national) regulation to the parallel application of national and European competition law cannot be understood as a replacement of administrative procedures by legal procedures (administration vs. judiciary) but rather as a complex process in which national administrative procedures are replaced by national legal procedures and by European administrative procedures. Transactions which affect trade between member states and which are covered by European competition law are in most cases the more relevant and important ones. Thus it may be argued that one type of administration is being replaced by another. It is then necessary to make a clear distinction between administrative procedures of regulatory authorities and administrative procedures by the EC competition authorities. The former focus on ex ante regulatory devices and cover all transactions of the industry at stake; the latter concentrate on critical cases ex post and selectively. One may regard the administrative procedures of the EC Commission as quasi-legal procedures.

After 1 May 2004, the picture may change somewhat because Regulation no. 17 of 1962 (which sets out the rules of the procedures for the application of Articles 81 and 82) will be replaced by Council Regulation (EC) no. 1/2003. According to art. 1, para. 2 of the new regulation, a system of legal exceptions will replace the current system of legal exemptions. This means that the courts have to interpret art. 81 para. 3 as a legal exception. Nevertheless, according to art. 10 of Regulation 1/2003, the Commission may under certain conditions decide that art. 81 EC will not be applicable to a given transaction.

5 Competition policy, regulation and the transformation of state monopolies

Transforming former state monopolies into competitive markets today is an essential part of economic policy in the European Union and its member states. Such transformation takes place mainly in so-called 'network industries' (like electricity, natural gas, telecommunication). Former 'natural monopolies' have to be broken up to pave the way for market integration on a European level. During the transformation process the relative weights of regulation and competition policy are changing. In order to better understand the complex problems of such transformation processes and the role of regulation and competition policy for their success, the case of the telecommunication sector will be taken as an example.[16]

The concept of breaking up former monopolies in the field of telecommunication rests on the assumption that, while the existing infrastructure will remain monopolized for a given period of time, competition can be introduced in downstream markets. In the telecommunication sector the argument goes that markets for telecommunication services (product markets) should be opened up, even if the network infrastructure remains in the hands of a monopolist. But then access to such networks (access market) has to be regulated. Thus regulated access appears to be indispensable for transforming former state monopolies into competitive markets. State ownership and monopoly are thus being abolished, but not state influence. Access regulation replaces state influence through state ownership.

Regulation comes into play because the introduction of competition on product markets can only be achieved by regulatory devices. Such regulatory devices are quite similar to an instrument in competition law, the access to so-called 'essential facilities' (essential facilities doctrine).[17] Despite this fact, transformers prefer regulation. The argument is that competition law may be strong enough to control market power – and maybe bottlenecks – in existing markets, but it is infeasible in a situation in which the market (that is the product market) has to be created. Furthermore, regulation provides the necessary ex ante instruments, whereas competition policy is an ex post mechanism.

The case for regulating access markets seems to prove no major concern. There is a second field, however, where regulation or competition policy are viable alternatives. In downstream markets the former monopolist enjoys a monopoly in the first transformation stage, after the abolishment of the legal monopoly and the introduction of competition by means of access regulation. Market power of the owner of the network could be controlled by sector-specific regulation or by means of competition policy. At first glance, one is inclined to argue that it is more effective to protect the new entrants who enter downstream markets because of access regulation rather than by means of competition law.

It has to be taken into account that access regulations focus on bottlenecks which are network-specific features, whereas market power in downstream markets no longer is a network-specific problem once the access problem has been solved. The choice between competition policy and regulation for dealing with problems of downstream markets boils down to a problem of which device is perceived to be more effective. This simple definition of the problem may be challenged if the dynamic process of transforming state monopolies into competitive markets is analysed in more detail.[18]

Transformation of state monopolies into competitive markets is a dynamic process which takes place in a number of distinct stages. In the first stage, when access regulation opens up downstream markets to new entrants, the position of the former monopolist will be contested by competitors which have to rely fundamentally on entry conditions on downstream markets granted by access regulation. Under favorable regulatory conditions new competitors will enter the downstream markets, where they are then confronted by competition from the former monopolist. The latter's position may be weakened if, as is often the case, the former monopolist is not yet fit for competition because of cost-inefficient organizational structures and contractual constraints (for example labor conditions). On the other hand, the former monopolist may have cost advantages from scale and scope economies which are not easily matched by the new competitors. In such an environment, it is decisive whether the former monopolist may drive the new competitors out of the market or whether he or she is not able to survive in the market owing to the comparative disadvantages mentioned. In such a situation, it makes a difference whether downstream markets are under a regime of sector-specific regulation or of general competition law.

Sector-specific regulation of downstream markets is effective insofar as the regulatory authority can simultaneously employ instruments of access regulation and control of market power in downstream markets. It has the opportunity to use these instruments in such a way that new entrants cannot be driven out of the market. This 'advantage' of double regulation (that is of access and of downstream markets) may turn into a disadvantage when institutional aspects become relevant. In a regime of sector-specific regulation the regulatory authority – in charge of access regulation – is tempted to protect the new entrants merely on the grounds of improving competition in downstream markets. Access regulation and protection of new competitors in downstream markets are two devices to guarantee the success of the transformation process. Such a concept may be helpful in the first stage of transformation, but it becomes more and more critical in later stages. By concentrating on competition on downstream markets (and neglecting potential competition on the level of networks) a vicious circle may threaten the dynamic evolution of competition in the overall market development.

Competition on downstream markets very much depends on conditions of market access. The more favorable the conditions are, the less incentive new entrants have for investing in infrastructure which would enable them to compete on the level of the network as well. Such entrants are totally dependent on access regulation and on protection in the downstream market as well. The regulatory authority has an incentive to protect the new entrants in the downstream markets in order not to endanger the transformation process. The overall incentive to invest in innovations at the network level is diminished. The potential for introducing competition at the network level thus cannot be tested in practice.

The regulatory authority may have an incentive to engage in this static approach of regulation because it may thus protect its own position over a long period of time. So long as competition is confined to downstream markets and access to these markets depends on access regulation, regulatory authorities enjoy a very strong position. New entrants depend on the double regulation mentioned above. They can only survive in such an institutional framework if regulation is guaranteed for a long period of time. Even the former monopolist may be interested in such a regulatory deadlock if, in accordance with capture theory, the relation between the regulatory authority and the addressee of regulation can be 'improved'.

The question then arises whether and how such a regulatory deadlock may be prevented or ended. The relationship between competition policy and regulation may play a major role here. If regulation is being confined to problems of network-specific market power, all problems of market power in downstream markets should be handled by competition authorities applying the tools of general competition law, if the access problem is handled effectively by sector-specific regulation. If investment in infrastructure leads to the erosion of bottlenecks, sector-specific regulation can be abandoned here as well. Under such institutional constraints new entrants could no longer hope that their market position, based on regulated access, would be protected against competition of the former monopolist merely on the grounds of keeping them in the markets. They would be confronted by an institutional framework also common to other markets. Thus, there would be strong incentives to enforce their own market position by turning from pure intra-network competition to a mix of intra-network competition and competition between networks, leading to competition based on infrastructure in downstream markets. A regulatory approach combining sector-specific regulation with the step-by-step introduction of competition policy depends on some modifications of the regulatory approach of access regulation. Such regulation should consider not only the incentives for competition in downstream markets as such but also the incentives for investments in infrastructure competition.

6   Concluding remarks
The relationship between competition policy and regulation turns out to constitute a highly complex problem. The process of deregulation (replacing regulation with competition policy) poses a much more complicated problem than is normally expected. In a process of transforming state monopolies into competitive markets, the initial introduction of sector-specific regulation may easily result in a regulatory deadlock which can only be prevented or ended if prudent regulatory devices are combined with the early introduction of competition policy in downstream markets.

Notes
1. Carlton and Perloff (2000, pp. 732, 782), Viscusi *et al.* (2000, ch.1).
2. See for example Kahn (1970), Scherer and Ross (1990).
3. See Martin (in this volume), for a detailed discussion of the nature(s) of competition.
4. For further discussion, see Canoy *et al.* in this volume.
5. For a detailed discussion of the underlying economic arguments, see for example Kaserman and Mayo (1995), Carlton and Perloff (2000), Neumann (2001), and Rowley and Rathbone in this volume.
6. See Neumann (2001) for an elaboration.
7. See, for a theoretical analysis, Tirole (1988, pp. 19–20). See also Kahn (1970, p. 11), Breyer (1982, p. 15), Sidak and Spulber (1998, p. 20).
8. Ehlermann and Laudati (1998, pp. ix–xii); see also the papers on 'competition policy objectives' in Ehlermann and Laudati (1998) by Jenny (1998); Casteñada (1998); Fels (1998); Fornalczyik (1998); Kobayashi (1998); Matte (1998); Neven (1998); Schaub (1998); Wolf (1998).
9. See Posner (1976) and The Chicago School.
10. On regulation and the efficiency goal, see Kahn (1970, p. 11), Berg and Tschirhart (1988, p. 236). See also Kaserman and Mayo (1995, p. 75).

11. See also Berg and Tschirhart (1988, p. 285).
12. See for example, Demsetz (1968), Stigler (1971), Posner (1974), Peltzman (1976), Berg and Tschirhart (1988, p. 287).
13. See for example Stigler (1971), Berg and Tschirhart (1988, p. 287).
14. See for example Kahn (1970, pp. 3, 11), Immenga *et al.* (2001, pp. 52–5).
15. See for example Peltzman (1976), Berg and Tschirhart (1988, p. 287).
16. See for example Laffont and Tirole (1999), Immenga *et al.* (2001), De Bijl and Peitz (2003) for the telecommunication industry.
17. See for example OECD (1996) for a survey.
18. The following discussion draws on Immenga and Kirchner (2002, pp. 354, 355).

References

Berg, S. and J. Tschirhart (1988): *Natural Monopoly Regulation – Principles and Practice*, Cambridge, UK: Cambridge University Press.

Breyer, S.F. (1982): *Regulation and Its Reform*, Cambridge, MA: Harvard University Press.

Carlton, D.W. and M. Perloff (2000): *Modern industrial organization*, 3rd edn, Reading, MA: HarperCollins Publishers.

Casteñada, G. (1998): 'Competition policy objectives', in C. Ehlermann and L.L. Laudati (eds), *European Competition Law Annual 1997, The Objectives of Competition Policy*, Oxford: Hart Publishing, pp. 41–52.

de Bijl, P. and M. Peitz (2003): *Regulation and Entry into Telecommunications Markets*, Cambridge, UK: Cambridge University Press.

Demsetz, H. (1968): 'Why regulate utilities?', *Journal of Law and Economics* 11, 55–65.

Ehlermann, C.D. and L.L. Laudati (eds) (1998): *European Competition Law Annual 1997, The Objectives of Competition Policy*, Oxford: Hart Publishing.

Emmerich, V. (1987): 'Die Problematik der Ausnahmebereiche im GWB', in H. Helmrich (ed.), *Wettbewerbspolitik und Wettbewerbsrecht. Zur Diskussion um die Novellierung des GWB*, Cologne: Carl Heymanns Verlag, pp. 237–50.

Fels, A. (1998): 'Competition policy objectives', in C. Ehlermann and L.L. Laudati (eds), *European Competition Law Annual 1997, The Objectives of Competition Policy*, Oxford: Hart Publishing, pp. 53–6.

Fornalczyik, A. (1998): 'Competition policy objectives', in C. Ehlermann and L.L. Laudati (eds), *European Competition Law Annual 1997, The Objectives of Competition Policy*, Oxford: Hart Publishing, pp. 67–9.

Immenga, U. and C. Kirchner (2002): 'Zur Neugestaltung des Telekommunikationsrechts – Die Umsetzung des "Neuen Rechtsrahmens" fuer elektronische Kommunikationsnetze und -dienste der Europaeischen Union in deutsches Rechts', *TeleKommunikations & Medienrecht* 54, 340–55.

Immenga, U., C. Kirchner, G. Knieps and J. Kruse (2001): *Telekommunikation im Wettbewerb*, Munich: Verlag C.H. Beck.

Jenny, F. (1998): 'Competition policy objectives', in C. Ehlermann and L.L. Laudati (eds), *European Competition Law Annual 1997, The Objectives of Competition Policy*, Oxford: Hart Publishing, pp. 27–39.

Kahn, A.E. (1970): *The Economics of Regulation: Principles and Institutions*, New York: John Wiley.

Kaserman, D.L. and J.W. Mayo (1995): *Government and Business. The Economics of Antitrust and Regulation*, Orlando: Dryden Press.

Kirchner, C. (1997): 'Kartellrecht und neue Institutionenökonomik: Interdisziplinäre Überlegungen', in J. Kruse, K. Stockmann and L. Vollmer (eds), *Wettbewerbspolitik im Spannungsfeld nationaler und internationaler Kartellrechtsordnungen*, Festschrift für Ingo Schmidt zum 65. Geburtstag, Baden-Baden: Nomos Verlagsanstalt, pp. 33–49.

Kirchner, C. (2002): 'Gemeinwohl aus institutionenoekonomischer Perspektive', in G.F. Schuppert and F. Neidhardt (eds), *Gemeinwohl – Auf der Suche nach Substanz*, WZB-Jahrbuch 2002, Berlin: edition sigma, pp. 157–77.

Kobayashi, H. (1998): 'Competition policy objectives', in C. Ehlermann and L.L. Laudati (eds), *European Competition Law Annual 1997, The Objectives of Competition Policy*, Oxford: Hart Publishing, pp. 81–4.

Laffont, J. and J. Tirole (1999): *Competition in Telecommunications*, Cambridge, MA: MIT Press.

Matte, F. (1998): 'Competition policy objectives', in C. Ehlermann and L.L. Laudati (eds), *European Competition Law Annual 1997, The Objectives of Competition Policy*, Oxford: Hart Publishing, pp. 85–109.

Neumann, M. (2001): *Competition Policy. History, Theory and Practice*, Cheltenham, UK and Northampton, MA, USA: Edward Elgar.

Neven, D. (1998): 'Competition policy objectives', in C. Ehlermann and L.L. Laudati (eds), *European Competition Law Annual 1997, The Objectives of Competition Policy*, Oxford: Hart Publishing, pp. 111–18.

OECD (1996): *The Essential Facilities Concept*, Paris: OCDE/GD (96) 113.

Peltzman , S. (1976): 'Towards a more general theory of regulation', *Journal of Law and Economics* 19, 201–17.

Posner, R.A. (1974): 'Theories of economic regulation', *Bell Journal of Economics* 5, 335–58.

Posner, R.A. (1976): *Antitrust law: An Economic Perspective*, Chicago: Rand McNally.

Schaub, A. (1998): 'Competition policy objectives', in C. Ehlermann and L.L. Laudati (eds), *European Competition Law Annual 1997, The Objectives of Competition Policy*, Oxford: Hart Publishing, pp. 119–28.

Scherer, F.M. and D. Ross (1990): *Industrial Market Structure and Economic Performance*, 3rd edn, Boston: Houghton Mifflin Company.

Sidak, J.G. and D.F. Spulber (1998): *Deregulatory Takings and the Regulatory Contract – The Competitive Transformation of Network Industries in the United States*, Cambridge, UK: Cambridge University Press.

Stigler, G.J. (1957): 'Perfect competition, historically contemplated', *Journal of Political Economy* 65, reprinted in G.J. Stigler (1965): *Essays in the History of Economics*, Chicago and London: The University of Chicago Press, pp. 234–67; page references are to reprinted version.

Stigler, G.J. (1971): 'The theory of economic regulation', *Bell Journal of Economics* 2, 3–21.

Tirole, J. (1988): *Theory of Industrial Organization*, Cambridge, MA: MIT Press.

Viscusi, W.K., J.M. Vernon and J.E. Harrington (2000): *Economics of Regulation and Antitrust*, Cambridge, MA: MIT Press.

Wolf, D. (1998): 'Competition policy objectives', in C. Ehlermann and L.L. Laudati (eds), *European Competition Law Annual 1997, The Objectives of Competition Policy*, Oxford: Hart Publishing, pp. 129–32.

10 Competition policy in a globalized economy: from extraterritorial application to harmonization

Jürgen Basedow

1 The worldwide boom of competition law and its harmonization

One of the conspicuous features of law and legal thinking in the recent past is the proliferation of legislation which purports to protect competition against private restrictions. Today, more than 80 countries are said to have some kind of competition law, and more than two-thirds of these statutes have taken effect since 1992.[1] While competition policy and antitrust law were concomitant with highly developed economies until 15 years ago, they are spread all over the world today. Competition statutes have been enacted in Latin America, in the former Soviet Bloc and in the Tiger States of Southeast Asia.[2] Even in the Arab world and China, competition law and policy are making some progress.[3] The worldwide trend towards competition law can of course easily be explained by the breakdown of the socialist economies a decade ago. Only one of the two traditionally competing models of economic order – competition and central administration – has survived, and the nations are now in a hurry to equip their legal systems with the standard outfit of successful market economies.

The increase in number of competition statutes is also favored by the continuing liberalization of international trade as evidenced by the agreement establishing the World Trade Organization of 1994 and its annexes. As trade barriers set up by states are being removed in the course of liberalization, private companies are becoming more and more exposed to foreign competition. This creates new incentives for private action designed to restrict this competition from abroad. A responsible policy for the opening of national markets must therefore go hand in hand with the enactment of statutes against private restrictions of competition. Otherwise, the former trade barriers put up by state law would be continued by private agreements.

In conjunction, the convergence of national laws and the need for antitrust statutes to supplement the liberalization of international trade give new momentum to the attempts directed at the international harmonization of competition laws. This is clearly expressed in Article 9 of the Agreement on

Trade Related Investment Measures (TRIMs) which forms part of annex 1A of the WTO Agreement.[4] Under this article the Council for Trade in Goods established by the WTO Agreement shall review the operation of the TRIMs Agreement and propose to the Ministerial Conference amendments to its text if that appears appropriate. It is explicitly provided that the Council for Trade in Goods 'shall consider whether the Agreement should be complemented with provisions on investment policy and competition policy'.

This announcement has given rise to an abundant literature and a vivid discussion over the last couple of years.[5] There are essentially three types of objections: the first advocates a consequent extraterritorial application of national laws which would reduce the need for an international harmonization considerably (see Wood, 1995; Hauser and Schöne, 1994, p. 217; Arhel, 1999, p. 88). The US Supreme Court has in fact prepared the field for such a policy in *Hartford Fire Insurance v. California* (see Symeonides, 1994, p. 615). A second type of argument questions the theoretical soundness of harmonization and favors a competition of competition statutes instead.[6] A third type of criticism doubts the feasibility of antitrust harmonization and fears perhaps the emergence of a bloated international bureaucracy.[7] The following discussion will elaborate on these objections. After a survey of the goals of harmonization I will outline what can be called a pragmatic approach for future international negotiations.

2   Is extraterritorial application sufficient?

The practical need for a harmonization of antitrust laws very much depends upon how effectively competition in transnational markets can be protected by national laws today. Only gaps in the protection of competition can justify the costly and time-consuming negotiations on harmonization. Such gaps may result from an overly lenient content of the substantive law, from restrictions to which its scope of application is subjected, and from difficulties in the international enforcement at the procedural level.

In the field of substantive law there are of course far-reaching differences between competition laws like those of the United States of America and the European Union which essentially build upon prohibitions which are to be applied directly by the courts, and other jurisdictions which grant a wide discretion to administrative authorities which may intervene against abuses if they think fit to do so; the majority of states do not even allow for such an administrative intervention.[8] However, the competition laws of the majority of the industrialized nations today converge towards a Western model consisting of prohibitions of abusive monopolistic behavior, cartels and concerted practices while most legislation, for the practical implementation, provide for specific competition authorities.

Except for the problem of export cartels, deficits in the protection of competition can hardly be ascribed to differences in substantive law. The exception of export cartels is equally approved by all nations, but it clearly is incompatible with the idea of an effective protection of competition in international markets: if every nation tolerates anticompetitive behavior as long as it is directed at foreign markets, the overall intensity of competition in the world will not increase.[9] Apart from the admission of export cartels, deficits in the implementation of competition law are rather the effect of rules on application and enforcement in the international arena.

The scope of application of the single antitrust laws is by no means regulated in a uniform way. Four types of conflict rules can be discerned:[10] strict territoriality, pseudo-territoriality, the effects principle and the balancing approach. The territorial approach was traditionally followed by Great Britain, before that country adapted its legislation to European Community standards in 1999.[11] Under the former legislation some territorial connection between either the acting persons or their acts and the British territory was required for the application of the British statutes. While the prevailing view in Britain was that only such a territorial approach could be reconciled with public international law, the country had to accept that anti-competitive conduct of foreign companies occurring in foreign countries, although affecting competition on the British market, could not be controlled by the application of British law. In the future, Britain will probably change her attitude and advocate the more expansive conflicts rule adopted by the European Court of Justice.

That rule amounts to an extraterritorial application of competition laws although it relies on considerations of territoriality; we may therefore speak of pseudo-territoriality. Thus the European Court of Justice has held that there is a sufficient territorial connection between an acting company established and incorporated in a non-member state and the European Community if a subsidiary of that company, although having distinct legal personality, is established in the European Community.[12] Even if that is not the case, conduct carried out outside the Community by a foreign corporation may still be subject to Community competition law if the restrictions of competition are to be implemented within the Community.[13] This approach has been characterized as an 'effects principle in disguise',[14] and it comes very close to the effects principle indeed, although some differences remain (cf. Schwartz and Basedow, 1995, s. 58). It appears that the view of the European Court of Justice is mainly influenced by objections pertaining to public international law. In particular, the United Kingdom repeatedly expressed the view that the pure effects doctrine has no basis recognized in international law.[15] The far-reaching reform of the British competition law in 1999 will perhaps stimulate a reconsideration of this issue in the Community since the United Kingdom no longer focuses on the isolated evaluation of single anticompetitive acts as it did under the former legislation; it will now rather depart from the restrictive effect that certain acts have on competition in Britain.

The third type of conflict rule is the effects principle. Its rationale is rooted in the substantive competition law which is concerned, not with the acts as such, but with their effect on competition. Therefore the appropriate connecting factor for the application of a competition statute is not the territorial link of an act or of the actor, but the effect of those acts on the competition of the home market. For the first time, the effects principle has been adopted, in the famous *Alcoa* case in the United States,[16] and it has recently been confirmed by the US Supreme Court. In *Hartford Fire Insurance Company v. California*, the court held it to be 'well established by now that the Sherman Act applies to foreign conduct that was meant to produce and did in fact produce some substantial effect in the United States';[17] such effects have to be 'direct, substantial, and reasonably foreseeable' in order to trigger the application of the US antitrust laws.[18] The claim of extraterritorial application having been severely criticized for many years, it can be taken for accepted by now. Beginning with the German statute against restrictions of competition of 1957,[19] many competition laws enacted all over the world have explicitly adopted the effects principle (cf. Schwartz and Basedow, 1995, s. 60, 67). Although not all of them are applied rigorously, they give evidence of a new state practice and of a new orientation of public international law.

The developments of the 1990s, in particular the Supreme Court judgment in *Hartford Fire Insurance*, have greatly diminished the significance of the so-called 'balancing approach' that had been adopted by the American Restatement 3rd of Foreign Relations Law. According to that restatement and to some circuit court judgments which it reflected, the claim of the American antitrust laws for extraterritorial application should only be accepted after a balancing of the various domestic and foreign interests, both public and private.[20] In *Hartford*, the Supreme Court neither accepted nor rejected the balancing approach, but it refused to follow that approach except for cases of true conflict between an American and a foreign statute;[21] this does not leave much room for the balancing approach.

The widespread acceptance of the effects doctrine appears to guarantee an effective protection of competition on the domestic market. Does that doctrine not allow for the prosecution of anti-competitive behavior wherever it occurs, provided that it has some effect at home? While this is true from a theoretical point of view an effective implementation in practice meets two types of obstacles. In the first place the assessment of one and the same anti-competitive behavior in two countries involved may be very different although it is based on similar rules. This has been clearly shown by the merger between Boeing and McDonnell Douglas which has practically transformed certain segments of the world market for civil aircraft into a duopoly. While that merger was readily approved in the United States, the European Commission imposed some severe conditions.[22] Moreover, the international enforcement of competition statutes very often requires an effective co-operation of foreign states in the service of proceedings, in the taking of evidence and in the enforcement of decisions. A harmonization debate would certainly help to reduce the significance of these obstacles.

3   Enforcement deficits

The effective enforcement of national antitrust statutes in the international arena invariably depends upon the assistance granted by foreign states. In many cases this assistance is already required for the initial service of proceedings, in others for investigations, the search of offices or the taking of other evidence. It is equally impossible to enforce decisions, whether injunctions or penalties, in foreign countries without the co-operation of the foreign state. While transnational economic activities by necessity imply that the parties involved, relevant witnesses and other evidence are spread over various countries, the powers of domestic antitrust authorities and courts are limited by the territorial scope of sovereignty as recognized under international law. Where states cross those limits they will often be confronted by 'blocking statutes' enacted by foreign countries which want to protect their spheres of sovereignty.[23]

The attempts to overcome those procedural limits have to be divided into two groups: the first is dealing with judicial assistance and the recognition and enforcement of foreign judicial decisions, while the second tries to establish rules on the cooperation of competition authorities (cf. Schwartz and Basedow, 1995, s. 92, 93). The first group embraces a number of instruments like the Hague Evidence Convention which are applicable, beyond the area of antitrust law, to all civil and commercial matters.[24] Since most antitrust proceedings conducted outside the United States of America are not judicial, but administrative, proceedings, the rules on the international cooperation of cartel offices are more important in this field. These rules have made great progress, but they are still far from being perfect.

Three generations can be discerned: the first generation is that of soft law consisting mainly of recommendations and other non-binding instruments elaborated by international organizations. Thus the Council of the Organization for Economic Co-Operation and Development (OECD) started as long ago as 1967 to draft recommendations for the reciprocal notification and the exchange of information in competition proceedings with extraterritorial effects.[25] And the code of conduct for restrictive business practices adopted in 1980 by the United Nations Conference on Trade and Development (UNCTAD), although mainly concerned with substantive law, also establishes certain procedural duties for states.[26] This code requires states to institute procedures for obtaining the information that is necessary for the effective control of restrictive business practices and to create mechanisms for the exchange of information and for the conveyance of information which is at their disposal, to other states. In addition the code provides for a duty of consultation between states which is often regarded as one of its central elements.

The second generation of procedural rules is that of bilateral treaties. Its forerunner was the Agreement between the Government of the United States of America and the Government of the Federal Republic of Germany relating to mutual cooperation regarding restrictive business practices of 1976,[27] which for the first time transformed the former soft law into binding rules. It was followed by similar agreements between the United States and Australia, between the United States and Canada and between the Federal Republic of Germany and France; the most important of these agreements was concluded in 1991 between the United States and the European Economic Community.[28] By and large these agreements all confine their attention to establishing duties of notification and consultation and providing more detailed rules on obtaining information. But they do not deal with investigations to be conducted by the competition authorities of one country in support of competition proceedings initiated in the other contracting state. Nor do they contain any rules on the service of proceedings abroad or on the enforcement in one contracting state of decisions taken in the other contracting state. Therefore the instruments of the second generation are still far from being effective rules for the extraterritorial application of competition law.

The third generation is characterized by the keyword of the so-called 'positive comity'. While 'negative comity' provisions purport to reduce the national claims to extraterritorial application in case of conflict of jurisdictions, 'positive comity' provisions entitle a contracting party to ask the other contracting party to take enforcement action against anti-competitive activity carried out on the latter's territory but affecting competition in the former state. While the EC–US Agreement of 1991 displayed first signs of a 'positive comity' approach,[29] it was only the agreement of 1998 between the same parties which contained a clear-cut rule on the matter. Article 3 of the new agreement makes it clear that the contracting party which is requested to initiate competition proceedings shall conduct them in accordance with its own competition laws and even if the anti-competitive behavior does not violate the laws of the requesting state.[30]

The latter clarification shows that 'positive comity' is far from being an equivalent to the taking of evidence in support of foreign proceedings, as is provided under the The Hague Evidence Convention.[31] Although the evidence collected in the requested state may also be useful for the conduct of proceedings in the requesting state, the competition authority in the latter state is not in a position to direct the foreign proceedings by its own questions and instructions. Moreover, the requesting party is under a certain obligation to stay its own proceedings until the end of the proceedings in the requested state.[32] These observations show that 'positive comity' does not purport to further proceedings in the requesting state; it rather gives prevalence to proceedings in the requested state. This may explain the fact that the 'positive comity' provisions have been invoked only once so far.[33] They do not provide help in the domestic proceedings of the requesting state, but rather transfer the responsibility for the enforcement of competition law to a foreign country. Although such surrender is not final and irreversible, it is difficult to understand why a national competition authority should leave the case to the cartel office of a foreign country whose substantive competition law may differ considerably from its own. The harmonization of substantive law standards appears to be a necessary precondition for the transfer of proceedings that is envisaged by the 'positive comity' provisions.

4   The competition of competition legislations

While the practical need for an approximation of antitrust laws and procedures should not be in dispute after the preceding considerations, some economists question the soundness of such a harmonization for theoretical reasons. In particular they point out the advantages of a competition of jurisdictions or of national legislations. They believe that, in open or integrated markets, enterprises will articulate their preferences for a certain jurisdiction by moving their establishment or seat towards that country. The migration of companies into the country indicates the economic superiority of its legal system, while the mass exodus of enterprises from a state reveals the inefficiencies of its institutions. In their view, it is not unrealistic to assume that the latter state will adjust its legal system to the standards set by countries which succeed in attracting foreign companies. Alternatively the less efficient states may keep their laws if they decide that the policy objectives behind the laws are worth the costs incurred by the emigration of enterprises. Whatever the reaction of business, differences between national legislations and the freedom of cross-border migrations are said to establish a competition of jurisdictions as a rational procedure for the discovery of more efficient national laws.[34] From this perspective the unification or harmonization of laws is criticized as a kind of conspiracy of legislators which prevents the procedure of discovery to produce its beneficent effects.[35]

The concept of legislative competition has originally been developed in areas such as labor law, social security and tax law which have a direct impact on costs, but it has been extended to other areas and also to antitrust law.[36] Some authors argue that it is not desirable for states to agree upon international minimum standards in competition law since this would prevent the institutional competition of antitrust policies. This competition is said to test different policies and to uncover the most appropriate one (Freytag and Zimmermann, 1998, p. 49).

The comparison of the unification of laws with a conspiracy of legislators appears, however, to be ill-founded.[37] This does not mean that the concept of legislative competition cannot help to explain the behavior of companies and/or legislators. But it has its practical significance in areas which are characterized by a territorial application of laws, that is, in areas where legal provisions are applied to acts committed in the legislating state or to persons established there. From the principle of territorial application of a certain statute flows the consequence that economic actors can avoid that statute by moving to a foreign country. While this condition essentially is fulfilled with regard to matters such as tax law and labor law, the starting point is entirely different in the case of antitrust. Whether competition laws are enforced on the basis of the effects principle, the balancing approach or some pseudo-territorial application, the migration of a company from one country to another does not change anything as long as the anti-competitive behavior produces effects on the market of the legislating state. The enforcement claim of that state's legislation remains equally immune against all attempts to avoid this legislation by committing the anti-competitive acts abroad.

Therefore one of the basic conditions for the successful functioning of legislative competition is absent in the area of antitrust laws. Although the abstention from harmonization in this field will keep alive a certain competition of ideas which are tested in different national statutes, it can by no means be compared to the competition of legislations as explained in economic theory.

Moreover, a competition of antitrust laws would appear highly questionable. If the assumptions of economic theory are correct, private business would opt for the country where it finds the legal framework which is most favorable to its own interests. In the area of antitrust laws this would be a state which admits anti-competitive agreements and practices to the greatest extent possible. The most appropriate competition policy to be 'discovered' in that process would allow hard-core cartels and even monopolization. If the idea of legislative competition is taken seriously in this area we would sacrifice competition on the markets for goods and services in favor of legislative competition.

To sum up, it can be said that the coexistence of different antitrust statutes all over the world has the advantage of providing the continuous stimulus to reconsider the pros and cons of a national competition statute. However, this advantage would not be sacrificed by a harmonization of minimum standards at the international level. Such a minimum harmonization which is the only realistic option at present would preserve the laboratory of comparative law and would leave many options for national legislators above the level of the minimum standard.

5 The feasibility of harmonization

Many opponents of the harmonization project refer to far-reaching differences between national competition policies which practically frustrate all international negotiations in this field.[38] At first sight, this objection appears to contradict the common observation that there is a 'remarkable convergence in national competition policies' (Scherer, 1996, p. 485). Is it not true that compulsory cartels which were so widespread before World War II are disappearing all over the world? And is the avalanche of antitrust statutes enacted in so many countries not evidence of a growing and spontaneous approximation of competition policies? While these observations are true, it cannot be denied that, up to the present, less than 50 per cent of the 200 independent states have enacted a statute against restrictions of competition, and even among those states competition policies are far from being in conformity with each other. They differ in the evaluation of vertical restraints, of merger control, of the impact of non-competitive public interest, in the sanctions to be inflicted and in the procedures to be followed. It should not be forgotten that antitrust statutes can be shaped and applied in a way which comes close to a direct regulation of industry, and that is what occurs in some countries.

Nevertheless, the existing differences do not appear to preclude the harmonization of competition laws and the coordination of national competition procedures. They rather call for a cautious and pragmatic approach, which should not fix the ideal target of a uniform world competition law, but rather describe the general setting of the harmonization process. As a consequence, the following limitations should be observed.

First, negotiations should only be conducted with those states which have already proved their interest in competition law by enacting a national statute. Other states should be admitted as observers, but should not be allowed to slow down negotiations with motions rooted in an anti-competitive national policy. If they want to participate with equal rights in the negotiations they can easily adopt one of the existing national legislations, the EC law or one of the international codes of conduct as a model for a national statute.

Secondly, at a first stage, the subject of negotiations should be confined to areas in which a convergence of national solutions can already be ascertained. This regards the so-called 'hard-core cartels', vertical price fixing and the prohibition of abuses of dominant positions.[39] Although the worldwide concentration process makes it desirable to include merger control in the negotiations, it is doubtful whether the fundamental differences in this area can be overcome. It is well known that the reservation of public interest in merger control proceedings is often used as a loophole for an industrial policy aiming at the creation of huge corporations which can survive in world-wide competition. Such policies have influenced merger control in many countries, even in the United States. As long as those policies are pursued, it is difficult to see how an effective merger control can be attained at the international level. Similar considerations apply to restrictions of competition inspired or supported by states, such as the business conduct of public enterprises and state aids.

A third limitation concerns the scope of harmonization. It should be confined to cases with an international dimension, that is, where cross-border trade is affected.[40] Harmonization and unification efforts in other areas of the law, such as the sale of goods[41] or transport[42] have proved successful because they did not endeavor to achieve unification across the board but only insofar as cross-border transactions are involved. Thus states retain the right to adopt different rules with regard to purely domestic transactions, which substantially lowers the opposition towards international unification. As those examples show, international conventions, even if limited in the aforementioned way, will have an impact on domestic legislation in the long run anyway.

Finally, negotiations should aim at an agreement on minimum standards. The worldwide debate on an international harmonization of competition laws gives rise to a certain fear in countries, such as the United States which dispose of very effective means to enforce competition law, that they will be bound to cut back on that enforcement and, in particular, to give up the extraterritorial application of their antitrust laws. Apparently, the idea of a minimum harmonization is neither discussed nor very well known in the United States. In the European Union, this concept has been implemented in a great number of directives, in particular in the field of consumer protection.[43] Community measures like the Council directive on unfair terms in consumer contracts often contain clauses under which 'Member States may adopt or retain the most stringent provisions compatible with the Treaty in the area covered by this Directive, to ensure a maximum degree of protection for the consumer.'[44] A similar approach in competition law would guarantee certain minimum standards such as the prohibition of vertical restraints under the rule of reason without depriving the contracting states of the right to subject those restraints to per se prohibitions.

After all, differences in national competition legislation may be an effective obstacle to an outright unification, but they cannot be said to prevent the international community from embarking upon negotiations on a minimum harmonization of certain rules for restrictions of competition which have an international dimension.

6 The goals of harmonization

The international harmonization of competition laws appears desirable for various reasons. Among the foremost objectives is the need to cure deficits in the enforcement of national competition laws. This need has already been explained. It requires an extension of the scope of national competition laws to export cartels and other restrictions which are primarily designed to affect foreign markets. In other words, we need a different conflicts rule for the application of competition statutes. The effect that anti-competitive behavior can have on the domestic market cannot be the sole decisive factor for the application of national competition law. The existence of alternative links, such as the place of conduct or the nationality or establishment of the actors should be sufficient. This is a delicate and crucial question since the contracting states would have to accept that protection of competition is in the universal interest of the international community and not only in the public interest of the particular state. At the same time the contracting states would have to agree that a restriction of competition on foreign markets cannot be justified by their national foreign trade interests.

In the second place, there are manifold interrelations between international trade policy and competition law. As pointed out above, the liberalization of trade in goods and services is not welcome to all competitors in the markets, and some may wish to perpetuate the former trade barriers by means of private agreements. A consistent policy must foresee such consequences and conceive appropriate remedies in competition law. A similar interaction can be observed in the field of intellectual property rights. By their very nature, their holders are entitled to monopolistic behavior and may wish to engage in monopolistic abuses. Since the Agreement on Trade-Related Aspects of Intellectual Property Rights (TRIPs)[45] puts the contracting states under a duty to respect intellectual property rights, it also had to envisage the possibility of such abuses. While Articles 8 (2) and 40 TRIPs give evidence of a corresponding consciousness, they equally show that the contracting states could not agree upon appropriate countermeasures in competition law.

A further interaction between trade and competition policies relates to dumping. As a form of predatory pricing, dumping depends upon the possibility of a company cross-subsidizing certain goods or services with extra profits made on the home market where it disposes of a dominant position. An effective and extraterritorial control of such abusive conduct under the competition laws of either the exporting or the importing country would therefore allow the importing state to repeal its anti-dumping laws. This has indeed happened in the framework of a bilateral agreement between Australia and New Zealand.[46]

Negotiations on the international harmonization of competition law would have to pursue other objectives as well. States would certainly embark upon the harmonization track in order to avoid conflicts of jurisdiction which have impaired international life so often in the past. Where former efforts have always focused on jurisdictional and conflict of laws issues, a solution might also be achieved by the harmonization of substantive competition laws. Only on the basis of such a harmonization would it be possible to concentrate the administrative competence and to implement the 'one-stop-shop' principle which is a major concern of private business in international competition law. An international harmonization project would finally serve as a model for future competition legislation at the national level. It would be particularly valuable for countries which have refrained from developing a competition policy of their own so far. A model approved by an international conference could give them guidance which they would probably accept more willingly than the adoption of a foreign competition law.

7   A pragmatic approach

What are the recommendations for political action which follow from the preceding considerations? At the outset I have to repeat that the harmonization of competition laws amounts to a taming of economic nationalism since states must no longer be allowed to tolerate, for the sake of domestic profits, anti-competitive conduct aimed at foreign markets. This is the most crucial point, and explains the difficulty of harmonization. The target cannot be expected to be achieved in one go, but only step by step. This is very different from other unification projects which may be negotiated for a number of years, but then are brought to an end at a single diplomatic conference. In antitrust law, states are well advised to embark upon the road towards harmonization with less ambition. What can be attained in the near future is the beginning of an open-ended negotiation process. At a first stage this process may lead to a first agreement on some basic issues which will then have to be tested in economic practice before the negotiations can be resumed and turn to further issues some years later. A successful model for that process could be the development of international trade law in the framework of the GATT[47] and its successor, the World Trade Organization (WTO). The close link between international trade and competition law would in fact suggest that the periodical WTO negotiation rounds should be used for the promotion of competition law harmonization.

The method of harmonization should be equally cautious. This does not mean that the international community should resume the former efforts to adopt soft law in this area; those efforts have not produced any perceptible effects. While international negotiations should aim at the drafting of binding provisions of law, they should respect national legislations and refrain from far-reaching interventions. As pointed out before, they should be limited to restrictions of competition with an international dimension and should aim at an agreement on minimum standards. This would imply the adoption of a non-self-executing treaty. The technique of self-executing conventions which is used for example, in the UN Sales Convention[48] and in the Warsaw Convention on air transport,[49] is difficult to reconcile with the intention of states to enact provisions at the national level which provide for a better protection of competition, but are applicable to the same fact situations. The resulting blend of international conventions and national provisions would be too confusing. A non-self-executing treaty would allow a contracting state to maintain, in its internal legislation, a single body of competition rules which implement the treaty and set higher standards at the same time.

As to the substance of competition law, the negotiations should be confined to such types of anti-competitive conduct which are regarded as harmful to the economy by all, or the vast majority of, states. This would include the prohibition of hardcore cartels, that is agreements on horizontal price fixing, on quota and other market shares, on the concertation of offers in public bidding and so on. In the area of vertical restrictions it would equally include a per se prohibition of vertical price fixing. With regard to other vertical restraints and to abuses of dominant positions, it should be possible to reach agreement on a prohibition under the rule of reason. As pointed out before, a similar consensus on the substantive criteria of merger control is less likely, but it would appear highly desirable and feasible to harmonize the essential rules on merger control procedures: the duty to notify certain mergers to the national competition authority, the time limits to be respected before the merger is put into effect, the kind of information to be supplied to the competition authority and so on. An international convention should also establish the obligation of the contracting states to set up national competition authorities for the enforcement of the substantive rules, and to provide for private law remedies such as damages or the invalidity of contracts concluded in violation of the substantive competition rules.

The enforcement of the harmonized laws should remain in the hands of national agencies. In order to increase the effectiveness of national enforcement proceedings, the states should conclude a plurilateral convention establishing some basic procedural duties of notification, information and consultation. An additional cooperation of national authorities with regard to the service of proceedings, the taking of evidence and even the enforcement of foreign decisions would be highly desirable, but the plurilateral negotiations would be overburdened by those topics; they may be negotiated in additional conventions, probably on a bilateral basis.

While the creation of an international competition authority with its own enforcement jurisdiction would not appear to be a realistic option for the time being, the international community would profit from an international agency which serves as a platform for the exchange of information and the discussion of world competition. It would have to register violations of the international competition law and publish periodical assessments of international competition in the different sectors of the economy. It might also be entrusted with the powers to conduct investigations and even with the right to bring suit in national courts, either against private companies for their anticompetitive conduct or against the respective state for tolerating violations of the international competition convention. The latter solution has been proposed in the Draft International Antitrust Code[50] which was elaborated by an international expert group some years ago. It is an original and inventive idea which may help to lead the debate on an international antitrust agency out of the dead end. This proposal might indeed allow putting some pressure on states which do not comply with the international competition convention without, however, encroaching upon the sovereignty of those countries.

The measures outlined above are not meant to form part of a whole which could only be approved as such. Many of them could be adopted individually but their overall effect on competition would certainly increase if the whole package could be agreed upon.

Notes
1. Cf. Pitofsky (1999); a similar statement can be found in Bundesregierung (1999). In a comparative survey completed in 1992, only 47 jurisdictions that have a competition statute are listed, see Schwartz and Basedow (1995).
2. For Latin America cf. Martí (1997, pp. 83–4). Accordingly, eight countries (Brazil, Columbia, Costa Rica, Jamaica, Mexico, Panama, Peru and Venezuela) have enacted new competition statutes since 1990. In Argentina and Chile, there already existed older statutes. For the former Soviet Bloc, see Varady (1999). As to the Republic of Korea, cf. Rittner (1988); for Taiwan, see Yu Wu (1999).

3. For a first and hesitant approach in an Arab country, see the legislation of Tunisia, in particular Loi no. 91-64 du 29 juillet 1991 relative à la concurrence et aux prix, J.O. de la République Tunisienne no. 55 du 6 août 1991, amended by Loi 95-42 du 24 avril 1995, J.O. de la République Tunisienne no. 35 du 2 mai 1995, p. 976. For the Chinese debate on the adoption of an anti-monopoly law, see Wang Xiaoye (2004, p. 285).

4. The WTO Agreement has been published in the *Official Journal of the European Communities* (OJEC) 1994 L 336; for the TRIMS Agreement in particular, see OJEC 1994 L 336/100.

5. See the references in Basedow (1998, p. 185).

6. See Freytag and Zimmermann (1998, p. 49); to a similar effect see Hauser and Schöne (1994, p. 216): 'we should follow a decentralized approach which allows some competition among rules'.

7. Cf. Möschel (1989, p. 462), Griffin (1997, p. 41), Wood (1995, p. 1297), Jackson (1994, p. 196), Hauser and Schöne (1994, p. 218).

8. Cf. the comparative survey presented by Immenga in Immenga and Mestmäcker (1997, Einleitung D no. 1 seq., 18 seq.) as well as Basedow (1998, p. 7-10).

9. Cf. Matsushita (1995, p. 1117), Immenga (1996, p. 603), Möschel (1989, p. 467).

10. For a thorough treatment cf. Schwartz and Basedow (1995, sect. 36 seq.).

11. On the new British Competition Act 1998, see the contributions in *European Competition Law Review* (1999, pp. 51–77).

12. European Court of Justice, 14 July 1972 (case 48/69, *ICI v. Commission*), EC Rep. 1972, 619, 662.

13. European Court of Justice, 27 September 1988 (joined cases 89/85, *Wood Pulp*), EC Rep. 1988, 5193, 5243 considerations 16–18; on the extraterritorial application of the EC merger control regulation see Fox (1999, pp. 334–6) with further references.

14. See in this sense, for example, Martinek (1989, p. 351), Schrödermeier (1989). For arguments *contra* see Lowe (1989, p. 11), Lange and Sandage (1989, pp. 160, 164).

15. Note no. 196 of the British Embassy at Washington, DC, presented to the United States Department of State on 27 July 1978: 49 *Brit. YBInt. L.* (1978) 390 (391). To a similar effect, see *Viscount Dilhorne* in *Rio Tinto Zinc Corp. v. Westinghouse Electric Corp.*, [1978] 1 All E.R. 434, 460 (H.L.): 'For many years now the United States has sought to exercise jurisdiction over foreigners in respect of acts done outside the jurisdiction of that country. This is not in accordance with international law'.

16. *U.S. v. Aluminium Company of America*, 148 F.2d 416 (2nd Cir. 1945).

17. *Hartford Fire Insurance v. California*, 113 S. Ct. 2891 = 125 L. Ed.2d 612, 638 (1993).

18. *Filetech S.A. v. France Telecom S.A.*, 157 F.3d 922 at 931 (2nd Cir. 1998); cf. Symeonides (1999, p. 359).

19. Gesetz gegen Wettbewerbsbeschränkungen of 27 July 1957, Bundesgesetzblatt (BGBl.) I, p. 1081 as amended; see s. 98 (2), which is now s. 130 (2) of the Act as promulgated anew on 26 August 1998, BGBl. I, p. 2546.

20. See American Law Institute (1987), in particular §§ 403 and 415.

21. *Hartford Fire Insurance v. California*, 113 S. Ct. 2891 = 125 L. Ed.2d 612, 640 (1993).

22. See the Decision of the Commission of 30 July 1997, OJEC 1997 L 336/16 at considerations nos. 114–19.

23. Various blocking statutes are reproduced in Vaughan Lowe (1983, p. 79); for a survey, cf. Pettit and Styles (1982).

24. See Hague Conference on Private International Law (s.d., p. 151).

25. Council Recommendation concerning cooperation between member countries on restrictive business practices affecting international trade of 5 October 1967: *International Legal Material* 8 (1969, p. 1309).

26. UNCTAD Set of Multilaterally Agreed Equitable Principles and Rules for the Control of Restrictive Business Practices, UN Doc. TD/RBP/Conf./10 of 2 May 1980.

27. Done on 23 June 1976, TIAS no. 8291 = Bundesgesetzblatt 1976 II, p. 1712.

28. Competition Laws Co-operation Agreement (EEC–USA) of 9 September 1991, *Comm. L. Eur.* 1991 I 383; for other bilateral agreements, see the references in Schwartz and

Basedow (1995, s. 91 at n. 530 seq.); see also the more recent agreement of 17.6.1999 between the EC and Canada, OJEC 1999 L 175/49.

29.   See Art. V, s. 2 of the Agreement of 17.6.1999 between the EC and Canada, OJEC 1999 L 175/49, at n. 35.

30.   Agreement between the European Communities and the Government of the United States of America on the application of positive comity principles on the enforcement of their competition laws of 4 June 1998, OJEC 1998 L 173/28.

31.   See Hague Conference on Private International Law (s.d.).

32.   See Art. VI of the Agreement of 17.6.1999 between the EC and Canada, OJEC 1999 L 175/49, at n. 37.

33.   Report from the Commission to the Council and the European Parliament on the application of the agreements between the European Communities and the Government of the United States of America and the Government of Canada regarding the application of their competition laws – 1. January 2000 to 31 December 2000, COM (2002) 45 final, no. 1.5. The follow-up report for the year 2001 does not refer to further applications, cf. COM (2002) 505 final of 17 September 2002.

34.   See von Hayek (1969).

35.   See Streit (1996, pp. 522, 527), Donges (1990, p. 178).

36.   See Freytag and Zimmermann (1998), Hauser and Schöne (1994).

37.   For the reasons, see Basedow (1998, p. 55).

38.   Cf. Möschel (1989, p. 462), Griffin (1997, p. 41), Wood (1995, p. 1297), Jackson (1994, p. 196), Hauser and Schöne (1994, p. 218).

39.   These subjects are also mentioned in European Commission (1995, p. 22, sub. 3.2); see also Basedow and Pankoke (2002, p. 55) on the basis of 15 national and regional reports; on resale price maintenance see Immenga (1996, p. 35, sub. III) and, to a similar effect, Matsushita (1995, p. 113) and Immenga (1996, p. 602).

40.   To a similar effect, see Draft International Antitrust Code in Antitrust & Trade Regulation Report (1993); Immenga (1996, p. 601).

41.   'United Nations Convention on Contracts for the International Sale of Goods Done at Vienna on 10 April 1981', *International Legal Material* 19 (1983, 668).

42.   Convention for the Unification of Certain Rules Relating to the International Carriage by Air Done at Warsaw on 12 October 1929, L.N.T.S. 137, p. 11 seq. as amended by The Hague Protocol Done on 28 September 1955, U.N.T.S. 478, p. 371 seq.

43.   See the papers collected in Everling and Roth (1997).

44.   Council Directive 93/13/EEC of 5 April 1993 on unfair terms in consumer contracts, OJEC 1993 L 95/29; see art. 8.

45.   Agreement on Trade-Related Aspects of Intellectual Property Rights, OJEC 1994 L 336/213.

46.   Cf. Protocol of 18 August 1988 to the Australia–New Zealand Closer Economic Relations – Trade Agreement on Acceleration of Free Trade in Goods, Australia Treaty Series 1988 no. 18, see Art. 4; cf. also Basedow (1998, p. 43).

47.   On the step-by-step liberalization of international trade in the framework of GATT (the General Agreement on Tariffs and Trade), see Petersmann (1981, s. 5, 23–5).

48.   'United Nations Convention on Contracts for the International Sale of Goods Done at Vienna on 10 April 1981', *International Legal Material* 19 (1983, 668).

49.   Convention for the Unification of Certain Rules Relating to the International Carriage by Air Done at Warsaw on 12 October 1929, L.N.T.S. 137, p. 11 seq. as amended by The Hague Protocol Done on 28 September 1955, U.N.T.S. 478, p. 371.

50.   The Draft International Antitrust Code is published in *Antitrust & Trade Regulation Report* (BNA) 64 (1993), Special Supplement no. 1628 of 19 August 1993; see also Basedow (1998, pp. 70, 142) and Fikentscher and Heinemann (1994).

References

American Law Institute (1987): *Restatement of the Law, Third Foreign Relations Law of the United States*, St. Paul, Minnesota.

Arhel, P. (1999): 'Droit international de la concurrence – s'oriente-t-on vers des négotiations?', *Revue du Marché Commun et de l'Union Européenne* 1999, 84–90.

Basedow, J. (1998): *Weltkartellrecht*, Tübingen: Mohr.

Basedow, J. and S. Pankoke (2002): 'General report', in J. Basedow (ed.), *Limits and Control of Competition with a View to International Harmonization,* The Hague: Kluwer Law International, pp. 3–62.

Bundesregierung (1999): 'Stellungnahme zum Monopolkommission zum Zwölften Hauptgutachten der Monopolkommission 1996/1997', Bundestags-Drucksache 14/1274 no. 96.

Donges, J. (1990): 'Wieviel Deregulierung brauchen wir für den EG-Binnenmarkt?, *Beihefte der Konjukturpolitik. Zeitschrift für angewandte Wirtschaftsforschung* 36, 169–87.

European Commission (1995): 'Competition policy in the new trade order: strengthening international competition and rules – report of the European Commission', Luxembourg.

Everling, U. and W.-H. Roth (eds) (1997): *Mindestharmonisierung im Binnenmarkt*, Baden-Baden: Nomos.

Fikentscher, W. and A. Heinemann (1994): 'Der "Draft International Antitrust Code – Initiative für ein Weltkartellrecht im Rahmen des GATT', *Wirtschaft und Wettbewerb*, 97–107.

Fox, E. (1999): 'The merger regulation and its territorial reach: *Gencor Ltd* v. *Commission*', *European Competition Law Review* 20, 334–6.

Freytag, A. and R. Zimmermann (1998): 'Muß die internationale Handelsordnung um eine Wettbewerbsordnung erweitert werden?', *Rabels Zeitschrift für ausländisches und internationales Privatrecht* 62, 38–58.

Griffin, J.P. (1997): 'The WTO study of the interaction between trade and competition policy: timely and controversial', *International Trade Law & Regulation* 3, 39–41.

Hague Conference on Private International Law (s.d.): 'Hague Convention on the Taking of Evidence Abroad in Civil or Commercial Matters of 18 March 1970', in Hague Conference on Private International Law (ed.), *Collection of Conventions 1951–2003*, The Hague: The Permanent Bureau of the Conference.

Hauser, H. and R. Schöne (1994): 'Is there a need for international competition rules?': *Aussenwirtschaft* 49, 205–12.

von Hayek, F. (1969): 'Der Wettbewerb als Entdeckungsverfahren', *Freiburger Studien*, Tübingen: Mohr, pp. 249–65.

Immenga, U. (1996): 'Rechtsregeln für eine internationale Wettbewerbsordnung', in U. Immenga, W. Möschel and D. Reuter (eds), *Festschrift für Ernst-Joachim Mestmäcker*, Baden-Baden: Nomos, pp. 593–609.

Immenga, U. and E. Mestmäcker (eds) (1997): *EG-Wettbewerbsrecht* I, Munich: C.H.Beck.

Jackson, J.H. (1994): 'Alternative approaches for implementing competition rules in international economic relations', *Aussenwirtschaft* 49, 177–200.

Lange, D.G.F. and J.B. Sandage (1989): 'The Wood Pulp decision and its implications for the scope of EC competition law', *Common Market Law Review* 26, 137–65.

Lowe, A.V. (1983): *Extraterritorial Jurisdiction. An Annotated Collection of Legal Material*, Cambridge, UK: Cambridge University Press.

Lowe, A.V. (1989): 'International law and the effects doctrine in the European Court of Justice', *Cambridge Law Journal*, 9–11.

Martí, R. (1997): 'La politica de competencia en America Latina', *Revista de direito econômico* 25, 77–98.

Martinek, M. (1989): 'Das uneingestandene Auswirkungsprinzip des EuGH zur extraterritorialen Anwendbarkeit der EG-Wettbewerbsregeln', *IPRax*, 347–54.

Matsushita, M. (1995): 'Competition law and policy in the context of the WTO system', *DePaul Law Review* 44, 1097–1118.

Möschel, W. (1989): 'Internationale Wettbewerbsbeschränkungen', in H. Leßmann, B. Großfeld and L. Vollmer (eds), *Festschrift für Rudolf Lukes*, Cologne: Carl Heymanns Verlag, 461–9.

Petersmann, E.-U. (1981): 'International governmental trade organizations – GATT and UNCTAD', *International Encyclopedia of Comparative Law*, XVII, ch. 25.

Pettit, E. and N. Styles (1982): 'The international response to the extraterritorial application of United States antitrust law', *Business Lawyer* 37, 697–716.

Pitofsky, R. (1999): 'Competition policy in a global economy – today and tomorrow', *Journal of International Economics and Law* 2, 403–11.

Rittner, F. (1988): 'Das Koreanische Wettbewerbsgesetz als kartellpolitisches Beispiel', in O.F. Freiherr von Gramm, P. Raisch and K. Tiedemann (eds), *Strafrecht, Unternehmensrecht, Anwaltsrecht. Festschrift für Gerd Pfeiffer*, Cologne *et al.*, pp. 555–68.

Scherer, F.M. (1996): 'Competition policy convergence: where next?', *International Business Lawyer* 1996, 485–7.

Schrödermeier, M. (1989): 'Die vermiedene Auswirkung', *Wirtschaft und Wettbewerb*, 21–8.

Schwartz, I. and J. Basedow (1995): 'Competition Law', *International Encyclopedia of Comparative Law* III, ch. 35.

Streit, M. (1996): 'Systemwettbewerb im europäischen Integrationsprozeß', in U. Immenga, W. Möschel and D. Reuter (eds), *Festschrift für Ernst-Joachim Mestmäcker*, Baden-Baden: Nomos, 521–35.

Symeonides, S. (1994): 'Choice of law in the American courts in 1993 (and in the six previous years)', *American Journal of Comparative Law* 42, 599–653.

Symeonides, S. (1999): 'Choice of law in the American courts in 1998: twelth annual survey', *American Journal of Comparative Law* 47, 327–92.

Varady, T. (1999): 'The emergence of competition law in (former) socialist countries', *American Journal of Comparative Law* 47, 229–75.

Wang, Xiaoye (2004): 'Issues surrounding the drafting of China's anti-monopoly law', *Washington University Global Studies Law Review* 3, 285–96.

Wood, D.P. (1995): 'The internationalization of antitrust-law: options for the future', *DePaul Law Review* 44, 1289–99.

Yu Wu, J. (1999): *Der Einfluß des Herstellers auf die Verbraucherpreise nach deutschem und taiwanesischem Recht*, Tübingen: Mohr.

Index